The Political Economy of
Mountain Java

The Political Economy
of Mountain Java

An Interpretive History

Robert W. Hefner

UNIVERSITY OF CALIFORNIA PRESS

Berkeley   Los Angeles   London

For My Parents

University of California Press
Berkeley and Los Angeles, California

University of California Press, Ltd.
London, England

© 1990 by
The Regents of the University of California

Library of Congress Cataloging-in-Publication Data

Hefner, Robert W., 1952–
    The political economy of mountain Java : an interpretive history
/ Robert W. Hefner.
        p.   cm.
    Includes bibliographical references.
    ISBN 0-520-08269-9
    1. Rural development—Indonesia—Tengger Mountains Region (Java)
    2. Tengger Mountains Region (Java, Indonesia)—Social conditions.
    3. Java (Indonesia)—Economic conditions—Regional disparities.
    I. Title.
    HN710.Z9C611454   1990
    307.1′412′095982—dc20   89-49222
                                                                   CIP

Printed in the United States of America
1   2   3   4   5   6   7   8   9

CONTENTS

TABLES

PREFACE

Modern social theory originated in the nineteenth and early twentieth centuries through the efforts of Western intellectuals to come to grips with three momentous events reshaping their societies: the emergence of industrial capitalism, the rise of the nation state, and the transformation of community and popular morality. From the start, this intellectual enterprise was historical and comparative. Even when the object of analysis was a particular case study, as with Weber's discussion of German bureaucracy or Marx's writing on English capitalism, conceptual insights were given analytic depth through comparisons with other periods and localities. Some writers developed these contrastive references more or less implicitly. Others—like Max Weber, with his lifelong effort to understand Western economic culture through research on religion and society around the world—sustained them in a rigorously systematic fashion. In either case, early social theory was thoroughly historical and comparative. To understand a society was to comprehend its distinctiveness relative to forms of life in other times and places.

In the years following World War II, important changes occurred in the mainstream of this intellectual tradition. In the 1950s and 1960s, first of all, a new consensus emerged on the nature of modernity and the processes of development that had brought it about. "Modernization theory," as it was called, drew an analogy between social and organic evolution. Specifically, it postulated that the emergence of more complex social forms depended on a dual process of, on one hand, structural specialization and differentiation, and, on the other, mechanisms of social integration and coordination. As societies advanced, their division of labor grew more complex, and their political organization broader and more participatory. Equally important, it was thought, they developed more universalistic symbols of nation and community. These cut across the parochial attachments of family, ethnicity, and religion, muting their potential divisiveness, and providing an overarching consensus for political life (Smelser 1971; Eisenstadt 1966; Hoselitz 1960).

As with the early pioneers of social theory, modernization theorists aspired to be historical and comparative. In practice, however, both qualities were severely compromised by the sheer muscularity of the modernization paradigm. By overgeneralizing from what was thought to have occurred in the West, the approach imposed a narrowly deterministic model of change on the non-Western world. The rigid power of the model was thus antithetical to the careful particularism required for historical or ethnographic observation. Rather than sensitizing observers to the realities of particular times and places, the model forced different experiences into common molds.

The narrowness of this theory became especially apparent as researchers set out to apply it to actual case studies. Economic anthropologists came forward with detailed monographs showing, among other things, that development often worked to reinvigorate extant social structures, rather than displacing them in favor of new and more specialized institutions (Epstein 1968; Geertz 1963b). Historical sociologists warned of the ethnocentrism of the modernization model, emphasizing that the paths to economic expansion and political innovation were many, not one (Bellah 1957; Bendix 1977). In effect, both critiques demanded that social inquiry return to its roots and craft a more careful history, with concepts sensitive to the cultural diversity of the modern world.

In the end, modernization theory went into decline, as the "orthodox consensus" (Giddens 1984, xv) that underlay its program was itself challenged. The decline was related to broader developments inside and outside the human sciences. In the West, conflicts centering around issues of race, lifestyle, religion, and gender impressed upon many observers that modern society had not reached as firm a "civic consensus" as once thought. In the Third World, political insurgency, ethnic violence, and imbalanced growth made it seem as if the promises of modernization were grossly premature. Researchers in the human sciences, meanwhile, awoke to the realization that there were analytic traditions other than structural-functionalism, some of which seemed uniquely well suited to the task of understanding the modern world.

Perhaps the most important influence on the "refiguration of social thought" (Geertz 1983, 19) in the late 1960s was the revival of interest in hermeneutic, or meaning-centered, approaches to the study of social life. These emphasize that, unlike the natural world, social reality is not objectively given, its processes unfolding independently of actors' understandings in a law-governed, deterministic fashion. On the contrary, social life is inextricably shaped by culture and meaning, since actors use their understandings to adjust to and change the world of which they are part. Inasmuch as this is true, the search for a natural science of society is misconceived, because the objects of social inquiry—human action and historical change—are irreducibly cultural, not mute natural facts. It follows from this insight that the interpretation of culture must be at the center of the sociological enterprise, not its periphery (Berger and Luckmann 1966:18; Geertz 1973a; Rabinow and Sullivan 1987).

The renewed emphasis on meaning at first had a salutary impact on social science's historical and comparative impulse. Rather than squeezing facts into a generalist framework, it encouraged researchers to attend to local histories and cultures, developing models of social change from the bottom up, rather than by deduction from heavy-handed abstractions. This emphasis reinvigorated ethnography and social history, both of which place local-level realities at the center of research. In line with the turn to meaning, new and more sophisticated methodologies for the analysis of cultural form were developed in linguistics, sociology, history, and anthropology (Marcus and Fischer 1986, 43; Hunt 1989).

The collapse of the orthodox consensus, however, was also accompanied by an overreaction against the generalized comparison and causal analysis that had been key features of social theory from its beginning; both concerns had been abusively overextended during the heyday of structural-functionalism and modernization research. The overreaction was perhaps most extreme in my own discipline, cultural anthropology. Earlier, in the 1960s, anthropologists like Scarlett Epstein (1962; 1968) and Clifford Geertz (1963a, 1963b) had drawn on concepts hewn in comparative social theory to focus and deepen their ethnographic narratives. By the 1980s, however, a particularistic spirit had seized the discipline. Many scholars now rejected the idea that concepts developed through comparative inquiry were either necessary or interesting. They rightly objected to mechanistic models of society, or what Clifford Geertz has called "laws-and-causes social physics" (Geertz 1983, 3). But many went on to infer that this implied a repudiation of any concept of social causality or constraint, or empirical data other than the frames of awareness through which actors see their world. Hermeneutics was not simply a central instrument in social analysis; it was the only legitimate one.

There was an irony to this turn of events. Inasmuch as they looked to anyone for precedent, interpretive researchers most often appealed to Max Weber, citing his emphasis on meaningful action, and his rejection of natural-science approaches to social reality. Though Weber objected to the conflation of society and nature, he did not believe that the search for causal generalization was misplaced, or that it amounted to the reduction of social inquiry to natural science. Weber believed that there are causal constraints on societal development, but that they operate differently than natural causes. Though they sometimes work behind the backs of actors, their broader impact is mediated by the understandings that actors have of their circumstances (see Giddens 1971, 150).

While rejecting the idea that social evolution is governed by mechanistic "laws," then, Weber nonetheless insisted that the final purpose of the "interpretive understanding" of social action is to arrive at "a causal explanation of its courses and effects" (Weber 1947, 88). At times, he added, such a global inquiry compels the analyst to move outside the perimeters of lived or self-conscious experience. "In all the sciences of human action, account must be taken of processes and phenomena which are devoid of subjective meaning," but influence behavior nonetheless (Weber 1947, 93).

Though neglected in contemporary interpretive research, Weber's insight points to one of the most poignant features of human life. It is what Anthony Giddens (1979, 7) has called "the escape of human history from human intentions, and the return of the consequences of that escape as causal influences on human action." The implications of this practical truth are simple but far-reaching. Among other things, it implies that recent attempts by interpretive scholars to represent social action as a "text," the significance of which lies in what the action "says" rather than what it "does" (Geertz 1973b, 19; Ricoeur 1979), are ill-conceived. The textual model overlooks the fact that social action can have practical consequences that affect the human condition even though unrecognized by actors. Hence it is not enough to look at the "said" of social action; we must also attend to the "done." In other words, even as we strive for a "hermeneutically informed social theory" (Giddens 1982, 5), we cannot confine our inquiry to meaning alone. To do so is to lose sight of the broader range of events that shape human history and culture.

This theoretical premise, and its related appeal for a broadening of interpretive inquiry, inform the argument of the present book. In most general terms, the approach I adopt here is both interpretive and circumstantial. It seeks, first of all, to understand a Southeast Asian peasantry's experience of politics and economic change from precolonial times to today. Equally important, however, the approach also aspires to account for the practical circumstances that have constrained that peasantry's economic actions and conditioned its awareness. Unlike a more exclusively symbolic or hermeneutic report, then, my account does not "refrain from causal or genetic hypotheses" in favor of a "purely descriptive account" of meaning (Berger and Luckmann 1966, 20). Instead, my perspective is sociogenetic, which is to say it examines the forms and meanings of a people's way of life and the circumstances involved in their sustenance and change. Only through such dialectical tacking between activity and constraint can we hope to "escape from the ritual either/or choice between objectivism and subjectivism" that continues to plague modern social inquiry (Bourdieu 1977, 4; cf. Keyes 1983a, 754).

A related concern informed my choice of research methods in the field and of narrative style in this book. Since the early 1970s interpretive theorists have repeatedly warned of "the danger that cultural analysis . . . will lose touch with the hard surfaces of life—with the political, economic, stratificatory realities within which men are everywhere contained" (Geertz 1973b, 30). There have been a few laudable efforts to apply interpretive methods to political-economic realities. Nonetheless, as a number of writers have noted, most interpretive scholars continue to neglect "issues of power, interests, economics, and historical change . . . in favor of simply portraying the native point of view as richly as possible" (Marcus and Fischer 1986, 77; cf. Ortner 1984, 131).

Interpretive theory's uneasiness in the face of these larger realities is in part related to the issue raised above: the mistaken conviction that the search for any kind of circumstantial constraint amounts to a conflation of social and natural science. But the limited application of interpretive methods to history and political economy was also an unintended consequence of one of the most promising trends of the 1980s: the growing use of micro-scale ethnographic methodology, not simply in anthropology, but in history, sociology, and psychology (Marcus and Fischer 1986; Hunt 1989; Biersack 1989). Perhaps no other recent intellectual development has had as salutary an impact on the substance and style of social analysis as has this one. None, certainly, has played a more important role in undercutting the excesses of general theories that "prematurely overlook or reduce cultural diversity" (Marcus and Fischer 1986, 33).

At the same time, however, the emphasis on micro-level ethnography has unwittingly reinforced what Eric Wolf (1982, 13) has called "the false confidence" of the ethnographer. Many anthropologists have treated "societies, even villages, as if they were islands unto themselves, with little sense of the larger systems of relations in which these units are embedded" (Ortner 1984, 142). To understand social reality, it is assumed, one need only attend to local microcosms of meaning, independent of any concern for history or material circumstance.

Particularistic sensitivity is, of course, a vital ingredient in history and ethnography. As Clifford Geertz has observed, good ethnography requires that theoretical formulations "hover so low over the interpretations they govern that they don't make much sense or hold much interest apart from them" (Geertz 1973b, 25). Left to itself, then, interpretive ethnography often refuses to "generalize across cases but . . . [only] within them" (Geertz 1973b, 26).

Such vigorous particularism can be a healthy antidote to the overgeneralized pretensions of grand theory. To assume that this methodological particularism is self-sustaining, however, is dangerously misleading. Among other things, it misrepresents the quality of intellectual engagement implied in historical and ethnographic reporting, and the way in which its requisite skills are developed. In the last analysis, after all, even individual case studies depend for their vitality on a regular infusion of concepts and sensibilities from comparative analysis. Why else would we immerse our students in history and ethnography before sending them off to do their research projects? The excellence of history and ethnography is not guaranteed, then, by their "complex specificness, their circumstantiality" (Geertz 1973b, 23). As Marilyn Strathern (1987, 5) has put it, our concepts must be "dually constructed." That is, they must advance comparative insight at the same time that they enhance our sensitivity to local realities (cf. Keyes 1983a, 754; Skocpol 1984, 368).

In the end, then, our knowledge of local worlds always depends on a larger learning. Even the most particularistic reports imply the structuring presence of this comparative knowledge. Conversely, social theory is perpetually renewed through its application to particular periods and places. It is the mutual and sustained engagement of general theory and localized research that makes our enterprise a discipline. We diminish the intellectual contribution of history and ethnography if we think otherwise.

All this is, again, related to the style and method of the present study. Ultimately, this local history decenters itself. Our encounter with this Javanese peasantry raises general questions on the concepts with which we understand economy and community, and social action in general. What are the bases for human solidarity and the sources of social power? What is the meaning of "class" in a peasant society dominated throughout much of its modern history by a European state? How does class here differ from that of an earlier industrializing Europe? What was its role in the making of this mountain peasantry relative to social groupings based on region, religion, or ethnicity? What are the implications of this analysis of economic change for a general understanding of culture, history, and social action? Though the historical narrative presented here focuses on Java, it is by necessity a general essay on the reality of politics, production, and meaning. It must be if this local example is to yield its truth.

Another generalist intent informs this local history. In recent years, a number of authors have commented that the study of political-economic change requires a new style of "middle-range" analysis. Such research would transcend the antinomy between, on one hand, village ethnography, and, on the other, sweeping macro-history. Faulting their fellow interpretive anthropologists for failing to do so, George Marcus and Michael Fischer (1986, 91), for example, have spoken of the need for new research methodologies, combining interpretive and political-economic research in the context of "multilocal" community studies. The sociologist Norman Long (1977, 190–92) has argued along similar lines. He emphasizes the need to link actor-oriented methodologies to history and calls for middle-range "regional studies" to bridge the gap between grand theory and village ethnography. It is only through such a combination of regional ethnography and reflective theorizing, I would add, that we can hope to break the impasse in social science between "those who claim the locality as a unit of analysis and those who focus on the determining power of exogenous and global forces" (Biersack 1989, 93).

When I set out for Java in the late 1970s, my intent was to carry out just such a program of research, combining multilocal ethnography with broader attention to national history and politics. I first traveled to East Java's Tengger highlands during weekend breaks from a language program in the nearby city of Malang in 1977. I returned to perform nineteen months of field research during 1978–80, and eight more during 1985. During the first period of research, I lived in two mountain villages in the "upperslope" portion of the Tengger highlands, the first for eleven months and the second for eight. In 1985 I went back to the second of these two villages for four months. At the end of those four months, I moved again, this time down the mountainside to a "midslope" mountain community, where agriculture, social organization, and religion were quite different from their counterparts in the upperslope area.

Though I lived in three upland villages over my twenty-seven months of fieldwork, I made weekly visits to another four villages, and two-to-four-day visits to another twenty. As I became familiar to people in this mountain region, I was invited to ritual festivals (*slametan*) in an eight-village area. In addition to being an opportunity to dance and relax, these gatherings provided me with a delightfully cordial setting in which to interview people and make contacts for future village visits.

My purpose in working over such a large area was to carry out a regional study rather than a more traditional village ethnography. In part, this choice was dictated by mountain Java's extraordinary social and ecological variety, which made generalizations on the basis of single-village research extremely problematic. Equally important, the method was dictated by the challenge of understanding the range of forces that had played a role in the making of this mountain peasantry. To this same end, I also drew on historical materials, mostly from Dutch scholars, dealing with the Tengger highlands in relation to Javanese history as a whole (see Ch. 2 and Appendix). The Tengger region is unique among upland areas of Java in having a rich body of commentary dating back over two hundred years. The historical and multicommunity study I have attempted in this book would have been impossible without this material.

My desire to link regional ethnography to history and political economy also explains the methodological eclecticism of my research. Though questions of experience and meaning were central to my inquiry, they were not its sole focus. I was also interested in such circumstantial processes as population growth, ecological decline, and long-term economic developments, the patterned complexity of which often escapes actors' awareness.

To this end I carried out a wide range of interviews to obtain quantitative as well as qualitative data. During 1978–80, for example, I conducted 342 interviews (of about two hours' length each) in two upperslope communities on household organization, property, production, and consumption. During 1985 I carried out the same interview in 150 households in two midslope villages. The results of these interviews provide the largest portion of the statistical data discussed in chapters 4–6 in this book. During 1985 I carried out an additional 150 interviews in midslope and upperslope villages on agricultural inputs and production. I also conducted a smaller number of structured interviews on traders and trading, store management, ritual festival expense (Hefner 1985, 216–38), wage labor, and the indigenous vocabulary for agriculture and plant growth. Unless a villager preferred to speak in Indonesian (which was rare), I conducted all interviews in Javanese, using a polite but relaxed "middle Javanese" (*kromo madyo*), or, as was the preference of most upperslope villagers, the mountain dialect of "Tengger" Javanese unique to this region (Smith-Hefner 1983, 1989).

I conducted these interviews only after several months' residence in each mountain region. They were an extension and systematization of a more general ethnographic dialogue, rather than a self-contained enterprise in their own right. The point is important, for it is only through sustained ethnography that one is able to direct one's attention to relevant issues and phrase questions in ways sensitive to villagers' concerns. At any rate, for the regional and comparative study I sought to carry out, this quantitative material was vital. The interviews through which it was obtained also proved to be a rich source of ethnographic insight in their own right, introducing me to people and problems I would not have otherwise encountered. I discuss these and other aspects of ethnographic method in the Appendix to this book.

This is, I should note, the second of two books that I have written on the culture and history of mountain Java. The religious issues occasionally touched on in this work are discussed at greater length in my *Hindu Javanese: Tengger Tradition and Islam* (1985), and a series of related articles on Islam and politics (Hefner 1983a, 1987a, 1987b, 1987c). In addition, I plan to address the topic of Muslim conversion and the religion of Java in a third and final book. In the present work, then, I have not tried to recapitulate the argument of these other writings. Readers interested in religious change or more detailed descriptions of social relations in the contemporary highlands may find these other works more illuminating than the present social history of economy, politics, and culture.

As the reader will note, the problems addressed in this book required a merging of history, ethnography, human ecology, and sociology. A generation ago, such methodological eclecticism would not have given anyone pause. Clifford Geertz's (1960, 1963a, 1965a) pioneering studies of Indonesian society, for example, demonstrated that rigorously empirical studies of politics and economics could and should be done in conjunction with interpretive ethnography.

Despite the pluralist aspirations of contemporary cultural theory (see Clifford 1986; Geertz 1983; Marcus and Fischer 1986), we have in recent years seen an unfortunate overreaction to the heavy-handed excesses of earlier grand theory. This has been expressed in, among other things, the neglect of comparative reflection, a loss of sociological rigor, and the repudiation of quantitative methods. Equally serious is the fact that unexotic topics once considered proper for culturally grounded social inquiry—economics, human ecology, and agriculture, among others— have been quietly stricken from our collective agenda. Perhaps this closure has allowed us a certain intellectual purism. But it has been achieved at the expense of interdisciplinary dialogue and a comprehensive understanding of the forces driving human history.

In writing this book, then, I have tried to go beyond anthropology's tradition of single-village study and to look at economy and society from both a regional and a historical perspective. My intent, in addition, was to bring a hermeneutically informed approach to bear on the complex realities of economic and political life. In part, this choice reflects my own hope that anthropology will make good on its comparativist promise and engage in a much-needed dialogue with history, sociology, and comparative politics. But it was also necessitated by the fact that, if these disciplines are to be done well, there can be no opposition between cultural meaning and material circumstance, or general comparison and local inquiry. The fact is that the understanding of particular worlds always raises general issues. This makes the task of historians and ethnographers more daunting. Happily, however, it also means that their work speaks to larger, more general, truths. Sustained excursion into the history and meanings of another way of life ultimately enhances our self-understanding. This book will have succeeded if it can convey something of that precious quality of cross-cultural research.

ACKNOWLEDGMENTS

Each of the two periods of research on which this book is based was supported by a Fulbright fellowship and a National Science Foundation research award (BNS 7806869; BNS 8317544). I am deeply grateful to both of these excellent programs. In Indonesia, I wish to thank officers of the Indonesian Council of Sciences (LIPI) for their support of scientific research. I owe special thanks to Masri Singarimbun of the Population Center and Sugeng Martopo of the Environmental Studies Center at Gadjah Mada University, both of whom generously agreed to sponsor my research. Michael Dove, an American anthropologist who worked with Pak Martopo at the time of my research, played a key role in making arrangements for my 1985 study. Hans Daeng of the Department of Anthropology, Gadjah Mada University, also helped to clear my research application and gave me the opportunity to meet Indonesian students. I am grateful to these men and the many Indonesian scholars who showed such kindness during my visits.

Though, for their protection, I must do so anonymously, I also wish to thank villagers in the Tengger mountains. They demonstrated great patience and humor in the face of my tiresome questioning. Rural Javanese have a social and moral sensitivity that is nothing less than extraordinary; the lessons I learned on interpersonal responsiveness challenged my American personality. I hope something of the lesson is visible in what I have written here.

A number of people read and commented on all parts of this manuscript, or helped in the earlier formulation of research ideas. In particular, I thank Conner Bailey, Dale Eickelman, Don Emmerson, Ricardo Godoy, Gillian Hart, Allan Hoben, Ray Kelly, Charles Keyes, Sherry Ortner, Toby Volkman, and Aram Yengoyan. I must single out two people for special mention. Dan Chirot, a historical sociologist at the University of Washington, urged me to bring anthropological ideas back to history and comparative sociology. For that I owe him much. Michael G. Peletz, an anthropologist at Colgate University, helped me to rethink portions of my argument in light of events elsewhere in Southeast Asia. Much of what I came to see in Java was helped by his careful eye.

Though neither was directly involved with this manuscript, Clifford Geertz and Hildred Geertz showed great kindness in commenting on my earlier research. My intellectual debt to them is apparent throughout this book. Though differing with him on several points of historical detail, I should hasten to add that the larger premise of this book seeks to respond to Clifford Geertz's (1984) "call to situate the general inquiry [into agrarian change] in the cultural context," and thus to reject all approaches that would render culture external to political-economic realities. I don't know that he would agree with the way I have told the story, but from beginning to end this study was informed by the weighty legacy of Clifford Geertz's work.

At the University of California Press, I owe special thanks to Betsey Scheiner, who first encouraged me to submit my manuscript to the Press, and Sheila Levine, who spirited the book and its author through the whole publication process with thoughtful intelligence and wonderful congeniality.

Finally, I must express my deepest gratitude to two people. The first is S. Sutrisno W.G., of Malang, my assistant during both periods of fieldwork. A naturalist already familiar to people in the Tengger highlands, Sutrisno was an indefatigable field-worker and a scholar in his own right. Without his long-established contacts in the mountains, the multicommunity study I have attempted would have been impossible. He taught me much about Java, Indonesia, and the Islamic faith he holds so dear. Lastly, I must thank my wife, Nancy J. Smith-Hefner. Her sociolinguistic research proved to be a vital complement to my own work. Her thoughts shaped everything I know about Java. Without her love, her humor, and her criticism, I would have been unable to carry out this research.

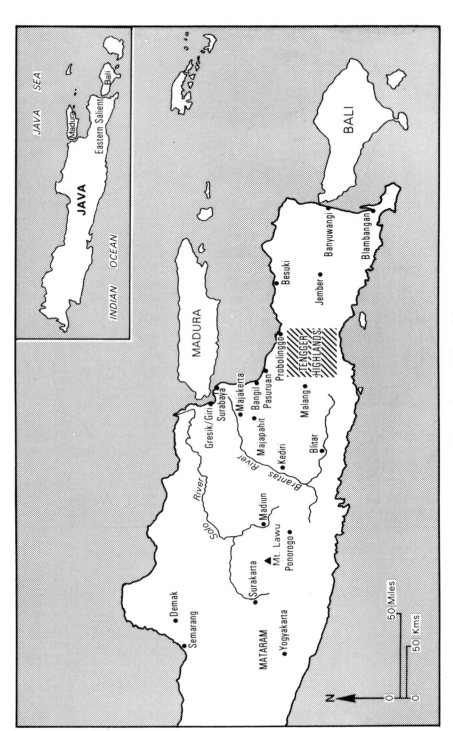

Map 1. East and Central Java

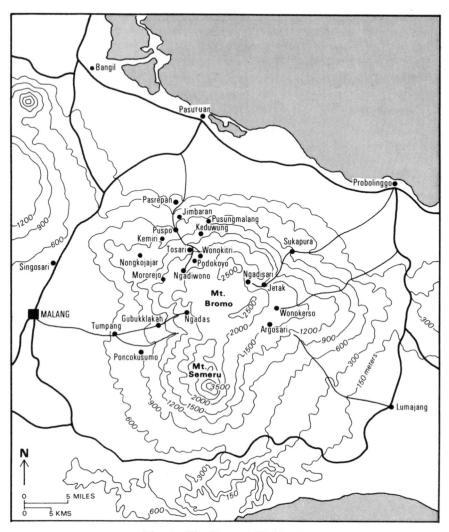

Map 2. The Tengger Highlands

ONE

Introduction

Mountain Java in History and Social Theory

It's not like before. In the old days people here were different from those in the low-lands [ngare]. *They weren't interested in wearing fine clothes that drew attention to themselves, or in eating special foods like those you see today. Even though some people owned more and some less, people dressed and ate the same. At harvest people of all backgrounds worked together in the fields. Nobody was ashamed of calloused hands or dirty feet. Now it's different. Those who are well off* [sing nduwe] *want to give orders and keep their hands and feet clean of earth. They keep track of every-thing they give and everything they get in return. It's just like the lowlands. Every-thing is counted up* [diperhitung] *and owned.*
                    —A TOSARI FARMER, 1985

Economic change is a moral as well as material process. Its impact is felt not only in the brute facts of income and production but in the reshaping of identity, aspirations, and authority. In the modern West, the growth of industrial capitalism undermined traditional values, challenged social hi-erarchies, and reorganized even the most intimate aspects of our daily lives. The more stable structure and needs of traditional society gave way to a world in which identity and tastes were continuously refashioned in the allied interests of production and status. Today, of course, this pecu-liar development is no longer restricted to the Western world. As the "great transformation" of economy and society has spread from the First World to the Third, so has its challenge to received attachments and mo-ralities. Witness to its material force, we are only beginning to compre-hend its cultural consequences.

This book is concerned with the reshaping of economy and commu-nity in one area of Southeast Asia, the Tengger highlands of East Java, Indonesia, where I first conducted research in the late 1970s. This was a time of great change on this densely populated island. A few years ear-lier, in the mid 1960s, Indonesia had witnessed the cataclysmic destruc-tion of the Indonesian Communist Party (PKI). Some of the most sustained violence of that period occurred in areas of East Java not far from the Tengger highlands. In the aftermath of the bloodshed, a more conservative, military-dominated "New Order" government, as it is called, took power. It quickly reversed Indonesia's restrictive policies on foreign investment and launched a number of ambitious, if sometimes controversial, economic projects. The new regime created programs for

1

the distribution of "green revolution" seeds, fertilizers, and credit. It improved roads and distribution networks. Luxury consumer goods soon flooded rural markets, accentuating the difference between rich and poor. At the same time, the government imposed tight restrictions on political activity, warning of the threat of communist subversion and Islamic extremism.

By the early 1970s the impact of these programs was being felt even in mountain areas of Java. In the Tengger highlands, roadbuilding brought motor transport, consumer goods, and a heightened government presence. Farmers who could afford green-revolution agrochemicals shifted from cultivation of food staples to lucrative cash crops. Japanese-made consumer goods began to replace traditional religious festivals (*slametan*) as the preferred indices of wealth and prestige. In every aspect of life, it seemed, a region that had once proudly distanced itself from the hierarchy and inequality of the surrounding lowlands awoke to find itself very much part of larger Java. A world was on the wane. Its passing was evident not simply in income and production, but in the altered bases of identity and authority.

Although my first concern in this book is to examine the history and consequences of this great transformation, from precolonial times to today, this local example is intended to raise general questions on the nature of economic life, the sources of social power, and the impact of development on both. In so doing, this study seeks to present a noneconomistic account of economic change.

My analysis departs from conventional economic approaches in several ways. It emphasizes, first of all, that individuals formulate and interpret their needs in interaction with others around them, rather than in the solitary introspection of neoclassical economics's "sovereign" consumer (Scitovsky 1976; Bourdieu 1977, 177). Second, it shifts the problem of identity and community to the center of research, recognizing that social practice is guided by a wider range of "commitments" than market utility alone, and by a more complex sense of self (Sen 1977, 328; Etzioni 1988, 11; Ortner 1984, 151). From this perspective, the rational actor of economistic analysis (Popkin 1979; Feeny 1983) is not so much wrong as woefully overschematized. Third, and finally, a noneconomistic approach to economic change stresses that, whatever their relative autonomy, the market and other economic institutions are ultimately dependent upon the moral, political, and legal institutions of society as a whole (Giddens 1987, 136). Hence economic change is never just a matter of technological diffusion, market rationalization, or "capitalist penetration." Deep down, it is also a matter of community, morality, and power. All of these are at issue in the great transformation reshaping our world.

COMMUNITY RECAST: MOUNTAIN JAVA IN SOCIAL CHANGE

In a less analytically self-conscious fashion, upland villagers in the 1970s and early 1980s were preoccupied with these same problems of identity and community in economic change. For centuries the inhabitants of this region had seen themselves as a "mountain people" (*wong gunung*) distinct from the "people of the lowlands" (*wong ngare*). Untrained in the abstract jargon of social science, villagers used this regionalist distinction to talk about differences of hierarchy and interaction. In their eyes, lowland society was characterized by great inequality, with high rates of landlessness, extremes of wealth and poverty, and a long history of religious intolerance. Highlanders were unpretentious and outgoing (*blater*), they would say; lowlanders were aloof and status-conscious. Lowland people were slow to invite visitors into their homes, they pointed out, and received them more formally when they did. Rather than the cooked food and easy discussion of highland etiquette, one received a glass of tea and stiffly conventional conversation. "Lowland people are more interested in preserving their status than making you feel at home," one uplander averred. "What they value," he went on, "is rank and position [*pangkat*], while people of the mountains like to think of themselves as all alike [*padha*], and of one descent [*sakturunan*]."

These, of course, were simplified characterizations, designed to prescribe a pattern of behavior as much as describe its contrary. In a certain sense, however, they did point to real differences between the two regions. Although in the nearby lowlands 40 percent of the rural population are without farmland, landlessness was unknown in most of the Tengger highlands until recently. Absentee landlordism has been common in the lowlands since the nineteenth century, but it was traditionally unknown in the mountains. In fact, until recently, the highlands had almost no sharecropping, land rental, or intravillage patron-clientage. "No person here is able to command [*kongkon*] another," villagers would say. While there was clear hyperbole in this characterization, it did capture a general truth. Highland society was less stratified than that of the lowlands. Villagers relied on independent access to land, not the "subsistence guarantees" of superordinate patrons (Scott 1976, 5), to meet their daily needs.

Interactional styles reflected these same values of inexclusivity and social independence. In talking among themselves, for example, mountain people spoke in what is, from a Javanese perspective, an unusually direct and unqualified manner. Their dialect emphasized the less formal speech of *ngoko* rather than the status-sensitive variant of "high" Javanese known as *kromo* (Smith-Hefner 1983). Rather than serving as the language of rank in interaction, as in much of lowland Java, *kromo* was used to address outsiders, which is to say, to speak with people who did not understand the more direct and solidary ways of upland Java.

Religion expressed this same general ethos. Mountain traditions were communally based. They spoke of the descent of all villagers from ancestral pioneers (*cikal bakal*) and the collective dependence of the living on guardian spirits of land and water. Some uplanders called themselves Muslim, and others Hindu or "Budha." But both worshiped ancestral and guardian spirits, stressed the importance of communal rites, and called for tolerance between Muslims and Hindus (Hefner 1985, 126–41).[1] Some communities in the nearby lowlands had once had a similarly inexclusive Javanist tradition. At the beginning of this century, however, it was suppressed in the wake of a broad movement for Islamic revitalization. The Muslim resurgence was itself prompted by the growing influence of wealthy Muslim traders. The association of Islam with social inequality only served to reinforce highlanders' estrangement from lowland ways.

The survival of this upland tradition was not a product of pristine isolation or unchanging traditionalism. The Tengger region was first incorporated into a lowland-based polity in the tenth century; thereafter, the region's inhabitants played a central role in state-sponsored worship of mountain deities. Eight centuries later, the first European reports from the area noted that uplanders engaged in extensive trade with the surrounding lowlands. Social contact further increased in the nineteenth century as the area was drawn into Dutch-imposed cultivation schemes. During that same century, the Tengger region assimilated an immigrant population larger than that indigenous to the area. Despite these trends, upland society remained less stratified than that of the lowlands and preserved distinctive social forms.

Recent developments have put this contrast in question, challenging both the cultural meaning and practical supports of this upland way of life. Even the simplest developments raise troubling challenges for old sensibilities. Is the owner of a new television set obliged to position it prominently in a front window so that neighbors can enjoy free viewing, as enjoined by traditional norms of entertainment? Should a wealthy farmer be spared the obligation of taking part in compulsory village-

1. The traditional term for the religion of non-Muslim people in the Tengger mountains was *agama Budha,* or "Budha [Buddhist] religion." Though historians are uncertain just why this was so, the same term was used by Javanese from the seventeenth century on to refer to the religion of the pre-Islamic period, even though Hinduism, and not Buddhism, appears to have been the religion of state (Pigeaud 1962, 4:68). The priestly tradition from which Tengger Javanese liturgies are descended was a cult of popular Sivaism with no Buddhist influences; in recent years, most of the upland "Budha" population has come to reidentify itself as Hindu. This religious history is discussed in Hefner 1985.

improvement projects (*kerja bakti*) if he can hire a coolie in his place? Should the much-admired son of a former communist be barred from assuming a leadership role in a farm extension organization because of state regulations against ex-communists?

These and other issues were the subject of an ongoing and sometimes heated debate concerning social relations in a fast-changing world. Although not cast in the technical vocabulary of Western ethical philosophy, these were moral issues, concerned with the nature of right and wrong, and the quality of commitment between people in relationships.[2] They were also political issues, concerned with the mechanisms by which certain interests and self-images were promoted and others denied or ignored. Far from being a pale reflection of realities whose real urgency lay elsewhere, these issues were at the heart of the political and economic transformation of this region. Tracing mountain society back in time, this book seeks to make their contemporary reality intelligible in light of their social and historical genesis.

THE REGIONAL BACKGROUND: RECOGNIZING A VARIED JAVA

Many of our impressions of this densely populated Asian island are built on what is, in fact, an astounding ignorance of its regional variety. When we speak of Javanese culture, we think of inland Central Java, heir to the

2. The concept of morality used in this book draws on recent interdisciplinary research that challenges the traditional view that an individual's moral judgment is the product of solitary reflection on abstract principles of right and wrong. Though not dismissing the influence of reflective reason (or certain universal moral dispositions), this recent work also emphasizes the pivotal role of personal identity, social relationships, and emotions in the development of moral sensibilities and in the determination of the categories of persons to whom different moral standards are applied. This research thus seeks to transcend the "too-sharp separation between self and other" characteristic of utilitarian and liberal philosophy, emphasizing that "our connections to others and our capacities for responsiveness are a central part of our identities, rather than being mere sentiments or voluntary commitments" (Blum 1987, 316-18; cf. Sandel 1982; Yack 1988). The quality of one's social connections, and their impact on one's self-image, thus become the point of departure for empirical investigation of moral growth. The implications of this approach extend far beyond ethical psychology, since issues of value and commitment are at the heart of all political, economic, and social inquiry. In place of such rarefied abstractions as economics's *homo economicus,* for example, we need to understand real people in particular worlds, exploring the social assistance they receive in developing their identity and values, and comparing the ways in which different social orders inflect this process of moral orientation. For literature relevant to this expanded understanding of the genealogy of morals, see, in psychology, Carol Gilligan 1982; in philosophy, Lawrence Blum 1987; in political theory, Michael Sandel 1982 and Bernard Yack 1988; in economic philosophy, Amartya Sen 1977 and Amitai Etzioni 1988; in anthropology, Maurice Bloch 1973, Mary Douglas 1970, and Richard Shweder et al. 1987.

richly refined and hierarchical traditions of the native courts (*kraton*) that ruled much of the island from the seventeenth to nineteenth centuries.[3] When we think of agriculture, we think of *sawah* (irrigated farm land), with its durable and neatly sculpted rice fields. Though both must be central to any account of Java, there are "other Javas away from the kraton" (Hatley 1984) and other dimensions to the island's agricultural ecology. In addition to analyzing the form and meaning of economic change, then, the present study is intended to enhance our appreciation of Java's diversity, and the historical conditions that have made it what it is.

The Tengger highlands are one of the most richly varied of these other Javas. Located to the south of the port towns of Pasuruan and Probolinggo, to the east of Malang and west of Lumajang, the highlands form a vast mountain wedge, some six hundred square kilometers in area. The mountains separate Java's central heartland from the far eastern territories known as the *ujung timur*, or "eastern salient." For most of the modern era, this eastern zone lay outside Central Javanese political control. From the seventeenth to nineteenth centuries, in particular, when inland Central Java was developing the features of social hierarchy that we today identify as quintessentially Javanese, the eastern salient remained a rebellious frontier characterized by populist mannerisms and less hierarchical ways. It retains a distinctive spirit to the present day.

Environmentally, too, our images of Java have been too simplistic. The Tengger region is one of twelve mountain complexes, consisting of some 120 mountains, that form the east-west backbone of the island. Despite their enormous expanse and critical ecological importance, these upland territories have been the object of little social research. Agricultural studies have focused on wet-rice *sawah* while neglecting rainfed agricultural land (*tegal*). Thus it is often assumed that, over the past 150 years, upland agriculture has followed the same pattern of intensification as that in the rice-growing lowlands. The history of the Tengger highlands, however, shows this not to be the case. Upland farmers have responded to commercial and demographic pressures quite differently than their *sawah* counterparts. The green revolution reshaping upland agriculture today is also having a markedly different impact. The combined effects of commercialization and environmental degradation, finally, promise to make for a very different future.

For all these reasons, then, the present study seeks to trace the history of one upland region relative to other parts of Java. The local example

3. When I speak of "Java" in this book, I, too, am guilty of heuristic simplification. I am primarily concerned with areas of ethnic Javanese cultural influence, especially the east and central provinces of the island, where about seventy million of Java's hundred million people live (Koentjaraningrat 1984, 3–30). West Java is home to Java's second largest ethnic group, the Sundanese.

speaks to larger truths: much of what greater Java was, and much of
what it is becoming, is clearer in light of this upland-lowland comparison. We see in it, too, a local expression of the broader changes in economy, community, and power occurring throughout modern Southeast
Asia.

The Cultural Ecology of Pasuruan

Today the Tengger mountain region is divided into four administrative regencies (*kabupaten*). Each has its capital in the lowlands and
stretches up into one quadrant of the highlands. The bulk of the research
on which the present account is based was centered in the regency of Pasuruan and one village just over its southern border in the regency of
Malang. My study reflects this emphasis, focusing especially on the
northwestern quadrant of the highlands located in the Pasuruan regency.[4]

Like its three sister regencies, Pasuruan is one of the most socially and
ecologically diverse regencies in all of Java. It stretches from the steamy
coastal littoral around Pasuruan, with its crowded towns, coconut groves,
and lush paddy fields, southward toward the Tengger mountains, which
loom massively above the quickly rising coastal plain. The upland terrain
is dominated by the Mount Bromo volcano, which lies at the center of
the Tengger mountains, and Mount Semeru, an enormous volcanic cone
(and, at 3,500 meters, Java's highest mountain) about twenty-five kilometers to the south.

Though settled more than a thousand years ago, for most of its history
the rugged territory around these volcanoes was home to only a few dry-
field farmers working deep soils in narrow valley bottoms. Land outside
their hamlets remained under tropical jungle or, at higher altitudes, cool
forests of temperate conifers. The forests were home to a rich variety of
game, including monkeys, tigers, eagles, wild pigs, flying foxes, buffalo,
and deer. In the nineteenth century, however, one saw a preview of what
would later occur in other parts of Southeast Asia. The forests were cut
and game was exterminated as the colonial government extended its
commercial operations and Java's exploding population sought out the
island's last cultivable lands. Though volcanic eruptions and government
restrictions prevented settlers from opening the southern forests immedi-

---

4. My wife, Nancy Smith-Hefner, carried out ethnolinguistic research in a third of
the four regencies, in the village of Ngadisari in the regency of Probolinggo. Her research and insights provided an essential comparison with my own, and I have drawn
on them extensively in this account. In the interest of brevity, however, I have not focused on that regency's history. During most of the nineteenth century, I should add,
Pasuruan and Malang formed a single residency, the capital of which was located in Pasuruan. The neighboring regencies of Probolinggo and Lumajang also formed a single
residency during that period.

ately adjacent to Mount Semeru, all the lands around Mount Bromo were put under cultivation. The rich tropical and subtropical forest was transformed into government estates and peasant farms.

Today little remains of Pasuruan's jungles or the diverse flora and fauna that once lived in them. The regency's ecology is dominated by dense human settlement, distributed over four agricultural zones: a low-land terrain with irrigated rice and sugarcane; a transitional hill region, where paddy (*sawah*) is intermixed with rainfed fields (*tegal*); and, finally, "midslope" and "upperslope" mountain zones, where all cultivable land is *tegal*. These last two regions are the primary focus of the present study.

Midslope settlement extends from about 600 to 1,200 meters above sea level. The region's primary crops are maize (the traditional staple), cassava, coffee, cloves, and a few other subtropical perennials. Upperslope cultivation extends from 1,200 to 2,500 meters. Thanks to Mount Bromo's periodic sprinkling of ash, soils in this area are thick and richly volcanic, among the most fertile in Java (Donner 1987, 98). The cool climate makes them ideal for an assortment of temperate vegetables, such as onions, cabbages, carrots, and potatoes. Though its growing life is twice that of the midslope region (ten months as opposed to five), maize is also grown here, and traditionally it was the region's staple.

The gradient from lowland to upland is also marked by extraordinary cultural variety. Lowland Pasuruan is one of the strongest centers of Islamic traditionalism in all of Java. The area is home to several influential Islamic religious schools (*pesantren*). Since the nineteenth century, teachers and patrons of these Muslim institutions have comprised the core of the lowland rural elite. Islam's influence remains strong today, and is evident in everything from women's dress to regency politics. In national elections, for example, the regency has consistently provided the largest bloc of votes in all of Java for the party of Muslim scholars, Nahdatul Ulama. Prior to 1965, this party's monopoly of power served to check the growth of the Indonesian Communist Party. More recently, it has hindered the post-1965 government's efforts to promote its own "functional" party, Golkar, to the detriment of Muslim ones.

The dominance of Islam in lowland Pasuruan reflects the regency's turbulent history. Coming from the island of Madura off East Java's north coast, Madurese have migrated to this eastern region since pre-Islamic times (Pigeaud 1967, 1:11). Until the eighteenth century, most were assimilated into the larger Javanese population. In the seventeenth and eighteenth centuries, however, Java's eastern territories were racked by brutal warfare, and this once-prosperous territory was depopulated. After winning control of the region in 1743, the Dutch made up for the shortage of population by encouraging migration from the impoverished island of Madura (Kumar 1979). The subsequent influx of Madurese eventually altered the ethnic balance here and in most of far-eastern Java. By the middle of the nineteenth century, almost half Pasuruan's population was Madurese (and though official statistics are lacking, the proportion appears roughly similar today). Far removed from Central Java's courts, Pasuruan's northern littoral thus took on the appearance of a plural society, combining elements of Madurese and Javanese culture. Transformed further by European colonialism, it also proved to be a fertile breeding ground for Islam, one of the few institutions capable of bridging the gap between ethnic Javanese and Madurese. Islam also proved uniquely effective in responding to the political and moral challenge of European domination.

Not all of the Pasuruan regency was transformed in this fashion. The highlands remained predominantly Javanese, and their religious traditions strongly Javanist (*kejawen*), with few orthodox Muslim influences. Mountain religion emphasized festivals at guardian-spirit shrines (*dhanyang*) rather than mosque services or daily *solat* prayer. Indeed, in the highest reaches of the Tengger mountains, an explicitly non-Islamic, Sivaite priesthood survived among a small portion of the Javanese population. It was the only such Hindu priesthood to have escaped the wave of Islamization that followed the collapse of Java's last major Hindu-Buddhist kingdom in the early sixteenth century (Robson 1981; Noorduyn 1978). According to local traditions, a portion of the vanquished Hindu population took flight to nearby Bali, which remains Hindu to the present day. A smaller number of people, however, are said to have sought refuge in the Tengger highlands. Legend would have it that it is from this population that the modern-day "Tengger" or Tengger-Javanese—the non-Muslim population of the upperslope highlands—are descended (Hefner 1985). Lacking castes, courts, high arts, or an aristocracy, this simple mountain peasantry was an unlikely heir to the glories of Javanese Hinduism.

In the eighteenth and nineteenth centuries, the colonial state set out to transform Java's economy, and the Tengger highlands were drawn into an islandwide extractive grid. This European expansion was not the result of a self-propelled "capitalist penetration." Nor, contrary to some models of modern capitalism (Frank 1969; Wallerstein 1974), were its effects on class and community structurally similar to those seen in western Europe. Java's incorporation into an international order was critically mediated by the policies of the colonial state, many of whose programs were specifically noncapitalist. Government initiatives, for example, relied heavily on forced rather than free labor. They protected government monopolies, forcibly reorganized native landholding, and reinforced noncapitalist relations of production among the peasantry. As on the nearby island of Sumatra (Kahn 1980, 155), the resulting socioeconomic formation was a complex hybrid of statist monopolies, private enterprise, and peasant smallholdings.

Although titularly established in 1743, European power in the eastern salient was only consolidated in the final years of the eighteenth century. In Central Java and Madura, this was a period of sustained population growth. After peace was proclaimed, therefore, the colonial rulers encouraged migration to the sparsely populated eastern territory by providing tax breaks and free farmland to immigrants. At first most of the newcomers settled in lowland areas where *sawah* could be established (Palte 1984, 18). By 1820, however, settlers were also moving into Pasuruan's Tengger highlands (de Vries 1931, 1:51).

The trickle turned into a flood after 1830. In that year, in an effort to generate more revenues through the production of export crops, the government introduced compulsory cultivation on upland "waste lands" (Geertz 1963, 52; Furnivall 1944). Once again, colonial power, not independent capital, led the way in this economic transformation. The cool mountain terrains of the Tengger highlands proved to be well suited for the most lucrative of the European government's cultivars, coffee. From 1830 to 1850, therefore, all territory between 600 and 1,200 meters above sea level was stripped of its jungle and transformed into one vast coffee stand. At first, the cultivated expanse was punctuated by only occasional native settlements. Soon, however, land-hungry migrants poured into the highlands. Between 1807 and 1930 the mountain population increased from 5,661 to 104,070, as compared with an increase of 37,000 to 322,033 in the regency as a whole (de Vries 1931, 2:table 6). Most of the upland growth occurred in the midslope coffee lands. The upperslope territories (above 1,200 meters) escaped the greatest portion of the influx, because they were too cool and cloud-covered to support coffee, and because the government wished to set aside reserves for the Hindus native to the area. Though they were spared the immigrant assault, it would not be long before these non-Muslim Javanese also felt the full impact of colonialism.

This migratory movement created the pattern of cultural distribution seen in today's highlands, with Javanist Muslims in midslope villages and Hindus in the upperslope area. The midslope population was at first only nominally Muslim, sharing ritual traditions with its Hindu neighbors. No mosque or Muslim religious school existed in the area until the beginning of the twentieth century. Developments, however, soon threatened to undermine this bastion of popular Javanism. The end of the nineteenth century brought roads and commerce to midslope villages. With them came a new influx of "merchant-farmers" (as highlanders called them) with strong ties to the Muslim lowlands, and little sympathy for upland religious customs. Commerce continued to expand through the 1920s. In fact, it briefly looked as if the Muslim entrepreneurs might be the pioneers of a new upland society, more Muslim and class-stratified in its ways.

Subsequent developments, however, cut short this growing differentiation. The Great Depression, Japanese occupation, and war of independence (1945–49) destroyed upland commerce and drove away many of the Muslim traders. Commerce revived slightly in the 1950s. At the end of that decade, however, political chaos and economic decline again conspired to undercut commercial expansion before it had had time to revolutionize production. Meanwhile, in the midslope region, population growth had shrunk agricultural holdings to a mean size inadequate to support families at any but the most minimal standard of living. Erosion had so devastated some hillside fields that the viability of agriculture itself was in question. Landlessness remained rare, however, and highland society did not break down into two opposed groups of landless proletarians and agrarian capitalists. Though real differences of class existed, the bulk of the highland peasantry remained involved in a minimally productive regime of subsistence agriculture and petty cash-cropping (cf. Kahn 1980).

By the 1960s, then, upland agriculture was stagnant and society was in crisis. The stagnation was the result of externally engendered policies and local ecological decline, not peasant irrationality or heavy-handed traditionalism. Tradition here showed the strong imprint of four centuries of change, and local farmers had long demonstrated their ingenuity in production and marketing. In the 1960s, although pushed into a grim subsistence agriculture, farmers again responded energetically, searching desperately for measures to reverse the region's disastrous downturn.

Not surprisingly, then, upland farmers were intrigued in the 1970s by reports of green-revolution innovations in the lowlands. Their response showed little of the myopic conservatism sometimes attributed to peasant farmers. Before the government had even promoted their use, upland farmers sought out new seeds and agrochemicals on their own. They experimented with cultivation techniques. Eventually they discovered several crops that held the promise of greatly increasing production. Independently of government directives, the highlanders launched their own green revolution.

Though their consequences were not uniform, these events eventually reshaped village society. They brought new wealth, consumer goods, and outside investment. With them came greater mobility, growing inequality, and pressures to conform to the social styles of larger Java. Village society was also affected by the reforms introduced by Indonesia's post-1965 government, with its drastic curtailment of rural political activity. In this instance, then, the green revolution was not an isolated adjustment in marketing or technology. It was part and parcel of a broader "integrative revolution" (Geertz 1973c) that drew this once-peripheral region into the economy, culture, and politics of modern Java.

THE NATIONAL BACKGROUND:
SOCIAL CHANGE IN NEW ORDER JAVA

Almost two decades after national independence, the mid 1960s witnessed the arrival of a New Order government determined to reorganize Indonesian politics and economics. More than anything else, this set the stage for subsequent changes in rural Java. The example requires us to "bring the state back in" (Skocpol 1985, 4) to agrarian analysis, recognizing the critical—if often pluralistic (Emmerson 1983)—impact of government on politics, production, and social differentiation.

The final years of the preceding Sukarno regime had seen ruinous hyperinflation (Arndt 1971; Mackie 1971), infrastructural decline, falling rice production (Timmer 1981, 86), and the flight of foreign capital (Booth and McCawley 1981b). In the political arena, parliamentary government had given way in 1957 to a more restrictive "Guided Democracy," dominated by President Sukarno and an intensifying three-sided rivalry between the Communist Party (PKI), Muslim organizations, and the armed forces (Lev 1966; Ricklefs 1981, 245–71). Political tensions increased in the 1960s. In response to the challenge, the PKI attempted to outflank its urban-based rivals through vigorous mobilization in the countryside. The party's campaign concentrated on implementation of recently passed land-reform legislation (Utrecht 1969). In the contest that ensued, the communists lost control of many of their rural supporters, and their Muslim rivals responded with surprisingly effective counterattacks (Mortimer 1974, 276–328). Some of the most extreme incidents of violence occurred in East Java. The political struggle took an unexpectedly bloody turn, however, in the aftermath of a failed left-wing officers' coup in Jakarta the night of October 1, 1965 (Crouch 1978, 97). In the months that followed, the PKI was banned and hundreds of thousands of its supporters were rounded up and killed. The stage was thus set for the New Order Suharto government.

The New Order government immediately set a different course than its predecessor. Opening the country to Japanese and Western investment, it soon managed to bring inflation under control, attract significant foreign capital, and achieve a positive balance of payments. It also launched new initiatives in agriculture, including programs for the distribution of fertilizers, pesticides, and newly developed modern rice varieties (Booth and McCawley 1981b). The programs expanded after 1973, when international oil prices climbed and government revenues swelled. After some initial setbacks owing to coercive administration

(Hansen 1973), the extension program began to take effect. By the late 1970s the majority of rice fields in Java were planted with new rice varieties and fertilizer use had become among the highest per hectare in Asia (Booth 1979; Timmer 1981). Yields increased dramatically. With annual increases of 3–5 percent, Indonesia's total rice production almost doubled in the 1970s to 18.5 million tons and reached 22 million in the early 1980s.

These achievements were offset by the poverty of Java's enormous population and by distributional trends that threatened to exclude the rural poor from the benefits of increased production. Despite an ambitious—and, by Third World standards, successful—family-planning program, the island's population continued to grow at a rate that ensured that it would double every 35–40 years (Hull and Mantra 1981). By 1985 Java's population was nearing 100 million, with "population densities . . . higher than any other agrarian region of comparable size in the world" (Husken and White 1989, 236). The weight of population on the land was reflected in shrinking landholdings. Between 1963 and 1973, the size of the average Javanese farm fell from 0.7 to 0.66 ha. (Booth and Sundrum 1976, 94). Although macroeconomic data indicate that landholding inequality remains moderate by Third World standards (Booth and Sundrum 1976, 95), these figures exclude the many rural people who own no land at all—usually more than 40 percent of the population in wet-rice areas of the island.

Other developments underscore the plight of Java's rural poor. Between 1924 and 1976 the proportion of the rural population identifiable as "very poor"—defined as all those with an annual per capita income less than the equivalent of 240 kg of rice, or roughly U.S. $50 (in 1985 dollars)—is estimated to have grown from 3.4 to 39.8 percent (Palte 1984, 85; Sajogyo 1977). Trends during the first years of the New Order also pointed to a situation of worsening distribution, with growing inequality between urban and rural areas. Despite increases in rice production, absolute consumption for the lowest 40 percent of the rural population did not improve, and indeed may have deteriorated (King and Weldon 1977, 708).

Employment trends raised troubling questions as well. From 1961 to 1980 the proportion of the work force identified as agricultural fell from 73.6 to 55.0 percent (Scherer 1980; Hart 1986, 62). The decline occurred at a time when there was little rural-urban migration, and the proportion of the island's population residing in rural areas fell only a few percentage points, to about 75 percent (Speare 1981). Half of the employment growth was in petty trade, services, and cottage industries, which are even less remunerative than rice farming (McCawley 1981; Hart 1986, 64). As Gillian Hart (1986) has argued, this pattern suggests that the decline in the agricultural labor force was at least in part the result of forcible displacement, not enticement into more lucrative off-farm enterprises.

Other evidence confirms that the lowland poor were being excluded from traditional farm employment. In East and Central Java, for example, the spread of modern rice varieties was accompanied by new, more restrictive labor arrangements. These barred villagers from harvests in which they had once had a right to work (Stoler 1977; Collier et al. 1973). Around this same time, many farmers replaced the hand-held harvest knife (*ani-ani*) with the sickle, reducing demand for harvest labor, and eliminating poor people's right to glean (Stoler 1977). The introduction of mechanical rice hullers, finally, made hand pounding obsolete. Although they lowered milling costs for people who paid to have rice pounded, the machines displaced some 7.7 million part-time pounders (Timmer 1973; Collier 1978). The majority of these were landless and land-poor women supplementing meager household incomes. Although recent surveys indicate that, for those able to find work, wages in rice farming increased in the late 1970s and early 1980s (Husken and White 1989), the sad fact is that large numbers of people are barred from farm employment entirely.

Many of these developments were also seen, of course, in other areas of Southeast Asia. There, too, gains in production have often been offset by more imbalanced patterns of employment and distribution (Bailey 1983; Ganjanapan 1989; Peletz 1988; Scott 1985). The situation in Indonesia, however, was further complicated by political events in the years just prior to the green revolution. As a number of scholars have noted (White 1976; Hull and Hull 1976), the opening of Java's rural economy coincided with the shutting down of most of the political organizations of the pre-1965 period. The watchwords of the New Order government have been "development and security" (*pembangunan dan keamanan*). Its overriding concern has been to avoid any recurrence of the agrarian conflict that characterized the final years of the Sukarno government. With this in mind, the regime initiated political reforms designed to reduce the influence of political parties and increase loyalty to the government. Government policies spoke of the need to transform rural society into a "floating mass." Under this policy, the rural population was encouraged to participate in national elections. Outside designated electoral periods, however, the populace was not to be bothered with politics. Instead, it was enjoined to devote its energies to the more pressing task of social and economic development (Crouch 1978, 272). Political parties were barred from organizing in villages.

Whatever their official intent, the New Order's programs have had a strong impact on all areas of Java and all aspects of rural life. Policy changes have made Indonesia's once-powerful political parties marginal players in a national arena dominated by the military. Equally serious, the programs have left rural people with little voice in the political process. At the same time, economic developments have increased rural differentiation and raised troubling questions as to the political and distributional consequences of development.

All of these changes have brought problems of equity and power to the center of attention in Javanese studies, which have recently reinvestigated Java's agrarian history in an effort to gauge the scale of recent changes by looking more closely at what preceded them. The results of this research challenge received images of rural society. Clifford Geertz's (1963a) pioneering study argued that the Dutch excluded Javanese from the capital-intensive export sector, forcing most of Java's growing population into an already "labor stuffed" (1963a, 80) *sawah* ecosystem. The resulting process of "agricultural involution," as Geertz calls it, did not split native society into opposed camps of "large landlords and a group of oppressed near-serfs" (1963a, 97). Instead, he argues, native institutions "maintained a comparatively high degree of social and economic homogeneity by dividing the economic pie into a steadily increasing number of minute pieces."

In line with this view, some scholars have interpreted the developments of post-1965 Java as a breakdown of long-established sharing arrangements. Traditional values stressing "social concern for the poor," it is argued, have been replaced with ones stressing efficiency and profit maximization (Collier 1978).

Though it does not contradict Geertz's primary thesis that colonialism did not produce a simple pattern of class polarization, more recent research indicates that class differences were more pronounced, and sharing values much weaker, than Geertz thought. It has been demonstrated, for example, that a large pool of landless and land-poor villagers existed in lowland areas even in the nineteenth century. Village officials and large landowners, it appears, thrived under colonial programs, often at the expense of their less-privileged neighbors. Rather than sharing poverty, those who played key roles in the colonial system appear to have used it to their benefit.[5]

Most of this recent research, however, has focused on the wet-rice lowlands, again neglecting upland agriculture and society. What was mountain Java like prior to this period? How has it changed? Has it experienced the same exclusionary pressures as the lowlands? More basically, what comparative lessons can we learn here about the processes of agrarian change? Mountain society remains to be incorporated into our understanding of Java's history and contemporary development; its lessons provide comparative insight into rural differentiation in Java and all of Southeast Asia.

5. Though this revisionist literature is vast, some of the most insightful contributions include Alexander and Alexander 1982; Breman 1982 and 1983; Elson 1978a and 1984; Hart 1986; Husken and White 1989; Knight 1982; Van Niel 1981; and White 1983.

HIGHLAND SOCIETY IN TRANSITION

There are, perhaps, good reasons for the analytic neglect of the rainfed uplands. Wet-rice is the most widespread of Java's cultivars, occupying about 40–45 percent of its agricultural lands (Montgomery 1981, 102). Although cassava and maize are important in Javanese diet (Dixon 1984, 69), rice is the most widely consumed and culturally preferred staple. The wet-rice lowlands are also the most densely populated of Java's agricultural regions, and the poorest and most economically stratified. During the Sukarno era, they were the site of the most pitched political battles. More recently, they have been the primary focus of government agricultural programs. For all these reasons, researchers and politicians alike have been especially concerned to monitor their development.

There are, nonetheless, compelling reasons for extending our research to the uplands. Besides their intrinsic interest for a broader understanding of Javanese culture, the highlands encompass about one-third of the island's total land area (Birowo and Hansen 1981, 1). Rainfed lands (*tegal*) and house gardens (*pekarangan*) account for over half of Java's cultivated land. In the drier and more rugged terrains of Java's eastern salient, the figure is usually higher. In the regency of Pasuruan, for example, dry-fields comprise nearly two-thirds of all agricultural land, and they are primarily located in mountain territory. Generalizations about upland agriculture are difficult, however, because it is characterized by such extraordinary diversity. The paddy field's homogenized ecology here gives way to a dizzying assortment of terrains. Upland farm practice reflects this fact, displaying dramatic variation according to altitude, temperature, cloud cover, soils, rainfall, groundwater, topography, and the resources of the resident population.

There is, however, one near-universal feature of upland agriculture: its susceptibility to erosion and fertility degradation. Upland *tegal* lacks the ecological resilience of irrigated *sawah*. Worked intensively, it loses its fertility. Exposed to winds and rain, it erodes. Cultivated without fallow, it becomes an ideal medium for fungi and insect pests. Not surprisingly, then, the history of agriculture in the Tengger mountains is one of ongoing ecological crisis. In the nineteenth century the deforestation accompanying extension of government coffee into upland "waste lands" caused widespread loss of topsoil. In this century population growth, shrinking landholdings, and commercial intensification have placed additional pressures on mountain lands. Though the green revolution of the 1970s reversed falling productivity, it did not stop soil erosion; in a few areas, in fact, it clearly exacerbated it (Palte 1984, 88; Roche 1985, 13; McCauley 1984, 10). As elsewhere in Southeast Asia (Peletz 1988, 160), this erosion has an impact far beyond the mountains. It worsens lowland flooding, pollutes drinking water, clogs irrigation channels, and destroys offshore marine environments. On environmental grounds alone, therefore, the study of upland agriculture is of compelling importance.

When, beginning in the late 1960s, the government began its rice-intensification programs, it at first paid little attention to rainfed or upland agriculture. As rice production increased some 41 percent from 1967–71, production of the major dry-field food staples—maize, cassava, and sweet potatoes—fell at an annual rate of 10, 7, and 5 percent respectively (Timmer 1981, 43). In Pasuruan's Tengger highlands, per-hectare yields for maize had, by the late 1960s, fallen to .80 metric tons, a low figure even by Javanese standards (Booth 1979, 49). Even worse, on some severely eroded fields, soil had become so infertile that maize could no longer be grown at all.

The introduction of green-revolution inputs to rainfed agriculture quickly reversed this decline. By the late 1970s average provincial yields for cassava and maize had risen over 50 percent (Roche 1985; Mink and Dorosh 1987, 44). In regions like the Tengger highlands, however, the increase was overshadowed by an unexpected development: the replacement of food staples with cash crops. In midslope villages farmers shifted from maize and cassava to coffee and cloves. In upperslope villages they replaced maize with potatoes, cabbages, and onions.

With the exception of cloves, all of these cash crops had been grown in the highlands prior to this time. Most, however, had been only secondary cultivars, grown alongside a primary crop of maize or, in the midslope region, cassava. Insect pests, soil fungi, low or variable yields, and market instability made farmers unwilling to cultivate these market crops more intensively. Now, for the first time, most of these problems were neutralized, and a truly intensive agriculture seemed possible. In just a few years, upland agriculture moved from subsistence cultivation marginally supplemented by cash-cropping, to capital-intensive commercial agriculture. A backwater of subsistence cultivation a few years earlier, the highlands became the site of Java's most aggressively capitalist agriculture.

The new agriculture depended upon massive applications of pesticides, fungicides, and fertilizers. Agrochemical inputs of this scale required capital expenditures several times those of wet-rice agriculture. Moreover, unlike paddy farmers, mountain farmers were not given government credit toward input purchase. As a result, they were obliged to turn to private sources of capital, financing the green revolution on their own. This organizational constraint proved to have a critical effect on the breadth of upland intensification. In the midslope region, the new agriculture became a monopoly of the wealthy. Unable to amass the capital required for new inputs, midslope smallholders remain trapped in an ecologically unstable, low-yield agriculture, even as their more affluent neighbors reap profits unimaginable ten years earlier. At the same time, the very success of the new agriculture has attracted a horde of outside investors, pushing land prices out of reach of the poor. In a region where the low price of land had long allowed for mobility between landholding groups, this development points to an ominous hardening of class lines.

In the upperslope region, by contrast, the accumulation of capital for new inputs was much easier, largely because vegetable cultivation allows for rapid turnaround on investments. Here, then, the benefits of the new agriculture have been shared by rich and poor alike. Demand for labor and, with it, wages and employment, have increased, and even the poor have enjoyed expanded incomes. Alienation of land to outsiders and wealthy villagers remains rare. Indeed, if anything, the green revolution here has strengthened the grip of smallholders on their land.

The example is instructive, because it shows that the social consequences of this upland green revolution are by no means uniform. A similarly varied pattern can be seen in the new agriculture's environmental impact. In the midslope region, tree crops have helped to reduce erosion, promising to stabilize this region's degraded topsoils. In the upperslope region, by contrast, the double- and triple-cropping of vegetables has resulted in unprecedented erosion. Farmers are aware of the crisis in fertility management. Yet as population grows and mean landholdings shrink, they are torn between the short-term interests of income and the long-term interests of the soil.

This unhappy tension between productive and environmental interests has long characterized upland agriculture, distinguishing it from the more durable paddy field. Upland environmental stabilization will remain one of the most critical challenges facing Java as it moves into the next century. The example reminds us that agricultural development must be assessed in terms of environmental sustainability, not just short-term returns.

The lesson is also relevant for other areas of the developing world, where commerce and population growth have pushed people into previously marginal mountain terrains. Though less widely studied than the world's dwindling tropical forests, these delicate mountain ecosystems are of crucial importance to the developing world. Their future is threatened, however, by population growth and agricultural programs that overlook their environmental fragility in the pursuit of short-term market rewards.

CLASS AND COMMUNITY IN ECONOMIC CHANGE

Recent changes in upland political economy have also widened the gap between rich and poor and linked the social forms of economic differentiation to national institutions and life-styles. As in much of the developing world, in other words, local economic culture is being recast along national lines. Here in the Tengger highlands, the change has been particularly striking, because this area was traditionally renowned for its relative equality and distinctive regional styles. A final goal of the present book, then, is to assess the practical and moral consequences of this incorporative change. While the discussion is grounded in a particular example, the issue is general, and my argument is intended to raise comparative questions for the analysis of class, community, and modern economic development.

Though a concern of economic theorists since the days of Ricardo, Smith, and Marx, the analysis of class has suffered in recent years. The topic has been caught between its close identification with Marxism (where the concept is by no means applied with great consistency), its wholesale neglect in cultural and symbolic studies (Ortner 1984, 131), and neoclassical economics's lack of interest in developing any more sociologically realistic units of analysis than "households" and "firms." In addition, as Lipset and Bendix (1953, 150) noted many years ago, discussions of class "are often academic substitutes for a real conflict over political orientations."

Despite renewed interest in political-economic topics in the 1980s (Marcus and Fischer 1986; Ortner 1984), then, the analysis of class is still fraught with conceptual problems. What is class, and how is it related to more general processes of social differentiation? What is its role in the structures and processes of political life? How does its influence differ from those of social groupings built around ethnicity, religion, or political ideology? As Bendix (1977, 362) and Nisbet (1965, 20) have noted, Western social thinkers were burningly preoccupied with these issues almost a century before Karl Marx, as they attempted to find answers to questions of rights and authority in a post-traditional world. Today, as class, status, and power are recast in the Third World, these same issues confront us on an even broader scale. Our inability to reach agreement on them is no trivial issue; it reflects a lack of consensus on the very meaning of modernity.

This same disagreement has handicapped empirical analyses of change in non-Western societies, where disputes as to the nature of class and status ensure that even simple events are subject to contradictory interpretations. This confusion is apparent, for example, in recent debates on Javanese agrarian history. In addition to disagreeing on the nature of class in colonial times (noted above), scholars have differed on the role of class in the anticommunist massacres of 1965–66, in which over half a million people died. Since some of the most intense violence pitted Muslims against nominally Muslim Javanists, some observers have concluded that class played a smaller role in the conflict than religion.

Others have rejected this view, arguing that the ferocity of bloodletting showed that religious and cultural cleavages, or *aliran*, overlapped with class structures. Hence, behind the facade of religious conflict, it is argued, the real issue was class struggle for control of economic resources.[6] Beyond this local debate on Javanese history lies a much broader question as to the nature of modern capitalism and its effects on solidarity and conflict.

The issue is an important one, not simply for Southeast Asian studies, but for a general understanding of political-economic change. The history of the modern world is littered with examples of economic transitions ultimately undercut by political disputes over life-styles, privileges, and social inequality. Over the long run, then, politics cannot be neatly separated from economics, however useful such a distinction might be for certain analytic exercises. Political analysis in turn, however, requires understanding of the "enduring attachments and commitments" (Sandel 1982, 179) that animate social life. It is just such an interactive approach—in which culture and social identity are seen as intrinsic to political economy, not external superstructures—that underlies the noneconomistic approach to economic change presented in this book.

This project requires a different perspective on economic life than normally entertained in neoclassical economics or conventional Marxism. In particular, it shifts the problem of identity and community to the center of investigation and demands a more sociologically and psychologically realistic model of economic actors. "The view of the person as a clear-headed maximizer over clearly defined preferences must give way to the image of a more complicated and less certain actor, attempting to sort out what is worth doing and what sort of person to be" (McPherson 1983, 111). Every preference, and every economic choice, in some sense evokes this issue of "what sort of person to be."

The consequences of this sociocultural insight for economic analysis are important. What economists call "preferences," first of all, are not immaculately conceived private mysteries independent of culture and society, as the neoclassical axiom of "consumer sovereignty" would imply (Scitovsky 1976; Hefner 1983b). Nor, as Marx would have it, are human

---

6 · The literature on *aliran* and class is extensive. The original formulation was Clifford Geertz's (1959; 1965a, 108–28). The distinction was subsequently appropriated by political scientists, even as Geertz distanced himself from some of its earlier associations (Geertz 1965a, 150). The single best collection of articles on the *aliran* dispute is found in Anderson and Kahin 1982, although King 1982, Wertheim 1969, and essays by Jackson, Emmerson, and Liddle in Jackson and Pye 1978 also represent important contributions. See ch. 7.

interests self-evidently given in relations of property and production.[7] Individuals receive social assistance in deciding what is valuable to them,
and why. They refer back to their sense of who they are and what seems
appropriate to their way of life. This sensibility is itself informed by what
social psychologists call "social referencing"—that is, assessment of the
evaluations of significant and powerful others in formulating one's feel-
ings as to the good and desirable (Shweder et al. 1987, 69; Feinman 1982;
Merton 1968). The social referencing of each of us as individuals is influenced by relations between groups in society, and the moral and political
history they imply. The resulting "commitments" (Sen 1977) that underlie human behavior are broader in scope than those attributed to the abstract individual of utilitarian theory; and they respond to interests more
varied than those of the marketplace alone. From this perspective, *homo
economicus* is, in fact, a thoroughly social being. A noneconomistic account of economic life begins with this complex truth.

   This approach to economic change does not mean that neoclassical
methods have no role to play in the analysis of economic life. Where
one's concern is to investigate the formation of prices through the interaction of supply and demand, and where consumer preferences are more
or less stable, for example, there is little need to invoke such a complex
model of identity and "socially organized forms of satisfaction" (Leiss
1976, 9). In the study of economic change, however, preferences are not
always stable, and even an understanding of supply and demand requires
that one attend to more than price signals in the marketplace. In such a
context, the "self" of which we talk in "self-interest" can no longer be
unproblematically equated with that of a fictional *homo economicus*. Nor
can it be reduced to a putative class interest simplistically defined as the
internalized expression of class position. To grasp actors' interests we
must understand their identity and commitments and the history and social structures through which they are sustained.

   These issues underlie the agrarian history presented in the following
chapters. It is clear, for example, that throughout much of this history intrasocietal class divisions were only one among the many forces shaping
rural solidarity and conflict. In the seventeenth and eighteenth centuries,

   7. As has been widely remarked (Etzioni 1988; Sahlins 1976; Leiss 1976), both Marxism and neoclassical economics are prone to simplistic characterizations of "self" and
"self-interest." Both use what is essentially a utilitarian model of human needs and
judgment, and—a few intriguing remarks by Marx aside (Marx 1973, 92)—both neglect investigation of the social formation of wants. When viewed as a psychocultural reality rather than a static attribute of an abstract economic man, self-interest can only be
understood in relation to actors' social involvements, with the life-style, needs, and political contests they imply. Economic development reshapes these social arrangements
just as much as it does income and production.

the political-economic landscape of rural Pasuruan was more critically influenced by interregional wars. These united the Dutch and a declining Central Javanese state against a loose alliance of Javanese rebels, Balinese princes, and independent-minded Tengger peasants. Although these regional contests had a clear economic dimension, they were not played out along simple class lines. They were interstate conflicts, and states can achieve organizational autonomy relative to domestic social structures. Hence they "are not simply reflective of the demands or interests of social groups, classes, or societies" (Skocpol 1985, 9).

In the nineteenth century, as the Dutch consolidated their power and effectively excluded their rivals, such state rivalries had a less direct impact on the Javanese countryside. Again, however, it was the state, not intrasocietal classes or status groups, that set the course for the transformation of larger Java. Government played a similarly pivotal role in the economic development of nearby Sumatra, Malaya, and Thailand (Kahn 1980; Peletz 1988; Keyes 1987).

By unifying a countryside earlier fractured by regional hostilities, the Europeans created a large-scale, interregional economy. Homogenizing the social terrain in this way, they brought into being an economy of scale in which local communities were no longer primarily self-sufficient; large masses of people in once-isolated regions were subjected to similar economic demands. In so doing, colonialism created in an Asian context some of the conditions recognized by both Marx and Weber as central to the formation of class groupings in modern Europe (Giddens 1973, 84).

In other respects, however, Dutch colonialism had a markedly different impact than industrial capitalism in Europe. The transformation of the countryside was pioneered by a foreign-dominated bureaucracy, not a vigorous native bourgeoisie. Colonial policies systematically discriminated against natives in enterprise, politics, and education. As a result, one saw no hint here of that "historically prior clearing operation" (Parkin 1979, 31) that, in Europe, Marx simplistically believed, would sweep away "premodern" status-group attachments such as ethnicity and religion, leaving the ground clear for a final showdown between workers and bourgeoisie. In Indonesia state policies were premised on ethnic distinctions. Rigidly reinforcing the status-divide between Europeans and indigenes, the colonial government created a nontraditional status category—the native Indonesian. It thus ensured that Indonesia's soon-to-emerge political movements would primarily espouse nationalist goals, not those of class struggle.

As noted above, there *were* important class divisions in rural Pasuruan and all of Java, most strikingly in wet-rice areas of the countryside. These divisions, however, were not simple products of domestic class struggles. In large measure, in fact, they were shaped by the mercantile state, which needed native elites to help direct its commercial programs, and a mass of peasant producers to work for them. Colonialism forced Java's peasantry into the world market. But it barred them from playing too active a role and forced most of them into a mixed pattern of small-holder production and forced labor on government estates. In both spheres, relations of production remained primarily noncapitalist, relying little on free wage labor.

Given these changes in rural institutions, the question still remains, How did native Javanese experience class? What was its role in their identity and commitments? As numerous scholars have noted (Weber 1968, 930; Giddens 1973, III; Parkin 1979), the objective reality of class in no way guarantees solidarity among its cohorts. Other social groupings can engender organizations and moral commitments of their own. Contrary to some models of class polarization, then, the colonial transformation of rural Pasuruan did not corrode all preexisting status-group attachments, leaving the field clear for a simple contest between capitalist peasants and landless proletarians. Its structural impact was more varied, and its effect on popular solidarity was mediated by preexisting social cleavages, the most important of which was the opposition between lowland Muslims and Javanist highlanders.

Though in native eyes this regional contest was often identified as a religious one, it was more complex than that. It was a conflict between two types of native community, and two ways of being Javanese, each characterized by its own forms of life. In this sense, the conflict was like that between modern nation states: Each side had its own elites and its own patterns of status, class, and power. Class influences were real enough, but, as in other societies, their influence was complex. Class groupings were crosscut by communally based status groups, enhancing regionalist allegiances, and working against the development of self-conscious social classes.

Whatever its complex role in identity and polity, class in its "objective" sense has always had a strong influence on welfare and social organization. This is evident still today in mountain Pasuruan. Wealthy farmers were the first to use new agrochemicals, and they continue to apply larger amounts to their fields today. They are better able than the poor to engage in soil conservation practices such as fallowing and manuring. They have less difficulty securing private credit, and are more likely to purchase or rent farm land. They more frequently hire coolies and, through the provision of credit and employment, often support dependent clients. Large farmers also divorce less frequently and adopt children more often. They have more children in general and fewer infant deaths. Their children go to school longer than do the land-poor, and more of them seek high-paying jobs outside agriculture and outside the village. In earlier years, the land-wealthy were more likely to invest their wealth in ritual exchange partnerships than the poor, and they sponsored larger and more prestigious religious festivals. Today, they lead the way in promoting new forms of conspicuous consumption, bringing television sets, motorbikes, and new foods, furniture, and dress into villages once renowned for their exclusion of "lowland" goods. They are also ardent promoters of linguistic and social styles once stigmatized as *ngare*-lowlander. In short, though its role is mediated by complex social arrangements, class does correlate with broad differences in life-style, rank, and power.

Given this pervasive influence, it might seem curious that political groupings have not been primarily organized along horizontal class lines. At least in an objective sense, after all, the majority of peasants in lowland and upland Pasuruan have long been members of the same economic class. In the nineteenth century the broadest segments of both peasantries were drawn into a regional colonial economy, and both came to occupy a similarly subordinate position in a colonial mode of production. Viewed circumstantially then, they comprised a single class. In terms of their day-to-day commitments, however, they did not. Differences of religion, life-style, and politics convinced people in both regions that they were to a significant degree separated by opposed interests. Whatever their common class situation, therefore, the two peasantries (or the lowest segments thereof) did not form a consistently solidary group. Even at the height of its 1964 land-reform campaign, the Indonesian Communist Party made little progress in its goal of uniting poor and middle peasants in the two regions.

One way to explain this lack of class cohesion would be to fault the awareness of the peasantry and speak of their "false consciousness" or inability to recognize their true (lateral) class interests. This was the tack adopted by Marx in his famous *The Eighteenth Brumaire of Louis Bonaparte*. In analyzing the political role of the peasantry in mid-nineteenth-century France, Marx at first notes that they are concerned with issues of religion and nationalism, not just economic reward. Tracing their ideological orientation back to the peculiarly fragmented conditions of peasant production, he seems on one hand to acknowledge the possibility that solidary groupings can be organized along lines more diverse than intraclass allegiance (Marx 1968, 171–72; Cohen 1982, 120). Indeed, at times he verges on an insight, later developed by Max Weber, that there are social interests and sources of power other than those engendered by relations of production.

In the end, however, Marx's excursion into a more heterogeneous world abruptly ends. He pulls back from the subversive lesson of his example, apparently sensing that it would imperil his primary faith that class interests take precedence over all others, and that they are ultimately derived from relations of production. Adopting an essentialist view of class interests, he ends by berating the French peasantry for being "incapable of enforcing their class interests in their own name. . . . They cannot represent themselves, they must be represented" (Marx 1968, 172).[8]

The negative lesson Marx provides is a general one. Time and time again in historical and ethnographic research, we encounter similar instances of agents acting contrary to their interests as specified in terms of an abstract model of property and production. Having determined the circumstantial contours of class, one assumes that they provide the key to actors' "real" interests. When agents act contrary to these putative concerns, one speaks of "fetishism" or "false consciousness."[9]

Building on comparative history and social theory (Giddens 1973, 1984; Cohen 1982; Chirot 1986; Weber 1968, 926–33), the approach I use in this book assumes that class is an important dimension of social reality, but not unitary in its effects. In the real world, actors' interests are never directly derivative of relations of production. There are other structures of power, other sources of interest, and other grounds for moral solidarity. With Weber (1968, 926–33; Giddens 1973, 43), then, the analysis of class

8. One of the finest discussions on this tension between Marx's empirical studies of class and his prior ideological commitments is found in Cohen 1982. Giddens 1973 and Parkin 1979 explore this same problem, noting Marx's tendency to reduce all sources of power and all social interests to relations of production.

9. As James Scott (1985) has best demonstrated, there is another way out of the "false consciousness" dilemma. It is to show that what looks like compliance on the part of peasants actually overlooks the less dramatic, "everyday forms of resistance" whereby peasant subordinates quietly but persistently defend themselves from superiors' demands. This argument is a useful corrective to conventional views of political resistance. But it raises the question of the nature of the solidarity implied in such acts. Though Scott wisely reminds us to attend to "the messy reality of multiple identities" (Scott 1985, 43), much of the literature on peasant and worker resistance appears reluctant to push this analytic injunction very far and devotes most of its attention to political struggles that conform to conventional models of class solidarity. Often it is assumed that class divisions are themselves sufficient to guarantee (lateral) class solidarity. Immanuel Wallerstein elevates this conceptual mistake to the status of an analytic axiom, insisting: "The traditional distinction between objective class status and subjective class membership . . . seems to me totally artificial. An objective class status is only a reality insofar as it becomes a subjective reality for some group or groups, and if it 'objectively' exists, it inevitably will be felt 'subjectively' " (Wallerstein 1979, 225–26). If one is to avoid projecting one's own values into political analysis, however, the problem of class allegiance has to be subsumed within the larger effort to understand the general structures and determinants of social solidarity. As Max Weber argued most forcefully, there can be no guarantee that class takes precedence over ethnicity, religion, nationalism, vertical patronage, or other social bonds in the structures of everyday life.

begins with the recognition that its influence can be, and usually is, pluralistic.

The implications of this thesis for the study of agrarian change are important. "Social differentiation" cannot be understood in terms of objective relations of production or "surplus extraction" alone.[10] It must also be grasped in relation to community and life-style—or what Weber calls "status groups"—and the identity and commitments they imply. This, of course, makes the analysis of class more difficult. No longer can we assume, as Marx did (Giddens 1973, 28), that class structures correspond directly with structures of political and intellectual domination. As here in rural Pasuruan, status groups based on noneconomic criteria such as region, religion, or ethnicity can cut across (circumstantially given) class lines. The differential control of resources can reinforce interclass alliances. Even where there is a strong awareness of class, therefore, the inequalities it entails need not lead to lateral class allegiances. Segmentary ties of patron-clientage are just as common a reaction to the scarcity created by differential control of market resources.

Recognizing that there are no universal formulae for understanding its influence on status and power, we must be careful in crafting a definition of class. In particular, the definition must avoid any hint of that teleology, so widespread in conventional interpretations of class (cf. Wallerstein 1979, 225), that would suggest that the objective structures of class automatically specify a particular social interest. The concept of class, in other words, must be a restrictive one, with no more entailments than can empirically be justified.

In keeping with these reservations, *class* as used throughout this book refers to aggregates of individuals who are similarly situated relative to control of the means of production and other market resources (Giddens 1973, 84). In this sense, I distinguish class from social stratification, or the evaluative system of ranking used by members of a society in attributing prestige (see Parkin 1978, 603). In line with Weber (1968) and Giddens (1973), this concept of class need not imply common identity, collective self-awareness, or any of the other cultural traits that sociologists associate with the concept of a "group." It is an objective influence on the life-chances of men and women, about which they become conscious only under certain conditions.

10. In an otherwise superb analysis of agrarian differentiation in Southeast Asia, Benjamin White makes just this mistake, defining differentiation in narrowly productivist terms. "Rural differentiation," he writes, is primarily concerned with the "process of change in the way in which different groups in rural society . . . gain access to the products of their own or others' labor, based on differential control over production resources" (White 1989, 20).

Whether class groupings do give rise to such collective identity and shared commitments—which is to say, whether they become what we might call "social classes" (Weber 1968; Giddens 1973)—is an important question. Indeed, as Giddens (1973, 105) has observed, it is in some ways the single most important question in our effort to understand the structure of modern society. Analytically, however, this question cannot be collapsed into the other as if objective relations of production always specify a single pattern of conflict and solidarity.

To put this argument slightly differently, one can distinguish two related, but nonetheless distinct, features of class, the one "circumstantial" and the other subjective or phenomenological. Of these, only the former is a necessary and universal feature of class.[11] As Anthony Giddens (1984, xix) has discussed more generally, "circumstantial" forces can exercise social influence without actors being aware of their existence. This is the dimension of class that I explore, for example, when examining infant mortality across different classes. High rates of infant mortality among the land-poor do not in any systemic way depend on actors' awareness of or identification with a given social class. The incidence of infant deaths is nonetheless profoundly influenced by a family's control of productive resources. Here, then, is an arena in which the circumstantial effect of class is quite significant, even though it appears to work largely independently of actors' awareness.

Alternately, of course, class can be viewed subjectively, through its influence on people's identity, interests, and solidary allegiances. This is the type of analysis involved, for example, in determining the degree to which the Communist Party in the Tengger highlands attracted followers because they viewed it as a defender of the poor. While the circumstantial reality of class can operate independently of actors' consciousness,

---

11. This restrictive view of class and class consciousness thus differs from those of Wallerstein (1979, 225) and E. P. Thompson (1978, 145), both of whom assume that the existence of class groupings in some sense implies, or depends upon, collective awareness of shared interests. As Anthony Giddens has noted (1973, 92–93), Marx himself vacillates on this point. In his theoretical writings on European capitalism, he implies that at least in the long run such a coincidence of objective position and consciousness will develop. In his historical writings on feudalism, the French peasantry, and oriental despotism, among other subjects, however, he seems to pull back from the view that objective class either engenders or depends upon common consciousness. Inconclusive as it is, the more serious shortcoming of Marx's approach, at any rate, is his failure to develop an adequate appreciation of the sources of power outside the production process. This failure meant that it would be all too easy for his followers to assume that class and class consciousness are intrinsically connected and comprise the hidden base on which political-economic power and social solidarity are grounded (see Parkin 1979; Giddens 1973; Bendix 1977).

class in this latter, subjective sense, cannot. It builds upon the acknowledged identities of social life.[12]

In the chapters that follow, I am concerned with both these dimensions of class. I am particularly interested, moreover, in "the blank spot
in class theory" (Giddens 1973, 105): understanding the processes whereby circumstantial classes do or do not become self-conscious social
classes, and the relationship of the latter to groupings based on ethnicity,
religion, or other features of social status.

This problem of class and *stand,* of course, is the same that underlay
Max Weber's entire life project. In recent years it has reemerged as a
central problem in modern social inquiry (cf. Bourdieu 1984, xi). The Pasuruan example provides us with an unusually rich terrain for exploring
its contours. Class here has been but one of the influences shaping social
conflict. Regional and religious differences have also played an important
role. The example indicates that class groupings need not be separated
by "mutual antagonism and the incompatibility of interests" (Parkin
1978, 608), as some essentialist definitions of class would insist. Our egalitarian biases aside, the influence of class is just as real, and just as legitimate, when it reinforces alliances between rich and poor, rather than
separating them in polarized class struggle. The history of modern nationalism demonstrates that communities built across class lines can engender allegiances every bit as compelling as those grounded on
intraclass solidarity (Anderson 1983a).

12. As I have described them here, these two qualities of class resemble the familiar
Marxist distinction between class "in itself" and "for itself" (see Giddens 1973, 94).
The former looks at class in terms of all those "similarly situated vis-à-vis means of
production" (Brow 1981, 34). Class "for itself," by contrast, explores the problem of
class as a "solidary group, conscious of common interests and organized to pursue
them" (Brow 1981, 35). In my opinion, the Hegelian connotations of these terms make it
preferable to use a different terminology, which avoids any hint of a dialectical teleology. In talking of "class consciousness," one might add, it is useful to distinguish between simple consciousness of kind and the conviction that those occupying common
class situations actually share common interests (see Bottomore 1965, 64; Giddens 1973,
111). As here in mountain Pasuruan, people can be aware of hierarchies of wealth and
power without thereby feeling committed to those who share a class position. Having
distinguished these two dimensions of class, I should also emphasize, as Giddens (1984)
does more generally, that the relationship between them is extremely unstable. Actors
catch glimpses of the circumstantial influence of wealth and power (and other aspects of
social life) all the time, and use this knowledge to adjust their behavior. In changing
their actions, they invariably restructure both their self-understandings and their circumstantial environment. The result is that the border between the circumstantial reality of "materialist" social science and the lived reality emphasized in interpretive social
theory is constantly changing. In the study of social reality in general, and of status and
class in particular, then, there can be no simplistic, or even stable, dualism of objectivism and subjectivism.

A general theory of social solidarity, then, requires that we reject the view that class position automatically specifies a unitary social interest. A pluralist alternative is particularly important if we are to avoid what the political theorist Jean Cohen (1982, 191–93) has called the "fetishism of class relations" that affects much contemporary social theory. In attributing a determinant influence to class, this view effectively "excludes the possibility that there might be other modes of domination than socioeconomic class relations, other principles of stratification in addition to class (nationality, race, status, sex, etc.)" (Cohen 1982, 193). It overlooks the possibility "that certain forms of political power can be generated independently of class power and can indeed annihilate the power of social classes" (Parkin 1979, 140).

The history of nation-state warfare makes the contrary truth all too clear. So, too, did the anticommunist violence of 1965–66 in East Java. The conflict was exacerbated by declining economic circumstances, which differentially affected rich and poor. Hence it had an important class dimension. But the practical impact of such pressures often forced poor peasants into alliance with local patrons rather than their fellow poor. The conflict was also affected by religious and social organizations whose motives and morality were in no way reducible to class interests. Finally, and in some ways most important, the force and direction of the violence were ultimately shaped by the machinery of state, an institution whose dynamic is never reducible to class interests alone. To describe the conflict as a simple "class war" substitutes a reductionist abstraction for the more sustained sociological analysis required to understand the plural bases of identity, morality, and power.

In attempting to write a history of economy and society in the Tengger highlands, then, I have felt compelled to subsume my inquiry under two larger projects: (1) investigation of the circumstantial influences that shape welfare and social relations, at times independently of human awareness; and (2) analysis of the solidary groupings through which men and women establish a sense of self and commitment to others. In studying social history, we are obliged to recognize that society has a practical integrity whose complexity often escapes actors' understanding. A purely cultural or interpretive analysis, therefore, cannot capture the range of forces that shape its development. At the same time, however, actors' self-understandings are integral aspects of social life. In the analysis of economic change, there can be no detour around the social world, with its varied patterns of solidarity and power. Herein lies the key to a noneconomistic approach to economic change.

These, at any rate, are the lessons from this small corner of Southeast Asia. Thrust into a national arena, these mountain Javanese sought not simply to maximize income or expand production, but to redefine community and "what sort of person to be." Not an ineffable mystery, this sense of community and commitment is socially and politically sustained. It is one of the most powerful forces at work in our modern world. It is for this reason that governments, parties, businesses, churches, and other institutions court it with such favor and expend such resources on its education and control. It underlies our political commitments and animates our economic aspirations. The contest to redefine its guiding sensibilities perpetually reshapes our world.

TWO

Politics and Community in
Premodern History

Few areas of Java bear such visible traces of Southeast Asia's complex history as do the Tengger highlands. Drawn into a lowland-based Hindu-Buddhist state a thousand years ago, this is the only region in modern Java to have preserved an indigenous Hindu priesthood. After Hindu Majapahit's fall at the beginning of the sixteenth century, the centers of power on the island moved west to Muslim courts in Central Java, and the influence of lowland powers in the eastern mountain areas waned. For the next two centuries, politics and religion worked to isolate these mountain Javanese from their Muslim neighbors to the west. Indeed, for a time, it looked as if the inhabitants of this upland territory might become a wholly separate ethnic group. Like highlanders in much of Southeast Asia (Keyes 1977, 19; Leach 1954), they preserved a dialect, a religious tradition, and a social order distinct from those of their lowland neighbors. Their mythology spoke of flight from the lowlands and an identity distinct from that of Muslim Javanese.

Ultimately, however, the upland-lowland contrast did not evolve into a full-blown ethnic cleavage, as the mountains were firmly drawn into events in the surrounding society. Isolated from the courtly influences that reshaped Central Javanese culture in the seventeenth and eighteenth centuries, the Tengger highlands awoke in the nineteenth century to find themselves forcibly reincorporated into a new and more powerful entity, the Dutch colonial state. It was this more than any other institution that shaped politics and community in the Tengger mountains at the dawn of the modern era.

THE PRECOLONIAL UPLANDS

Prior to the tenth century the most important centers of state power on the island of Java were located around the rich wet-rice terrains of inland central Java. Much of the spectacular architecture of this region—at Buddhist Borobudur and Sivaite Prambanan, among other sites—dates from this period. In the tenth century, however, court power shifted eastward, first to the Kediri region, in the western portion of what is today the province of East Java, and, early in the thirteenth century, to Singosari, a town located at the western edge of the Tengger highlands. The shift east may have been owing to the growing importance of trade with eastern Indonesia's spice islands, for which the eastern Javanese authorities acted as brokers. As Schrieke (1957, 2:301) has speculated, the move may have also been the product of flight from Central Java by peasants seeking to escape the onerous burden of forced labor required for the construction of Central Java's monumental architecture.

Political rivalry among eastern Java's new principalities was intense. Kediri was conquered in 1222 by Singosari, a state founded by a commoner with no prior dynastic genealogy. Seventy years later, Kediri forces returned to avenge their defeat by capturing the Singosari court. Kediri's victory was itself short-lived, however, as Singosari armies returned quickly to rout the invaders. Consistent with Javanese tradition, Singosari's leaders were reluctant to reestablish their capital at a site once seized by their enemies. Hence a new court was built about ninety kilometers (as the crow flies) to the northwest, at a site known as Majapahit. Situated a small distance from the coast in the Brantas River valley, the location was ideally suited for control of the agrarian hinterland and for easy access to the important port of Surabaya at the river's mouth (Robson 1981, 262). The old Singosari court, meanwhile, appears to have remained in use; fourteenth-century chronicles, for example, report that King Hayam Wuruk of Majapahit stayed in its central compound at the end of his tour of the realm in 1359 (Pigeaud 1962, 4:104). For the next two centuries, Singosari-Majapahit was Java's most powerful kingdom; it would be remembered in modern times as the most glorious of the island's pre-Islamic states. It declined in the final decades of the fifteenth century, however, and its eventual conquest in the 1520s by Muslim principalities (Noorduyn 1978; Robson 1981) was an important watershed in premodern Javanese history.

Our knowledge of the Tengger highlands during this pre-Islamic period is fragmentary. Literary and epigraphic evidence indicates that the mountain region played an important role in state-supported religious cults. It was home, for example, to both Sivaite and Buddhist clerical communities, as well as to a smattering of freeholder villages involved in the worship of mountain spirits (Pigeaud 1962, 4:443–44; Hefner 1985, 25). The most important of these spirits was that associated with the massive volcanic cauldron at the center of the Tengger massif, known as Mount Bromo. Rising some 300 meters from the desolate wastes of a rolling "sand sea" (*segoro wedi*), this smoldering crater is itself located at the center of a larger, extinct crater, some ten kilometers in diameter and four hundred meters deep. Historical evidence indicates that in Majapahit times the Bromo complex was the focus of important ritual activity, as it is still today for the upperslope Hindus. Each year, non-Islamic highlanders come together on the slopes to throw offerings into the volcano and to remember the flight of their Hindu ancestors from Muslim armies (Hefner 1985, 46).

Religious texts from the pre-Islamic period make numerous references to this unusual mountain terrain, indicating that at least some of the local population were involved in state cults. Several texts, for example, link the sand sea around the Bromo caldera to sacred territories in classical Hindu cosmology. One text, for example, describes how the souls of the dead must pass through the sand sea's barren wastes on their way to the fiery hell of Bromo (Gonda 1952, 148). The same purgatorial image appears in prayers of ritual purification still used today by Hindu priests in the upperslope highlands (Hefner 1985, 176–82). An important work of the late Majapahit period, the *Tantu Panggelaran* (see Pigeaud 1924), also mentions this region, identifying Mount Bromo as the spot where the Indic god of fire, Brahma (from whom the volcano's name, Bromo or Brama, is derived), does his smithing.

The most intriguing references to the Tengger highlands, however, occur in the fourteenth-century *Nagarakertagama,* an account of a "progress" through the countryside by Hayam Wuŕuk, ruler of Majapahit at the height of its power (Pigeaud 1962). The king's journey skirted the Tengger highlands, and on several occasions he made forays into its midslope regions. For example, the royal procession visited a *mandhala* religious community in the district of Tongas, Probolinggo (on the northern slopes of the Tengger massif), performed water devotion at a nearby shrine, and received tribute from eleven Buddhist communities, including three located in or near present-day mountain communities.[1] Although today all of these villages lie just below the territory inhabited by upperslope Hindus, ethnographic evidence suggests that several of them remained non-Islamic into the early nineteenth century.

The importance of the Tengger mountains for Majapahit religion raises the question as to the precise relation between this earlier tradition

1. The three villages are Lumbang, Pancur, and Tenggilis; see Pigeaud 1962, 4:68; de Vries 1931, 1:17.

and that of today's upperslope non-Muslim "Tengger." This issue has long fascinated scholars, who have hoped that modern Tengger traditions might provide clues as to the nature of popular religion in Majapahit times. J. E. Jasper's (1926) influential work on modern Tengger, however, counseled pessimism in this regard. He argued that in earlier times the upperslope population was a tribal enclave that had held itself apart from the rest of Java. This people's conversion to Hinduism occurred so late in Majapahit's history, Jasper speculated, that they were only superficially Indicized. Hence their traditions tell us little about pre-Islamic religion as a whole.

In his brilliant work on fourteenth-century Java, Theodore Pigeaud relied heavily on Jasper's account to reach a similar conclusion. "In fact even in the pre-Islamic period," he wrote, "the Tengger highlanders seem to have formed a separate community, worshipping the spirit of a volcano who (by outsiders, probably) had been given an Indian name, Brahma" (Pigeaud 1962, 4:244). The ritual texts preserved by Tengger priests, he concluded, are "apparently of relatively recent date," and thus are "disappointing to scholars seeking information on Old Javanese religion" (1967, 1:49). Rather than linking the present-day Tengger tradition to the Sivaite communities discussed in the *Nagarakertagama* or the *Tantu Panggelaran*, therefore, he thought it more likely that modern Tengger are related to the "spirit servants" (*hulun hyang*) mentioned in the Walandhit charter discovered near Mount Bromo at the turn of the present century (1962, 4:443–44). These people, he speculated, were probably "simple worshippers of local Spirits or tutelary deities residing on mountains or in springs, not wholly identified with the great Indian gods, especially Shiwa" (1962, 4:486).

More recent research, however, refutes these arguments and indicates that the ancestors of today's upperslope Hindus were mountain Javanese whose priests in Majapahit times were members of a Sivaite clergy found throughout East Java and Bali.[2] Even today, there are strong parallels in ritual performance and paraphernalia between Tengger and Bali. Indeed, some Tengger prayers show a word-for-word correspondence to those found in modern Bali, describing a richly detailed Sivaite cosmol-

2. Jasper's (1926) historical reconstruction reached a different conclusion in part because he, like many scholars in colonial times, regarded the upperslope "Tengger" population as a cultural and racial survival of an earlier proto-Javanese population. Even in Jasper's time, however, there was strong evidence of earlier cultural ties between Tengger and Bali (Scholte 1921), suggesting that the isolation of the upperslope Hindus was the product of political conflict, not of putative racial distinctiveness (Rouffaer 1921; de Vries 1931). The Hindu population, one should note, are physically indistinguishable from people in other areas of East Java, and they certainly think of themselves as Javanese (Hefner 1985).

ogy.[3] This and other evidence indicates that clerics in the Tengger mountains were once associated with a popular Sivaite order known as the *resi
pujangga*, genealogically related to the non-Brahmanic *resi bujangga* of
modern Bali.

For an understanding of politics and community in the premodern
Tengger highlands, this apparently obscure information is of critical importance. It shows that from early on the people of the highlands and
those of the plains had strong cultural ties. This is in striking contrast
with many other areas of Southeast Asia where mountain peoples maintain ethnic and religious identities apart from those of the state-
dominated lowlands (Leach 1954; Keyes 1977, 27). That this was not the
case in the Tengger highlands testifies to the cultural cohesiveness of the
early Javanese state. It also helps to explain why in Java, unlike neighboring areas of Southeast Asia, there was such a remarkable degree of
ethnic homogeneity from an early period. Even in Majapahit times the
lowland-based state exercised a dominating influence on upland affairs.

After reaching its zenith in the fourteenth century, Majapahit fell into
decline just a hundred years later, in part as a result of the rise of Muslim
mercantile states in the western and central regions of the Malay archi-
pelago. The court itself was overrun in 1478, apparently by a rival Hindu
principality. It was then recaptured by what was probably a legitimate
dynastic line in 1486 (Noorduyn 1978, 255). Shortly after its reestablish-
ment, the court was moved inland, away from the increasingly powerful
Muslim principality of Surabaya at the mouth of the Brantas river (Robson 1981, 279). The mercantile economy of the now-Muslim coast was
slowly becoming ascendant over the inward-looking, rice-growing, and
largely feudal interior. Eventually, the alliance of Muslim merchants and
potentates proved too strong. In the 1520s Majapahit fell to Muslim
forces from north coast principalities, under the spiritual and political
leadership of Demak (de Graaf and Pigeaud 1974, 34–71). The process of
Islamization that had followed insular trade routes through Northern Sumatra (converted in the late thirteenth century), northeastern Malaya
and the southern Philippines (fourteenth century), and Malacca and the
Malay peninsula (fifteenth century) had achieved its greatest prize yet.

Majapahit's collapse marked the beginning of a long and uneven
process of Islamization in Java's eastern territories, one that would not be

3. The content of the old prayers says nothing about either priestly or popular understanding of their meaning. Historical evidence shows that this non-Islamic population experienced considerable cultural disorientation as it came under the influence of
its Muslim neighbors (Hefner 1983a). The relationship between the Tengger and Balinese prayers is discussed in greater detail in Smith-Hefner 1983 and Hefner 1985, 163–
88. The corresponding liturgy of the Balinese *resi bujangga* is found in Hooykaas 1974.
Other information on these *resi* is found in Hooykaas 1964 and Pigeaud 1924, 248–49.

completed for another 250 years. In the middle of the sixteenth century, the north coast principality of Demak took the lead in coordinating the campaign against the few remaining Hindu-Buddhist principalities on the island, relying on a shifting alliance of Muslims from Java's north coast. The port of Pasuruan fell to Demak's forces in 1535 (de Graaf and Pigeaud 1974, 180). The victors quickly appointed a Muslim administrator for the region, and in 1546 Pasuruan, now Islamized, played a leading role in the Muslim campaign against the still heathen court of Panarukan, just to the east. Despite these advances, large interior areas to the east and south of Pasuruan remained non-Islamic. The most important center of resistance was the small principality of Blambangan at the far eastern tip of Java. The last of Java's Hindu-Buddhist courts, Blambangan was attacked in the 1540s, 1580s, 1590s, and early 1600s. The population of the Tengger mountains appear to have been drawn repeatedly into this contest. They had the unfortunate distinction of lying smack dab in the middle of the no-man's-land separating Muslim Central Java from Hindu Blambangan to the east (de Graaf and Pigeaud 1974, 193).[4]

The turmoil in this eastern region was soon complicated by a changing balance of power in Muslim Central Java. Beginning in the late sixteenth century, the inland agricultural state of Mataram rose to power, ultimately dominating the trading ports of the north coast. While Mataram was nominally Islamic, and even used Islam as a rallying cry against its Dutch enemies, it greatly restricted the political influence of the once-powerful Muslim clergy. Court literati also revived some of the aesthetic styles of the pre-Islamic period (Ricklefs 1974) and created many of the distinctive ritual forms still associated with "Javanist" Islam.

Like its north-coast predecessors, Mataram looked east after consolidating its power in Central Java. It conquered Pasuruan in 1616, Madura in 1624, and Surabaya, its most powerful coastal rival, in 1625. Still non-Islamic, Blambangan was repeatedly attacked between 1635 and 1640, when Mataram forces finally managed to occupy its court. Like earlier Muslim powers, however, Mataram failed to develop administrative control of the eastern territory, and, with the help of forces from Hindu

---

4. Even in the nineteenth century, legends collected in the countryside spoke of the violence of former times and the role of Tengger priests in resisting Islamic armies (de Graaf and Pigeaud 1974, 179; Hefner 1985, 53–57; Rouffaer 1921, 300). Few of these tales are remembered today. Interestingly, the image of Islamization that emerges from these accounts is quite different from the relatively gentle process described in some Central Javanese myths (Geertz 1968, 29). Here in the eastern salient, or Oosthoek, Islam's advance was anything but a quiet process of personal conversion.

southern Bali, the wily Blambangan court eventually resurfaced and again challenged Mataram's authority (Ricklefs 1981, 44).

As a non-Islamic population, the Tengger highlanders were fair game for enslavement by Muslims. Between 1617 and 1650 Mataram forces made repeated forays into the mountain territories around Mount Bromo and nearby Mount Kawi to seize slaves. The prisoners were among the famous *gajah mati* ("dead elephant") population taken from eastern Java to Central Java to work as royal footmen and forest workers (Rouffaer 1921, 300).

While it could periodically devastate the region, however, Mataram was unable to establish a stable administration, and eastern Java's mountains provided shelter for anti-Mataram rebels. In the 1670s, for example, a Madurese prince by the name of Trunajaya mounted a powerful challenge to the Mataram court. It was suppressed only after the Dutch East Indies Company—which in 1619 had established a fort at the western end of the island—came to the aid of imperiled Mataram (Ricklefs 1981, 75). Once defeated, Trunajaya's forces took refuge in the Tengger mountains, where they were pursued by Dutch forces. This was the first European intervention in the highland area.

Around this same time a Balinese ex-slave by the name of Surapati was involved in several attacks on the Dutch, first in West Java and then in Central Java (Kumar 1976; Ricklefs 1981, 80). After the latter incident, he too fled east, and in 1686 he established a court near the port of Pasuruan at the northern foot of the Tengger mountains. Surapati's Pasuruan quickly became a political force in its own right, providing the organizational momentum for an anti-Mataram alliance linking Pasuruan, Tengger, Blambangan, and the Balinese. This brazen challenge to Mataram's authority could not long go unanswered. In 1706–7 the inland court forged an alliance with the Dutch East Indies Company, and some 60,000 VOC (Vereenighde Oostindische Compagnie), Mataram, and Madurese troops attacked Surapati's stronghold near Pasuruan (de Vries 1931, 1:20). Surapati was killed in the first weeks of battle and the powerful garrison overcome. Pasuruan was seized and turned into a Dutch fort—the first in East Java and just twenty kilometers from the Tengger mountain range. For years Surapati's descendants continued to put up resistance from hideouts in the Tengger mountains and Blambangan. The last rebel leader in Tengger was captured by Dutch forces only in 1764 (Jasper 1926, 11). When Blambangan fell in 1771 (Ricklefs 1981, 96), there followed one of the most peculiar events of Javanese history. So as to split the long-rebellious Blambangan court from its south Balinese allies, the Dutch took the unusual step of encouraging the Islamization of Blambangan's royal family. Although some villages are reported to have remained Hindu into the nineteenth century, this marked the effective end of Hinduism in the Blambangan area (Pigeaud 1932). Henceforth Javanese Hinduism was restricted to the small peasant population of the Tengger highlands.

Dutch cooperation with Mataram, first against the Trunajaya rebels and then against Surapati, exacted a high price. In November 1743, in the aftermath of the Surapati campaign, the Dutch were granted full sovereignty over most of Java's north coast and all of the eastern salient (Ricklefs 1981, 89). The era of eastern Java's political autonomy thus finally came to an end. Even prior to the capture of the last Tengger rebels, the Dutch established a small presence in the upperslope village of Tosari. From 1743 to 1751 they laid out vegetable gardens there to provide food supplies for the Pasuruan garrison (de Vries 1931, 1:133). In the late 1760s native farmers in the region were given vegetable seeds and instructions for their cultivation, and between 1772 and 1790 a German worked as an agricultural extension agent in the village. Although its influence was at first only modest, European power had nonetheless penetrated the mountains, ending the long middle ages that had begun with Majapahit's fall. This also signaled the beginning of a new era in relations between upland society and the lowland state.

Several facts relevant to our understanding of the modern uplands stand out from this overview of precolonial history. Some 250 years of political violence, first of all, help to explain the unusual distribution of population in the Tengger mountains on the eve of colonial rule. Although the religious communities of the Majapahit era had been located in the more temperate midslope highlands, by the end of the eighteenth century these territories had been depopulated. The surviving mountain population took refuge in the less temperate—but militarily defensible— upperslope regions. Village settlement patterns were also influenced by this troubled history. Early visitors to the region consistently report that native settlements were located on steep ridges, high above cultivated valley floors, and often inconveniently remote from the springs on which villagers depended for water (Domis 1832, 327). Houses were built on terraces (*gampengan*), clustered tightly together, without the home gardens characteristic of lowland settlements (van Lerwerden 1844, 82; Raffles 1965, 1:329). These hilltop hamlets provided protection from the predatory attacks that plagued this region well into the nineteenth century.

This same history explains certain cultural anomalies of the eastern salient as a whole. Many of the distinctive features of language, etiquette, politics, and art today identified as classically "Javanese" really developed only recently, in the course of the cultural renaissance that occurred at Central Java's courts in the eighteenth and nineteenth centuries (Pigeaud 1967, 1:7; Moedjanto 1986). The later diffusion of these styles to other areas of the island helped to reverse the trend toward cultural regionalization evident in the early post-Majapahit period. Since it was never under effective Central Javanese control and was ceded to the Dutch in 1743, the eastern salient at first escaped many of these standardizing influences. It remained a stronghold of nonstandard dialects, the last bastion of popular Hinduism, and a region in which such quintessentially Central Javanese art forms as *wayang* puppetry and *wayang wong* theater were less popular than bawdier local arts (Pigeaud 1932; Hefner 1987b).

There was, however, a price to be paid for such cultural independence. The warfare that plagued the eastern territory for much of the post-Majapahit period effectively depopulated large areas of the countryside. We know something of the cultural traditions of Tengger and Blambangan because in these regions a critical mass of people and institutions survived. It is probable that indigenous eastern Javanese populations remained in other areas too at the end of the eighteenth century. Their ranks were so depleted, however, that they would soon be overwhelmed by the Madurese and Javanese who migrated to the area beginning in the late eighteenth century. In these regions a frontier culture emerged that incorporated Madurese, Malay, and Javanese traditions, obscuring what remained of eastern Javanese customs. In a region where Muslim religious schools (*pesantren*) provided one of the few popular organizations capable of cutting across ethnic and communal lines, Islam would become the most influential of these post-traditional forces. Although its mountain regions remained non- or only nominally Muslim, lowland Pasuruan became one of the strongest centers of Muslim traditionalism in all Java.

SOCIAL CHANGE UNDER COLONIAL RULE

The Dutch administrators who visited Pasuruan in the eighteenth century saw a territory rich in economic resources but poor in what was needed to realize their promise for Europeans: a sedentary and controllable labor force. The rural population that had survived (just over thirty thousand people) was largely concentrated in the lowlands. The few residents of the Tengger highlands were located in isolated upperslope villages. A 1746 report from Pasuruan spoke enthusiastically of the regency's potential. But it bemoaned the area's poverty, its small population, and a banditry problem that brought ruin to the countryside (de Vries 1931, 1:22).

Dutch efforts to revive the local economy were aided by developments in Java as a whole. Between 1757 and 1825 Java experienced its longest period of peace since the early sixteenth century (Ricklefs 1981, 94). Both inland and coastal areas of Central Java enjoyed new prosperity. Population grew, and the general peace allowed for freer movement of goods and people (Meijer Ranneft 1916, 64). The heavy burden of taxes and labor services imposed on the peasantry in the native districts of Central Java meanwhile created pressures for flight to less oppressive territories. The native regents who now worked under Dutch authority in Java's eastern salient took advantage of the population movement by encouraging settlement in their districts. Taxes were waived on new settlers for the first three or four years of their residence (Palte 1984, 18). Already in the 1750s, therefore, Dutch reports spoke of a visible increase in Pasuruan's population (de Vries 1931, 1:22). Although in Central Java population growth resulted in a significant movement of people into the rainfed uplands (Palte 1984, 19), most of the pre-1830 immigrants to the thinly populated Pasuruan regency were able to settle in *sawah* districts or on the fringes of the Tengger mountains (de Vries 1931, 1:51).

Pasuruan's highlands were at first little affected by the immigration. European activity was confined to vegetable cultivation and the operation of a hostel for European visitors (de Vries 1931, 1:133). Coffee—cultivated under Dutch rule around Batavia since the 1700s and in western Java's Priangan highlands since the 1730s (Geertz 1963a, 58)—was introduced into a few lower-lying villages only in the final years of the eighteenth century (Rouffaer 1921, 301). Officials were delighted, however, by the success of the crop. In 1793 production was 3,750 lbs; just two years later, it had increased to 31,250 (de Vries 1931, 1:71). The crop was cultivated around existing centers of population, not in the thinly populated mountains. But compulsion was already used to recruit labor for its cultivation. By 1811, 4,361 people—about 12 percent of the regency's population—were involved in forced coffee cultivation (de Vries 1931, 1:71).

Production here and in other parts of Java grew steadily in the years prior to 1830. Despite a slump in world coffee prices in 1823 (Furnivall 1944, 96), coffee exports from Java to the Netherlands reached 17 million kilograms in 1825 and 25.6 million in 1828; they then dipped to 17.7 million in 1830, following a fall in prices. Even at its low point, the value of these exports exceeded that of sugar, the other major commercial export, by a ratio of three to one (Furnivall 1944, 104). In short, on the eve of the implementation of one of the largest systems of compulsory cultivation in all of colonial Asia, the infamous Cultuurstelsel ("Cultivation System"), rural Java was already being drawn into a powerful extractive grid. Most of Java's eastern uplands, however, still lay outside its grasp, and the colonial government was at a loss as to what to do with its vast "waste lands."

Political and demographic circumstances combined to provide a solution to this problem. The Javanese aristocracy, under the leadership of Prince Dipanagara, made a last effort to defend its authority against colonial encroachment, and war raged in Central Java between 1825 and 1830 (Carey 1979, 63–77), killing 200,000 Javanese and sending thousands more fleeing into the upland areas of Central Java and the eastern salient (Palte 1984, 19). After the war, the colonial government introduced the Cultuurstelsel, under which Java's peasants were supposed to pay their taxes in produce, rather than cash, by cultivating commercial crops on a portion of their lands or, in the case of coffee (and some other minor crops), on nearby government forest lands (Geertz 1963a, 52–82; Van Niel 1972). The system of compulsory coffee cultivation that had proved so profitable in western Java's Priangan highlands was thus extended to upland areas of eastern and central Java. A similar program was launched in West Sumatra (Kahn 1980, 164). While in theory the new policy was supposed to lighten the burden of taxation on the peasantry, in actual fact it was administered in a dizzying variety of fashions and with widespread inequities (Van Niel 1981, 41).

The Dutch introduced several commercial crops, but the two most successful during the life of the system proved to be coffee and sugar. Sugar was grown primarily on peasant *sawah* fields, and, except where estates were established on newly opened tracts, this required temporary appropriation of native rice lands. The result was a drop-off in rice production and, in a few areas, famine (Van Niel 1981; Elson 1984; Breman 1983). Coffee, by contrast, was an upland crop, and its impact on food-crop cultivation was at first less serious. Most of Java's mountain peoples practiced a variant of shifting cultivation, and it was easy enough to confine them to smaller land areas without immediately threatening their subsistence. The overall impact of coffee on the highlands was still nothing less than revolutionary. In just a few years it replaced a complex forest ecosystem, in which human agriculture was but a small component, with commercial enterprises that dominated the mountain environment.

Prior to the implementation of the Cultivation System, most coffee outside West Java was grown in hedgerows at the edge of fields and in small gardens in the lower reaches of Java's mountains. The new system took advantage of Java's growing population, however, to channel people into the uplands, transforming previously unworked "wastelands" into lucrative coffee stands. The scheme was so effective that by midcentury government officials had to report that there remained no additional forest land to open for coffee (Fasseur 1975, 62). Mountain areas throughout Java, including the Tengger highlands, were ringed with a "coffee belt," extending from 600 to 1,200–1,400 meters in altitude. An entire forest ecosystem had disappeared.

At the height of the Cultivation System, the number of peasants mobilized for coffee cultivation exceeded the number involved in cane cultivation, at times by a ratio of three to one (White 1983, 28). The amount of labor required was massive. The number of coffee trees planted grew from about 116 million in 1833 to 242 million in 1835 and 330 million in 1840 (Klaveren 1953, 123). During the 1840s from four to five hundred thousand families were involved in coffee cultivation, and each year from two to ten million new trees had to be planted (Van Niel 1972, 100). Although only about 5 percent of the total *sawah* was under sugar cultivation at any one time, 70 percent of all Javanese families were involved in compulsory cultivation, more than half of whom worked with coffee. Quite simply, coffee was the most important export for most of the Cultuurstelsel period (Furnivall 1944, 129), and its impact on Java's agricultural ecology was second to none.

In part because of its extraordinary profitability, coffee remained a government monopoly longer than any other cultivar. From January of 1833 on, private trade in the crop was outlawed, and all coffee had to be sold to the government at fixed prices (Furnivall 1944, 120). While private production of other commercial crops grew in importance after 1850, the state maintained its monopoly control of coffee. Only at the end of the nineteenth century did it relax its hold, when declining world prices and an islandwide coffee blight (which began around 1878–80 and eventually destroyed most of the government's *arabica* trees) made all but the most fertile government stands unprofitable (Furnivall 1944, 200). Even then, however, the state was reluctant to relax its control. Pressured by capitalist entrepreneurs in the Netherlands, it announced plans to privatize production and abolish forced cultivation. But the program of liberalization was blocked by war with the Sultan of Aceh, in northern Sumatra, which drained government coffers. Compulsory cultivation did not end until 1915 in Central Java and the 1920s in East Java. By then, mountain Java faced new demographic and ecological challenges.

COLONIAL PASURUAN

The impact of nineteenth-century colonialism on Pasuruan was consistent with this islandwide pattern, underscoring the manner in which lowland political economy dominated the evolution of the highlands. Although coffee and sugar were grown in the regency prior to the Cultivation System, their cultivation really took off only after 1830. The northern littoral stretching from Pasuruan to Surabaya became Java's largest sugar region, and would remain so for the life of the Cultivation System (Elson 1978a, 9). Immigration from Madura and Central Java in the preceding decades had tripled the regency's population from 37,000 in 1807 to 113,000 in 1831 (de Vries 1931, 1:37), providing just the labor force required for colonial schemes. In the same period, the area devoted to irrigated *sawah* doubled (de Vries 1931, 1:54), providing more land for cane cultivation.[5]

The introduction of the Cultivation System shocked the sugar districts so severely that their population actually declined during the first four years of the program (Elson 1978a, 26). Most of the fleeing population moved south, away from the sugar-growing coast. A significant proportion of this population moved into the Tengger highlands, whose rainfed lands were unsuitable for cane cultivation. Thus the temporary decline in the regency's total population hid what was in fact a sudden increase in the population of the regency's non-sugar-growing districts, most of which lay in or adjacent to the Tengger highlands. The flight of ethnic Javanese was offset by the movement of an almost equal number of Madurese into coastal areas, continuing a process of Madurization that had begun in the prior century (Elson 1978a, 27).

The flight of population testifies to the fact that, in the early years of the Cultuurstelsel, the burden of compulsory labor was greater in the sugar districts than in others (de Vries 1931, 1:99). Elsewhere in Java, too, regional inequities in forced labor resulted in population flight from sugar to coffee districts (Onghokham 1975, 215). The migrations only accelerated the incorporation of Java's once-peripheral uplands into the islandwide colonial economy.

Pasuruan did not experience calamities as severe as those in other parts of Java under the Cultivation System. The regency never suffered famines like those in Central Java during the 1840s (Furnivall 1944, 138; de Vries 1931, 1:94). The milder impact of the Cultuurstelsel here was largely because of the greater availability of land in the regency and its smaller population. By comparison with inland Central Java, in particular, Pasuruan enjoyed an abundance of land. During the last half of the nineteenth century (1855–1905), the regencies of Pasuruan and Malang experienced the greatest expansion in arable land in all of Central and Eastern Java (Palte 1984, 21). Despite a growing population, this expansion ensured that at the beginning of the twentieth century the region's population density remained the lowest in all of East and Central Java: a "mere" 580 persons/km² of farm land, as opposed to 835 for East and Central Java as a whole (Palte 1984, 29). In nineteenth-century Java, it would seem, Pasuruan was one of the regencies best suited to endure the rigors of colonial enterprise.

The impact of forced cultivation on the regency was severe nonetheless. Contrary to some accounts of the Cultuurstelsel (e.g., Geertz 1963,

5. Between 1807 and 1827 the average annual increase in the regency's population was an astonishing 4.7–5.6 percent, much of it no doubt owing to immigration. From 1831 to 1900, by contrast, the average annual rate of population increase slowed to a modest 1.5 percent (de Vries 1931, 1:37–38).

38), recent research indicates that Pasuruan's paddy farmers did not respond to the annual loss of their land to cane-growing by intensifying
rice cultivation on their remaining lands. Instead, both the quantity and
quality of labor in rice declined as more and more workers were forced
onto government fields. Rice production per capita actually fell until
midcentury, and the sugar districts of Pasuruan's northern littoral—rice
exporters a generation earlier—became net importers (Elson 1978a, 18).
Non-sugar-growing districts in this same part of Java were better able to
meet their staple needs, and as a result net population movement into
these areas was greater than that into the sugar districts. It was only toward the end of the Cultivation System in the 1860s that labor intensification was sufficient to reverse the sugar districts' decline.[6]

Colonial policies also reinforced rural inequities. Although early in the
nineteenth century the English governor Sir Thomas Stamford Raffles
had reported that Pasuruan knew almost no landlessness, by midcentury
about 40 percent of the sugar districts' population was without land
(Elson 1984, 90). Equally important, the mobility previously available to
peasants—as in other parts of Southeast Asia, a critical influence on
their bargaining power relative to superiors (Adas 1981; Scott 1976)—had
greatly diminished. By the late 1830s agriculture had absorbed the remaining lowlands (de Vries 1931, 1:95). At the same time, colonial policies
strengthened the authority of traditional aristocrats and village chiefs
(Furnivall 1944, 140; Elson 1978a, 8). Drawn from the ranks of the wealthy,
village leaders were given broad authority in the allocation of village
lands and were bribed or given percentage payments for cooperating
with government officials. Instead of social leveling and the equalization
of poverty, the Cultivation System served to "reinforce, exaggerate, and
harden the lines of social standing and wealth which had existed before
1830" (Elson 1978b, 55).

An Advancing Capitalism?

Did these policies effectively support the advance of rural capitalism,
as some observers have suggested (Alexander and Alexander 1979; White
1983; Knight 1982)? Or, by excluding native farmers from capital-
intensive sectors of the rural economy, did colonial enterprise impede the
development of a capitalist peasant class (Geertz 1963; de Vries 1931, 1:37)?
The answer to this question in part depends on how one defines capital-

6. Citing the decline in rice production of the 1830s and 1840s, some scholars have
speculated that the increase in average family size seen later in the century was an effort
on the part of the peasantry to compensate for labor lost to government enterprise by
increasing its fertility (Alexander and Alexander 1979, 35; for Central Java, see White
1976).

ism in a colonial context and what sort of social hierarchy one deems central to its development.

Events in Pasuruan do not fit neatly into either model. The Cultivation System more consistently supported the interests of European capital than it did those of native Javanese. In rice-growing villages, for example, villagers' rights to land were regularly abrogated in favor of European enterprise. In the early years of the system, shares of communal land were homogenized (they had earlier been more inequitably divided) and distributed more widely so as to expand the pool of workers liable to compulsory labor; in theory, only landowners were subject to such labor taxes (de Vries 1931, 1:97). At least in the short run, the policy stripped rural elites of their economic autonomy, reinforced communalism, and undermined private enterprise. While eroding some aspects of rural hierarchy, however, the system reinforced others. Lower-level aristocrats and village chiefs saw their privileges greatly expanded. In exchange for their help with government programs, they were rewarded with large cash payments, labor services, and access to government lands (Van Niel 1981, 43; Elson 1978a, 8; Furnivall 1944, 140; Breman 1982, 16). The result was growing landlessness and inequality among those who did own land.

Although economic inequality increased, then, it was not the result of the growth of free labor or the jockeying of entrepreneurs in the marketplace. Though it linked the rural population to international markets, in the domestic sphere Dutch colonialism did not support native capitalism. Much of the labor mobilized for government enterprise was coerced, not free. The state monopolized the market in land, guaranteeing itself final authority over its disposition. What native elites there were depended more for their influence on powers selectively accorded them by the colonial authorities than on independent control of the means of production. Contrary to some models of capitalist expansion (Frank 1969; Wallerstein 1974), then, Java's incorporation into the international capitalist system was not itself a guarantee that local relations of production would be recast along capitalist lines. Excluded from ownership of large-scale enterprise, and forced into a holding pattern on their own farms, the native Javanese were, in the end, a dominated population. They were linked to international markets by state power rather than by the dynamism of a native bourgeoisie (cf. Kahn 1980).

The cumulative effect of these changes was an administrative structure never before seen in Java: a systematically coordinated grid for the extractive control of labor and produce. On this point Clifford Geertz's characterization of social change in colonial Java as a kind of "advance toward vagueness," in which traditional social patterns were not so much transformed as "elasticized" (Geertz 1963a, 103), risks overlooking the revolutionary changes in rural administration, especially in district and village government. Politically and economically, colonial Java was very different from the society that had preceded it. Its political structures governed the rhythms of rural life more directly. The Dutch, of course, eventually departed. But this powerful state structure would remain and play an important role in modern agrarian development.

A DOMINATED HIGHLANDS

Although prior to 1830 the Tengger highlands were still a colonial backwater, after that time coffee and population growth rapidly transformed the region. As coffee cultivation spread to the midslope highlands, production in the regency increased. Between 1832 and 1836, production grew from 278,000 to 1,220,000 kilograms (de Vries 1931, 1:73). The number of new trees planted each year increased from 71,400 in 1832 to 253,000 in 1836. Between 1836 and 1849, finally, the number of trees harvested increased 500 percent, to 4,300,000.

The method of compulsion used here was similar to that in other areas of Java (Geertz 1963a, 56; Van Niel 1972, 99). Each family was given responsibility for a certain number of trees; at midcentury, the average in Pasuruan was 1,250 (de Vries 1931, 1:74). The annual harvest from these trees could be sold only to the government at collecting warehouses located in three midslope villages. The price was fixed by the colonial authorities, and the bulk of it was in fact never paid out, but deducted from the farmer's land tax. Nonetheless, people who carefully nurtured their trees could sometimes earn a modest profit; throughout the life of the system the potential for individual gain appears to have been greater than was the case with sugar. This fact served, of course, to attract immigrants from the sugar-growing lowlands.

The other attraction for immigrants was the availability of forest land for family agriculture. The government attempted to regulate forest opening, but did so largely to protect its own commercial interests. It set aside the flattest and most fertile mountain lands for its own coffee, leaving the native population to cultivate marginal hillside lands. Nonetheless, during most of the nineteenth century, the Tengger highlands had at least some frontier areas where immigrants could acquire land. With the exception of native officials, most families received smallholdings of one to two hectares. By restricting peasant differentiation in this manner, the government guaranteed itself a large pool of workers, since, as in the lowlands, landowners were subject to the highest labor tax. Overall, then, government programs served to reinforce a pattern of peasant smallholding rather than differentiating rural society into capitalist farmers and landless workers.

Toward the end of the century, the amount of open land diminished as roadbuilding and land scarcity brought land-hungry immigrants from the lowlands. The influx was so great that, by 1910, there was in effect no more land to be had. In an effort to control lowland flooding, the government returned a large portion of its coffee stands to natural forest and relocated their native cultivators downslope. Between 1910 and the mid 1920s private lands were surveyed, village borders were demarcated, the forests were replanted, and the remaining government land was redistributed to local farmers. An era of highland frontier mobility had come to an end.[7]

Highland Population and Landholding

It is difficult to create a precise statistical portrait of population and landholding in the Pasuruan highlands during the nineteenth century. Government censuses were even less accurate in highland areas than they were in the lowlands. In addition, the boundaries of upland administrative districts changed several times in the nineteenth century, making precise comparisons with later periods difficult (de Vries 1931, 1:11). One can nonetheless get a general impression of changes from census information taken from the nineteenth-century upland district known as "Tengger," in which the districts that form the focus of the present study were located.[8]

On the eve of the Cultivation System in 1828, the Tengger district was inhabited by just 2,204 persons, most of whom were Tengger-Javanese Hindus concentrated in the inaccessible reaches of the upperslope highlands. The midslope region was even more sparsely populated, with only a handful of residents in its entire expanse. As table 2.1 shows, however, during the remainder of the century population grew steadily.

As the figures in table 2.1 indicate, the population of the Tengger district increased most rapidly during the peak years of coffee cultivation

7. It is clear that this legacy of open land also influenced the system of tenurial rights found in the highlands. While much of Pasuruan's *sawah* and at least a small portion of its *tegal* dryland was under communal ownership, all of the land in the Tengger highlands was private heritable land, subject to only residual village restrictions on sale to outsiders (de Vries 1931, 1:123). Communal landholding was not found even in the indigenous Hindu communities of the upperslope region. I discuss the history of land tenure further in chapter 5.

8. The Tengger district changed its borders several times in the course of the nineteenth century, and was broken up into several smaller districts at the beginning of the twentieth. The district included only about 60 percent of what can properly be regarded as Pasuruan's highlands. All of the communities in which ethnographic research for the present study was conducted, however, once lay in this district, and developments there in the nineteenth century were more or less typical of most of Pasuruan's highlands. There was also a Tengger district in the neighboring regency of Probolinggo.

TABLE 2.1   Nineteenth-Century Population Growth

Year	Tengger District	Pasuruan Regency	Tengger as % of Pasuruan Regency	All Java
1830	2,234	109,847	2.0	7,000,000
1840	3,711	131,792	2.8	8,700,000
1850	10,314	142,293	7.2	9,600,000
1860	12,025	170,141	7.0	12,600,000
1870	12,899	187,819	6.9	16,200,000
1880	—	—	—	19,500,000
1890	24,920	261,788	9.5	23,600,000
1900	40,167	305,910	13.1	28,400,000
1930	49,873	322,033	15.5	41,700,000

SOURCES. Adapted from de Vries 1931, 2: tables 3 and 6, and Geertz 1963a, 69.

from 1840 to 1850, and then again at the end of the century, just prior to the final closing of the uplands. The end of the century saw economic recession in Pasuruan's lowlands, as the sugar industry went into decline. The resulting "formation of a new class of poor" (Elson 1984, 154) contributed to upland flight. Mountain roadbuilding facilitated its movement.

Figures on agricultural land similarly underscore the far-reaching changes in the mountain district during the nineteenth century. In 1816 the region is estimated to have had 438 hectares of agricultural land, all of it rainfed *tegal*. This represented 10.5 percent of the regency's rainfed land (4,186 ha), but a mere 2.5 percent of its total agricultural land (17,182 ha). At this point in history, in other words, rainfed land played only a minor role in regency agriculture. Covering some 12,996 hectares, irrigated *sawah* was more than three times as extensive (de Vries 1931, 2:table 8). By 1927 all this had changed. The total area of rainfed *tegal* had grown to 32,500 hectares, about eight times its area in 1816. Total *sawah* area, meanwhile, had increased only 37 percent, to 17,800 hectares (de Vries 1931, 1:164). There was thus now almost twice as much *tegal* as irrigated land.

A substantial portion of the growth in rainfed *tegal* occurred in the Tengger district. By 1929 its *tegal* area had increased to almost 7,000 hectares, one-fifth of the regency total, and about sixteen times the area in 1816.[9] The figure underscores an important feature of Pasuruan agriculture in the nineteenth century. The greater portion of its expansion oc-

9. The figures cited here do not include European-owned land or, when estimating the total dry-land area cultivated, house lands (*pekarangan*) planted with gardens.

TABLE 2.2 Land Use on Java and Madura, 1883–1980
(thousands of ha)

	1883	1913	1938	1980
Sawah	1,845	2,200	3,368	3,491
Tegal	640	1,775	3,251	3,271

SOURCES. Palte 1984, 22, and Roche 1985.

curred on rainfed fields, not irrigated *sawah*, and a significant portion of this rainfed land was in the mountains.

Similar changes were occurring throughout Java. Between 1880 and 1920 the native population of Java and Madura almost doubled in size, growing from 19.8 million to 35.0 million (Furnivall 1944, 347). Though much of this population was absorbed into an already "labor stuffed" *sawah* system (Geertz 1963a, 80), there was also widespread expansion on to rainfed lands. Between 1883 and 1938, for example, total *sawah* on Java and Madura increased 19.2 percent, from 1,845,000 to 2,200,000 hectares. In the same period, the total area of dry farmland more than doubled, from 640,000 to 1,775,000 hectares (Palte 1984, 22).

During that same thirty-year period, rainfed land grew from 26.0 percent of Java's agricultural land to 44.7 percent. Today the area of rainfed *tegal* slightly exceeds that of *sawah* on the island (Booth 1985, 122). By the beginning of the twentieth century, in other words, Javanese agriculture was no longer exclusively or even predominantly *sawah*-based. Expansion had created a more heterogeneous agroecology and brought the island's last remaining arable lands under cultivation. In areas like Pasuruan, rainfed *tegal* was characteristic of this transformation.

As table 2.2 shows, between 1913 and 1938, there was another period of wet-rice expansion in Java, spurred on this time by government investment in irrigation projects. *Sawah* increased 53 percent, to an area roughly equal to its total today. Once again, however, rainfed land experienced an even more dramatic expansion, growing 83.2 percent, to a total land area also almost equal to its expanse today. The upland expansion begun in the nineteenth century was thus largely complete by the fourth decade of the twentieth. Only a few peripheral areas remained to be opened to cultivation. From this point on, Java's expanding population would have no choice but to intensify cultivation on a fixed land base.

An Advancing Infrastructure

Agricultural change was only one of a range of developments that reshaped rural Pasuruan at the end of the nineteenth century. Roadbuilding also had a notable impact. In the eighteenth century the only carriageway in the entire regency was that between the coastal towns of Pasuruan and Bangil. A few side roads were added with the beginning of sugar cultivation in the 1820s and 1830s, but the greatest expansion in roads occurred during the "spatial outburst" (Palte 1984, 20) of Java's population from 1860 to 1925. For the first time ever, roads were built connecting Pasuruan with the foothills of the Tengger mountains to the south. Shortly thereafter two small feeder roads pushed higher into the mountains, reaching the midslope communities of Puspo and Nongkojajar. Markets were soon opened in both villages, the first ever seen in the highlands. The upperslope region, meanwhile, remained without roads, and it had no markets either. There were two small horse paths to Tosari, but neither was suitable for vehicle traffic. Since the government had no estates in the area, it had little reason to invest in roadbuilding.

In the last years of the nineteenth century, however, upperslope Tosari became an important rest-station for Europeans. There were three hotels in Tosari and a fourth in nearby Ngadiwono, with accommodations for over two hundred guests and facilities for tennis, golf, croquet, and mountain tourism. It was tourist development, not an interest in native welfare, that spurred the government to construct vehicle roads into the rugged upperslope region. A dirt road was opened in 1914. It was given a stone foundation in 1919 and asphalted in 1935–36. Although the colonial government originally intended to extend roads into other upperslope villages, the Great Depression and, shortly thereafter, the Japanese invasion shattered these plans. Only with the expansion of government oil revenues after 1973–74 would roadbuilding again take place. Until that time Tosari was the only upperslope community accessible by vehicle. Even in the midslope region, more than half of all villages lay four to fifteen kilometers from vehicle roads.

The final years of the nineteenth century saw further evidence of the incorporation of the highlands into a national political economy. The Agrarian Law of 1870 opened "waste lands" to private European farmers, who were awarded lease rights for periods of up to seventy-five years. The resulting influx of European farmers occurred just prior to the closing of forests to native cultivators, thereby worsening the shortage of land. Although there were two small European farms around Tosari (specializing in dairy products and flowers), the more significant European holdings were in the temperate midslope region. Even here European settlement was unevenly concentrated around Puspo and Nongkojajar. Europeans preferred these areas because of their mild temperatures, fertile soils, and accessibility. Nongkojajar had the largest number of estates and was the only area that saw the formation of a resident class of landless laborers, recruited from the ranks of lowland immigrants.

The ecological problems associated with deforestation eventually led to the passage of a law (in 1874) requiring that permission for opening wasteland be secured from district-level officials rather than local village chiefs. Motivated by a similar concern for its fast-dwindling forests, the government established a Forestry Department in 1879 to manage upland forests devastated in large part by earlier colonial enterprise (Furnivall 1944, 180–201; Donner 1987, 346). This same legislation sought to control erosion by requiring those farming hillside land to build terraces (Palte 1984, 38). This stipulation was widely ignored, however, and, in the decades that followed, upland erosion worsened.

In a related development, the government in 1899 introduced a Land Rent Law that reorganized village boundaries, consolidating smaller villages into larger administrative entities (Furnivall 1944, 387; Ricklefs 1981, 148). In Pasuruan, the number of administrative villages was reduced from about 500 to 241 (de Vries 1931, 1:35). The same program surveyed lands, demarcated village borders, and closed vast areas of forest to cultivation. The program represented a reversal of government policies on midslope settlement. At the height of the Cultivation System, peasants had been encouraged to live dispersed in remote settlements, adjacent to the government coffee stands they tended. With its withdrawal from coffee cultivation, the government forced midslope peasants into nucleated settlements like those in the upperslope highlands. Its intent was to enhance control of the rural population and monitor forest use.

In Pasuruan the resettlement project took nearly two decades to complete. It coincided with the abolition of compulsory coffee cultivation, which wound down in this regency between 1917 and 1922. The "coffee belt" that had been created in the middle of the nineteenth century thus disappeared, and the upland frontier was forever closed. From this period on there would be no significant opening of additional forest land to cultivation.

With all these changes, the stage was thus set for the events of the later twentieth century, when population growth, political turmoil, and commerce would further transform the social landscape. Whatever the direction of those changes, they would occur in a social environment now characterized by high population densities rather than low ones, a strong state structure rather than a diffuse, indigenous one, and an agrarian economy strongly linked to external markets. Pasuruan's highlands had been thoroughly integrated into the structures and processes of European colonialism. Developments in the twentieth century would reflect the consequences of this incorporative revolution, and present new challenges to the residents of this once-remote highland territory.

Plate 1: Mt. Bromo (crater with smoke left of center)
with Mt. Semeru Rising in the Background

Plates 2–6: The Faces of
Upland Society

Plate 2

Plate 3

Plate 4

Plate 5

Plate 6

Plate 7: Upperslope Villages
Are Typically
Nucleated

Plate 8: Midslope Household Drying Cassava

Plate 9: A Traditional–Style Kitchen (*Pawon*):
Domestic Space and Guest Space as One

Plate 10: The Tosari Market

Plate 11: A Madurese Peddler

Plate 12: Wage Laborers (*kuli*)

Plate 13: Consumption Communities:
Female *Tayuban* Dancer in Traditional Festivity

Plate 14: Male in Festival
Dance

Plate 15: Child in Festival
Costume

Plate 16

Plates 16–18: The Ruinous Effects of Erosion in Upperslope Vegetable Fields

Plate 17

Plate 18

Plate 19: New Instruments of Production: Truck Farming

Plate 20: A New Muslim Orthodoxy: Nightly Classes in Qur'anic Reading

Plate 21: Agencies of Resocialization: Village School

Plate 22: Village Culture as National Community: Girl Scouts

THREE

Agricultural History
Intensification and Degradation

In his *Agricultural Involution,* Clifford Geertz observes that the "extraordinary stability or durability" of wet-rice agriculture allowed it to absorb a large proportion of colonial Java's growing population. Although it provided no more than a minimal income, *sawah's* ecological resilience ensured that that livelihood would not be jeopardized by environmental degradation. "Given the maintenance of irrigation facilities, a reasonable level of farming technique, and no autogenous changes in the physical setting, the *sawah*...seems virtually indestructible" (Geertz 1963a, 33; cf. Donner 1987, 66).

The paddy field's ecological qualities contrast sharply with those of upland rainfed land (*tegal*). Under ideal conditions, *sawah* is an eminently sustainable agriculture, capable of long-term intensive cultivation. *Tegal,* by contrast, is dangerously susceptible to degradation, especially in terrains as rugged as the Tengger mountains. The history of agriculture in this region demonstrates this somber reality all too clearly. Farmers here have had to adapt, not only to population growth and a changing political economy, but to the ominous ecological consequences of their own agricultural intensification.

THE DEMOGRAPHIC BACKGROUND

By the 1920s, the spatial expansion of migrants southward into Pasuruan's Tengger mountains was essentially complete. Once sparsely and unevenly populated, the entire highland region now had a substantial resident population. Statistics on population in the mountain subdistricts in the 1920s reveal this fact clearly (table 3.1). With 321 people per square kilometer of agricultural land in midslope Puspo, and 234 in upperslope Tosari, the mountains had themselves begun to feel the

TABLE 3.1   Population Growth, 1807–1927

Subdistrict	Population		Density/km² Agricultural Land, 1927
	1807	1927	
Midslope villages			
Puspo	37	1,693	334
Jimbaran	44	1,512	364
Kemiri	—	1,264	337
Palangsari	68	734	303
Janjangwulung	—	1,432	276
Pusungmalang	—	798	399
Keduwung	—	758	260
Total	149	8,191	321
Upperslope villages			
Tosari	228	2,503	336
Wonokitri	210	3,156	186
Podokoyo	136	1,028	265
Ngadiwono	185	1,276	211
Mororejo	—	1,389	252
Total	759	9,352	234

Source. Adapted from de Vries 1931, 2: table 2.

weight of population. The burden was especially heavy in the midslope region. Among upperslope villages, only Tosari, with its European hotels and sizable immigrant community, had population densities comparable to those in the midslope area.

Population continued to grow steadily, of course, after 1927. Curiously, however, the rate of increase was greater in the more densely populated midslope region (table 3.2). Between 1927 and 1985 that subdistrict's population grew almost 150 percent, while that in the Tosari subdistrict grew by only 60 percent. Densities climbed to 675 people per square kilometer of agricultural land in midslope Puspo and 406 in upperslope Tosari. About 20–30 percent of the agricultural land against which these figures are measured, one should note, has an inclination of more than 40 degrees. From a hydrological perspective, therefore, it should probably never have been opened to cultivation at all. The growing weight of population on the land had, however, pushed villagers to cultivate even the most marginal lands. The same pressures would soon engender changes in agricultural practices as well.

The upperslope region's lower rate of population growth was in part related to the fact that subsistence cultivation here was less productive,

TABLE 3.2   Population Growth, 1927–85

Subdistrict	Population in 1985	% Incr. 1927–85	Density/km² Agricultural Land, 1985
Midslope villages			
Puspo	4,128	144	678
Jimbaran	4,744	214	955
Kemiri	2,385	89	616
Palangsari	1,949	166	611
Janjangwulung	3,167	121	612
Pusungmalang	2,711	240	928
Keduwung	1,300	72	327
Total	20,384	149	675
Upperslope villages			
Tosari	3,907	56	529
Wonokitri	4,607	46	329
Podokoyo	1,361	33	367
Ngadiwono	2,274	78	421
Mororejo	2,602	87	446
Total	14,751	58	406

SOURCES. Adapted from de Vries 1931, 2: table 2, and village records.

since maize, the area's staple, required twice the time to grow there that it did in the midslope region. As a result, double-cropping of maize was impossible, and the same land area could not support as large a population as in the midslope region. There is also evidence to suggest that infant mortality rates were higher and fertility lower in the higher-altitude region (see ch. 6).

Government policies probably played a more important role in limiting population growth in the Tosari subdistrict, however, by making it difficult for outsiders to acquire land. In the nineteenth century the government had set aside large tracts of land in this region (where coffee did not grow well anyway) as reserves for the native inhabitants of the Tengger mountains, and then discouraged sale of this land to outsiders. After its surveying and registration in the 1910s, the private sale of land became technically legal. Most upperslope communities, however, informally continued to restrict sale to outsiders, apparently at the urging of government officials. At the turn of the century, European officials had expressed alarm at the spread of Islam into this previously non-Islamic region (La Chapelle 1899; Bodemeijer 1901; von Freijburg 1901). Though, in fact, government reports from the period (and the accounts of old villagers today) indicate that land sale did occur, the colonial government clearly hoped to—and did—slow the flow of Muslim immigrants to the higher-lying region. In the majority of upperslope villages, local restrictions on land alienation remained in force until the 1970s, when most communities moved to allow rental and sales to outsiders.

Policies on land alienation in the midslope area, by contrast, were always more liberal. A few villages forbade the sale of land to nonresidents, but most allowed it when immigrants were willing to take up residence. At the beginning of this century, in fact, some officials in the midslope region were reportedly eager to take advantage of the expanding demand for upland land. With the closing of government stands at the turn of the century, most ex–estate workers had been given just two hectares of private land, but a handful of district and village officers had managed to secure tracts as large as twenty or thirty hectares. With the continuing influx of lowland migrants, they reaped profits from the sale of this land. Village chiefs and district officials were also entitled to a percentage of the cash exchanged in land sales by villagers in their domains.

The market for midslope land varied, however, according to village location. Demand was greater for prime plots situated on or near vehicle roads, and land prices there were four to five times those for remote mountain terrains. Not surprisingly, then, migrants to such choice communities tended to come from affluent, nonfarm backgrounds; many had acquired the wealth they needed to purchase land through upland trade. In more isolated midslope communities, by contrast, transportation was difficult and commercial opportunities limited. These villages attracted less affluent immigrants, and for most of this century land remained relatively inexpensive. In the 1920s profits from the sale of one cow were sufficient to buy half a hectare of fertile land in these remote communities. Poor people who lacked capital could share-raise a cow for its owner in exchange for its first offspring, and, in so doing, amass the wealth to purchase land.

Through these and other arrangements, mobility into the ranks of landowning villagers remained relatively fluid. The consequences of this segmented market are still reflected in patterns of land distribution today. Land is far more equitably distributed in remote midslope villages than in those that were already major commercial centers in the first decades of this century (see ch. 5).

This history of migration and population growth in the Tengger highlands shows, then, that agricultural change was shaped not only by environmental constraints, but by government policies, commerce, and class. A similarly complex interaction between environmental and social forces was evident in the processes of agricultural intensification that accompanied population growth.

AGRICULTURE IN THE PREMODERN HIGHLANDS

In precolonial times agriculture in the Tengger highlands was organized around primary cultivation of maize (*jagung*), the region's staple, and secondary cultivation of an assortment of commercial crops sold outside the region. Uplanders' involvement in lowland markets appears to go far back in time; "traditional" agriculture, in other words, was not a wholly noncommercial endeavor. Mythic narratives collected by Raffles early in the nineteenth century, for example, report that the god Bima had cursed the highland population for siding with Krisna in his contest with Bima. As punishment for their role, Bima forbade the weaving of cotton cloth and the growing of rice (Raffles 1965, 1:333). By implication, the myth would suggest, commerce with the lowlands to obtain these goods was enjoined (cf. de Vries 1931, 1:131).

Until the late nineteenth century there were no market sites in the entire highlands. Commercial crops had to be marketed in the lowlands at sites that specialized in the bulking and transport of upland goods. Early colonial reports speak of uplanders' total dependence on these lowland markets for salt, fish, pots, cloth, and metal (Domis 1832, 328; van Lerwerden 1844, 81). The highlands had none of the cottage industries (blacksmithing, mat-weaving, pottery) so familiar in the more economically diversified rural lowlands. To be a highlander was synonymous with being a *wong tani*, a "farm person." Everyone worked the land, and everyone earned their livelihood from its fruits.

Although trade goes far back in time, the range of crops grown for market sale has changed over the years. One of the first Dutch reports from the region, in 1785, noted that highland peasants sold onions and *jarak* in the lowlands. *Jarak* is *Ricinus communis*, the castor bean, from which lamp oil was made in old Java (de Vries 1931, 1:131). The onions and *jarak* were both intended for Javanese consumers in the lowlands. Reports seventy years later, however, paint a very different picture. No mention is made of *jarak*. Instead, the primary cash crops are those introduced by Europeans at the end of the eighteenth century; the most important are said to be potatoes and cabbages. Reference is also made to specialized cash crops like artichokes, wheat, strawberries, grapes, and various leafy greens. Virtually all of these crops were intended for European and Chinese consumers in the fast-growing towns of Surabaya, Malang, Pasuruan, and Probolinggo (Domis 1832, 328; van Lerwerden 1844, 81; de Vries 1931, 1:134).

Even at this early period, upland peasants seem to have adapted quickly to new commercial opportunities. Colonial policies did not require Tengger peasants to grow these cash crops; they did so willingly and with little evidence of wariness of market involvements. The dual emphasis on food and cash crops, of course, provided them with a subsistence safety net; were market demand to diminish, they always had their maize crop to carry them through. From this time until the end of the colonial era, upperslope peasants were heavily involved in extraregional markets, earning most of their disposable income raising crops for European and Chinese consumers.

Highlanders consumed little of this commercial produce themselves. Their staple was maize, supplemented on festival occasions by rice, which they obtained through purchase or barter in the lowlands.[1] Originally an American cultigen, maize is thought to have been introduced into Indonesia by Spanish or Portuguese mariners sometime between 1521 and 1568 (Wigboldus 1979, 23). If it made its way to Java shortly after this time, which seems likely, it may have played a role in facilitating the slow retreat of Hindu farmers upslope into the less accessible terrains of the Tengger highlands in the aftermath of the Muslim conquest of Hindu Majapahit. In the earlier pre-Islamic period, when most of the area's population lived at lower altitudes, its diet may have resembled that of the peoples of eastern Indonesia today (Wigboldus, 1979, 19). It probably included dry-field rice, bananas, sago, millet, and taro (cf. Donner 1987, 57). Of these crops, only taro (called *tales* or *mantri*) still grows abundantly in the highlands today. Despite good yields and easy cultivation, market demand for taro is low, and no farmers cultivate it as anything other than a snack item for home consumption.

The maize cultivated in this early period, and still grown by upperslope farmers today, was a white-kerneled "Indian" variety. Its stalks are taller, its cobs longer, and its kernels larger and starchier than today's modern strains. By comparison with these new varieties, it is also more pest- and mildew-resistant. Placed in large unhusked bunches (*pocong*) on outside platform walls (*sigiran*), the grain can be stored for as long as twelve months. This is three to four times the storage life of new varieties. Its slightly cheesey taste is also preferred by highlanders. The primary disadvantage of the old maize is its long growing life: eight to twelve months in upperslope regions (1,200–2,500 meters altitude) and five to seven months in midslope terrains. As mean landholdings shrank in the late nineteenth century, this long growing season made traditional maize ill-suited for double-cropping. Working their fields more intensively,

---

1. Though a traditional staple in upland areas of central and western Java (Palte 1984, 44), dry-field rice (*padi gogo*) was never widely cultivated except in the lowest reaches of the Tengger highlands. It does not produce seed anywhere above 1,100 meters in these mountains. Though technically cultivable in most of the midslope region, its lower energy yield per hectare and inability to grow on infertile soils ensured that most farmers preferred maize as their staple.

farmers were forced to turn to new strains of corn, or different, quicker-growing cultivars entirely.

In the early colonial period, of course, when the highlands' small population was concentrated in the upperslope region, the need to maximize yields per hectare was not as pressing as it would be a century later. Early European travelers reported that, where there was any population at all, peasants confined their cultivation to valley bottoms, leaving hillsides and hilltops thick with forests rich with game (Domis 1832, 325). Farmers practiced a system of extended grass and bush fallowing, growing crops for one or two years on one plot of land, then shifting to another while the first piece lay fallow for six or seven years.

Little or none of the agricultural land was cultivated using full-blown swidden. With swidden, a plot is used for a year or two and then fallowed for fifteen to thirty while other forest areas are brought under cultivation (Geertz 1963, 22; Freeman 1955, 40). At the beginning of the nineteenth century there was sufficient land to allow this, but the mobility it required contradicted the defensive need to concentrate settlement in one corner of the highlands (north of Mount Bromo) and locate villages atop inaccessible hillsides (Domis 1832, 327). More distant terrains—particularly those to the south of Mount Bromo, in what are today the regencies of Malang and Lumajang—were suitable for agriculture; indeed, historical evidence indicates that they were already settled in Majapahit times. They would have been eminently well suited for swidden. In the aftermath of Majapahit's fall, however, settlement in this southern area disappeared, victim, no doubt, of bandits and slave raiders.

With the establishment of colonial peace, highland farmers again responded quickly to new opportunities, and there was extensive movement of Tengger Hindus from the main areas of settlement north of Mount Bromo to the south. Although only two survived late-nineteenth-century Islamization, most of the southern Hindu settlements noted in colonial reports (Jasper 1926) date from this period, having been founded by Hindu pioneers from the northern regencies of Pasuruan and Probolinggo. This Hindu expansion was small, however, by comparison with the Muslim migration from the lowlands that was about to take place as a result of the government's program of compulsory coffee cultivation.

The ecological impact of the lowlanders' migration was also more serious than that of native settlers. The colonial government reserved the flattest lands for its own coffee gardens. Immigrants to the midslope region were thus forced to work steep hillside fields, resulting in widespread erosion. Other features of the government's program also contributed to topsoil loss. While some coffee workers were assigned permanent plots, during the first years of the program many were not, since their labor was needed to cut still-virgin forest elsewhere. After cultivating lands for two or three years, workers would be relocated to another forest site and given a new plot of land. Under these circumstances, farmers had little incentive to invest in labor-intensive soil-conservation techniques such as terracing or contour farming (cf. Donner 1987, 120).

Even the government's coffee stands suffered from extensive erosion. As throughout Java (Palte 1984, 25), two modes of planting were used in establishing government tracts. The one, preferred by Dutch officials, was the "orderly garden," in which the entire forest was cut. Coffee and shade trees (required to regulate the coffee bush's growth) would then be planted on the bare land. Although visually neater, this pattern of deforestation exposed soils to the harsh sun, winds, and rains of the East Javanese monsoon.

The other technique for establishing coffee stands, said to be preferred by Javanese farmers, was the *monosuko* system, in which large and middle-sized trees were kept in place and coffee planted in between. This pattern of cultivation produced a field in some ways similar to that of swidden agriculture, with its protective forest canopy (Geertz 1963, 16). Food crops might also be planted around the coffee bush during the first two or three years of its growth. Since coffee trees do best if grown under a gentle shade cover (Ruthenberg 1980, 298), the *monosuko* system is in fact ideally suited to the production of coffee. More important from an environmental perspective, the system is also erosion-resistant. It maintains tree and plant cover during the delicate transition from natural forest to coffee grove.

Despite persistent reports of erosion, however, the government preferred its system to that used by native Javanese. The unfortunate result was that upland regions experienced disastrous rates of erosion, "the consequences of which are felt even in our time" (van Klaveren 1953, 124; cf. Donner 1987). Compulsory cultivation of coffee appears to have had a similarly disastrous environmental impact in nearby Sumatra (Kahn 1980, 176).

Although in the 1870s the government sought to counteract deforestation and erosion by restricting forest cutting and requiring peasants to build terraces (Furnivall 1944, 180, 201; Palte 1984, 38), these measures were widely ignored. They were, whatever the case, too little too late. The fertility of vast areas of mountain land had been permanently degraded. When the government redistributed a portion of its coffee lands to native farmers at the beginning of this century, much of this land showed signs of serious fertility exhaustion.

The example illustrates another difference between upland *tegal* and lowland *sawah*. In the highlands, there was no equivalent to the ecologically beneficial investments made by the government in *sawah* irrigation works. In keeping with its earlier identification of them as "waste lands," the government treated mountain lands as expendable resources, valuable only if human labor was channeled into their development. Government policies ignored the fact that highlanders regarded much of this land as their own. In uplanders' eyes, of course, the land was not a "wasted" resource at all. They harvested game in its forests and periodically cultivated its gentler slopes.

During most of the nineteenth century, however, the state's interest in the highlands was limited to maximizing whatever returns it could get from cash crops. The government's attitude would change in the final years of the nineteenth century, as it grew aware of the pace and consequences of Java's population growth. It had also come to regard industrial resources like oil (discovered a few years earlier in Sumatra) as a more lucrative source of revenue than the forced cultivation of agricultural produce; the colonial economy was orienting itself toward industrial capitalism rather than mercantile trade. In addition the profitability of coffee had itself finally declined. Yields had fallen drastically as more and more groves were destroyed by the leaf blight that spread across the island in the last three decades of the nineteenth century. Lowland flooding and the siltation of irrigation channels also pointed to the large role of mountain forests in environmental management. The limits of upland exploitation were becoming clearer even to the colonial government. They would become all the more apparent in the twentieth century.

AGRICULTURAL TRANSITION IN THE EARLY TWENTIETH CENTURY

With the closing of forests in 1910 and the parceling out of the last government land, upland farmers had nowhere to turn to for more land except their own villages. From 1910 to 1925, then, they opened even the most marginal lands to cultivation. The forested slopes around upland communities were stripped bare and planted with food crops. "You planted crops anywhere a man could stand," one elder explained. Trees were removed because they shaded plants and diminished yields. At the end of this final phase of expansion in 1927, the average family farm in the midslope region consisted of 1.59 hectares. In the upperslope region, the mean was 2.13 hectares. As population grew and per-capita landholding declined, the challenge was to secure higher yields from less land. It was only at this point, a century after the first mass migrations to the highlands, that upland agriculture faced intensification challenges comparable to those experienced decades earlier in the wet-rice lowlands.

Tegal *Intensification*

There are important differences between intensification techniques with *sawah* and those on rainfed land. With *sawah,* everything depends upon the regular and controlled supply of water. If this can be assured, and such problems as salt damage avoided, *sawah* makes possible the highest and most sustainable yields of any preindustrial agriculture (Ruthenberg 1980, 184–87).

The control of water, of course, requires substantial investments of labor and capital, but although the construction of irrigation works is expensive, it also provides high marginal returns to labor. Less dramatic intensification measures follow in the wake of such construction, including pregermination and nursery sowing of seeds; transplanting rather than broadcast sowing; more precise row planting; more frequent and systematic weeding; terrace draining and aeration; more thorough plowing, raking, and leveling of terraces; the application of vegetable and manure fertilizers; and more precise harvesting techniques, such as those associated in Java with the use of the hand-held harvest razor (*ani-ani*).

Most of these measures had already been introduced into Javanese agriculture by the end of the nineteenth century. From an agroecological perspective, however, none was as important as *sawah*'s basic requirement: construction of irrigation works. The beauty of traditional *sawah* is that a labor that assures high marginal returns also guarantees the long life of the system itself. The interests of production and sustainability converge in the practical elegance of water moving through sluices onto irrigated terraces.

Tegal intensification rarely achieves this happy balance of interests. The pursuit of higher short-term yields frequently occurs at the expense of fertility and topsoil management. This was already apparent in the Tengger highlands during the 1920s. The ratio of population to agricultural land was so high that average fallow periods had fallen to only a few months, and many smallholders could no longer afford the luxury of fallowing at all. For them, permanent cropping was becoming the norm. As the geographer Jan Palte has emphasized, such intensive cultivation poses serious environmental problems:

> The permanent use of unirrigated land presents one of the most troublesome problems of tropical agriculture. . . . The typical climatic difficulties (esp. variation and intensity of rainfall), edaphic difficulties (i.e. extensive leaching, rapid breakdown of organic matter, poor soil structure), and biotic difficulties (viz. flourishing of weed, fungi, and parasites) cause the quick exhaustion of the fertility of the soil and make continuous dry-field farming subject to the high risks from prolific weed growth, pests, and disease. . . . Upland fields are usually found on sloping grounds, so that they are, moreover, exposed to the danger of erosion. Going eastward on Java, this danger is increased because of the ever pronounced monsoon character of the climate, marked by heavy rainfall concentrated in one season. (Palte 1984, 33)

Farmers in the Tengger highlands were not passive in the face of this crisis; they took strong measures to meet its challenge. From early on, rocks were removed from fields to make tillage easier. Single-run plowing with oxen gave way to double- and triple-plowing so as to better aerate soils. By 1930 plowing had itself given way to hoeing (*bencar*) with the short-handled hoe (*pacul*). Hoeing allowed farmers to dig deeper, aerating soils better, and bringing up subsoil nutrients.[2] Greater care was also shown in planting and weeding. Broadcast or plow-line planting of crops like maize gave way in the 1920s to dibble stick (*gejik, coblos*) planting in neatly arranged rows. Rather than simply discarding grasses after weeding, they were placed around the base of crop plants in a technique known in local dialect as *njurug*. *Njurug* uses grasses as green manure, and strengthens stalks against the treacherous monsoon winds of January and February. As weeds proliferated on permanently cropped lands, weeding also increased in frequency, from once a season for maize and potatoes to two or three times.

One of the most critical fertility-management measures adopted by upland farmers was the application of green and animal manures. Village elders today insist that in earlier times animal manures were not used on crops. "If an animal dropped manure someplace, we just left it there; the soil was fertile [*subur*] without it," one explained. Manure use became widespread only at the beginning of this century, and even then only with vegetable crops, not maize.

In earlier years, the preferred way of rejuvenating soils was fallowing (*njar gaga*), usually in conjunction with the cultivation of fertility-restoring plants.[3] As Ruthenberg (1980, 172) has noted, with adequate fallow times, such techniques can maintain the fertility of dry-field lands indefinitely. With the decline of per-capita holdings in the Tengger highlands, however, the opportunity costs of fallowing increased. Only large landholders could afford to pull whole fields out of cultivation for the year or so required to grow a thick fallow cover.

2. For as long as can be determined, plows have never been used in upperslope agriculture. Hoeing was the norm, apparently because steep and narrow fields make plowing impractical. The hoeing technique traditionally used in the upperslope area, however, was not nearly so intensive as the deep-dig technique used today, known in local dialect as *bencar*. *Bencar* hoeing goes to depths of 60 to 80 centimeters. By contrast, the traditional shallow-hoe technique, known as *molah* or *dangir*, worked soils to only 25 or 30 centimeters (see ch. 4).

3. Farmers were familiar with several especially effective fallow plants. The two most important were *lobak*, a thick-growing grass, and *rupina*, a nitrogen-fixating plant (called *eceng-eceng* in lowland dialect); I was unable to determine their botanical names. Both plants grow wild in the uplands, and farmers harvested their seeds for planting in their fallow fields. With the decline of fallowing, these plants are rarely used today, though farmers are still aware of their restorative properties.

In place of fallowing, farmers resorted increasingly to green and animal manures. Manuring is more labor-intensive than fallowing, since the transport of grasses or manures from distant locales can be an arduous task. On midslope fields—where the mixture of volcanic and clay soil created a less fertile medium than the richly volcanic soils of the upperslope region (see Donner 1987, 98)—plant and animal manures were applied to both coffee and maize. In the upperslope region, by contrast, green manures were less widely used, and animal manure was applied only to vegetables. When, after one or two vegetable crops, the field was rotated to maize, it was considered sufficient to let the maize plant "live from" (*urip teka*) the earlier manuring.

Although de Vries (1931, 1:30) reports that Tengger farmers used ammonium sulphate in the 1920s, villager today insist that the chemical fertilizer was restricted to a handful of farmers in Tosari, where there was a sizable European population. In actual rupiah equivalent (measured relative to the price of rice), ammonium sulphate in the 1920s was ten times as costly as the chemical fertilizers available to farmers in the 1970s. Among native farmers, moreover, it was rumored that if one used the chemical fertilizer and then stopped, the soil would be ruined for later cultivation. "We believed that chemical fertilizers make the earth lose its fragrance [*ora wangi*]," an elder farmer explained, "and when the fragrance is gone the earth is not good."[4]

Animal manures, by contrast, were widely available, since the Tengger highlands had long been an important center for cattle raising. In his 1844 report, for example, J. D. van Lerwerden (1844, 87) commented that residents of the mountain region were among the regency's most ardent cattlemen. Eighty years later this was still true. In the Tengger district as a whole, half of all families owned two or more head of cattle (de Vries 1931, 1:129). The figure was higher in the midslope region than in the upperslope area, suggesting that farmers in the less fertile midslope area had greater access to manure. Since wealthy farmers owning several head of cattle usually farm out their livestock to poor farmers, and the tender under such arrangements obtains rights to the manure (ch. 4), the large cattle population probably brought ecological benefit even to poor farmers.

Finally, upland farmers undertook two other intensification measures early in this century: intercropping and terracing. Intercropping is the

4. Tracing the history of agricultural intensification in modern Java, Anne Booth (1985, 132) notes that prior to World War II ammonium sulphate was used almost exclusively by Dutch-owned estates. She calculates that its use by paddy farmers could have been profitable, but its supply was unstable. The availability of fertilizer declined further after Indonesian independence. Though domestic production began in 1964, the input became available to upland farmers only in the 1970s (see ch. 4).

planting of two or more crops in a mixed pattern in a field. A variant of the technique had been used in the highlands even before the transition to permanent cultivation at the beginning of this century. Reports indicate that in low-lying areas of the Puspo subdistrict, for example, dry-field rice and maize had been intercropped since the early nineteenth century; in the upperslope region, potatoes, vegetables, and maize were also regularly intercropped (de Vries 1931, 1:138). Throughout the highlands, too, root crops like taro (*mantri*) and sweet potatoes (*tela*) had always been intercropped with maize, usually at the edges of fields, where the low-growing tubers could secure sunlight.

Intercropping, then, was not new to the highlands. At the turn of the century, however, farmers began to use it in a more systematic fashion to obtain larger outputs from a diminishing land area. If done effectively, the practice can increase yields, reduce erosion, control pests (which are less likely to spread than in a single-stand field), and make better use of fertilizers. The technique's major drawbacks are that it accelerates depletion of soil nutrients and requires painstaking labor. Planting must be staggered, with the lower-growing crop planted first so that it has a chance to grow before being shaded by the taller plant. Plants are laid out in neat rows so that they do not compete with each other for nutrients or sun. During weeding and harvest, workers must move carefully through the densely packed field to avoid damaging one crop while working on the other. Although such tedious labor raises labor inputs per hectare, its benefits are real, since it allows larger and more varied yields than possible under monocropping methods.

The final and most dramatic fertility-management innovation introduced to the highlands was terracing. Of all the intensification measures discussed here, this one most directly resembles those typically associated with wet-rice agriculture. It is expensive of both time and labor, and it massively reshapes the landscape. The colonial government first tried to introduce terracing in the rainfed uplands in the 1870s, with legislation requiring recipients of government land to build terraces (ch. 2; Donner 1987, 120). The rule was not enforced, however, and terrace construction really began, again under government pressure, only after 1910.

As is the case with paddy fields, the labor required to build *tegal* terraces is substantial. Egbert de Vries's (1931, 1:140) research on "showcase" terraces around Tosari early in this century indicated that construction there required an average of 700–900 workdays per hectare; other studies report figures as high as 1,500 workdays (Donner 1987, 163). Additional labor is then required to maintain the terrace year after year. This is no easy task, particularly in areas with soils as soft as those in the upperslope highlands. Terraces constructed on thick volcanic soils tend to collapse during heavy downpours. (Stone-wall terraces are found only in extremely rocky regions on the northern face of the Tengger mountains.) The terraces constructed in the Tosari region in the 1920s appear to have suffered just this fate; none lasted into the independence period.

Terrace construction began again in the 1970s, once more as a result of government pressure. Resistance to the program was widespread. Farmers protested that on steeply inclined fields, terraces reduce the total land area available for cultivation. In addition, in fields where deep volcanic soils are soaked with monsoon rains, terrace walls (*bebatur*) frequently collapse, sending their soils downslope in massive mudslides. In general, terraces work best on only moderately inclined lands and with thinner, coarser soils than those found in the upperslope highlands. Ironically, then, terraces have proved most durable where the land is already so heavily eroded that its rich topsoil has given way to a less fertile, denser subsoil.

The example is illustrative of broad differences in the form and consequences of agricultural intensification in *tegal* and *sawah*. From its beginning, wet-rice agriculture obliges the farmer to invest in an infrastructure that increases production while enhancing agricultural sustainability. By happy coincidence, developments that undermine the long-term viability of the paddy field tend to be quickly reflected in diminishing harvest yields, thus providing farmers with corrective feedback that improves farm management. With dry fields like those in the Tengger highlands, however, there is no such consonance of short-term productive and long-term ecological interests. Many of the innovations that produce immediate gains in output—like deep-dig hoeing rather than plowing, or permanent cropping rather than fallowing—also have deleterious ecological consequences. Other intensification initiatives, like the construction of terraces or the planting of trees, hold the promise of improving *tegal*'s ecological resilience. But they do so at the price of short-term declines in production.

It is this ongoing and unfortunate trade-off that so distinguishes the history of agricultural intensification in the Tengger highlands from that of lowland *sawah*. *Sawah* unites the interests of productivity and ecological resilience, while, to put it a bit too simplistically, *tegal* constantly obliges unhappy compromise. As landholdings shrink, land-starved smallholders are inevitably forced to neglect ecological concerns. In the face of small or declining income, they have little choice but to choose cultivation regimens that guarantee immediate returns. In the Tengger highlands, the consequences of this tragic trade-off would become more apparent after 1930, when intensification initiatives foundered on a combination of economic, ecological, and political obstacles.

1910–1950: COMMERCIAL INTENSIFICATION AND COLLAPSE

During the 1910s and 1920s, it looked for a while as if the Tengger region were about to enter an era of sustained commercial growth. Roadbuilding had just opened new areas of mountain territory to vehicle traffic and traders, and developments in the lowlands increased demand for upland farm products. In the last half of the nineteenth century, Java's European population had increased from 17,200 to 62,447. Over the same period, the Chinese population had almost doubled, going from 150,000 to 277,000 (Furnivall 1944, 212). The growth of both communities had a direct impact on upland agriculture. Chinese and Europeans were the primary consumers of upperslope vegetables. Native laborers on European estates consumed midslope corn. Although they did not control production or first-stage trading in upperslope produce, Chinese merchants indirectly provided the greatest portion of the capital used by upland traders.

The commercial expansion of the 1910s began in the midslope region. With the growth of the maize-eating labor force on lowland estates, and with government efforts to encourage more of the rural population to consume staples other than rice, demand for upland maize skyrocketed. During these same years, agricultural extension officers provided farmers with new, quicker-growing strains of corn. (None proved cultivable, however, in the cooler upperslope region.) With the coffee crop blighted by disease, midslope farmers turned to maize as their primary commercial crop and responded eagerly to market demand. Double-cropping the new strains of corn, the average family could meet its subsistence needs (about 650 kg of unmilled corn annually for 4.5 individuals) on just one-third of a hectare of land. Since the average midslope farm had an area of 1.59 hectares, the remaining land could be devoted to maize for market sale. This harvest figure assumes yields of one metric ton per hectare, the mean midslope yield during those years. On more fertile lands, however, yields as high as 1.7 metric tons were not uncommon. In short, roadbuilding, growing market demand, and new strains of corn all allowed midslope farmers to enjoy a small boom in commercial cultivation beginning in the 1910s.

At first the upperslope highlands lagged behind the midslope region in this commercial growth. New strains of corn could not be grown there, and double-cropping was impossible. The roads constructed at the turn of the century did not penetrate upperslope terrains. Although, with its hotels and resident Europeans, Tosari was already a major center of market activity, commerce in other upperslope villages was still limited. Production for market picked up considerably, however, with further road improvements. Between 1909 and 1912 roads from the lowlands to the two

most important midslope centers, Puspo and Nongkojajar, were asphalted. Shortly thereafter construction began on a road designed to link
these midslope communities with Tosari. Completed in 1914, the new Tosari road reduced the trip to Pasuruan from two days to twenty hours (by
oxcart). Not only was the trip shorter, it was also half as expensive as
transport by horse or *pikul*-pole porters. The infrastructure had been laid
for a new wave of commercial expansion.

Once again, upland farmers showed little shyness in the face of new
commercial opportunities. Reports from Tosari during the 1920s underscore the enormity of the change. According to one study, a third of Tosari's farmers had given up cultivation of maize entirely for permanent
cultivation of potatoes, cabbage, and other commercial crops (de Vries
1931, 1:138). Although vegetable cultivation was less intensive in more isolated villages, even in these communities a ripple effect could be seen.
Merchants in midslope Puspo, for example, competed with Tosari's traders for a share of the trade, stimulating commercial expansion in nearby
upperslope communities. Almost overnight, the Puspo market became
as big as that in Tosari. In the next two years, general stores were opened
in other mountain communities, especially in the prosperous upperslope
region. Seven were opened in Tosari alone, two in Ngadiwono, and one
each in Wonokitri and Mororejo.

Unlike the vegetable trade, store operation was dominated by outsiders. About half the stores were run by Chinese, the others by lowland
Javanese and Madurese. The presence of the outsiders excited little an-
tipathy, however. In general, highlanders were more tolerant of ethnic
Chinese than their lowland counterparts. There was, in addition, a dizzy
sense of optimism in the air, a feeling that the time had come for new institutions like dry-goods stores. Uplanders referred to the period as the
"era of prosperity" (*zaman kemakmuran*). Finally, they said, the highlands
could become modern like the lowlands.

The trade also sparked the growth of a small transport industry. It
grew to include some twenty animal-drawn vehicles and employed about
four times as many part-time packers and drivers. Unlike the recently
opened stores, moreover, the oxcart (*cikar*) industry remained firmly in
local hands. By renting vehicles on credit, the transport enterprises also
enabled producers to carry their own crops to lowland markets. This
made it easier for local farmers to compete with large merchants if they
wished to carry vegetables to market themselves. The competition raised
farm-gate prices paid to farmers, bringing benefit to all.

Around 1929 the *cikar* carts were joined by motor vehicles. A lowland-
based Chinese merchant bought the first such truck, but he was followed
a year later by three highland natives. The native traders operated on a
scale never before seen in the highlands. They shipped vegetables to Ban-

dung in West Java (a major center of European population), Solo and Semarang in Central Java, and to the East Javanese port of Surabaya, where produce was packed on ships for Kalimantan. Although most of the urban merchants with whom they dealt were Chinese, the upland traders enjoyed considerable independent wealth and were not mere tools of outside capital.[5] Their weekly shipments exceeded hundreds of dollars in value, an extraordinary amount by the standards of Java. They were also heavily involved in borrowing from banks. The volume of loans in Tosari, Puspo, and Nongkojajar was among the highest in the regency (de Vries 1931, 2:38–40). In short, the Tengger highlands were in the midst of a true commercial revolution, spearheaded by a new class of wealthy produce traders.

New Relations of Exchange

The impact of the new commerce was not limited to the expansion of trade. Although preharvest purchase of coffee had been common in midslope villages since early in the nineteenth century (de Vries 1931, 1:141), in upperslope villages such arrangements appeared only with the commercial expansion of 1910–29. There were two types of preharvest purchase: (1) *ijon* or *ngijo,* purchase of crops long prior to their harvest, at a correspondingly discounted price, and (2) *tebasan,* or purchase a few days prior to harvest at prices close to normal market rates. Under *tebasan* the farm family was not obliged to participate in the harvest; under *ngijo* they were. *Ijon* was, in effect, a disguised form of credit at extremely unfavorable interest rates. With *ijon* (and unlike *tebasan*), it was the farmer who sought out the trader. Inevitably he or she did so in response to a sudden need for cash; the further in advance of harvest the request was made, the more imbalanced the terms of the contract. As competition for upland produce increased, however, the incidence of *ngijo* is said to have declined. The commercial expansion was accompanied by the growth of regularized trading partnerships between farmers and traders, and the replacement of *ijon* with more benign credit institutions.

The most important of these new arrangements was that known as *bakul langganan,* a "regular" or "habitual" trade partnership. Under the terms of this relationship, a trader (*bakul*) provided cash to a farmer in

5. Contrary to the pattern seen in midslope villages and most of rural Java (see Stoler 1978; Alexander 1987, 35), women in the upperslope region do not play a large role in agricultural trade. This appears to be related to the historic isolation of highland communities from produce markets. Until the 1920s, most markets were one to three days' travel from upland communities, and traders had to stay overnight in distant towns, a serious matter for women charged with childcare responsibilities. Uplanders insist that it was this that led women to play a minor role in long-distance trade. Today upperslope women are key figures in store management, work that does not require them to spend nights outside the village.

exchange for exclusive rights to that farmer's produce. The loan was repaid the next few times the farmer sold crops to the creditor, by deducting a portion of the principal from the sale price. Once repaid, the
creditor invariably followed up his earlier loan with another. Indeed, the
buyer was expected to provide loans throughout the life of the *langganan*
relationship. By doing so, he excluded competitors and assured himself
of a steady share of local produce. Equally important, he also obtained
goods at a 10–20 percent discount over ordinary farm-gate prices.[6] In a
region where credit was scarce and extraordinarily expensive (interest
rates of 100 percent on a 3–4 month loan), such loans were an important
and not prohibitively expensive source of capital.

As time went on, *langganan* traders expanded their operations to include the marketing of consumer goods. Renting an oxcart or truck in
lower-lying market towns, the *bakul* would transport goods to highland
villages and sell them at a price below that of local stores, often on credit
to his clients. The *langganan* merchant was a key agent in the introduction
of new consumer goods into the highlands during the 1920s.

Most *langganan* traders, however, only operated within a small radius of
Tosari or midslope Puspo. Resenting the growing influence of lowland
merchants in their villages, officials in Wonokitri—long a center of upland traditionalism—banned *langganan* trade from their community. Traditionalists in other villages also sought to exclude these merchants and
their "lowland" goods. Traders themselves found it inconvenient and un-
necessary to seek out producers too far from the central Puspo-Tosari
road. Indeed, in general, the full impact of the commercialization of the
1920s was restricted to villages near vehicle roads. The majority of upland
communities still lay between four and thirty kilometers from the nearest
roads. High transport costs put them at a disadvantage relative to their
counterparts in Tosari or Puspo. Hence, although they also marketed
vegetable crops or (in the midslope region) new strains of corn, farmers
in remote communities remained more heavily involved in subsistence
cultivation of maize than their counterparts in Tosari and Puspo.

For these and other reasons, then, the impact of the 1920s' commercial
expansion was unevenly felt throughout the highlands. Some communities preserved the characteristics noted by outsiders in earlier times:

6. The *langganan* or *langganan tetep* ("regular customer") relationship is found in a
wide range of commercial transactions in Indonesia. Jennifer Alexander's (1987, 177–20)
insightful discussion of the arrangement in Central Java's cloth trade indicates that
there the indebted customer is allowed to make purchases from other suppliers. In addition, customers are not subject to direct or indirect credit charges on their loans, as
seemed to be the case in the vegetable trade of the 1920s. My research on *langganan* in
the vegetable trade today showed that both patterns—restrictions on trading partners
and sellers' tacit acceptance of a reduced price for their goods—are still the norm.

homes were "without distinction" (Domis 1832, 331), with fewer visible differences of wealth than typical of the lowlands; *gamelan* orchestras rather than industrially produced commodities were the most highly esteemed luxury goods (van Lerwerden 1844, 85); and the villager of most ample means was more likely to be the hereditary Hindu priest or a Javanist ritual specialist (*dhukun*) than a savvy merchant capitalist (Kreemer 1885, 347).

Nonetheless, in the 1920s, both mountain regions appeared to be in the early stages of a genuine commercial revolution. Trade profits underwrote the formation of a new class of wealthy villagers in upland commercial centers. At least in these communities, mountain society seemed on the verge of a new social order, more affluent and class-stratified than the old.

The Depression and Japanese Occupation

In the 1930s several developments cut short this commercial expansion. The international depression reduced demand for upland produce. Prices for corn and vegetable crops fell dramatically. Declining government revenues (Furnivall 1944, 442) prompted the government to abandon its plans to extend vehicle roads to more remote villages. The intensification of commercial activity sparked by roadbuilding in the Tosari region stalled; eventually it would stop entirely.

In the upperslope highlands ecological problems also contributed to the commercial decline. Between 1930 and 1933 a potato blight spread across the highlands, destroying most of the crop. Extension officers investigating the blight discovered that it rarely affected cultivation on long-fallowed or recently opened land. But where fields were permanently cultivated without fallow, the blight reached epidemic proportions. That part of the potato plant that lay above ground would become spotted, blacken, and die a few weeks after sprouting. Officials concluded that the blight was caused by a fungus that thrived in intensively cultivated soils. The fungus blemished but did not destroy cabbages; it did not affect onions or maize. In an effort to combat the problem, extension officers introduced hardier strains of potatoes. While at first these proved more pest-resistant, eventually they too succumbed to the disease. Desperately searching for alternatives to potatoes, farmers were obliged to cultivate less lucrative crops such as cabbages and onions. They were also instructed to return to their earlier practice of fallowing and to alternating vegetable cultivation with maize. Both policies required that farmers accept a drastic reduction in their incomes.

In some respects, this ecological problem was more serious than the economic downturn of the 1930s. Even if trade were to revive, there would be no going back to the intensive cultivation of a few years earlier. The example is one more reminder of important differences between wet-rice and dry-field agriculture. While annual irrigation in *sawah* serves to control pests and stabilize soils, there is no such control in dry-field agriculture. Double-cropped year after year, vegetables deplete vital nutrients and create a soil environment ideally suited for fungi and pests. For Tengger farmers the economic consequences of this simple fact were quite serious. They would be unable to revive permanent cultivation of vegetables until the introduction of chemical fungicides, pesticides, and fertilizers in the 1970s.

The crisis of the 1930s did not bring upland commerce to an end. Trade with the lowlands continued, and most of the leading entrepreneurs in Puspo and Tosari managed to continue their operations on a reduced scale. Many turned to charcoal trading. The charcoal was produced by poorer farmers seeking to supplement declining farm incomes. As throughout Java during the 1930s (Palte 1984, 37), most of the trees they cut were illegally taken from government forest lands.

Events soon conspired, however, to destroy even this last remnant of the once-thriving upland trade. In January 1942 the Japanese invaded the Dutch East Indies and established an occupation government. The occupation would revitalize the political fortunes of Indonesian nationalism and Islam (Benda 1983; King 1982, 74–85). From the perspective of upland agriculture, however, the Japanese impact was unequivocally negative. By the time they left in 1945, the Japanese had wiped out what had remained of upland commerce and driven the local population to the brink of famine.

The Japanese advance into the highlands began favorably enough. The first step the Japanese took was to encourage squatter occupation of European farms. As in other areas of Java (Palte 1984, 27), they also ordered farmers to cut down commercial trees on European estates and turn them into charcoal, an initiative that was warmly received by the local population. As Japanese farm policy proceeded, however, other directives came forward that were less favorably received by the population. Farmers were told to limit their cultivation of commercial crops, and become self-sufficient once again in food staples. Only a few staples were allowed: maize, cassava, and bananas in the midslope region; maize and (astoundingly, since in modern times it had never been widely cultivated) taro in the upperslope region. All coffee trees were destroyed, and cultivation of specifically "European" vegetables was forbidden. The restrictions were designed to free land for a cultivar of greater interest to the Japanese: *jarak* (the castor bean), which they hoped to use for fuel oil.

Japanese farm policies did more than stipulate cultivars. They reorganized upland marketing as well. At the heart of the reform was a system of cooperatives designed to regulate farm production and the distribution of consumer goods in an effort to generate revenue for the occupying government. With this goal in mind, the mountain region was divided into three economic zones. Each was administered by a Japanese advisor assisted by native staff. Together they formed a *kumiyai*, a cooperative for the marketing of produce and distribution of goods. All cash crops had to move through the *kumiyai*, where they were taxed and sold at government-specified prices. Black market activities were brutally suppressed. The public beatings that several traders suffered at the hands of Japanese officials shocked villagers and succeeded in restricting black market trade.

Besides providing tax revenues and allowing for a more controlled distribution of scarce consumer goods, cooperative regulations, it is said, were also designed to eliminate Chinese involvement in rural trade. Anti-Chinese restrictions were a feature of the Japanese occupation throughout Southeast Asia (cf. Peletz 1988, 117). Highlanders had always been tolerant of the Chinese, however, and many correctly recognized that their forced evacuation would deal a further blow to upland commerce.

In the highlands, then, the *kumiyai* replaced a system of private commercial trade with a corporate entity controlled by government directive. In theory the cooperative system was not supposed to discriminate against native traders. Those who wished to market produce could still do so, as long as they restricted themselves to government-stipulated crops. In practice, however, the impact of the cooperative system was ruinous, effectively destroying an already-weakened trading community. Before transporting their wares to the lowlands, traders were obliged to take them to the Tosari cooperative (or, in the midslope region, to Puspo or Nongkojajar) and pay a 5 percent sales tax on the goods, which could then be resold only at fixed prices. Under these circumstances, of course, the opportunities for profit were severely restricted. The arrangement eliminated the advantage of timing and information management so critical to Javanese traders' profits (Alexander 1987, 143). In addition, there was little reason for producers to deal with local traders, since they could sell their produce just as well at the cooperative center.

As the occupation continued, the burden on the mountain populace increased. During the first years of the war, livestock were subject to forced sale at low prices, and by mid 1944 they were being confiscated outright. Not surprisingly, farmers responded by slaughtering most of their animals. In late 1943 native-owned oxcarts (*cikar*) and trucks—the shining symbols of a once-proud trading class—were also seized by occupation officials. They were to be used in the transport of local laborers, recruited under compulsion, to the Jurangkwali region near Batu, seventy-five kilometers away, where the Japanese were constructing cave fortifications in anticipation of an Allied invasion. The construction effort was onerous, lasting the length of the war, and several upland men perished under the rigors of forced labor. The merchants' oxcarts and trucks were never returned. What remained of upland commerce was slowly but systematically obliterated.

The situation only worsened in the final year of the war. Consumer goods were scarce. Cloth was in such short supply that some people were forced to clothe themselves in old tire tubing. Corpses were buried in tattered clothing, without the white linen shroud required by religious custom. By 1944 the *jarak* trees cultivated by government mandate were large enough to compete with the maize that had originally been intercropped alongside the saplings, and further maize cultivation was forbidden. Hunger spread through the highlands. While the food shortages did not result in deaths, as in some areas of Java, upland farmers were forced to transport furniture, heirlooms, and anything else of value to the lowlands, where they bartered for food and clothing. Livestock herds had been totally wiped out. Young men fleeing compulsory labor left the area to take refuge in the more anonymous environment of lowland towns. Official prices paid to farmers were so low as to discourage production.

To provide fuel for railroads and charcoal for industry, the Japanese also began clear-cutting trees on government and private lands. The trees were essential for soil and water conservation, and the sudden deforestation is said to have had a devastating impact. Upland villagers can still today point to barren ravines created, they say, by the Japanese. Around upperslope Tosari no trees were left standing, and many springs went dry. Desperate to cultivate food staples, squatters seized recently denuded government forest land, which only exacerbated the problem of erosion and landslide.

The end of the war in August 1945 brought temporary economic relief. Farmers quickly cut down the *jarak* trees mandated by the Japanese. The hated cooperatives in Tosari, Puspo, and Nongkojajar were dismantled, and farmers were once again allowed to plant whatever crops they wished. Independence also brought war, however, as the Dutch (at first with the aid of Asian-theater English forces) returned and attempted to reimpose a colonial administration. Having seized cities and some rural areas in late 1945 and early 1946, the Dutch found themselves unable to suppress popular resistance, since much of the countryside remained under republican militias. In the Pasuruan regency, Dutch forces controlled most of the lowlands, but republican guerrillas dominated the highlands.

The three most important militias in the mountains were Hizbullah, the Muslim militia (which operated only in the midslope region, and even there was the smallest of the three militias); Banteng, the militia of nationalist forces; and Pesindo, a left-wing militia with ties to the Indonesian Communist Party (see Reid 1974, 77–103). The militias' economic policies were wildly irregular and did little to stabilize the rural economy. One guerrilla group might allow farmers to transport produce to the Dutch-controlled lowlands, while another, farther down the road, would forbid all trade. In addition to the militias, however, the highlands were plagued by gangs of roving bandits (*rampok*). Armed with rifles and knives, these groups posed as militia members to attack, rob, and even kill upland traders. Hoping to win support by taking advantage of farmers' difficulties, the Dutch organized several convoys to Puspo and Tosari to purchase produce and court the goodwill of the people, but these had no lasting impact on the deteriorating highland economy.

In short, for the duration of the independence war (1945–49), upland agriculture ground down to a grim subsistence regime. The prosperous trade in corn and vegetables was now a thing of the past. Roads fell into disrepair or were destroyed by local militia. Local merchants had lost their oxcarts and trucks, and their trading capital had been wiped out. Virtually the entire stock of upland cattle had been destroyed. Deforestation was rampant. As has been reported in the rural lowlands (Elson 1984, 248), these developments reversed the trend toward economic expansion seen two decades earlier. The commercial revolution of the 1920s had given way to economic collapse.

The Europeans were gone too. The elegant hotels around upperslope Tosari and the private homes near Puspo and Nongkojajar survived the early years of the revolution, empty monuments to the colonial past. After an infamous "police action" by Dutch forces in July 1947 (Ricklefs 1981, 213; Reid 1974, 112), however, the militias—fearing that the colonial armies would use the buildings for deeper penetration of republican territory—put them to the torch. Estate land was also seized. By the time peace was proclaimed and order restored, the crisis of upland agriculture had only worsened, fueling the tensions that played a major role in the political contests of the 1950s.

EARLY INDEPENDENCE: REVIVAL AND DECLINE

The treaty ending the war for independence was signed in December 1949, bringing peace and the expectation of prosperity. The 1950s saw a small revival in upland commerce, but, relative to prewar levels, production stagnated. In 1950 not a single road into the highlands was still passable. Those in the midslope region were reopened in 1951, but the road to Tosari remained closed until late 1953.

Commerce was slow to revive. In the midslope region the Japanese had destroyed the last stands of coffee. Although a few large farmers replanted coffee in the early 1950s, it would be five years before the first harvests, and another eight before mature yields began. A second obstacle to the revival of upland commerce was the flight of Chinese from the region. The Japanese had closed all Chinese-operated stores in rural areas and forbidden the Chinese to engage in trade. During the independence struggle republican militias continued the exclusionary policy. A few years after independence several Chinese store owners returned to the Tengger highlands, and some even tried to rent farmland, but their renewed presence was short-lived. In 1959 the military governor of East Java ordered all Chinese out of the countryside and into regency towns. Once again, Chinese stores were closed and with them went a vital source of capital.

By 1955, however, there were a few signs of commercial revival, especially around upperslope Tosari. Potato and vegetable exports from Surabaya to Sumatra and Kalimantan had been started again the year before, and the reopening of the Tosari road allowed farmers to contribute to the trade. Ties with Chinese merchants in Semarang, Solo, and Bandung were also renewed, providing vitally needed capital. There was no going back, however, to the halcyon days of the 1920s. Potato cultivation still suffered from fungal infestation, and with the Europeans gone, there was no demand for vegetables with especially high profit margins, such as artichokes, green beans, and cauliflower. Cabbages and leeks (*bawang teropong*) became the upperslope region's primary cash crops.

From 1955 to 1957 a national antimalaria campaign made DDT widely available. Applied in massive doses, the chemical improved vegetable yields—while decimating populations of insect-eating birds and killing fish (which poor people harvested) in lowland paddy fields.[7] During this same period, chemical fertilizers remained expensive and hard to find; almost no farmers used them. Although in the late 1950s the government's Padi Centra rice program created a small black market in ammonium sulphate, the chemical remained expensive and only intermittently available. Fertility management was further complicated by the lack of manure, the result of herd destruction during the Japanese occupation. The cattle population did not revive to 1930 levels until the late 1960s.

It was at this same time, farmers say, that some midslope fields became so infertile that they could no longer sustain maize cultivation. On severely eroded hillside fields, in particular, maize would not fruit. For the first time in the region's history, therefore, poor farmers shifted to cassava as a food crop. A similar shift from maize to cassava had begun

7. Although technically a controlled substance, DDT remains one of the most widely used pesticides in highland areas. Farmers appreciate its low price (about U.S. $2.00 per kilo in 1985) and ruthless efficiency in killing pests. Distressingly, it is also dusted in high doses on stored potatoes to fend off mice and insect pests and increase storage life.

in some poor communities below the Puspo subdistrict in the 1920s.[8] In the midslope highlands, however, cultivation of cassava became common only after the war. Grown without manure or chemical fertilizer, cassava can quickly exhaust soils, draining them of potassium and phosphorous. The plant also provides limited canopy during its early growth, and harvesting it seriously disrupts the topsoil, increasing the likelihood of erosion (Palte 1984, 46; Roche 1984, 14). For farmers hoping to earn a living on infertile lands, however, there was little choice but to cultivate whatever crop would grow.[9]

Farmers showed great resolve in the face of these difficulties and managed to reverse the economic decline in some spheres. In 1954–55 the vegetable market was reopened in Tosari. In 1957 two local merchants in Tosari and one in Puspo managed to purchase World War II–vintage trucks. In the midslope region commercial cultivation of cassava sparked a modest trade expansion. In both mountain districts, however, the commercial revival was overshadowed by growing political controversy. The most serious dispute centered around some 250 hectares of European land seized by squatters after 1942. The squatters had not yet been given title to the lands, and there were rumors that they might have to return them to the government. Communist organizers repeatedly warned of just that possibility, saying that if the squatters did not join forces with them, they would lose their lands to greedy officials. In the early 1960s their warnings appeared to be confirmed when officials in one village seized squatter lands and gave them to relatives and district officers (see ch. 7).

The annihilation of communist cadres during 1965–66 brought a sort of resolution to the squatter problem. At the same time, the introduction of new inputs a few years later led to the first real expansion of commercial agriculture since the 1930s. The 1970s would bring new economic opportunities and new challenges.

8. The colonial government had introduced cassava into Java in the nineteenth century, but peasant resistance to its cultivation remained strong until the food crisis of the 1880s (Palte 1984, 45).

9. Commercial opportunities also played a role in cassava's expansion. A key factor was the opening in 1955 of a tapioca factory in Pandaan, about 65 kilometers from this mountain area. Another factory was established shortly thereafter in nearby Probolinggo. Both developments were part of a broad expansion in East Javanese cassava production that began in the prewar period and continued to the early 1980s, when falling prices resulted in production cutbacks. Over the years, cassava came to play a role in the diet of rural East Javanese greater (in terms of grams consumed per day) than that in any other part of the island, with the exception of Yogyakarta (Dixon 1984, 69).

CONCLUSION

One point clearly emerges from this brief history of upland agriculture. Although driven by related political, commercial, and demographic pressures, upland dry-field agriculture (*tegal*) followed a different course of intensification than lowland *sawah*. Both remained small-scale and labor-intensive. But *tegal* lacked the ecological durability of *sawah*. Extended to the limits of available land area, cultivated with little or no fallow, and deep-hoed to bring up subsoil nutrients, upland *tegal* falls prey to erosion, landslides, leaching, soil fungi, insect pests, and, ultimately, declining production. Faced with shrinking landholdings, or enticed by higher profit margins, upland smallholders have little choice but to maximize short-term yields, whatever the long-term consequences. The happy consonance of interests between productivity and sustainability seen in *sawah* gives way in *tegal* to continuing unhappy trade-off.

The evolution of upland agriculture also differed from *sawah* in that intensification involved new commercial crops, not increased production of food staples. It therefore implied greater dependence on outside markets. The involvement of upland farmers in produce markets was nothing new, of course; "traditional" agriculture had always included cultivation of cash crops. Commercialization did not revolutionize production, then, as much as it adjusted the relative ratio of food staples to commercial cultivars.

Can one say, therefore, that the commercial activity in the twentieth-century highlands was really incipient rural capitalism? The question is of comparative interest, inasmuch as some students of economic history assume that incorporation into the international economic order automatically sets in motion a process of development in which relations of production and exchange are recast along capitalist lines (Frank 1969; Wallerstein 1974). Certainly Java's highlands had been incorporated into such an international economy, although, as seen in chapter 2, that process was mediated more by the colonial state than it was by an independent class of capitalist burghers. The example raises the serious question of what it means to say that development in such a colonial context was "capitalist" at all.

Leaving aside the European farmers, a critical evaluation of this question yields a complex and tentative answer. If capitalism involves no more than the capitalization of exchange—with traders securing profits by buying cheap and selling dear—then one can confidently say that between 1900 and 1960 there were major periods of capitalist expansion. If this is all that is meant by capitalism, however, then capitalism has existed for thousands of years all around the world, wherever merchants have sought trading profits. Such a view adds little to our understanding of modern agrarian change.[10]

If, in line with Marxian views (Wolf 1982, 78; Mandel 1978), one thinks of capitalism as the growth of wage labor and the extraction of surplus by owners of the means of production, then the answer to this question is even more qualified. During this half-century period, wage labor was not the motor that drove native commerce forward. Most farmers who shifted from subsistence to commercial crops continued to work their land using family labor, occasionally assisted by neighbors and friends. As in G. van der Kolff's (1936) example from south-central Java, the incidence of wage labor did increase slightly. But it was intensively utilized by only a small number of affluent merchants who had bought land in the midslope area after their migration at the beginning of the century (see ch. 5).

On the whole, then, wage labor was not the primary cause of commercial intensification, but one of its secondary symptoms. Like so many separate potatoes in Marx's famous sack, the majority of farmers continued to operate independent farms exploiting their own labor. They benefited from none of the advantages of scale or industry associated with true capitalist production. At the same time, however, they were not forced into the ranks of Java's landless poor. Like upland areas of Sumatra (Kahn 1980), Java's highlands remained a bastion of an inaffluent, but durable, middle peasantry.

If, finally, one adopts a more neo-Weberian view and sees the rational application of capital-intensive technology to commercial production as one of the keys to capitalism, then, again, there is little evidence here of a true capitalist takeoff. With the exception of DDT and a few hybrid

10. This equation of capitalism with market sale is sometimes assumed to underlie Max Weber's views on capitalism. In fact, his analysis is more complex. Weber (1968) used the term *capitalism* less restrictively than did Marx, suggesting capitalism had existed for thousands of years, everywhere people undertook economic enterprise in anticipation of profit through market exchange. Marx by contrast limits the concept of capitalism to the modern era. He argues that its most critical feature is the development of "free labor," deprived of the instruments by which it could make an independent living, and thus obliged to sell its labor power on the market. Despite his more liberal usage of the term, Weber distinguished "capitalism" from "modern capitalism." The latter, he recognized, had many unique features and involved more than just market sale; moreover, he dated its birth to approximately the same period that Marx did (Giddens 1987, 129). Though he agreed with Marx that the emergence of free labor was an important event, Weber stressed that other innovations were also critical to the development of modern capitalism, including (a) the organization of rationally coordinated business bureaucracies, (b) the dependence of the majority of consumers on markets for the provisioning of their needs, and (c) the growth of capital-intensive productive technology.

seeds, most of the technology used during this half-century period was little different from that of one hundred years earlier. A short-handled hoe, a sickle, an axe, a shoulder pole and basket—these were the primary instruments of production. Where they occurred at all, therefore, productive increases were the result, not of the rational application of industrial technologies, but of simple shifts in cultivation made possible by expanded opportunities for lowland trade.

In short, during the first half of the twentieth century, the changes seen in native agriculture were related less to the capitalization of production, with its characteristic investment in wage labor and technology, than they were to expanding market opportunities. What was so fitfully occurring in the native sector, then, was less a capitalist revolution than a miniature "mercantile" one. As Eric Wolf (1982, 88) has observed, in Europe mercantilism was a trade-oriented commercial system that preceded the development of industrial capitalism. It was based on control of markets, not on the industrial transformation of labor and technology. In the Tengger highlands too (but again, speaking only of the native sector), commercial expansion was driven forward by market trade, not by the transformation of production.

For the most part, in fact, production arrangements were left as they were. The expansion did affect choice of cultivars, and in some areas it altered harvesting practices too. But any broader assault on the organization of production was impeded by the desperate hold of thousands of smallholders on their land. Contrary, then, to certain models of agrarian capitalism (Lenin 1899), there was no simple polarization here between an impoverished class of landless proletarians and a wealthy group of "kulak" landlords. The heart of this development was mercantile, reshaping relations of exchange, not relations of production. This fact is reflected in the nature of the technical innovations that did occur. They consisted of instruments for moving produce to market—oxcarts, motor vehicles, and merchant credit. These stimulated, but did not otherwise transform, a largely noncapitalist agriculture.

In the end, not even this modest expansion could be sustained. No sooner had a merchant elite established itself in the 1920s than circumstances conspired to bring about its decline. The commercial devolution began with the ecological and economic crises of the 1930s and accelerated with the Japanese occupation and independence struggle. In the early 1950s it looked as if the crisis had passed. But it reemerged with the hyperinflation and political turmoil of the 1950s and early 1960s. Reports from other parts of Java point to a similarly cyclical pattern of commercialization and decommercialization during the first decades of this century (Geertz 1965a; Husken and White 1989, 247; Elson 1984; Husken 1979).

Only after 1965 would the conditions exist for more sustained accumulation.

The enduring recession did not entirely eliminate differences of class or status. These survived. Four decades of economic instability, however, prevented the trading elite from expanding their activities very far. Unable to consolidate even their own businesses, they were in no position to "invade the productive process and ceaselessly alter the conditions of production," as Eric Wolf has put it in describing Europe's capitalist revolution (Wolf 1982,79). By the early 1960s, meanwhile, it looked as if there was little more that could be done to increase production with existing technology. A class of traders survived, but a growing portion of the peasantry was stuck in a vicious circle of economic decline.

Suddenly and profoundly, all of this changed with the emergence of the New Order government. In the early 1970s roads were built and new agricultural technologies introduced. Shortly thereafter the highlands commenced a phase of commercialization that dwarfed that of the 1920s and raised the possibility of a more substantial transformation of production, class, and community. The green revolution had begun.

FOUR

The Green Revolution in
Mountain Agriculture

The changes seen in mountain agriculture in the mid 1970s were in part the unintended consequence of developments begun in the wet-rice lowlands in the late 1960s and only marginally concerned with upland or rainfed agriculture. In the first five-year development plan (1969–74), "food policy *was* rice policy" (Mears and Moeljono 1981, 23). Preoccupied with *sawah* production, the government paid little attention to the rainfed uplands, and production there stagnated.

Indirectly, however, state policies had a powerful impact on mountain agriculture. Programs for distributing chemical fertilizers to wet-rice farmers created a thriving black market. Government efforts to expand production eventually created supplies sufficient to allow deregulation, providing upland farmers with legal access to fertilizers. Roadbuilding and the manufacture of a new fleet of light trucks brought transportation to even remote mountain communities, allowing farmers to market their goods quickly and more cheaply. With increased mobility came new consumer goods and outside investment. Benefiting from the growth of revenues made possible by the oil price increases of 1973–74 (Booth and McCawley 1981b, 7), the government built schools, clinics, and administrative offices, broadened farm extension programs, and launched an ambitious family-planning program (Hull and Mantra 1981). It also imposed strict limits on rural political activity (Mahoney 1981). Slowly but systematically the New Order government reshaped rural society.

Mountain villages experienced these changes with particular intensity. Less economically stratified than their lowland counterparts, highland communities were suddenly exposed to a new range of social influences. Inward-focused cultural traditions were undermined as the movement of people, capital, and goods became easier and radio and television brought home new images of identity and well-being. Government policies linked village structures all the more firmly to the machinery of state. Even the most basic changes in mountain agriculture were related to broader shifts in national politics and culture.

BACKGROUND TO GREEN REVOLUTION

Between 1965 and 1981 Indonesian production of milled rice increased from 10.2 to 22.3 million metric tons (Mears and Moeljono 1981, 26; Republik Indonesia 1983–84, 257). The actual area of *sawah* increased only slightly during this time, from 7.5 million hectares in 1967 to 8.8 million in 1978. Most of the production increase was thus a product of growing per-hectare yields. The dimensions of the change were remarkable. Between 1954 and 1966 national yields had remained stagnant at about 1.18 metric tons per hectare. Between 1967 and 1978, however, they grew from 1.20 to 1.99 metric tons. On Java the increase was even greater, with yields rising from 1.24 to 2.25 metric tons. This expansion occurred on an island that had seen rice production decline by 15 percent and per-capita rice consumption decrease from 107 to 92 kilograms during the politically troubled 1960–64 period (Mears and Moeljono 1981, 25). Of all of Southeast Asia, Java most desperately needed the changes promised by the green revolution.

As in other countries, the green revolution was associated with the introduction of new, faster-growing, and potentially higher-yielding "modern rice varieties" (MRVs) (Barker, Herdt, and Rose 1985, 62). The success of these new rice strains depended on better water control and the abundant application of chemical fertilizers and pesticides. Hence, in all of the countries where they were introduced, the MRVs required parallel efforts to improve irrigation and to increase distribution of chemical inputs at affordable prices (Hart et al. 1989, 4; Peletz 1988, 169). In Indonesia the intent of the credit programs was to provide farmers with capital at the beginning of the rainy season, when they are most severely strapped for cash and are thus unable to buy farm inputs. After several trial arrangements (Hansen 1973), the Bimbingan Massal ("mass guidance"), or BIMAS, program became operative throughout most of Java and Bali by the mid 1970s. By 1978 about two-thirds of Indonesia's rice fields were planted with the new varieties.

During the early years of the BIMAS program, seeds and fertilizers were available through government channels only, and farmers outside of official programs had great difficulty securing inputs. Fertilizer distribution was in theory deregulated in 1971. Production lagged behind demand, however, and many farmers were still unable to obtain inputs. Cooperatives designed to help in the production and procurement of rice

(Mears and Moeljono 1981, 33) were given first priority in fertilizer distribution, further restricting public access. With demand exceeding supply, a lively black market in agrochemicals developed, some of whose most active consumers were farmers in Java's vegetable-growing uplands (Palte 1984, 42).

This was the case, for example, in the Tengger highlands. In 1969, once again showing their entrepreneurial initiative, farmers from upper-slope Tosari and Ngadiwono established an illegal fertilizer distribution network. In late 1971 subdistrict officials uncovered the operation and briefly jailed its organizers. The incident is illustrative of important differences between intensification initiatives in the uplands and those in the rice-producing lowlands. In the latter region, the government was the main promoter of green-revolution technology. It subsidized agricultural credit, organized agricultural extension programs, and helped in procurement and marketing (Husken and White 1989). In the Tengger highlands, by contrast, the entire effort was a grass-roots initiative, at first undertaken in the face of government opposition. It was organized by local entrepreneurs, financed by private capital, and only acknowledged, approved, and regulated by the authorities several years after its inception.

Government neglect of rainfed and upland agriculture was dramatically evident in production figures from the early years of the New Order. Rice production during this time increased, but production of staples other than rice declined, in some cases even precipitously. For example, maize production fell 10 percent, cassava 7 percent, and sweet potatoes 5 percent a year between 1968 and 1971 (Timmer 1981, 43). Government policy during the 1970s kept the ceiling price of rice low relative to other staples, and from 1970 to 1977 the prices of maize, cassava, and sweet potatoes rose 59, 80, and 100 percent respectively relative to rice. Despite their potential profitability, production of dry-field staples increased only slightly. In 1975, after several years of bumper rice harvests, maize yields in Indonesia were still only 1.09 metric tons per hectare. This was 15 percent greater than production per hectare in the early 1960s, but still only 77 percent of the all-Asia average, and less than half of the mean yield in nearby Malaysia (Mears and Moeljono 1981, 53). Cassava production remained similarly stagnant, with yields of about 8 tons per hectare, no greater than in the early 1950s (Roche 1984, 9). Farmers on rainfed land lacked access to new technology, it seemed, and their agriculture stagnated.

The government began to show a greater interest in other crops when it became clear that agricultural self-sufficiency could not be guaranteed through rice alone. In 1972–73 maize, soybeans, peanuts, and cassava were included in the BIMAS extension program, so at least some *tegal* farmers could obtain credit for fertilizers. During Repelita II, Indonesia's second five-year development plan (1974–79), BIMAS support for staples other than rice was supposed to expand from 388,000 to almost 2 million hectares (Mears and Moeljono 1981, 35), 70 percent of which was to be devoted to maize. The area actually covered by the program proved to be considerably smaller than the official goal, but the target figure nonetheless indicated that the government was finally concerned about non-rice staples.

Ultimately, the impasse in dry-field agriculture was resolved through greater fertilizer production. By 1977 Indonesia had achieved near self-sufficiency in production of urea (for nitrogen), with annual production of about 787,000 tons (Mears and Moeljono 1981, 41). Large government subsidies allowed the product to be sold at prices that were among the lowest in Asia (Barker, Herdt, and Rose 1985, 88; Husken and White 1989, 252). Although subsidies were primarily intended to help rice producers, the growing availability of inexpensive fertilizer also benefited other farmers. Between 1970–71 and 1978–79 application of chemical fertilizer to cassava and maize on Java increased by 250 percent and 135 percent respectively. Actual dosages per hectare remained small, averaging, for example, only 21.7 kilograms for cassava and 71.2 for maize in 1979 (Roche 1984, 12). The impact on production was nonetheless notable, reversing the decline seen between 1968 and 1971. Nationally, maize production increased an average of 4 percent a year during the 1970s. By the end of the decade, mean yields per hectare were 1.7 tons, up from .95 ton in the 1960s (Mink and Dorosh 1987). Cassava yields per hectare also increased more than 50 percent (Roche 1985, 6). After years of neglect, Java's rainfed lands began to feel the benefits of new programs and technologies.

Other government programs also brought unintended benefits to upland areas. In the early 1970s assembly factories were built to manufacture "Colt" light trucks to replace an antiquated fleet of postwar American vehicles (Booth and McCawley 1981b, 8). By the late 1970s there were so many of these privately owned trucks that competition for customers along Java's main highways had become fierce, and drivers were forced to seek out clients on less heavily traveled roads. Many operators moved their services to recently opened mountain roads.

The expansion of roads was itself related to broader changes in Indonesia's economy. Much of the nation's road system had never been fully rehabilitated after the war of independence, and it had deteriorated even further during the economic crises of the late 1950s and early 1960s. Flush with new oil revenues, the New Order government in the 1970s made road expansion a priority. In Java a significant portion of the new construction occurred in remote upland areas. In midslope and upperslope portions of Pasuruan's Tengger highlands, for example, the area of asphalted road increased from 47 to 92 kilometers, and the number of villages with access to vehicle roads (stone-surfaced or asphalt) increased from about 20 to 80 percent.[1]

Road improvements brought immediate benefits to Java's farmers. Agricultural surveys during the 1970s revealed that the difference between farm-gate and rural market prices actually narrowed, in large part because road improvements had lowered transport costs and increased competition for farm goods (Booth 1979, 51). In four communities in the midslope Tengger highlands, for example, real transport costs declined 37 percent in the first year after the opening of a road in 1980. In nearby upperslope communities, costs fell by almost half. The availability of inexpensive transport also gave farmers the option of selling crops themselves in the lowlands, avoiding middlemen and securing a larger share of the profits.

If one can talk, then, of a green revolution in mountain Java, it involved not just the introduction of new inputs to agriculture, but changes in transportation, marketing, consumption, and, as we shall see in chapter 7, politics. Focusing for the moment, however, on the diffusion of new productive inputs, one notes several important differences between the highland experience and that in the wet-rice lowlands. First, as noted above, responsibility for securing the new technology lay with local farmers, not the government. Indeed, at times local farmers acted contrary to government directives, as when they attempted to secure fertilizer stocks through irregular channels. Second, fertilizers and pesticides would prove to be as important as new varietal strains in the uplands, where some of the most critical obstacles to agricultural intensification were agroecological, the unfortunate consequence of permanent cultivation on rainfed lands. New agrochemicals allowed farmers to neutralize or reverse these ecological problems, at least in the short run.

Finally, and most dramatically, while new inputs facilitated increased production of maize or cassava, they also allowed some farmers to substitute lucrative cash crops for food staples. In Pasuruan's midslope highlands, maize and cassava gave way to coffee and cloves. In the upperslope area, maize was replaced by the permanent cropping of commercial vegetables. Although we lack accurate islandwide figures, observers in other parts of Java have also noted a significant decline in the area planted with maize and cassava (Roche 1985, 8). During the same period, vegetable

1. As in much of Java, the main access roads in these areas were constructed with subsidies from the national Inpres program (see Booth and McCawley 1981b, 8). Feeder roads linking individual communities with the main road were the responsibility of individual villages, often requiring several years of weekly village labor (*kerja bakti*) to complete.

cultivation increased, as did the area planted to commercial perennials like coffee, cloves, and citrus fruit.[2] Events in the Tengger highlands help to explain the economic logic of this shift away from food staples. As we shall see, they also illustrate the new agriculture's ambiguous impact on an agricultural environment that was already imperiled.

THE ECONOMICS OF COMMERCIAL INTENSIFICATION

None of the modern varieties of corn introduced into Java in the 1970s have yet proved suitable for cultivation in the cool, cloud-covered, upper-slope highlands (i.e., areas above 1,200 meters). Farmers there grow the same strain of white maize used for centuries and are able to plant only one crop a year. Per-hectare yields remained low in the 1970s despite small applications of chemical fertilizer. Production surveys of twenty-one upperslope maize farmers in 1985 revealed that farmers were obtaining harvest yields of almost 1,100 kilograms per hectare (table 4.1). This is notably less than the national average of 1.7 tons, but is consistent with other low-productivity areas of East Java such as Madura and the southern limestone highlands (Mink, Dorosh, and Perry 1987, 71).

Although their input costs were low, profits (exclusive of costs to land and family labor) for upperslope maize farmers were small too, providing average gross yields equivalent to only Rp 164,400 per hectare, or, at 1985 rates, $150. Returns to land and family labor averaged only Rp 123,970 per hectare. Dividing these net profits by the number of days families spend cultivating a maize crop, this comes to only Rp 611 for each family-worker day. This is enough to buy 4 kilograms of maize meal, or 2.2 kilograms of milled rice. While not intolerable by Javanese standards, returns of this magnitude were less than the average (upperslope) field laborer's daily wage in 1985. Table 4.1 provides a more detailed overview of inputs and outputs, using 1985 prices. I have not included the cost of renting or buying land in estimating returns to cultivation; nor have I taken into account the costs of family labor. In this and later tables, a "day's field labor" has been standardized as 5.5 hours and does not include travel time

2. Frederick Roche (1985, 12) observes that between 1974 and 1983 the area planted to smallholder coffee in Indonesia increased from 346,700 to 738,400 hectares. In the same period clove stands expanded from 171,600 to 548,900 hectares. A large portion of this extension, he notes, occurred in upland areas of Java, and it did so at the expense of maize and cassava.

to fields, which, on average, adds an additional 45 minutes to a worker's day.[3]

These figures confirm upperslope farmers' views on maize. Its primary virtue, they note, is that it requires little capital and only moderate amounts of labor. Farmers produce their own seeds, and poorer farmers hire no labor. Cash costs are thus kept to a minimum. Fertilizer use can also be cut considerably below the mean. Poor farmers apply none, letting the maize live off fertilizer applied to vegetable crops grown earlier on the same land. Through these and other measures, they keep their capital expenditures to a minimum, making maize an inexpensive, if not particularly lucrative, crop.

By contrast, the two main cash crops in the upperslope region, potatoes and cabbages, require considerable outlays of capital and labor. Seeds (or, in the case of pregerminated cabbages, seedlings) are expensive; chemical fertilizers are applied at rates several times higher than in any other kind of Indonesian agriculture; and pesticides and fungicides are abundantly applied. Manures also add to input costs.[4] As table 4.2 indicates, the total cost of nonlabor inputs (again excluding imputed costs to land) for potatoes and cabbages is fifteen to twenty times that for

3. Several points of information in table 4.1 require additional explanation. Though their cost is included in figures here, maize seeds are usually taken from one's own harvest rather than being purchased. They are all unimproved varieties. Their value in table 4.1 is calculated as equal to unprocessed maize kernels, which sold in 1985 for Rp 150 per kg. The only chemical fertilizers used in maize cultivation were TSP (trisodium phosphate) and urea, with urea application usually two to three times that of TSP. No upperslope farmers used ammonium sulphate; nor did any apply manure (which is used in the midslope region). Finally, it is important to note that the average of 246 workdays per hectare of maize is considerably higher than the figures from other parts of Indonesia provided by Mink, Dorosh, and Perry (1987), even adjusting for the fact that they standardize the workday to 8 hours, while I use a figure of 5.5 hours. If one adjusts Mink et al.'s figures to 5.5-hour days, labor inputs for one hectare of monoculture corn averaged 73–124 workdays per hectare in their findings, less than half the total in mountain Pasuruan. Some of the difference may be related to Mink et al.'s figures on women's work. These indicate that women provide only 10–25 percent of total labor in corn production. My research in the Tengger highlands revealed no such pattern of low female participation. Quite the contrary, women accounted for slightly more than half the maize labor in the upperslope region and just under one-half in the midslope region. In an otherwise superb study, Mink et al.'s low figures for women strike me as curious, and they invite further study.

4. When the shift to intensive vegetable cultivation began in the mid to late 1970s, many farmers stopped using animal manures entirely (see below). A significant decline in harvest yields since those years has prompted leaders of local farm organizations to promote their use again, in conjunction with chemical fertilizers. The move back to animal manures was just beginning in 1985. To judge by the amounts of manure used with vegetables in other parts of Java, it is likely to continue.

TABLE 4.1 Inputs and Outputs for Upperslope Maize

	Amount	*Cost/Value (Rp)*
Nonlabor inputs		
Seeds	16 kg	2,400
Chemical fertilizers	84 kg	10,080
Manure	0 kg	0
Pesticides	0 kg	0
Total nonlabor costs		12,480
Labor inputs		
Hired labor	43 days (17%)	27,950
Family labor	203 days (83%)	
Total labor use	246 days (100%)	
Total labor costs		27,950
Total costs		40,430
Returns		
Yield	1,096 kg	164,400
Total returns[a]		123,970
Daily returns per family-worker		611

NOTE. Sample size: 21. In 1985, when this survey was done, U.S. $1.00 = Rp 1,100.
[a] Returns to land, family labor, capital, and management.

maize. By Javanese standards, in other words, these are extraordinarily capital-intensive crops.

In a Javanese context capital inputs of the magnitude seen here with cabbages and potatoes are almost unbelievable. While manuring is relatively light, chemical fertilizer is applied at about thirteen times the rate of the maize crop, or ten times the all-Java average for maize in 1981. Even by the standards of Asia's green revolution, the volume of fertilizer is extraordinary—almost seven times the amount, for example, used by farmers in government rice programs in 1975 (Booth 1979, 61). Even Japanese rice farmers apply only about 340 kilograms of chemical fertilizer per hectare (Barker, Herdt, and Rose 1985, 77).

Pesticide and fungicide expenses are also substantial. Potatoes have to be sprayed an average of six times in the dry season, and eight to twelve times during the rainy season, to protect them from the soil fungi that curtailed their cultivation decades earlier. By comparison with these material costs, expenditures for wage labor are modest, about 9 percent of total input costs for potatoes and 19 percent for cabbages. Keeping in mind that vegetables can be double- or triple-cropped, one sees that a hidden social benefit of the new crops is that they increase annual de-

TABLE 4.2 Inputs and Outputs for Upperslope Potatoes and Cabbages (per ha)

	Potatoes		*Cabbages*	
	Amount	Cost/ Value (Rp)	Amount	Cost/ Value (Rp)
Nonlabor inputs				
Seeds	1,041 kg	156,000	20,540 seedlings	35,349
Chemical fertilizers	1,115 kg	133,800	1,224 kg	146,880
Manure	1,710 kg		3,326 kg	
Pesticides/fungicides		90,240		23,591
Total nonlabor costs		388,590		222,450
Labor inputs				
Hired labor	57 days (19%)	37,050	78 days (33%)	50,700
Family labor	242 days (81%)		157 days (67%)	
Total labor use	299 days (100%)		235 days (100%)	
Total labor costs		37,050		50,700
Total costs		425,640		273,150
Returns				
Yield	7,315 kg	731,500	25,500 kg	765,000
Total returns[a]		305,860		491,850
Daily returns per family-worker		1,264		3,133

NOTE. Sample sizes: potatoes, 50; cabbages, 35. The survey was done in 1985.

[a] Returns to land, family labor, capital, and management.

mand for labor by 200–400 percent over what it is for maize. The new agriculture thus provides rewards for landholders and wage laborers alike (ch. 5).

If input costs for vegetables are high, so too are returns to family labor and resources. Upperslope fields currently produce a respectable average of 25.5 tons of cabbages per hectare. The mean for potatoes is 7.3 tons per hectare, a relatively poor yield by Javanese standards, but still sufficient to provide returns to family labor, land, capital, and management twice those of maize. Potato yields in this region have declined substantially over the past ten years, from a 1977 average of 13 tons per hectare. This is largely a result of inadequate crop rotation and significant fertility degradation (see below).[5] In 1985 the farm-gate price of both vegetable crops was about two-thirds what it was in the early 1970s, when competition from Java's other vegetable-producing highlands was weak. Even using today's figures, however, both crops remain profitable. On a per-harvest basis alone, the average family-worker earns the equivalent of 4.6 kilograms of milled rice per day cultivating potatoes and 11.4 kilograms for cabbages. That is two-and-one-half to five times as much as one earns each day cultivating maize.

Both of the new cultivars, moreover, require considerably more labor per season than the old maize crop. Even as they generate higher returns per day, therefore, they also provide more days' work, work that is shared by landowners and wage laborers alike. In addition, finally, both crops can be double- or triple-cropped each year, rather than the one crop possible with maize. The consequence of this extraordinary intensification is that while increasing the demand for wage labor, cabbages and potatoes also provide landowners with annual farm incomes five to ten times those possible with maize. Given these facts, it is easy to understand the enthusiasm with which upperslope farmers took up the new cash crops in the 1970s.[6]

Midslope Intensification

In midslope regions of the Tengger highlands, a similar transition from primary cultivation of food staples to intensive cultivation of commercial crops began in the mid 1970s. Here, however, farmers concentrated on tree perennials, especially coffee and cloves. As with upperslope vegetables, the new agriculture became possible only with the availability of chemical fertilizers and pesticides in the 1970s.

Coffee has long been grown in the midslope highlands, but in the 1970s farmers were introduced to new strains of *Coffea robusta* and *arabica*, and came to rely heavily on chemical fertilizers and pesticides. New cultiva-

5. Discussions with villagers revealed that in recent years many poor farmers have begun to triple-crop potatoes without fallow or crop rotation. They do so because a third crop can be planted during the dry season even without irrigation. By contrast, dry-season cultivation of cabbages requires abundant irrigation, an arduous labor. With potatoes, one can also neglect to use manure, thereby reducing costs. This is impossible with cabbages; without manure, the cabbage head cracks and spoils. For reasons of economy, therefore, poor farmers prefer to cultivate potatoes, since, if short of cash, they are better able to economize on chemical and manure inputs. As a consequence, though, their yields are much lower than the mean.

6. In Java the ability to double- and triple-crop temperate-climate vegetables decreases as one moves down the mountainside into warmer and less cloud-covered terrains. In the Tengger highlands, the limits of potato and cabbage cultivation are reached between 1,100 and 1,200 meters altitude. The climatic transition coincides with a change from deep, well-drained volcanic soils to poorly drained clay soils ill-suited for vegetables. Between 600 and 1,000 meters, however, farmers can double-crop maize. They can also grow cassava or coffee, neither of which grows well in the upperslope region.

tion techniques were also introduced, including heavier manuring, more regular weeding, and careful pruning of the coffee bushes and the shade trees that regulate coffee growth.

Although cultivated for centuries on the "spice islands" of eastern Indonesia, cloves were introduced to the Tengger highlands, and indeed to Java as a whole, only in the 1960s. Between 1964 and 1985 Indonesian clove cultivation increased dramatically, expanding from 60,000 to almost 600,000 hectares, and 97 percent of total production was by smallholders (Bennett et al. 1987, 6). In the Pasuruan highlands cultivation of the crop was impossible without heavy applications of fertilizers and pesticides. Failing either, the tree fell victim to termites, stem-boring insects, red ants, root diseases, leaf drop, or tree fungi; or it simply failed to blossom.

Comparison of the new agriculture with the old in the midslope region is complicated because the mix of crops grown here has always been varied. Before the 1970s, for example, the majority of midslope farmers cultivated maize as their primary staple, using whatever surplus they could produce as a cash crop. In the 1950s, however, poor farmers had begun to substitute cassava for maize, since the crop provided more profitable yields even on infertile lands. Some smallholders also grew a little coffee, but, given fluctuating yields and uncertain prices, few owned more than a handful of trees. Larger landholders sometimes cultivated much larger tracts of coffee in addition to a small backup subsistence crop.

For poor or middle peasants, the primary advantage of maize and cassava is that neither requires much capital and both provide steady returns (table 4.3). The general intensity of cultivation is similar to that seen with upperslope maize, with the notable exception that midslope farmers use larger amounts of both chemical fertilizers (urea and trisodium phosphate) and manure. Midslope farmers insist that their maize will not bear fruit unless given small amounts of *both* animal and chemical fertilizers, since their soils are less fertile than those of the upperslope region.

Exclusive of land and family labor, capital inputs to the midslope maize crop are still small, totaling only Rp 26,000 per hectare, or (at 1985 exchange rates) U.S. $23.60. Yields are low: 937 kilograms per hectare as opposed to the upperslope's 1,096. Midslope farmers can double-crop their maize or intercrop it with cassava, however, providing higher annual yields despite poorer soils.[7] At just over Rp 710 per family-worker

---

7. The figure for mean maize yields in table 4.3 is for single-stand maize and cassava only. If farmers intercrop maize and cassava, they do so at the beginning of the rainy season in late October or early November. The density of cultivation reduces mean maize yields per hectare by about one-quarter and rules out planting a second maize crop that same year. The total labor required for maize and intercropped cassava is nonetheless less than that required for two separate maize crops.

TABLE 4.3   Inputs and Outputs for Midslope
Maize and Cassava (per ha)

	Maize		Cassava	
	Amount	Cost/ Value (Rp)	Amount	Cost/ Value (Rp)
Nonlabor inputs				
Seeds	16 kg	2,400	4,000 cuttings	4,000
Chemical fertilizers	120 kg	14,400	24 kg	2,880
Manure	1,830 kg	9,150	0 kg	0
Pesticides	0 kg	0	0 kg	0
Total nonlabor costs		25,950		6,880
Labor inputs				
Hired labor	22 days (9%)	12,100	14 days (19%)	7,700
Family labor	215 days (91%)		140 days (91%)	
Total labor use	237 days (100%)		154 days (100%)	
Total labor costs	12,100		7,700	
Total costs		38,050		14,580
Returns				
Yield	937 kg	140,550	7,600 kg	114,000
Total returns[a]		102,500		99,420
Daily returns per family-worker		478		710

NOTE. Sample sizes: maize, 17; cassava, 12. The survey was done in 1985.
[a] Returns to land, family labor, capital, and management.

day (about U.S. $0.65), cassava provides better returns to farm families
than maize, despite the fact that its farm-gate price has fallen from Rp
25–30 a kilogram to Rp 15 since 1980.[8] On the whole, though, both cassava
and maize in this midslope region generate relatively little employment
and provide only meager daily returns, much like maize in the upperslope region.

8. The figure in table 4.3 on total workdays for cassava excludes harvest labor, because it is undertaken by the trader (*penebas*), who purchases the crop in the field. In
1985 the purchase price for such cassava was Rp 15 per kg: Prices paid to the farmer are
renegotiable should the trader err to his own disadvantage.

Coffee and Cloves

The "traditional" cultivation of coffee in the midslope region also requires little capital or labor. Surveys of ten coffee smallholders in 1985 indicated that average per-hectare inputs of labor, including harvest, were only about 120 workdays annually. In this area of Java the coffee plant is (under customary cultivation techniques) not pruned but allowed to grow as "forest coffee" (*kopi alas*). No effort is made to regulate the amount of light the tree receives through the careful planting and pruning of shade trees, a critical variable in the regulation of production and the long-term health of the tree (Ruthenberg 1980, 298). Although when the tree is first planted farmers sometimes apply a shoulder-pole load (about 40 kg) of manure, most fertilize only every six or eight years, and even then they use only 10–20 kilograms of manure per tree. Harvest is carried out in one or, at most, two phases, rather than several, as would be required to guarantee higher bean quality.

Although maintenance costs are low, so too are yields for this unintensively produced coffee. Surveys of ten traditional growers revealed that, even excluding crops ravaged by pests, annual yields averaged only .28 of a kilogram of dried beans (*kopi berasan*) per tree. With 900 to 1,000 trees per hectare (the usual density), this means that a hectare of coffee produces only 252 to 280 kilograms of dried beans. This is well below the national smallholder average of 429 kilograms per hectare (Booth and Sundrum 1981, 194). With the farm-gate price of low-to-medium-quality *robusta* beans at Rp 1,000 per kilogram, average gross returns were only Rp 250,000 to Rp 280,000 per hectare in 1985. In bad years returns can be considerably less, a fact that explains smallholders' reluctance to rely too heavily on the crop.

The uncertainties associated with coffee are legion. Besides the vagaries of weather and annual yield fluctuations, crops are regularly attacked by berry borer worms. In normal years, these destroy or damage about one-sixth of the crop. "Bad years," when they destroy twice this amount, usually occur every five or six years, however. To reduce the risk of attack, farmers harvest coffee while it is still green. Green beans fetch a lower price, but the price loss is offset by the more secure yield. As has been reported from elsewhere in Indonesia (Godoy and Bennett 1987a, 10), theft of beans is also a problem. During 1985 two stands near Puspo were stripped of their harvest, reportedly by professional thieves, who make regular forays into the area from the nearby lowlands.

To prevent theft, farmers allow their bushes to grow tall in the manner of "forest coffee." Harvesting forest coffee requires scaffolds, which makes the process more conspicuous. These theft-resistant trees, however, also provide smaller yields than well-pruned bushes and require more work. Processing of the berries introduces additional uncertainties.

Harvest takes place at the beginning of the dry season, and, not uncommonly, an unexpected late rain can hamper drying. Inadequate drying results in fungal decay, destroying the beans or lowering their quality and sale price. Improper hulling similarly damages the coffee bean, further lowering its price.[9] Finally, on top of these technical difficulties, the price of coffee fluctuates widely from year to year.[10]

In the face of all these difficulties, it is easy to understand why poor farmers opt for cultivation of maize or cassava. Whatever their mediocre yields, these staples provide consistent returns; whatever their fate in the market, they can, if need be, be consumed by farmers themselves.

Cultivation techniques for cloves and new strains of coffee differ markedly from the rather casual cultivation of old. Both crops require large amounts of capital and, at least initially, of labor. Farmers who choose to put either crop in on existing coffee lands, for example, are obliged to rip out their old trees. Grafting of saplings onto the trunks of old trees is not practiced. Even after removing old trees, the labor required for the planting and first-year care of a hectare of new bushes is substantial, averaging about 535 workdays for coffee and 470 for cloves. The work involved under ideally intensive conditions includes digging a hole, planting the sapling, manuring, fertilizing, spraying, weeding, and pruning. For a hectare of coffee, farmers also plant 200–300 shade trees, which protect the young saplings from the sun and are later used to regulate production. While exposure to unshaded sunlight may temporarily increase production, continued over several years it kills the coffee bush. Cloves may also be protected with shade trees during the first three or four years of growth, but these are eventually removed.

In short, the amount of labor required to get these new crops established is substantial. As table 4.4 shows, nonlabor costs are also much higher than for maize or cassava. As with vegetables in the upperslope region, in other words, the green revolution in the midslope highlands is expensive of both labor and capital.

After the first year, inputs to intensively grown coffee and cloves decline, but they still involve significantly more capital and labor than traditional coffee. Saplings, for example, are remanured annually during these first years, with at least half a *pikul* load (20–30 kg) of manure for coffee and a full load or even two for cloves. Chemical fertilizers and pesticides are also abundantly applied—fertilizers (1/2–1 kg per tree per year, plus fertilizer sprays for leaf growth) twice per year, and pesticides four

9. Godoy and Bennett (1987a, 1987b) provide an overview of some of the difficulties in cultivating coffee and maintaining high berry quality in other parts of Indonesia.

10. Surveying coffee prices from 1976–86, Godoy and Bennett (1987a, 22) show that the real price of *robusta* grade A1 coffee fell from Rp 1,925 per kg in 1976 to Rp 815 in 1982. It has risen again in recent years.

TABLE 4.4   Nonlabor First-Year Start-Up Costs for New Coffee and
Cloves, 1985 (per ha)

	Coffee		Cloves	
	Amount	Cost (Rp)	Amount	Cost (Rp)
Saplings	1,000	75,000	200	200,000
Chemical fertilizer	550 kg	66,000	200 kg	24,000
Manure	22,000 kg	110,000	8,000 kg	40,000
Pesticides		48,000		60,000
Total		299,000		324,000

NOTE. Sample size: 8 per crop.

times, or as may be required. Exclusive of labor, the total cost of inputs averages about Rp 200,000 per year for a hectare of intensively cultivated coffee and about Rp 130,000 for cloves.

Not surprisingly given these start-up costs, affluent farmers took the lead in introducing cloves and intensive coffee. They were the farmers, after all, who could best afford to pull fields out of food-staple cultivation, expend the capital to nurture the young trees, and wait out the long period from planting to first harvest. In this cool midslope region, yields do not begin for four or five seasons for coffee and five to eight for cloves. Even then yields remain small for three to four more years.[11] Total expenditures from planting to harvest for each crop can equal one million rupiah per hectare; this assumes that coffee produces yields in five years, the clove in six. The figure does not yet include the cost of land and labor. Labor costs, of course, diminish after the first two years.[12] The conclusion

11. Coffee provides small yields 4–5 years after harvest and good yields after 8–10 years. The time lag from planting to first harvest for cloves, by contrast, varies significantly with altitude and cultivation techniques. Working from Moluccan data, Bennett et al. (1987, 1) note that the lag is 4–7 years below 700 meters altitude and 10–15 years between 700 and 1,000; it can be reduced to 6–7 years at the latter altitude with fertilizers. These estimates broadly correlate with farmers' experience in upland Pasuruan, where the tree is grown between 600 and 900 meters altitude. Most farmers have obtained harvests after 5–6 years, but some have had to wait as long as 8. With both coffee and cloves, I should note, small amounts of maize or cassava may be intercropped with the young trees during the first 2 years, thus providing some income from the field. In the case of cloves, the cassava is also used to provide shade for the young saplings. Such intercropping is always notably sparse, however, for fear of its competing with the saplings for nutrition. It rarely extends beyond the second year.

12. Surveys of five large landowners revealed annual labor inputs (including harvesting and processing) of about 270 workdays for mature coffee and only 235 for cloves. These are rough figures, but they nonetheless point to a disturbing consequence of the new agriculture: diminished demand for wage labor, a vital source of income for many poor villagers (see ch. 5).

to be drawn from all these data is thus clear: the start-up and opportunity costs of coffee and cloves are high enough to make their intensive cultivation impossible for the poor.

In actual practice, of course, coffee and cloves are cultivated to varying degrees of intensity. With coffee, cutbacks on fertilizers, manure, pesticides, semi-annual pruning, and cultivation of shade trees are quite common, and do not always have disastrous effects. Coffee, after all, has been cultivated in this region for years. If it survives its first three years without being blighted by fungus or attacked by termites, red ants, or stem borers, it will usually live to produce a small harvest, even under less-than-ideal conditions.

Variation in cultivation technique does, however, result in variable yields. Surveys of farmers cultivating new coffee hybrids with light or irregular use of pesticides and fertilizers revealed that their per-hectare yields had increased about 40 percent, to just over 400 kilograms of dried beans per hectare. Farmers using the full range of new cultivation techniques, however, achieved average harvests of 1,000 kilograms of dried beans per hectare. With a 1985 farm-gate value of over one million rupiah, this is considerably better than traditional coffee farmers do. Excluding costs to land and labor, this implies returns of Rp 800,000 (U.S. $727) per hectare, which is impressive by Javanese standards. Among households cultivating coffee, however, only one in five was doing so intensively, and all of these had more than two hectares of land. This is but one more indication that the green revolution in midslope coffee is largely an affair of the wealthy.

The degree of technical latitude possible with clove cultivation is even smaller than with coffee. Household and field surveys in the midslope region revealed that farmers who had not made regular applications of pesticides to their cloves ultimately lost most of their trees to insect pests, fungi, or Sumatran leaf blight. In this area of Java, termites, stem borers, and red ants attack virtually every sapling planted. As happened in 1982, the occasional extended dry season also exacts a toll, killing trees too far from mountain springs for hand irrigation. Under these uncertain circumstances, losses to farmers have been staggering. Among the survey population in Puspo and Jimbaran, 82 percent of the trees planted between 1974 and 1979 had died. No farm family with less than a hectare of farm land saw more than 25 percent of its trees survive, and about half saw all their trees killed. Among landholders owning more than two hectares of land, by contrast, use of pesticides was widespread, and the majority saw two-thirds or more of their trees survive.

For those who can bring their trees to maturity, clove profits are very good. In Puspo in 1985, the price of dried cloves averaged Rp 7,000 per kilogram. Clove stems (used in poorer-quality clove cigarettes) could also be sold for about one-tenth this price. Three years earlier clove prices had achieved highs of Rp 11,000 per kilogram. While the midslope crop was still too young to provide definitive longitudinal data on harvests (the first trees having been planted only in 1975), a handful of trees in 1985 were providing yields as high as 7.5 kilograms of dried blossoms. Mean yields from six farmers cultivating these ten-year-old trees were much lower— about 920 grams per tree, averaged over four years. As is generally the case with cloves, yields fluctuate in a biannual pattern, high-yielding years being followed by one or two years of much lower production. Unlike some clove-producing regions in south Malang and Lumajang, however, the tree produces blossoms even in these alternate "off" years in highland Pasuruan, a fact that has made these midslope terrains all the more attractive to urban investors lured by reports of cloves' profitability (ch. 5).[13]

Even at the relatively immature age of ten years, then, cloves have begun to provide what are by Javanese standards very high returns. At two hundred trees per hectare and Rp 7,000 per kilo, the above figures imply gross returns of Rp 1,288,000 (U.S. $1,170) annually. Even after deducting start-up costs and the moderate annual labor expenses, this figure still implies very good returns. Reports from nearby south Lumajang, where the crop has been cultivated for fifteen years, indicate that average yields can increase to as much as 1.5 kilograms of dried cloves per tree. Yields stabilize at about twenty years of age, and trees can remain productive for several more decades.

Given a potential for profits of this magnitude, it is not surprising that the new agriculture was immediately welcomed with great excitement in both mountain regions. When I visited the region in the late 1970s, there was a dizzy optimism in the air. Poor and rich alike proclaimed that a way had finally been found to breathe new life into a tired agriculture and break out of the grim cycle of ecological and economic decline. Time and time again I heard ordinary farmers say, "We don't have to be poor anymore; people won't be able to call highlanders backward." As it turned out, however, one essential ingredient in this agricultural revolution is capital, and its distribution is anything but uniform. The sociology of capital accumulation differed between the two mountain regions,

13. Biannual fluctuation has been calculated into the above averages. One should add here that yield estimates for mature cloves are notoriously irregular, since production varies widely. Bennett et al. 1987 cites government data showing that 1984 yields per hectare in East Java averaged about 282 kg. In most other areas of Indonesia, however, official yield figures per hectare varied from 60 to 190 kg, with a national average of only 76.8 kg. Godoy and Bennett (1987c) themselves estimate that average yields per hectare for mature stands in Maluku vary from 205 kg for unfertilized trees to 436 for fertilized trees. The figure for fertilized trees is far higher than anything I ever encountered in Pasuruan and south Lumajang.

and ensured that the benefits of agricultural change were distributed very unevenly.

THE SOCIAL ORGANIZATION OF AGRICULTURAL INTENSIFICATION

It is important to understand how enormous the above start-up costs are in a Javanese context. Exclusive of labor, average per-hectare inputs for one crop of potatoes were about Rp 390,000 (U.S. $355). The annual cost of intensive coffee cultivation averaged about Rp 220,000 (U.S. $200). In 1985 male field laborers in the vegetable-producing upperslope region earned an average daily wage of Rp 700–800, sometimes including one meal; women earned Rp 600–650. Their workday lasted from 9:00 A.M. to 3:30 P.M., with a half-hour lunch break at midday. In the midslope region male and female laborers earned about Rp 550 and Rp 500 respectively, working from 7:00 A.M. to 12:00 or 1:00 P.M.; wages were lower if a meal was included.[14]

These figures illustrate the expense involved in growing new cash crops. The mean value of nonlabor inputs to one hectare of potatoes is equivalent to a male field laborer's wages for 557 days! The average value of the annual nonlabor inputs required for intensive coffee cultivation equals a midslope male's wages over 400 working days. Given these expenses, one may rightly wonder how any but the very rich could afford to make the transition to intensive cultivation of commercial cultivars. This is a question of capital accumulation, of course, and the way in which it was resolved in each of the two upland regions helps explain important differences in the social scope of the new agriculture.

In the upperslope highlands commercial intensification was at first regionalized and limited to a handful of families in Tosari and Ngadiwono, communities that had been commercial centers since the nineteenth century. All of the pioneer families were vegetable traders as well as farmers; since the small revival of trade in the 1950s, they had had extensive contacts with lowland traders. Several of them had accumulated sufficient wealth to purchase trucks and operate small stores.

The introduction of new fertilizers, pesticides, and seed varieties in the early 1970s was not the first time these farmer-traders had sought to ex-

---

14. In both regions, wages were lower in communities not involved in the new agriculture. There was also some variation in wages according to the season and the regularity of employment. In the midslope region, in particular, laborers accept lower wages for the promise of regular employment. Thus, for example, in Puspo a laborer will accept a reduction of Rp 100 per day when she or he is offered employment for more than two weeks.

periment with new agricultural techniques. Around 1955, for example, one of them managed to secure seeds for a new cabbage strain that had been imported from Europe to Indonesia. Acting entirely on his own, the farmer bought them from a Chinese store in Surabaya, planted them for two seasons, and eventually determined that they were more pest-resistant than earlier strains. Other farmers had shown similar initiative, experimenting with new seed potatoes, and various nontraditional crops, such as apples, oranges, melons, squash, and wheat. None of these proved very profitable. These same farmer-traders were the first to acquire DDT and market it in their stores. After 1969 they had taken the lead in securing chemical fertilizers through the black market. Seen from this perspective, far from being a novel initiative in an otherwise traditional agriculture, their introduction of agrochemicals in the early 1970s was but the latest in a series of initiatives undertaken to resolve the problem of low productivity that had plagued upland agriculture since the 1930s.

The first chemical pesticides were spin-offs from the government's rice-intensification program. After they were obtained in small quantities in 1969, their use was at first restricted to a small circle of people with ties to the trader families. By late 1972, however, pesticides and fungicides were freely available in stores, and taking note of the efforts of their more progressive neighbors, other farmers in the region also began to experiment with their use. The innovators made no secret of their new techniques; indeed, in good entrepreneurial fashion, several used their own fields as demonstration plots for seeds and chemicals that they then sold in their stores. In late 1972 a Ngadiwono farmer planted the first crop of an improved variety (*bibit unggul*) of potatoes using pesticides and fertilizers. It yielded a harvest equivalent to 21 tons per hectare, almost ten times the amount obtained without agrochemicals. Although subsequent experiments achieved less spectacular yields, the new technology made possible continuous cultivation of vegetables on the same plot, something not possible since the fungal blight of the 1930s. The longstanding impasse in commercial intensification seemed broken.

Word of the new agriculture spread quickly to other communities, and once again upland farmers responded with entrepreneurial verve. By 1975-76 the majority of farmers in Tosari and Ngadiwono had shifted from primary cultivation of maize to the new regime of multicropped potatoes and cabbages, growing maize only in their more distant fields. By the late 1970s the technology had spread to every one of some forty upper-slope communities in the regencies of Pasuruan, Probolinggo, Malang, and Lumajang. Invariably, the first families to adopt the new technology were wealthy farmers or, as had been the case in Tosari and Ngadiwono, farmers active in trade. Some inputs like new seeds or sprays were at first expensive, precluding their use by poor farmers. Wealthy farmers were also more likely to have trade ties through which information on new technology became available. In addition, of course, they could better afford the risk involved in experimenting. Contrary to the lowland pattern, the government provided no extension programs to familiarize farmers with the new technology (it began to do so on a very limited scale only in the late 1970s). Given the expense and uncertainty, then, it was the wealthier villagers who were best prepared to lead the way in adapting the new agriculture to local conditions.

Though pioneered by the affluent, the new technology quickly spread to other farmers. The process was nicely illustrated in the southern Tengger community of Ngadas, where I conducted research in 1978 and 1979. Ngadas had always been one of the last upperslope communities to respond to new social trends. It was only in early 1978, just a few months prior to my arrival, that the first farmer experimented with pesticides, fertilizers, and a new strain of high-yielding potatoes, all of which he had acquired from relatives in Ngadiwono. As had happened in other villages, news of his initiative spread quickly, and everyone eagerly awaited its results. In the end, the farmer lost half his crop because of overfertilization. The remainder, where he had used a slightly different dosage, survived, and the yields were so impressive that the new technology was proclaimed a great success. Whereas just one farmer had used agrochemicals in early 1978, ten months later my survey of two hundred farmers revealed that one-third were using chemical fertilizers and one-fourth chemical pesticides. A few farmers had even begun to use chemical fertilizers with their maize crops (table 4.5). The great transition had begun.

The figures in table 4.5 show that, as had earlier been the case in Tosari and Ngadiwono, large farmers in Ngadas took up the new technology more quickly than their poor neighbors. When I returned to the village just a year later, however, almost 90 percent of all farmers were using chemicals, although the number fertilizing maize remained low (12 percent).

Ngadiwono provides a longer perspective on the same process of technological diffusion. Chemical inputs had been illegally marketed in the village in 1969, and by the mid 1970s most farmers used them. Surveys of 142 farm households in 1980 revealed that all of them were using chemical inputs and over half were applying fertilizers to their maize. There were still important differences among farmers in the amount of agrochemicals actually used. With potatoes, for example, fertilizer application among smaller farmers (with less than half a hectare) averaged fully 46 percent less per hectare than was the case for farmers controlling more than two hect-

TABLE 4.5   Percentage of Households Using Agrochemicals in Ngadas and Ngadiwono, by Size of Holding

Input Used	Landholding (ha)						All House-holds
	.01–.19	.20–.49	.50–.99	1.00–1.99	2–3.50	>3.50	
In Ngadas							
Fertilizers	0	11.1	14.3	36.2	51.4	90.0	29.4
Pesticides	0	6.7	7.1	27.7	43.2	80.0	22.3
Fertilizing maize	0	4.5	3.6	4.3	16.2	20.0	7.2
In Ngadiwono							
Fertilizers	100	100	100	100	100	100	100
Pesticides	100	100	100	100	100	100	100
Fertilizing maize	50.0	46.7	48.0	58.3	70.0	75.0	57.5

SOURCE. Survey of 342 upperslope households, 1979–80.

ares of land. Nonetheless, as the figures in table 4.5 show, use of capital-intensive chemical inputs was no longer an elite prerogative.

The broad diffusion of this technology was made easier by the rhythms of vegetable cultivation itself, in particular, the relatively short time lag from planting to harvest. Although the prewar "Javanese potato" (*kentang jowo*) had a growing season of 200 days, the new high-yield strains (*bibit unggul*) require just 100 to 120 days. New strains of cabbages require 90–130 days, with an additional month during the dry season. This short growing life guarantees a quick return on investment. Over the course of several harvests, therefore, small farmers can accumulate the capital needed to expand the area they cultivate, plowing the profits from one harvest back into the purchase of more inputs. Villagers have terms for such incremental cultivation—*bak-bakan, ceklekan,* or *petakan*—words that literally mean "small plot," or, more accurately, "plot by plot." In this context, however, the terms refer to the staggered cultivation of fields throughout the year so as to balance the demand of one field for capital inputs with harvest yields from another. During the shift to intensive vegetable cultivation, farmers used this plot-by-plot method to accumulate a growing reserve of capital with which to extend the area devoted to vegetable cultivation. In this fashion, even poor farmers acquired the new inputs.

Poor farmers could also acquire new seeds and inputs through sharecropping arrangements, which, though historically uncommon in this area (see ch. 5), flourished briefly in the 1970s. The most common arrangement required capital-poor landowners to promise half of their potato or cabbage harvest to a farmer who provided seeds and fertilizers. The landowner paid for pesticides, or their price was deducted from profits at the time of harvest. The landowners performed all labor except harvesting, when they were helped by a representative of the seedowner. The harvest was then sold, and its price divided evenly (*diparon*) between the seedowner and landowner.

All these factors—the relatively quick returns to capital, the high profitability of the crop, and the availability of sharecropping credit if necessary—ensured that in the upperslope region the new commercial agriculture diffused rapidly and evenly among the farm population.[15] Though introduced by elite farmers, the new cultivars eventually brought benefits even to the poor.

Midslope Accumulation: Imbalanced Growth

Circumstances were less conducive to such broad-based change in the midslope highlands. With high start-up costs, fierce pest problems, and delays of four to eight years before harvest, intensive cultivation of the new tree crops was limited to affluent farmers. The poor were understandably unwilling to pull their fields out of food-staple cultivation for several years before meaningful harvests began and unable to afford the volume of inputs required for intensive cultivation.

Larger landowners had an additional advantage. Where necessary, they could turn to outside investors for capital for clove and coffee cultivation. As word of the new crops spread, lowland merchants (many of them ethnic Chinese) came forward offering to "rent" (*nyewo*) large fields. The usual arrangement covered a period of ten to twenty years. During this time, the renter paid for all nonlabor inputs, from the original purchase of saplings to annual applications of fertilizers and pesticides. The landowner performed some but not all of the labor on the rented land, including, most especially, protection of the crop at harvest. In addition to the original rental payment, the landowner received a small share of the harvest. At the end of the contract period, the land was

---

15. There was also an element of good timing to the diffusion of the new technology. Upland Pasuruan was one of Java's first high-altitude areas to pioneer intensive vegetable cultivation. It developed its industry when competition was weak and prices were high. Since 1982–83 the real price of vegetables (especially potatoes) has fallen considerably, while pesticide and fertilizer prices have climbed; with decreasing government subsidies, prices of agrochemicals are likely to increase. Other upland areas may find it more difficult to imitate the broad pattern of intensification seen in upperslope Tengger.

TABLE 4.6   Percentage of Midslope Households Using Agrochemicals, by Size of Holding

Input Used	Landholding (ha)						All House- holds
	.01–.19	.20–.49	.50–.99	1–1.99	2–3.50	>3.50	
Fertilizers	51.9	90.2	97.2	100	100	100	86.4
Pesticides	22.2	37.3	41.7	70.6	100	83.3	44.9
Fertilizing maize	50.0	90.2	96.7	93.3	100	100	85.0

SOURCE. Survey of 150 midslope households, 1985.

to be returned to its owner, who, in theory, would reap the benefits of the capital improvements on it.[16]

Investors offered such rental arrangements only to large landholders. They claimed it was too expensive to operate dispersed gardens under several small owners, and more difficult to protect one's investment. In addition, they said, poor farmers were likely to steal crops or sell inputs intended for use on trees.

For all these reasons, smallholders in the midslope region have had great difficulty accumulating the capital required for intensive cultivation. They have not been entirely barred, however, from the benefits of new technology. As table 4.6 indicates, many have begun to use small amounts of fertilizer. Even at levels that are less than ideal, the application of fertilizers and pesticides to coffee and maize allows for at least moderate increases in production.

The experience of farmers in both areas of the Tengger highlands illustrates what is by now a familiar story in Asia's green revolution. The social and economic consequences of new technologies are not uniform. In strictly economic terms, a key influence on a farmer's success is the ability to sustain proper levels of input application over periods and at

16. This *sewo* contract was a benevolent variant of a kind of land rental, also called *sewo*, practiced in the midslope region since the 1950s. Under the terms of this older contract, a landowner rents out his land at a low rate in exchange for a loan. Typically, no interest is paid on the loan, but the rental fee is nominal. The landowner then sharecrops the land on a "halves" (*paron*) basis; the debtor-landowner is responsible for all labor and inputs. If at the end of the contract period the loan is still not repaid, or another is needed, the contract is renewed. Where the value of the loans exceeds the estimated value of the land, the landowner may eventually have to forfeit ownership entirely. Such rental contracts are rare in the upperslope region, but were common in the more class-stratified communities of the midslope region (see ch. 5). Gillian Hart (1986, 101) reports that similar arrangements were common among the destitute in north-central Java.

rates that ensure returns adequate for recovery of start-up costs. While this is a truism of any economic enterprise, its implications for the success of agricultural programs can be quite complex, as the comparison of vegetables and tree perennials shows. The relatively quick returns to capital in vegetable farming have allowed poor and rich farmers alike to adopt new technologies. The incomes made possible by the new agriculture have actually strengthened the hold of small farmers on their lands and allowed a dramatic across-the-board increase in the standard of living.

In the midslope region high start-up costs and the long lag between planting and first harvest have combined to make commercial intensification a more uneven development. Poor farmers are unable to sustain the investments required for lucrative returns. Nonetheless, access to chemical inputs has increased harvests of food staples and seems likely to continue to improve coffee yields even if trees are not cultivated under ideal conditions. If the social side of this agricultural system were in equilibrium—without the current doubling of the population every forty years or competition by capital from investors and wealthy farmers—the position of poor farmers might eventually improve significantly. Unfortunately, rural society knows no such steady state, and other forces in the midslope region threaten to worsen distributional patterns.

A similar lesson applies to the study of the ecological effects of farm technologies. In different environments new technologies can have very different impacts. This is clearly the case in the Tengger highlands. In the midslope region, the new agriculture has helped to reduce erosion and landslides. In the upperslope region, by contrast, recent events raise troubling questions about the long-term viability of the new agriculture.

COMMERCIAL AGRICULTURE AND THE ENVIRONMENT

One of the qualities that distinguishes upland dry-field agriculture from *sawah* has always been the latter's ability to maintain high yields over long periods without any significant diminution of fertility. The *sawah* pond stabilizes or, in some instances, even improves soils, but the permanent use of unirrigated land "presents one of the most troublesome problems of tropical agriculture" (Palte 1984, 33). The general problem is the same in dry-field agriculture as in *sawah*—to secure greater outputs from a diminishing per-capita land area—but in the former case the techniques for its resolution often only defer fertility-management problems.

The agriculture introduced into upland Java in the 1970s did little to change this basic problem. What it did do was alter the mix of techniques used in fertility management. Examination of these techniques in the midslope and upperslope regions illustrates how, in intensifying produc-

TABLE 4.7   Fallowing Practices of Midslope and Upperslope Farmers, by Size of Holding

	Landholding (ha)						
	.01–.19	.20–.49	.50–.99	1–1.99	2–3.50	>3.50	All House-holds
Midslope							
% farmers fallowing some land	0	0	0	0	11.1	16.7	2.0
Fallowed land as % group total	0	0	0	0	3.7	2.2	.3
Upperslope							
% farmers fallowing some land	0	2.7	13.6	23.0	40.0	72.7	21.9
Fallowed land as % group total	0	1.0	3.1	6.0	9.9	15.1	5.2

SOURCE. 1980 and 1985 surveys of 492 households.

tion, some farmers have managed to improve the sustainability of agriculture, while others have placed it in jeopardy.

Traditionally, fallowing was one of the most important ways to rejuvenate soils (ch. 3). Statistics on the practice today, however, show how small a role it now plays in upland agriculture. Although they universally acknowledge its benefits, only 2 percent of the survey households in the midslope region indicated that in the last year they had had any land fallow (*dijar*) for three or more months, the minimum time required to grow a small cover of green grasses. As one would expect, those who were able to do so were from the ranks of larger landowners, although even among them the practice is rare. All together, a mere 0.3 percent of all midslope farmland had been fallowed in the year prior to the survey. Fallowing is more widespread among upperslope farmers. But even there its incidence is for all intents and purposes restricted to large landholders (table 4.7). In today's Tengger highlands, in short, fallowing plays an only minor role in fertility management. The great majority of farmers just cannot afford it.

TABLE 4.8   Ownership and Share-Raising of Livestock among Midslope and Upperslope Farmers, by Size of Holding

		Landholding (ha)						
	0	.01– .19	.20– .49	.50– .99	1– 1.99	2– 3.50	>3.50	All House- holds
Midslope farmers								
% owning cattle	0	42.9	45.1	69.4	76.5	88.9	50.0	56.0
% owning cattle or goats	33.3	53.6	60.8	75.0	76.5	88.9	83.3	66.7
Mean no. cattle or goats owned	.8	1.4	1.5	2.7	4.0	6.0	8.3	2.6
% share-raising other house- holds' cattle	33.0	25.0	45.1	36.1	17.6	0	0	31.3
Upperslope farmers								
% owning cattle	0	0	4.1	13.6	29.9	41.7	54.5	22.8
% owning manure- producing ani- mals	0	42.9	47.9	54.5	66.7	98.0	86.4	62.6
Mean no. ma- nure animals per household	0	.6	1.0	1.0	1.6	3.1	5.5	1.8
% share-raising other house- holds' cattle	0	28.6	20.8	6.8	9.2	3.3	0	9.7

SOURCE. 1980 and 1985 surveys of 492 households.

Besides fallowing and the application of chemical fertilizers, the other technique for rejuvenating soils is the use of manure. Although a few wealthy farmers have begun to purchase chicken manure from a poultry plant in the nearby lowlands, for most, access to manure still depends upon control of livestock, especially cattle. Goats, pigs, and horses play an only minor role in manuring.

Table 4.8 shows that the midslope region has maintained the high level of livestock ownership that characterized the area even in the last century (de Vries 1931, 1:129). More than half of all households own at least one head of cattle, and the mean is 1.62 per household, a remarkable figure by Javanese standards. Two of every five households own two or more head of cattle; 20 percent own three or more. When goats are included, a full two-thirds of all households own some kind of manure-producing animal. The high incidence of livestock ownership extends to even the land-poor, 43 percent of whom own one head of cattle. More than a third of this same group share-raise one or more head of cattle using a "halving" system known as *paron*. Under the terms of this contract, the animal-tender gets to keep all the manure produced by the animal. At sale, the original purchase price of the animal is deducted from the sale price, and the remaining cash is then divided equally between the tender and owner. Through share-raising and ownership, a large number of mid-slope farmers get access to vital manures.

There is only one exception in the midslope region to the positive correlation between land assets and livestock ownership. Among the largest landholders (controlling more than three and a half hectares), cattle ownership actually declines. In conversation, these large landholders insist that high maintenance costs and low returns make cattle an unattractive investment. In 1985 a young "Australian" cow (the preferred breed in the highlands) cost Rp 200,000 when purchased at 10–12 months of age. It would sell two years later for only twice that amount. Profits would then have to be shared equally with the share-tender. In addition, the cattle owner would have to pay a commission (of Rp 5,000–10,000) to the cattle trader (*blantik*) who arranged the animal's sale and transport to the low-lands, and a 5 percent tax to subdistrict government. All together, the cattle owner might make Rp 90,000 on a two-year investment. Given the risk involved in cattle-raising, and the high returns possible with cash crops, this level of reward was not considered attractive.

Surveys revealed that all of these large farmers continued to use manure, indeed abundantly with coffee and cloves. But they now buy it. Although this means that there is a local market for manure, the people who sell it are invariably smallholders. For them, the income from manure means cutbacks in its application on their own fields. In this instance, then, the calculating eye of large landholders inadvertently contributes to the infertility of poor farmers' lands.

The upperslope region has a much lower rate of livestock ownership, and the contrast between classes is even more pronounced. Only about one-fifth of all upperslope households own cattle, and the mean number per household (.444) is about one-fourth of that in the midslope area (1.62). Only 10.5 percent of all households own two or more head of cattle, and only 5 percent own three or more. Though smaller, the pool of manure-producing animals is more varied than in the midslope region, with a large pig population, a moderate goat population, and even a few horses. The presence of these livestock lifts the mean number of animals to 1.8 per household. Only one-fourth of this mean figure, however, consists of the most effective manure-producers, cattle.

As table 4.8 shows, livestock ownership here is also more unevenly distributed across classes than is the case in the midslope region. Only 3.5

percent of the land-poor own cattle (as opposed to the midslope's 42.7 percent). Share-raising occurs, but again among only 9.7 percent of all households, as opposed to 31.3 percent in the midslope region. Most of the share-raising is done by the land-poor, one in five of whom have access to cattle through such tending arrangements. This distributes animal resources more widely, but still not as broadly as in the midslope region.

In short, there are fewer cattle here than in the midslope highlands, and the relative shortage is reflected in cultivation practices. If they have access to manure at all, most farmers reserve it for vegetables. About 77 percent of all farmers in the upperslope sample reported using manure in the past year for vegetables, but only 18.6 percent bother to use it for maize. On the less fertile lands of the midslope region, fully 54.3 percent of all farmers apply manure to maize. A similar pattern obtains, interestingly, with chemical fertilizers and maize. In the midslope region, 93.6 percent of all farmers regularly apply chemical fertilizers to their maize, while in the upperslope region only 24.9 percent do. Although poorer than their upperslope counterparts, midslope farmers have adopted a more flexible mix of techniques to meet the challenge of fertility management.

Erosion

Fallowing, fertilizing, and manuring are all elements in a management regime that seeks to restore fertility to hard-worked soils. Erosion is the other side of this management story, of course, and in the long run it presents the most serious challenge to upland agriculture. As Roche (1985), McCauley (1984), Palte (1984), and Donner (1987) have all stressed, reduction of soil erosion is as important an element of Java's upland farm programs as is the raising of farm incomes. Indeed, it is one of the most serious problems in Javanese—and Southeast Asian (cf. Peletz 1988, 158)—agriculture as a whole. The interests of soil preservation and output maximization have often been at odds, and recent evidence suggests the problem may be getting worse, not better, in upland Java. Here again, the benefits of agricultural technology must be assessed within an environmental framework larger than that of short-term returns on labor and capital.

In the midslope region, the interests of sustainable agriculture have been well served by the recent shift to tree crops. Here, finally, is an agriculture that provides a happy consonance of interests between income and topsoils. The new perennials greatly reduce the need to bare the earth and keep its surface clear of plant growth. As practiced in recent years, by contrast, the double-cropping of maize requires farmers to "deep hoe" (*bencar*) prior to planting the maize crop, and to strip the soil surface of weeds twice more during the plant's growing season. Deep-hoeing has been necessitated by the leaching and depletion of topsoil nutrients. Where maize is intercropped with cassava, the impact on soils is all the more deleterious, because soils must be opened again at harvest time.

By contrast, intensive cultivation of coffee or cloves requires that topsoils be turned only when planting the tree or dumping manure and fertilizers around its perimeter each year. In neither case is soil massively and regularly exposed to the elements. From this perspective, cultivation of tree perennials promises to greatly reduce topsoil loss, and improve retention of water, an important element in lowland flood control.

In the vegetable-growing upperslope region, the environmental situation is far less promising. Although viable on valley bottoms or gentle hillsides, on steep hills vegetable cultivation increases erosion and the incidence of mudslides. Staff from the Department of Farming at Brawijaya University, Malang, made several visits to upperslope Pasuruan in 1985. They estimated that 25–30 percent of the land now under cultivation is in fact too steeply inclined (having a slope greater than 40 degrees) to be planted with anything other than trees and bushes, let alone crops as disruptive of topsoils as potatoes or cabbages. Extension agents from the regency set the figure at 30 percent of all farmland, but added, with understandable resignation, that there was little chance of returning these lands to forest or bush. As upperslope farmers know all too well (having experimented with the crops), none of the tree perennials that thrive in the midslope region grow well in this high-lying region; similarly, the returns from wood crops such as rattan or commercial trees would be insufficient to support the present population, let alone double the number, who will live here in another forty years.

From the perspective of topsoil preservation, vegetable crops represent one of the worst choices for these steep-sloped lands. The contrast with soil treatment under the old maize crop is telling. In earlier times maize was planted only once a year, at the beginning of the rainy season. Soils were hoed only prior to and during the first rains, and at depths (about 25–30 centimeters) shallower than required for today's "deep-dig" *bencar* hoeing (40–80 centimeters). Though they weeded the crop two or three times prior to harvest, farmers were careful not to open the soil during the heavy rains of February and March, and often deliberately left a small layer of grass on the ground between plants to stabilize the topsoil. Harvest occurred only at the end of the rainy season in May or June.

The new agriculture shows no such cautious regard for soils. Vegetable plants are extremely sensitive to competition from weeds. They also require quick and effective drainage. Standing water stunts plant growth, rots roots, and makes the plant more susceptible to worms and insect pests. In the 1970s, farmers began to use a wet-season technique for potato cultivation that helped to move heavy rains quickly away from plants, but with disastrous consequences for soils. Rather than planting crops in *melintang* (across-slope) contour patterns, they placed them in large, long mounds *(gulutan)*, running downhill *(mbujur)* with the contour of the land. The drainage channel between such mounds *(selokan)* was made deeper and straighter and kept clean of weeds to ensure a quick flow of water and keep plant roots above standing water. The ideal depth from the bottom of this down-sloping channel to the top of the potato mound was a full 35 centimeters, more than twice the height of the less regularized mounds earlier used for vegetable crops.

Constructed on even the steepest hillsides, these channels have predictably disastrous results. During heavy rains, even the most casual observation reveals large amounts of soil and water moving downslope in the drainage channel. More seriously, fields are more deeply hoed than before, and hoed during all seasons rather than just at the beginning or end of the rainy season. As a result, rains soak into the loose soils and create a mobile, floating mass of mud ready to slide into the valley floors below. Mudslides have become commonplace. In Ngadiwono in the early 1970s, eight homes were destroyed and three people killed during one downpour. During field research in March 1985, four days of torrential rains created mudslides that closed roads into every community in upperslope Pasuruan and sent hundreds of tons of topsoil into valley bottoms. Village officials appealed to the government for help in responding to the event, which they rightly referred to as a "natural disaster" *(bencana alam)*. In the village of Ngadiwono alone, where I had been monitoring sheet and gulley erosion on twenty fields, I counted forty mudslides involving soil loss at least a half meter in depth, fifteen meters wide, and fifty meters in length. Many were larger than this, moving down whole mountainsides and destroying everything in their path. Streams in valley bottoms were dammed by the landslides, and on twelve of the twenty quarter-hectare field sites I had been monitoring, topsoil loss was so great as to expose clay subsoils or hard subsurface rock. All of the large mudslides observed on these sample tracts came from vegetable fields, while damage to maize fields, while visible, was slight.

Without measurement of soil sediment load in rivers, it is difficult to provide compelling quantitative measures of erosion.[17] But it is clear nonetheless that soil loss is advancing at unprecedented rates. Subdistrict

17. The quantitative evidence we do have, however, confirms that erosion is advancing at disastrous rates. Donner (1987, 125) cites data on sediment load in river water indicating that erosion rates in Java greatly exceed those of continental Asian rivers, with the exception of those in the highly eroded Himalayas. Studies of the upper Solo watershed in Central Java indicate that 50 percent of the surface has been severely eroded. Throughout Java as a whole, rates of erosion appear to be three to four times greater than those recorded one hundred years ago (Donner 1987, 118–25).

officials are aware of the problem, but confess that, short of forbidding vegetable cultivation, they cannot control it. Their efforts to introduce coffee and tea cultivation have proved unsuccessful, since neither crop does well in this cool, cloud-covered region, and the incomes they would allow in such a climate are, whatever the case, no match for those currently available with vegetables. Extension agents have also failed to convince farmers to stop constructing downhill drainage channels. The agents point out (as farmers had earlier acknowledged in our conversations) that in fact the downslope drainage was originally a method designed to be used with reverse-slope bench terraces. Rainwater was supposed to drain backward, away from the terrace lip into a small channel at the back of the terrace, which then flowed to a larger side channel running downhill. However, farmers found it impossible to build bench terraces on any but the most gently sloping hillsides. As a result, they constructed downslope "black terraces" (*teras ireng*), which proved less effective in controlling erosion. Combining these downslope terraces with vertical drainage channels allowed for quick runoff of water, but caused considerable topsoil loss as well. With soils hoed to depths of two-thirds of a meter and with few bushes or trees to break the fall, farmers had created floating topsoils ideally suited for landslides.

Eventually, of course, some kind of equilibrium will be reached. Erosion of this magnitude can continue for only so long, until a harder, and less fertile, subsoil or bedrock is reached. In a region once legendary for its rich, thick volcanic soil, bare rock and hard yellow clay are visible on steeply inclined fields. After rain showers, streams run thick with topsoil and roar down the mountainside, taking silt to irrigation channels and offshore reefs. What is happening to these hillside fields is nothing less than an environmental disaster. But it is one that no one at the moment seems able to resolve.

Farmers are well aware of the problem. Government officials have suggested banning cultivation of vegetables on steep hillsides, replacing them with maize. With diminishing landholdings, however, the land-poor see little attraction in this option, since the crop provides annual returns one-fifth to one-tenth the size of those possible with vegetables. Larger farmers, of course, might be better able to sustain a return to maize. But this would undermine the social gains they rightly feel they have earned, and would relegate them once more to the status of backward uplanders. In short, unless an alternative cultivar can be found for the region, it seems likely that the momentum for agricultural change will be the result of passive adaptation to declining circumstances rather than expansive innovation. The impact on popular welfare will be grim.

The example is a powerful reminder of the ecological problems that have always plagued upland *tegal*. The short-term interests of production again run contrary to those of soil preservation. Today's situation, however, is especially serious. Triple-cropping of potatoes opens the earth six times a year, which is to say, six times as often as was once the case with maize. Soils are hoed to twice the depth of old and reshaped to make vertical drainage channels. Because of the low height of the vegetable plant, soils are stripped of all grasses, regardless of season. The consequence is massive erosion.

These problems are not unique to the Tengger highlands. Surveys of vegetable cultivation in other upland areas of Java also warn of an alarming increase in erosion (Roche 1985; McCauley 1984; Palte 1984). They caution that preservation of the upland environment is one of the most important issues facing the island today. "Java's uplands cannot be allowed to further degrade with high soil erosion rates eventually eroding their production potential, with downstream siltation hampering the further development of the lowland agricultural system, and with upland residents increasingly faced with the option of either migrating to Java's already overcrowded urban areas or transmigrating in order to survive" (McCauley 1984, xi). The tragedy here is that a technology that brought economic benefit to small and large farmers alike in the upperslope region has created ecological problems likely to give it only a short life.

The new agriculture's impact has not been restricted to the agroenvironment. New methods of production are vitally dependent upon social, as well as natural, resources. These arrangements have a history as complex as that of agricultural ecology. They, too, were changing in the 1970s and 1980s, with a breadth and intensity unparalleled in contemporary Java.

FIVE

Relations in Production
Social Change in Land and Labor

Statistics on landholding provide sobering insight into Java's economic plight. In Indonesia in 1973, mean farm size was 0.99 of a hectare, and in Java the figure was a mere 0.66 of a hectare (Booth and Sundrum 1976, 94); 57 percent of all Javanese farms are less than half a hectare in size, 25 percent are 0.5-1.0, 17 percent are 1-5, and only 1 percent are 5 hectares or more (Booth and Sundrum 1981, 184). Urban and residential development, meanwhile, continues to nibble away at farmland. Between 1963 and 1973, the total area diminished by 3 percent, even though the number of farms increased by 4.3 percent. Whatever the success of farm programs, the sheer weight of population presents a daunting challenge to the island's future.

Population pressure itself, however, determines neither land distribution, the social organization of labor, nor the allocation of its product. Earlier studies were sometimes so impressed by the massiveness of Java's population and the miniscule scale of its farms that they concluded that land distribution and labor relations must be relatively equitable. Comparative research today suggests a more complex picture. Though the degree of land concentration in Java is only moderate by world standards, it is no more equitable than in most of East and Southeast Asia, where class differentiation is quite real (Booth and Sundrum 1981, 183).

Equally important, such gross statistics provide no information on the landless or the near-landless. Though they comprise 40-60 percent of the population in Java's lowlands (Hart 1986, 100; Penny and Singarimbun 1973; Husken and White 1989, 257), neither group is included in statistics on the farm labor force, since they are rather arbitrarily classified as "nonagricultural."[1] Historical and ethnographic studies, however, show that this "nonfarm" population has long depended on sharecropping and agricultural employment. This dependence is not just an economic fact. It is also a source of power for patrons, who use the selective extension of rights to land and labor to consolidate their political position. By failing to investigate the situation of the landless, analyses that emphasize "poverty-sharing" (Boeke 1953; Geertz 1963a) have inevitably misperceived the nature of agrarian hierarchy and overlooked the profoundly differential effect of inequality on welfare and politics.

Recent research has helped to revise this view of landholding and labor organization in lowland Java. Their history and organization in the highlands, however, remain poorly documented. We know little of how colonialism affected upland labor organization and even less about the impact of commercial agriculture today. The present chapter is intended to provide just such a chronicle, examining the social processes that have shaped landholding and labor relations in the Tengger highlands. Neither reality is a pure market phenomenon. Both show the dramatic influence of broader shifts in Indonesian politics and society. Both illustrate the general truth that market conditions are always shaped by the legal, moral, and political circumstances of society as a whole.

Several things distinguish this upland social history from the more familiar lowland story. First, and most important, the primary guarantor of household welfare here has never been sharecropping, privileged access to work, or any of the other patronage arrangements so widely reported from wet-rice areas of Southeast Asia (Scott 1976; Hart 1986; Husken 1979). Household welfare has instead depended on the ability of a man and woman to reap the fruits of their own piece of land. In precolonial times, population densities in this peripheral region were so low as to allow open access to forest land. Even with colonialism's advance, mountain land remained widely available, though access to it was now mediated by the colonial government rather than upland communities. Land scarcity became severe only at the beginning of the twentieth century, as coffee declined, the government launched reforestation programs, and the last remaining land was parceled out to private owners.

These economic facts had broad social consequences. In the lowlands the colonial authorities supported communal landholding so as to make easier their periodic appropriation of native rice lands. In so doing, they reinforced traditions whereby villagers were divided into named classes differentiated by hereditary rights to land (Jay 1969, 313; Breman 1983,

1. The "near-landless" are defined as those owning amounts of land below a certain, very small, farm size, usually less than 0.10 ha. See Montgomery and Sugito 1980, 351.

9). In the Tengger highlands, by contrast, the government reinforced a pattern of smallholder farming, and there were, as a result, no such named class groupings.

The logic of this upland policy was clear. At the dawn of the colonial era, the highlands were still lightly populated. The challenge for colonial planners was to recruit people for work on remote "waste" lands. The more people the government could lure to the mountains with the promise of land, the more laborers it could conscript for work on its coffee estates. Having set aside a small land area for indigenes, then, colonial officials divided the remainder between government estates and peasant parcels. As in coffee-growing areas of Sumatra (Kahn 1980), therefore, colonial policies reinforced extant patterns of smallholder appropriation. Although a few district and village officials were rewarded with large plots of land, virtually all villagers owned farmland, and the great majority earned the bulk of their livelihood from it.

Twentieth-century changes challenged this heritage but did not obliterate it. Despite commercial growth and growing land concentration early on in this century (de Vries 1931, 1:179), access to land remained far more fluid than in the lowlands. In all but a few heavily commercialized villages, land was inexpensive, and even immigrants to the region could hope to buy a plot. Absentee landlords were rare. Where sharecropping occurred at all, it usually linked kin and took a relatively benign form. The sharecropper retained at least 50 percent of the harvest, and often more. With widespread access to land, labor was similarly organized in a self-reliant fashion emphasizing household labor, only occasionally supplemented by that of neighbors and kin. The lowland system of "open" harvests and harvest shares—key elements in rural patronage (Stoler 1977; Hart 1986)—was unknown here. In its place, there was a curious tradition of festival labor, or *sayan*. Rather than reinforcing economic inequality, *sayan,* like the system of ritual festivals (*slametan*) to which it was related, tended to diffuse it. The affluent were enjoined to channel their wealth into conspicuous giving. This served the interests of prestige well, but worked against the sustained accumulation of capital. As in so much of upland life, economic preferences showed the clear imprint of local politics and community.

Events since 1965 have had a mixed impact on this agrarian order. As in wet-rice areas of Southeast Asia (Hart 1986; Scott 1986; Ganjanapan 1989), the upland elite are becoming more and more involved in political and economic affairs outside the village and outside agriculture. This has had an effect on their ability to manage their farms and the labor they need to run them. As in much of Southeast Asia (Hart 1989), new forms of dependent labor have emerged as this new class of "managerial" farmers has become more active. Both developments are especially striking here in the Tengger highlands, since prior to 1965 such hierarchical arrangements were rare.

In other respects, however, this upland region still stands apart from its lowland counterparts. Contrary to the pattern of wet-rice Southeast Asia (Hart 1986; Collier et al. 1973; Scott 1985), there has been no displacement of the poor out of agricultural employment. In fact, in the upperslope region, vegetable cultivation has actually increased demand for labor and pushed up wage rates. Whatever its unfortunate ecological consequences, commercial expansion in much of this region has actually strengthened the grip of smallholders on their lands and slowed the development of a wage-laboring underclass.

The situation, then, is not as grim as in much of the lowlands, where there are too many people for available employment and what jobs there are are selectively extended by patrons to dependent clients. Though they are not the most dynamic sector of the farm economy, the majority of uplanders are still heavily involved in smallholder agriculture. This cushions their dependence on wage labor, mutes class tensions, and informs the aspiration of even the poorest villagers to establish enterprises of their own so as not to be "ordered about" (*dikongkon*) by others. Even as elites set a new course for village society, this simple desire for autonomy continues to exercise an important influence on upland life. The example provides insight into the economic culture of one of Southeast Asia's most neglected social groupings: the middle peasantry.

LAND TENURE AND DISTRIBUTION

Two measures of landholding are especially relevant for assessing its social distribution: ownership and control. By "land owned" I refer to land over which a household has legal rights of ownership, use, and disposal, as defined by Indonesia's agrarian land laws and qualified by residual rights exercised by the community. By "land controlled" I refer to the total land area from which a household derives income, whether rented, sharecropped, borrowed, or owned. In the statistics provided I have followed Gillian Hart (1986, 96) in calculating "land controlled" as area owned plus half the area rented in minus half the area rented out. For sharecropping, the area added to or subtracted from the total controlled is based on the proportion of the crop a sharecropper pays out or that a landlord receives. Thus, for example, a landlord who receives half of a field's harvest is said to control half its land area, while one who receives two-thirds controls two-thirds of the land area. As the example of sharecropping indicates, the distinction between ownership and control is important, because title to land by no means guarantees its effective control. As in other areas of Southeast Asia (Hart 1986; Scott 1985, 21), other people may gain partial or effective control over a household's land through rental, sharecropping, or loan-pawning.

Table 5.1 shows patterns of land ownership and control in midslope and upperslope villages, as determined by a random survey of 492 households.[2] Areal figures include house-yard land (*pekarangan*) and dry-field agricultural land (*tegal*). House yards in the upperslope district are small and uncultivated, since villages here are densely nucleated (*nglumpuk*). In the midslope region, by contrast, settlements are more dispersed (*mencar*). House yards are larger and cultivated, although not as intensively as has been reported for some areas of the wet-rice lowlands (Stoler 1978). Of the two measures of landholding, land controlled is the more accurate index of farmers' access to land, and in subsequent correlations of class with other social variables, it is this figure on which I most consistently rely.[3] The fact that the percentage of households in each ownership group is identical to the percentage in the land-control groups illustrates that rental, sharecropping, and other tenancy arrangements do not significantly alter the overall distribution of land.

These statistics illuminate several important features of upland landholding. First of all, on an island where average farm size is 0.66 of a hectare, these mountain farms are above average in size, though only slightly so in the densely populated (and less fertile) midslope region. As one might expect given its history of settlement, land concentration is higher in the midslope region than it is in the upperslope area. Disaggregating the statistics somewhat differently than they are presented in table 5.1, one can see this more clearly. In the midslope region, the top 10 percent of the population control almost 50 percent of all village land; the top 4 percent control over 25 percent. The top quintile of landholders control 66 percent of the village lands. Land concentration at the high end of the sample is paralleled by land poverty at the low end. The land-

2. The distribution of households is as follows: 342 are located in the upperslope communities of Ngadas and Ngadiwono (200 and 142 respectively), while 150 are located in the midslope communities of Puspo and Jimbaran (100 and 50 respectively).

3. Landholding, of course, is at best an indirect measure of class. It is inaccurate inasmuch as the quality of land (and thus its value as a productive resource) varies independently of land area. More seriously, as White and Wiradi (1989, 268) have recently emphasized, it is an incomplete measure inasmuch as other social and material resources serve as productive assets. In much of Southeast Asia, off-farm activities are becoming increasingly important for both rural elites and the poor, further diminishing the accuracy of landholding as a clear indicator of class. Fortunately for the present study, the highlands are still characterized by a much lower degree of "occupational multiplicity" (White 1976) than is the case in the lowlands. For most households, land is still the most critical productive asset. Landholding thus provides a general measure of class, albeit an incomplete one. And it does yield some fruitful comparisons.

TABLE 5.1   Land Ownership and Control, by Region

		Ownership		Control	
	Size Groups *(ha)*	% All Households	% All Land	% All Households	% All Land
Midslope communities					
1.	0	2.0	0	2.0	0
2.	.01–.19	18.7	1.8	18.7	1.7
3.	.20–.49	34.0	11.6	34.0	13.3
4.	.50–.99	24.0	18.8	24.0	20.7
5.	1.00–1.99	11.3	17.8	11.3	18.2
6.	≥ 2.00	10.0	50.0	10.0	46.1
6a.	2.00–3.50	6.0	18.9	6.0	17.5
6b.	>3.50	4.0	31.1	4.0	28.6
Upperslope communities					
1.	0	1.5	0	1.5	0
2.	.01–.19	2.0	.3	2.0	.2
3.	.20–.49	21.3	6.0	21.3	5.3
4.	.50–.99	25.7	13.8	25.7	13.2
5.	1.00–1.99	25.4	26.4	25.4	24.6
6.	≥ 2.00	24.0	53.5	24.0	56.7
6a.	2.00–3.50	17.5	33.0	17.5	32.4
6b.	>3.50	6.4	20.4	6.4	24.4

NOTE. Mean land owned midslope, all households: .72 ha; mean controlled: .81 ha. Mean land owned upperslope, all households: 1.15 ha; mean controlled: 1.38 ha. Sample sizes: midslope, 150; upperslope, 342.

SOURCE. 1980 and 1985 surveys.

less comprise only 2 percent of the population, but fully 20 percent of all households own less than 0.20 of a hectare land. More than half own less than 0.50 of a hectare land, and 14 percent control only 0.10 of a hectare. Keeping in mind that part of this (usually about 0.05 ha) is occupied by a house site, households controlling less than a tenth of a hectare can be considered near-landless. For all intents and purposes, agriculture for them is a tiny complement to a livelihood earned elsewhere. In sum, while the situation in the midslope highlands is somewhat better than in most lowland villages, especially inasmuch as absolute landlessness is rare, land poverty is still widespread. Much land is concentrated in the hands of large holders.

In the upperslope region land concentration is less severe. By Javanese standards, there are a good number (almost 25 percent of the total) of large farms, comprising two or more hectares of land. Altogether they control about 57 percent of the surveyed village lands. An elite 6 percent of the population control about 25 percent of all village land. These figures still compare quite favorably with the more severely stratified pattern found in the wet-rice lowlands, where on average an elite 10–20 percent of households control 70–80 percent of the farmland (Husken and White 1989, 258). At the lower end of the landholding spectrum, the situation in this upperslope region is also less grim. Only 1.5 percent of the population control no land. Most of these people are elderly villagers who have deeded their land to their children, not people who have never owned land. (The average age of the male head of household in these landless households was seventy, as opposed to fifty in the midslope region). Only 3.5 percent of all households control less than 0.20 of a hectare, as opposed to 20.7 percent in the midslope region. About 25 percent of the population own less than 0.50 of a hectare, as opposed to almost 55 percent in the midslope region. By Javanese standards, in other words, land distribution in the upperslope region is only moderately inequitable.

The data on landholding also reveal several interesting facts about the tenure arrangements through which land is controlled. Sharecropping has long been important in Javanese agriculture and, indeed, most of wet-rice Southeast Asia (Bailey 1983, 32; Geertz 1963a, 99; Peletz 1988, 174; Scott 1985, 71; White and Wiradi 1989, 280). The fact that in the Tengger highlands there is so little difference between land owned and land controlled, however, indicates that neither sharecropping nor land rental is widespread. Ethnographic evidence confirms that the incidence of rental and sharecropping is very low, even among wealthy farmers.[4]

Another tenurial arrangement that reinforces landholding inequality in larger Java is also notably weak in this upland region—"salary lands," or *bengkok*. This is village land given on a usufruct basis to officials while they are in office. Because it is among the best in a village, and because village officials are usually drawn from the ranks of large landholders, *bengkok* concentrates additional land in the hands of wealthy villagers. A

4. For some landholding groups, the statistics do show a slight difference between land owned and land controlled. In the midslope region, landowners controlling two or more hectares of land appear to own a bit more land than they control, because they rent out small parcels of land to smallholders. In the upperslope region, large landowners control slightly more land than they own. Most of the additional land use here is from temporary cultivation of government forestry lands by these villagers. As throughout highland Java, the Department of Forestry periodically opens small areas of national forest to residents of nearby villages for the purpose of reforesting denuded lands. For two or three years, recipients of the land are allowed to cultivate maize (but no other crops) on the land alongside saplings planted for the regreening effort. While, in theory, access to these Forestry lands is open to all villagers, in practice village officials and other members of the elite often receive larger shares than do the poor. In line with this fact, control of these lands has a more noticeable impact on the holdings of large landholders in the upperslope region than on smaller ones.

study of late-nineteenth-century Javanese land tenure indicates that, where communal ownership of *sawah* land was the norm, 5–15 percent of this village rice land was at that time reserved for village officials (Kano 1977, 31). In modern East and Central Java, salary lands account for 9 and 15 percent respectively of all arable land. In some areas of lowland Central Java, the figure is as high as 30 percent (Booth and Sundrum 1981, 186).

The institution of salary lands is not found in any of the regencies in Java to the east of Pasuruan. Pasuruan itself is a transitional area. While salary lands exist in part of the regency, they are among the smallest in all Java (Kano 1977, 24). In the highlands, most communities lack the institution entirely. Of those examined in the present study, for example, only Ngadas has salary lands, and they comprise a moderate 4 percent of the total agricultural land.

In summary, then, land distribution in this mountain region is characterized by moderate inequity in the midslope region, but only light concentration in upperslope villages. Two facts, however, complicate this picture. The first is that in the midslope subdistrict land concentration varies greatly by village, while in the upperslope subdistrict it does not. Disaggregating the figures for each of the two village complexes surveyed in the midslope region (table 5.2), for example, it becomes clearer that in the first village, Puspo, land concentration is especially severe. The top 14 percent of the population control almost 58 percent of the land, and the top 6 percent of the population control 37 percent.[5] Meanwhile 25 percent control less than 0.20 of a hectare, and 56 percent control less than half a hectare. Though absolute landlessness is much less, the inequity among those who own land here rivals patterns of land concentration in the wet-rice lowlands (cf. Husken and White 1989, 258).

Meanwhile, only four kilometers from Puspo, the village of Jimbaran shows no such imbalance. There are no really large landowners in this community; middle farmers owning from 0.20 to 0.99 of a hectare of land comprise a full 80 percent of the population and control 75 percent of the land. Although it is the subdistrict's most destitute and densely populated village, Jimbaran is also the least economically stratified. Clearly, as other researchers have observed (White 1976), population density is not the cause of landholding inequity.

In this instance, the inequality seen in midslope landholding is related to an earlier history of roadbuilding, immigration, and commercial investment. Since the beginning of this century Puspo has been a magnet for investment by nonresident landlords and immigrant merchants, largely as a result of its abundance of water and its location on a well-

---

5. I have not included comparable figures on "land owned" in the figures shown in tables 5.2 and 5.3, because they are broadly similar to those listed for land controlled.

TABLE 5.2   Land Controlled, by Village

	Size Groups (ha)	Puspo		Jimbaran	
		% All Households	% All Land	% All Households	% All Land
Midslope villages					
1.	0	2.0	0	2.0	0
2.	.01–.19	23.0	1.7	10.0	2.0
3.	.20–.49	31.0	9.8	40.0	24.9
4.	.50–.99	16.0	11.8	40.0	50.3
5.	1.00–1.99	14.0	19.1	6.0	15.2
6.	≥ 2.00	14.0	57.7	2.0	7.6
6a.	2.00–3.50	8.0	20.5	2.0	7.6
6b.	> 3.50	6.0	37.2	0	0

	Size Groups (ha)	Ngadas		Ngadiwono	
		% All Households	% All Land	% All Households	% All Land
Upperslope villages					
1.	0	1.5	0	1.4	0
2.	.01–.19	1.0	0.1	3.5	0.4
3.	.20–.49	22.5	5.8	19.7	4.7
4.	.50–.99	28.0	15.0	22.5	10.8
5.	1.00–1.99	23.5	23.5	28.2	26.0
6.	≥ 2.00	23.5	54.5	24.6	58.2
6a.	2.00–3.50	18.5	36.1	16.2	27.5
6b.	> 3.50	5.0	19.5	8.5	30.7

NOTE. Sample sizes: Puspo, 100; Jimbaran, 50; Ngadas, 200; Ngadiwono, 142.

SOURCES. Upperslope data are from 1980 survey; midslope data, from 1985.

serviced vehicle road. Jimbaran, by contrast, has poor water resources and was linked to a vehicle road only in 1983. The divergent pattern of land concentration in these two villages today is thus a product of the "two-tiered" process of immigration and commercialization that took shape in this region in the first decades of the century (see ch. 3). Such discrepancies in patterns of land distribution between adjacent mountain villages are typical of the midslope region.

In contrast to the midslope region, the overall pattern of land distribution in the two upperslope villages is more similar (table 5.2). This is remarkable given the fact that Ngadiwono has long been a center of commercial cultivation, and lies only four kilometers from the market center of Tosari. Ngadiwono was already a stronghold of commercial activity in the 1920s, and was the first upperslope village to adopt new agro-chemicals and seeds after 1969. About sixteen kilometers to the south, Ngadas, by contrast, has always been one of the most isolated and eco-nomically conservative of upperslope communities. The village first ex-perimented with agrochemicals and high-yielding potato varieties in 1978 (ch. 4) and was opened to vehicle traffic only in 1979. Despite these histor-ical differences, patterns of land distribution in the two villages are simi-lar, with only a slightly higher degree of land concentration in the more commercial community. These and other data lend credence to infor-mants' comments that commercial agriculture has not contributed to landholding inequity in the upperslope region.

A final shortcoming of the landholding statistics is that, in carrying out surveys, I was unable to interview absentee landlords. Most ap-peared rarely in the community, and none wanted to have an outsider take note of their holdings. In the midslope region, their reluctance was reinforced by the questionable circumstances under which many had ac-quired their holdings during the political conflict of the 1960s (see ch. 7).

The above figures, then, do not include any land controlled by outsid-ers. In the upperslope region, ethnographic information indicates that absentee landlords control less than 1 percent of the available land. In the midslope subdistrict, however, absentee landholders appear to own 20 percent of Puspo's land and about 2 percent of Jimbaran's. The figure for Puspo is typical of midslope communities with a long history of commer-cial agriculture. In some midslope villages, then, land distribution is sig-nificantly worse than the figures in tables 5.1 and 5.2 would suggest. As in other long-commercialized communities, large areas of land here have been lost to outside investors through sale, pawning, and political in-trigue. Not coincidentally, these were the communities that were shaken by political movements for land reform in the pre-1965 period (ch. 7).

THE SOCIAL ORGANIZATION OF ACCESS TO LAND

Statistics on landholding are an incomplete indicator of economic strati-fication unless examined in relation to employment opportunities outside agriculture and the broader range of social relations through which peo-ple gain access to land and other resources. I shall examine the former problem later; here I wish to explore the social organization of tenure rights.

Inheritance is the single most important channel of land rights. There are others, however, and an understanding of their relative influence is critical for determining just how much mobility there is across class lines in this region, and how and where it occurs.

TABLE 5.3   Mean Land Inheritance for Males and Females, by Region and Landholding Group

			Landholding Groups (ha)					
	No Land	.01–.19	.20–.49	.50–.99	1–1.99	2–3.50	>3.50	All Households
Midslope								
Males	0	.11	.11	.25	.65	1.06	1.92	.33
Females	.09	.04	.14	.24	.23	.64	1.44	.24
Upperslope								
Males	.40	.14	.18	.35	.54	.98	.82	.50
Females	.13	.16	.23	.35	.48	.86	1.26	.50

Source. 1980 and 1985 surveys of 492 households.

Inheritance

Villagers in the Tengger highlands use a system of kinship and marriage similar to that reported from other areas of Java (Koentjaraningrat 1960; H. Geertz 1961; Jay 1969). Kinship is cognatic, and there is no corporate kin group larger than the family (Jay 1969, 174). Similarly, there is no concept of corporate kin rights, ritual responsibilities, or ancestral properties other than those associated with individual families.

Both male and female children are accorded rights in the parental estate (inheritance is discussed more fully in ch. 6). In most instances, there is no bias in favor of older or younger children, and boys and girls receive equal land shares. A small minority of midslope Muslims, however, insist that, "men carry twice as much on shoulder poles [*pikul*] as women carry [*nggendong*] on their backs, so a man should receive two shares for the woman's one." In practice, however, even those who invoke this rule implement it very loosely. Rather than being applied as a strict two-to-one ratio, it is more often cited to justify what is only a small male bias in inheritance. For the 492 households interviewed (each of which was asked to distinguish paternal from maternal land in its total holdings), statistics reveal that women almost always inherit as much land as men (table 5.3). Only in the midslope region is a small male bias evident, and it is clearest there among larger landholders, among whom the influence of Islam tends to be stronger.

The role of inheritance in establishing rights to land is underscored by the proportions of men and women who inherit land. Here there is no visible male bias at all. In the midslope region, 53.3 percent of all male household heads have inherited land, as opposed to 59.3 percent of all

TABLE 5.4   Percentage of Households Purchasing Land and Mean
Amounts Purchased, by Region and Village

Location of Household	% Households Purchasing Land	Mean Amount of Land Purchased per Household	Land Purchased by All Households as % of Total Village Land
Midslope communities			
Puspo	41.0	.85 ha	37.8
Jimbaran	46.0	.43 ha	35.0
Upperslope communities			
Ngadas	45.5	.74 ha	25.3
Ngadiwono	47.2	1.14 ha	37.0

SOURCE: 1980 and 1985 surveys of 492 households.

women. In the upperslope regions, the figures are even higher: 72.1 percent of all men and 83.6 percent of all women. In both mountain areas,
inheritance is the most important social avenue to landholding.

Land Purchase

Purchase also plays an important role in villagers' access to land. In
fact, its role is greater than those of either rental or sharecropping, the
two tenure arrangements most commonly providing rights to extrahousehold land in the lowlands.

Land is usually purchased by husbands and wives jointly; in the event
of divorce, it is divided evenly between the two partners as "property acquired in joint effort" (*gono-gini*). The percentage of households that
have acquired land in this fashion is remarkably high: 43 percent of all
survey households in the midslope region and 46 percent in the upperslope district. As table 5.4 indicates, the incidence of land purchase
varies little by village. There is notable variation in the mean amount acquired, however, ranging from a low of .43 hectares in Jimbaran, the
poorest and least commercialized of the communities, to a high of 1.14
hectares in Ngadiwono, the most affluent. Even when divided among all
the households in the survey rather than among those who actually buy
land, the amount purchased per household is still quite large: .35, .20,
.34, and .54 of a hectare in Puspo, Jimbaran, Ngadas, and Ngadiwono
respectively. Since the average couple inherit only .57 of a hectare in the
midslope region and 1.0 hectare in the upperslope area, the ratio of purchased to inherited land is remarkably high.

What is one to make of this high incidence of land purchase? Minimally, the figures indicate that land property is more mobile than one might expect from research in Java's lowlands (White and Wiradi 1989, 283) and from villagers' strenuous insistence that they would never consider selling their lands. Without exception, villagers speak of land in terms indicating they regard it as anything but an ordinary commodity. Its sale is an unthinkable disaster. The fact is, however, that land is the only good that most people can use to raise sizable amounts of cash. While everyone speaks with horror of having to sell land, then, many nonetheless do so. Unfortunately, my inquiries on the incidence of land sale ran up against a wall of moral valuation, and I was unable to gather accurate statistics from any but my most intimate acquaintances. From those examples, however, it was clear that land is sold almost exclusively to meet family emergencies. Speculation in land through its purchase and resale is rare; even those who own large landholdings display a dogged determination to keep what they have acquired and to pass it on to their children.

Regional averages obscure the fact that some households purchase large amounts of land while others purchase none. To assess the problem of class and economic mobility, we need to separate those who buy land from those who cannot. Are those who inherit little or no land destined to form a permanent underclass? To what degree are landholding groups closed classes between which there is no real social mobility? Grouping households by the inherited land husbands and wives bring to their union, table 5.5 provides a general indication of just how strongly prior inheritance influences one's ability to buy land.

Table 5.5 provides a remarkable, if complex, indication of the life-chances of people of different inherited means. Excluding for the moment households that have inherited no land at all, the basic picture is clear. As land inheritance increases, so too the percentage of households purchasing land grows, at least up to the ranks of the largest landholders. Not only do people of greater inherited means buy land more often, they also buy more than their poorer neighbors.

This pattern is only to be expected. In a densely populated region where there is little lucrative off-farm employment, land is the most important factor of production, and access to it allows one to generate the income needed to buy more. It is only among the largest inheritance groups that this direct correlation declines. The scale of their inheritance dampens their urge to acquire more land. Perhaps more important, as we shall see, the wealthy are leading the way in the diversification of economic enterprise, shifting their investments outside agriculture, a pattern seen in other parts of Java (White and Wiradi 1989, 299). Interestingly, then, it is the middle landholders inheriting 1.0–2.0 hect-

TABLE 5.5 Mean Land Purchased and Controlled, by Region and Inheritance

				Land Inherited (ha)				
	None	.01–.19	.20–.49	.50–.99	1–1.99	2–3.50	>3.50	All House-holds
Midslope								
Mean area purchased, all households in group	.29	.03	.24	.23	.70	.14	.16	.30
% households purchasing land	63.00	919.20	38.60	45.20	61.50	40.00	25.00	42.70
Mean area purchased, buying households only	.47	.16	.62	.52	1.13	.35	.80	.70
Mean land controlled	.33	.25	.56	.81	1.37	2.40	4.69	.81
Sample size	27	26	44	31	13	5	4	150
Upperslope								
Mean area purchased, all households in group	.42	.14	.16	.35	.60	.69	.34	.42
% households purchasing land	70.60	30.00	29.90	47.20	48.80	56.50	83.30	46.20
Mean area purchased, buying households only	.56	.46	.52	.74	1.24	1.22	.41	.91
Mean land controlled	.63	.34	.55	1.06	1.76	3.04	3.12	1.38
Sample size	17	10	77	106	80	46	6	342

SOURCE. 1980 and 1985 surveys.

ares of land among whom the incidence of land purchase is highest. Their aspiration to join the ranks of the large landholders seems readily apparent.

Excluding for the moment those who inherit no land, the struggle to acquire land is also evident among those who inherit smallholdings. Among those inheriting 0.01 to 0.49 of a hectare—47 percent of the total sample in the midslope region, and 25 percent in the upperslope area—only about 30 percent have been able to buy land. Age is not the critical factor here, since the range of ages represented for each inheritance grouping does not vary significantly. The low incidence of land purchase testifies to the simple fact that, for most people, being land-poor makes it difficult to buy additional land. Among those of the poor who do manage to buy land, however, the amount acquired is often substantial—up to 0.50 of a hectare. This is sufficient to lift its owners out of the ranks of the land-poor. Most people of limited inherited means stay put, however, neither buying land nor otherwise adding to the area they control. The conclusion to be drawn from these facts is clear. Land purchase does provide some people with upward economic mobility. Not surprisingly, though, those who inherit small amounts of land usually lack the resources to embark on this path to economic improvement.

There is one startling exception to this pattern. In households where neither spouse has inherited land—18 percent of the midslope sample and 5 percent of the upperslope—a larger proportion of families purchase land than is the case among almost any other inheritance group: 63 percent in the midslope region and 71 percent in the upperslope region. This is more than twice the percentage who purchase land among those who inherit between 0.01 and 0.49 of a hectare. The average amount of land purchased by these once-landless people, moreover, is remarkably large: almost half a hectare, an amount sufficient to catapult these people into the ranks of middle landholders. There is real economic mobility, in other words, precisely where one would least expect it: among people least well endowed by inheritance.

The broader data on the buying of land thus present a paradoxical image. On one hand, most of the statistics indicate that land purchase is a prerogative of those who have already inherited a sizable amount of land. For example, aggregating the data somewhat differently, we can see that, in the midslope region, among those who inherit only 0–.49 of a hectare, 60 percent never manage to buy land. While the mean amount of land purchased by those who do buy is an impressive 0.48 of a hectare, the figure is swelled by a small number of people who manage to purchase one or more hectares of land. Only 19 percent of the households in this land-poor inheritance group actually manage to buy over 0.25 of a hectare. The same general pattern obtains in the upperslope region. There, some

63 percent of households inheriting 0–.49 of a hectare have not been able to purchase additional land. But the mean amount purchased among those who do is a more impressive 0.53 of a hectare. Again, however, a few successful entrepreneurs swell the mean figure. In fact only 22 percent of households in this land-poor group have managed to buy more than 0.25 of a hectare. Most of the land-poor, quite simply, remain poor. Poverty creates its own self-perpetuating cycle.

This class-stratified pattern is contradicted, however, among those who inherit no land yet somehow still purchase sizable plots. Interviews with these people revealed that the key to their ability lies in their greater occupational mobility. Landlessness frees them from the constraints of residence associated with land ownership, and emboldens them to seek out new entrepreneurial opportunities. In this mountain region— particularly the midslope territory, where a larger proportion of villagers inherit no land—landless villagers show little reluctance to move to wherever economic opportunities are available. Occasionally their search takes them to the lowlands. Since there is already a large pool of resident poor there, however, and wages are very low, the more common course is to seek one's fortune in upland communities. Sometimes this involves work in petty trade, an arena where upperslope farmers have long deferred to midslope entrepreneurs. A small number of people have done sufficiently well in trade to do what successful entrepreneurs have traditionally done with windfall wealth—buy land.

More commonly, however, work in the upperslope region involves such status-demeaning tasks as tending cattle or performing live-in wage labor. When calculated on a daily basis, tending cattle pays very poorly. But the manner of payment—half of the animal's price at time of sale, after deducting its original purchase price—creates an ideal mechanism for accumulating capital, as long as one can otherwise meet one's daily subsistence needs. Since the labor of cattle-tending occupies only one or two hours a day, however, all cattle-tenders are able to engage in other income-generating activities.

Live-in coolies work under similar conditions. They are paid on a monthly basis and receive room and board in the interim, an arrangement also, in effect, creating a disciplined savings mechanism. Despite low daily returns, then, over the course of two or three years cattle-tenders and coolies can, if they are lucky, accumulate enough money to purchase a small plot of land. This was especially true prior to the mid 1970s, when the real price of land was much lower than it is today (see below).

The larger pattern, at any rate, stands in striking contrast with that characteristic of much of Southeast Asia. Rather than accepting subordination and seeking the "subsistence guarantees" of patron lords (Scott

1976, 5), the poorest of the poor here are driven to aggressive entrepreneurism. Equally astoundingly, they often succeed in their quest for independence.

The End of an Era of Upward Mobility?

Although this occupational eclecticism has allowed the landless to aspire to purchase land, recent developments have cast a cloud on their situation. Two stand out. First, between the mid 1970s and 1985, the number of traders working the upperslope communities increased tremendously, as midslope and lowland traders learned of the profits to be made selling to nouveau riche farmers. Peddlers who had been working in the area since the early 1970s complained bitterly about this trend, saying that competitors were driving down profits. In random surveys of peddlers coming daily to the central hamlet of Ngadiwono in April of 1979 and 1985, I found that the total had increased 69 percent, to some forty-four a day. Since over the same period the income of most farmers had fallen because of the recent decline in vegetable prices, the increase was owing to growing supply competition, not expanding demand. Traffic was so large that a small market had formed in an open space in the middle of Ngadiwono that was staffed exclusively by people from outside the village. The nearby Tosari market was also jammed, and a third market had sprung up in nearby Wonokitri. In the crowded world of Javanese petty trade, no new market stays uncompetitive for very long, and, as they told me repeatedly, many peddlers have seen their profit margins shrink (cf. Alexander 1987).

Second, and more ominous for the land-buying ability of the poor, land prices have skyrocketed in recent years with the expansion of roads and commercial agriculture. As word spreads that cloves do well in one village, coffee in another, potatoes and cabbages in still another, outside investors pour in, pushing up land prices. In Ngadiwono in 1985, adjusting for inflation and using 1985 rupiah values ($1.00 = Rp 1,100), the real price of prime vegetable land had tripled since the mid 1970s, to Rp 3–4 million per hectare (U.S. $2,730–3,640). Remote or infertile terrains could still be had for 60–70 percent of that, but even this represented a sizable absolute increase. In the southern village of Ngadas in 1978, before the opening of the vehicle road, the price of a hectare of good land (again using 1985 rupiah) was Rp 300,000–500,000. By 1985, when the region had proved itself well suited for vegetables, the price had risen to Rp 2 million. A similar escalation in real prices had occurred in midslope communities. There, in fact, a hectare of established coffee now sells for Rp 8 million, and one planted with cloves for Rp 15–18 million. Prices for lesser quality, remote land with no established perennial crops are much less, averaging about 1–1.25 million rupiah per hectare, but that figure still represents a quadrupling of prices since the early 1970s.

Right up through the late 1960s, cheap land had been a distinctive feature of upland society. As has been reported elsewhere in Southeast Asia (Scott 1985, 69), the green revolution has changed this. Of all recent developments, in fact, this was the one I heard most complaints about during my research. For the land-poor, the escalation in land prices represents a development as significant as the closing of forest lands at the beginning of this century. A small window of opportunity has closed. The very developments that have brought prosperity to more affluent farmers have reduced economic mobility among the poor. Long more permeable than in lowland society, the boundary between landed and landless has become firmer.

Rental and Sharecropping

Households also gain access to land by means other than inheritance or purchase. In Java as a whole, the most common such ways are rental and sharecropping. Though recent studies show its incidence is declining, sharecropping in greater Java is still common, with as much as one-fourth of all farmland controlled under some kind of sharecropping arrangement (Booth and Sundrum 1981, 184; White and Wiradi 1989, 280). The data on sharecropping and rental in highland Pasuruan, however, present a very different picture. Neither is or has ever been important in upland tenure.

Before independence, land rental was uncommon in all but a few highland communities with a resident Dutch population and an immigrant community of landless natives to work for them, as in Tosari and Nongkojajar. In those communities, it is said, some of the immigrant laborers rented small plots of land from local farmers to grow food for themselves or corn and vegetables for sale. More commonly, however, immigrants preferred to purchase land outright rather than rent it, or to acquire access through marriage to a local villager. Compared to lowland prices, land was not expensive. There was a steady trickle of immigrants from the ranks of the landless to those of landowners.

Sharecropping was equally uncommon. As is still the case today, where it occurred at all, it linked people bound by a prior tie of kinship or, more rarely, residential propinquity. Rather than a contract negotiated between opposed social classes (Scott 1976), tenancy mediated kinship relationships. It was a mechanism through which people helped their less affluent relatives. Poor people without kin were unlikely to receive such tenancy lands.

Then and today, the usual division of sharecropping rights was a simple arrangement known as *maro* or *paron,* "to divide in half." Under the terms of this agreement, the landholder (*sing nduwe tegal*) supplied the land, and would sometimes participate in planting and harvest (*mecok*), although this was an optional gesture of courtesy rather than a contractual obligation. The tenant (*sing nggarap*) was responsible for providing seeds and all other labor. When the *maro* system is used today, the tenant and landowner usually share the expense of fertilizer and manure. In theory, the harvest is divided evenly between the two parties. In practice, however, the 50 percent share to the tenant is a minimum. Particularly where they are bound by close family ties, many landowners give the tenant two-thirds or even more of the harvest.

This rather generous arrangement, one must note, was intended for maize cultivation only; commercial crops were not supposed to be sharecropped. Midslope cassava was the one exception to this rule, being a market crop that could also be sharecropped. Sometimes it was sharecropped using a halving system similar to that used with maize. When the price of the crop was low, however, the tenant received two shares for the landholder's one, under a "thirds" system known as *telon*.

By lowland standards, of course, both the "halves" and "thirds" arrangement are extremely generous to the tenant. Moreover, they have changed little over the years, even during periods of commercial expansion. Once again, as in other parts of Southeast Asia (cf. Peletz 1988, 174; Scott 1985, 72), the benevolence of the relationship is related to the fact that it most commonly links kin, not patrons and a servile underclass. Its benign qualities illustrate that, as Maurice Bloch (1973, 76) has noted generally, close kinship builds on a moral calculus different from the short-term investments of the marketplace. Its commitments are of longer duration, and they tolerate imbalances that would be unacceptable to those involved in a more rigidly economistic transaction. In this sphere, as others, uplanders demonstrate their responsiveness to a wider range of interests than market maximization alone.

Rental in the highlands is also uncommon. In the past, a few outsiders rented land in the more commercialized communities of the midslope region. And in recent years there has been a small increase in the incidence of rental by local people. With these exceptions, however, rental is not particularly common, and it does not appear to have ever been much more widespread than it is today, when about 5 percent of all households rent (table 5.6).

The statistics on sharecropping and land rental underscore several important facts. First, the landless and land-poor are less successful at securing sharecropping tenure than are middle peasants. The groupings in table 5.6 are based on land owned, not land controlled, in order to show whether rental or sharecropping increases access to land for the poor. In the aggregate, neither does: those who own little land still find themselves

TABLE 5.6 Incidence of Rentals and Sharecropping, by Region and Landowning Groups (Percentage)

	Land Owned (ha)							
	No Land	.01–.19	.20–.49	.50–.99	1–1.99	2–3.50	>3.50	All Households
Midslope								
Sharecropping	0	0	3.9	13.9	6.7	0	0	4.0
Rentals	0	0	3.9	2.8	8.0	11.1	0	4.0
Upperslope								
Sharecropping	0	0	5.5	3.4	0	0	0	2.6
Rentals	0	0	2.7	5.7	4.6	3.3	31.8	5.8

SOURCE. 1980 and 1985 surveys of 492 households.

unable to rent or sharecrop. Indeed, in the entire sample of almost five hundred households, not one landless or near-landless household managed to sharecrop or rent. Sharecropping is effectively a prerogative of lower-middle peasants owning between 0.20 and 1.00 of a hectare. Another statistic confirms this impression: with the land they sharecrop (the average area of which is 0.23 ha), the mean landholding of sharecroppers is almost three-quarters of a hectare. Sharecropping serves to push smallholders into the ranks of the middle peasantry, rather than to extend land rights to the poor.

There are several reasons for the exclusion of the poor. First, and most important, the majority of those receiving sharecropping concessions are kin of the landholder. In these cases, the tenancy relationship is not designed to maximize returns to the landowner. It is intended to provide assistance to a kinsman. Many of the poorest villagers, by contrast, come from families without a supporting network of kin. They are caught in a cycle of poverty precisely because they have few relatives to whom they can turn for this or other forms of assistance.

A second reason for the poor showing of the land-poor in the ranks of sharecroppers is that the poor lack the capital required to profitably cultivate land or maintain its fertility. Farming is now seriously dependent upon the application of manure and chemical fertilizers. Fertilizers are expensive, and the poor are less likely to own the livestock from which manure can be obtained. Even where they share-raise an animal, they are likely to sell its manure for cash rather than use it to rejuvenate their land. Landholders say they fear that if they were to provide fertilizer or manure, the poor would attempt to sell or exchange it for household necessities. For all these reasons, poor villagers are less likely candidates for sharecropping concessions than their better-endowed neighbors.

The relationship of landowner and tenant in the Tengger highlands is very different from that commonly reported in the lowlands, or, in fact, from much of wet-rice Southeast Asia. What few tenants there are do not become servile dependents of powerful patrons, expected, as in lowland society (Jay 1969, 264; Husken 1979, 144), to provide free services outside agriculture. The relationship here is less asymmetrical and is supposed to have something of the quality of relations between elder and younger siblings, rather than of those between servant and lord. It is characterized by polite reserve rather than servile deference. Although the sharecropper commonly volunteers to help the landowner during ritual festivals or house raisings, he is not otherwise reduced to the status of an "errand boy" (*wong kongkonan*), providing free services on command (cf. Jay 1969, 264).

In a Javanese context, the distinctiveness of this situation is best seen in light of examples from the wet-rice lowlands. There, ethnographic studies show that as much as two-thirds of the local population are in some kind of dependent tenurial arrangement with wealthy patrons (Jay 1969, 266; cf. Hart 1986, 111).[6] Where dependency relationships are developing in the mountains, they are more likely to work through wage-labor contracts (see below). This underscores once again that, here in the high-

---

6. There is one historical exception to this otherwise mild portrait of sharecropping in the Tengger highlands. In some midslope communities, there used to be a harsher sharecropping arrangement known as *bawon* or *majek*. The former term is used in lowland society to refer to the share of the crop received for harvest labor, as occurs, for example, in traditional "open harvests" (Stoler 1977; Collier et al. 1973; Hayami and Hafid 1979). Open harvests are not found in the Tengger highlands, and are reportedly also rare in upland areas of Central Java (Palte 1984, 83). In this midslope region, then, the term *bawon* referred to a different kind of harvest share: that paid to tenants for their help to a landowner in planting, weeding, and harvesting a maize crop. In other words, *bawon* or *majek* sharecropping was an upland variant of the infamous *kedokan,* an extremely imbalanced sharecropping arrangement found in wet-rice areas of East and Central Java (van der Kolff 1936, 17; Hart 1986, 186). As in some of those lowland areas, the sharecropping relationship here is said to have been introduced by immigrant farmers in the aftermath of the closing of forest lands in the period from 1910 to 1920, with the resulting land scarcity. But its fate in recent years has been different from that reported in the lowlands. Lowland *kedokan* has survived. It is common today even in highly capitalized wet-rice agriculture, for example, although now the tenant often receives a smaller share of the harvest (Hart 1986, 186; Husken 1979, 147). In the midslope highlands, however, this imbalanced sharecropping arrangement has disappeared. It was first introduced to the midslope region by Muslim "merchant-farmers," and tenants were recruited from the ranks of the lowland poor, brought to the highlands in part, it seems, because wealthy immigrants found it difficult to recruit local people to work on such disadvantageous terms. With the decline of the merchant-farmers in the 1930s, this sharecropping arrangement also disappeared.

lands, sharecropping is usually an arrangement whereby the affluent help their relatives, rather than a mechanism of "economic interdependence between agrarian classes" (Scott 1985, 77).

The low incidence of landlessness and dependent tenancy is related, of course, to the highlands' earlier history of open access to land. Today, however, mountain society is burdened with growing land scarcity, competition from outside investors, and rising land prices. Under these circumstances, it seems clear that patterns of land tenure are in transition to a new, more restrictive social organization. In the future, those who fall out of the protective net of landowning will find it more difficult to get back in.

LABOR ORGANIZATION IN AGRICULTURE

From a technical perspective, upland maize is not characterized by a periodic high demand for labor, as is the case with Southeast Asia's wet-rice agriculture. There, harvest may mobilize dozens or even hundreds of workers in a single field. With wet-rice agriculture, too, the flow of irrigation waters places strict constraints on the scheduling of cultivation (cf. Peletz 1988, 167). Rainfed maize, by contrast, can be worked in a staggered, plot-by-plot fashion (*bak-bakan, petakan*) that allows farmers to avoid the labor congestion so typical of *sawah*. In earlier times, most of the labor needed for an upland farm could be supplied by the landholding family itself. Extrahousehold labor might also be used, but this was not just a matter of physical need, but of status and prestige. While the forms of extrahousehold labor organization have changed little over the past fifty years, their relative role in the overall economy of agriculture has. The social history of extrahousehold labor provides another perspective on broader changes in upland class and community.

Cooperative Labor

Prior to the commercial expansion of 1910–29, the most common way of mobilizing extrahousehold labor was through one of several forms of cooperative labor. The different types were distinguished in terms of the size of the work crew, its social composition, the obligation to reciprocate, the presence or absence of food, and the general seriousness of the labor itself. With one exception, all of these forms of cooperative labor are still utilized in highland agriculture today. Their incidence and social importance have fluctuated greatly over the years, however, largely as a result of the waxing and waning of commercial intensification in the decades since 1920.

Kroyokan keluarga ("family gathering") is, as the term indicates, a relatively small, informal gathering of very close kin, mobilized to perform a task intimately associated with the domestic needs of the household. In its most common form, *kroyokan* involves parents and their children or grandchildren; or it may involve siblings and their spouses and children. They assemble for tasks like the husking and storing of maize after harvest; repair of a house roof; or the rebuilding of the *sigiran* platform, the vertical platform on which maize has traditionally been stored. In short, *kroyokan* is utilized for labor of an explicitly domestic sort, carried out in a family's house yard, and characterized, as its name indicates, by an air of relaxed familialism. Generational seniority is the primary principle of stratification, and the diffuse and enduring morality of close kinship displaces any concern for tit-for-tat reciprocity (cf. Bloch 1973).

The sponsoring family usually provides a few snacks for assembled kin, but these are never presented as a formal meal; they are set out casually on a table for each to enjoy when he or she so desires. Sponsors are thus spared the formal etiquette obligatory in receiving less familiar guests. Because *kroyokan* is confined to close kin, it entails no subordination other than that of children to parents, or younger to older siblings. Where kin of this sort are mobilized to help in less domestic tasks such as planting or harvesting, *kroyokan* merges with the second type of cooperative labor, known simply as "helping out" (*rewang*). The use of *kroyokan* in field labor is uncommon, however, except among adult siblings once members of the same nuclear family. In general, then, *kroyokan* is used only among very close kin and implies the informality of relaxed, undemanding tasks.

As its name suggests, *rewang*, or "helping out," is an only loosely coordinated and intermittently organized form of cooperative labor. Unlike *kroyokan*, *rewang* can be used for vigorous tasks, such as weeding or preparing a field for planting, repairing a house, or helping in the preparations for a ritual festival. Unlike rotating labor exchange, or *gentenan* (see below), *rewang* assumes no immediate tit-for-tat returns, and the hosts are not obliged to provide a meal, although they sometimes do. Nonetheless there is a greater concern for balance and reciprocity here than in "family-gathering" labor. *Rewang* need not be immediately repaid— indeed, it would look rather dourly calculating to do so—but, in a loose and enduring way, people do count on their *rewang* friends for mutual favors. People who *rewang*, in other words, are those upon whom one can depend without having to worry about immediate repayment of the favor or the etiquette associated with more elaborate forms of cooperative labor. At a work site, the sponsor will refer to most *rewang* as relatives (*dulor*). In fact, however, one's most important *rewang* helpers are usually neighbors and more distant relatives of the same generation, not the immediate family involved in "family-gathering" work.

Because of its informal, uncalculated nature, *rewang* help is not widely used for serious agricultural tasks, except among close social cohorts. Neighbors are likely to *rewang* only in the context of special events like ritual festivals, funerals, or house repairs. Among kin, as Robert Jay (1969, 251) has noted of Central Java (where much the same labor form is found), only people of equal or junior standing come to *rewang*. It would be considered unseemly for married children to expect their parents or elder kinsmen to provide help in this way, since the labor involved is often quite demanding, and thus inappropriate for a senior kinsperson. In those instances where elder kin do come, they are given some kind of supervisorial role, not identified by the work sponsors as *rewang*.[7]

Gentenan (literally, "turn-taking" labor) is the most rigorously reciprocal of cooperative forms of labor. It involves none of the casual, good-natured banter of family-gathering labor or *sayan* festival labor (see below). The rule in *gentenan* is reciprocity and hard work. To ensure that both principles are respected, *gentenan* teams are restricted to small groups of three to six farmers of equal status, all with near-equal needs for the task at hand. Rarely does the labor involve close kin, since its overt preoccupation with quid pro quo violates the less calculating eye of the close kinship tie.

Turn-taking labor is sometimes used for weeding or hoeing fields before planting. These are large and tedious tasks, and they lend themselves to the tit-for-tat calculation expected in *gentenan*. To ensure such a balance, a household is expected to "repay" (*nyaur*) the *gentenan* favor quickly. Having weeded one woman's plot, for example, a *gentenan* team will often move on to a field of equal area on the lands of another member, continuing in this fashion until all fields have been worked and all "debts" (*utang*) are repaid.

Although a few families regularly engage in this reciprocal labor with more or less the same group of neighbors, *gentenan* is best thought of as a temporary task group, dissolved after the completion of its rounds. It never becomes a corporate group with fixed leadership, stable membership, or more varied interests than the completion of the specific task at

7. Jay also notes that, in his east-central Javanese village, sharecropping dependents of wealthy patrons may be obliged to provide *rewang* help for some events with no expectation of direct payment or return. In cases such as these, the *rewang* relationship is indicative, not of a tie so close that precise calculation of return is obviated, but of subordination so severe that the junior party is obliged to provide services beyond those of the sharecropping contract. This asymmetrical *rewang* is uncommon in the Tengger highlands.

hand. Workers bring their own food, and the mood of the labor is serious and matter-of-fact, with little of the gay levity of *kroyokan* or *sayan*. Because of the equality demanded in the exchange, moreover, kin who join a *gentenan* crew are almost never of different generations, since the asymmetrical kin tie would interfere with the no-nonsense accounting and interactional equality demanded in *gentenan*.

According to the reports of elder villagers, when the last forests were felled early in this century, *gentenan* was the preferred way of carrying out the arduous work of clearing the land. With the closing of the forests after 1910 and the shrinking of landholdings, however, *gentenan* became less common. It was used more widely again, it is said, during the economically depressed years from the late 1930s to 1950. Today, however, it is again uncommon, confined to poor households too short of cash to hire wage laborers. It is virtually extinct in the more heavily commercialized vegetable-growing upperslope communities. With the large amounts of capital used in this region's agriculture today, even smallholders find it more convenient to hire wage labor rather than bother with the reciprocal calculus of *gentenan*. The latter, they say, is too difficult to coordinate, and the quality of the labor is inferior to that provided by closely supervised coolies. Besides, some farmers point out, unpaid reciprocal labor is really proper only when the crop cultivated is for "eating" rather than market sale. "That which is for eating can be reciprocally cultivated," says an oft-cited aphorism, "but not that which is for money" ("Sing ditedo tok saged gentosan, tapi sanes kangge pados donyo"). One way to respect this norm but still cultivate cash crops is to use reciprocal labor but pay those who participate in the exchange. This eliminates the tedious obligation to make sure that the amount of work performed on the lands of each farmer is equal to all the rest. If more labor is required for work on one farmer's land, a larger wage can be paid. The arrangement also neutralizes the negative connotations of wage labor for one's prestige. Such reciprocal wage labor, however, is widespread today only among the midslope poor (see below).

A fourth and final form of cooperative labor is the most distinctive of all; however, it has also experienced the most severe decline in recent years. This labor is known as *soyo* in the midslope region and as *sayan* in the upperslope area, best translated as "festive cooperative labor." As this translation implies, *sayan* is supposed to be a large, enjoyable affair, with abundant and special foods, a relaxed schedule of work, and conspicuous disregard for the normal standards of hard work. While turn-taking labor assumes strict reciprocity, the food and festive air of *sayan* free its sponsors from the responsibility of repaying laborers. Since in earlier times *sayan* required that a meat dish be served, *sayan* parties were expensive. In fact, one of the reasons *sayan* has declined is that its high-status sponsors have found better things to do with their wealth than court the good regard of their neighbors.

The style and organization of work in *sayan* illustrate the logic of a labor organized toward ends greater than utilitarian production alone. The number of workers, first of all, is supposed to exceed that technically required for the task at hand. In the most celebrated events there are so many laborers that the pace of work is relaxed and jovial, with some workers always on the margins of the work site chatting and joking, or sharing a cigarette. Extra hands, of course, are only an index of *sayan*'s more properly social function: to provide evidence of its sponsors' ability to attract large numbers of workers and, once they have arrived, to provide them with the lavish fare and amusement *sayan* requires.

Sayan, in other words, is a spectacular mélange of production and conspicuous consumption. Its form and meaning are determined by concerns other than technical efficiency. Distinction or prestige is the other concern, and the model for how it is to be achieved is borrowed from the most esteemed of upland social events, the religious festival (Hefner 1985, 104). The sponsors of *sayan* personally invite workers to the event several days prior to its occurrence, just as they do with workers for a religious festival. As is also the case with festivals, the sponsors assume the role of hosts on the actual day of the labor party. They are not supposed to give directions or otherwise supervise the work, since this would introduce an air of servility into an event that is supposed to give evidence of the comradely cooperativeness of all. On the day of a *sayan* party, therefore, the hosts appoint a "representative" (*wakil*) to direct mundane work, while the husband and wife focus their attention on the presentation of the meals that are the festival's social center. The withdrawal of sponsors from direct supervision of labor is a feature of festival organization throughout rural Java (cf. Hefner 1985; Keeler 1987).

There are two or three festival meals during *sayan,* the routines of which are strictly conventionalized. The first meal consists of white rice and a light vegetable, tofu, or meat dish, always completed with sweet coffee or tea and a cigarette. The second meal, which may be sent to the work site, consists of a sticky rice (*ketan*) and coconut milk delicacy known in the highlands as *pasilan.* This is also followed by coffee or tea. The third meal is the most elaborate, and is consumed in the evening back at the home of the labor sponsor, usually after the laborers have had time to wash up and relax. It consists of white rice, one or several meat dishes, rice sweets or store-bought cookies, and the usual coffee and cigarette. Workers file into the home of the sponsor and sit on mats (in the midslope region) or around tables (in the upperslope). While the guests take their meal, the host and hostess—who do not themselves eat with their guests—walk about, enjoining their guests to eat "abundantly" and "without embarrassment." Although the circumstances are a good deal less formal, both the etiquette and elaboration in the *sayan* party are modeled on religious festivals (Hefner 1985, 110). Lavish meals occur in no other context.

In earlier times, only maize and dry-field rice were cultivated using *sayan,* and even for them it was resorted to only during planting and harvest. For those of limited means, moreover, *sayan* at planting time was optional, since many people lacked the money to sponsor such lavish events at the beginning of the growing season. At harvest time, however, everyone was supposed to hold some kind of *sayan* festivity, and affluent farmers were obliged to make theirs particularly elaborate. While smallholders might invite ten or fifteen people, a large farmer would invite fifty, sixty, or more, so that the labor for each worker became lighter and the festivity greater. Meals, too, were expected to be more elaborate, rivaling religious festivals in their abundance of meat, eggs, and sweets. For large farmers, then, *sayan* succeeded in achieving its prestige ends only inasmuch as it displayed a conspicuous disregard for petty economizing.

Sayan parties, it should be emphasized, did not expand their sponsors' control over labor or land. They were far too inefficient an instrument for that. Contrary, then, to Popkin's (1979, 59) economistic claim, the prestige conveyed by festivals like these was not directly reducible to market gain. This labor recognized a larger utility—one's standing in the village—and this was a compelling concern in its own right.

In short, *sayan* was as much involved with the production of prestige as it was agricultural profit. In an earlier era, we must remember, extreme differences of dress, food, furniture, or house style were identified with the inequality of the lowlands and deemed unsuitable for mountain society (ch. 6). Differences of status and class existed, but there were restrictions on their social expression. Rather than striking at the productive arrangements that created inequality, these and other customs channeled wealth into prestige goods identified with mountain traditions. In using their wealth in this way, of course, affluent farmers were not motivated by blind allegiance to a collective norm. The resilience of this system depended on their continued willingness to invest in what was, in effect, a local prestige good, with little value in the outside world. Here again, private preference bore the imprint of a distinctive social community (Hefner 1983b; Etzioni 1988, 8).

At the beginning of this century, this regionalist commitment was severely tested in the midslope region by immigrant Muslim merchants who purchased land to operate commercial farms (see below). These men, it is said, refused to sponsor *sayan,* just as they refused to put on expensive religious festivals at *dhanyang* spirit shrines. Theirs was a different view of investment, status, and piety, one that denied the authority of local ways and looked to outside markets and a community of Muslim brethren beyond the parochial confines of the village.

Other forces also worked against festival labor. Small and large landholders alike complained that *sayan* workers did their work poorly, damaging topsoils and failing to attend to the detailed labor required for intensive agriculture. Poor villagers sometimes complained that they would have preferred a wage to a meal, since then they could decide how to spend their earnings. The combination of high cost, poor-quality labor and the attraction of new status goods ultimately eroded *sayan*'s appeal. The process began earlier in the midslope region, with the rise of the merchant-farmers in the 1920s. By the early 1950s agricultural *sayan* had become rare there, though it was still widely used in house construction. By the 1970s even housebuilding *sayan* was becoming a thing of the past. Wealthy villagers came to prefer urban-style, brick-and-mortar homes to the traditional wooden-frame house. Since villagers lacked the technical skills to construct the new buildings, carpenters from nearby towns were hired and paid on a contract (*borongan*) basis.

In the upperslope region, large-scale agricultural *sayan* survived longer, but ultimately suffered a similar fate. The crisis of the 1930s and 1940s imposed such severe economic hardship that the incidence of *sayan* labor and ritual festivals declined. Religious festivals revived in the 1950s, but *sayan* was presently to be dealt a fatal blow. In the first years of Indonesian independence, village chiefs were instructed by district-level superiors to put an end to wasteful festivities and commit their resources to the task of national development. Most (but not all; see Hefner 1987a) village leaders were unwilling to attack the religious festivals at the heart of mountain religion. They did, however, take steps to curtail *sayan*. In village after village, leaders banned the consumption of meat in *sayan* parties, insisting that wealthy villagers invest their cash in productive goods. Festival labor without meat, of course, is not festive at all, and the prohibition ultimately achieved its goal of bringing large-scale *sayan* to an end. In the 1970s I encountered full-blown agricultural *sayan* in only two highland communities, and even there it was dying. It had fallen victim to a more open social economy, responsive to the valued investments of larger Indonesia.

Wage Labor

If *sayan* festival labor has experienced the most severe decline in this century, wage labor (*mburuh; nguli*, "to work as a coolie") has seen the greatest expansion. Its social history reflects the broader course of political-economic change in this mountain region with unusual clarity.

Under the Dutch Cultivation System (1830–70), most of the labor mobilized for government estates was conscripted, with free wage labor playing a relatively minor role. With the rise of liberalism after 1870, however, private European estates were opened in mountain regions, and wage labor grew in importance. Around Puspo and Nongkojajar in the midslope highlands, the demand for labor was sufficient to attract a community of full-time resident workers. Most migrated to the mountains from lowland Pasuruan, Bangil, and regions to the west. In areas of less extensive European settlement, there was no such need for migrant labor. The occasional hiring of local farmers satisfied what European demand there was.

In the midslope highlands, Javanese and Madurese "merchant-farmers" (*bakul sing tani*), as local people called them, moved to the region on the heels of roadbuilding at the turn of the century. They, too, made extensive use of wage labor. Rather than hiring local villagers, however, they brought landless laborers with them from the lowlands. These client-coolies shared a common religious orientation with their patrons, being Muslim *santri* rather than staunch Javanists like most of the mountain population. More important, they were also linked to their patrons by debt, having contracted to work indefinitely in exchange for loans extended at the beginning of the contract period.

To work as a dependent coolie in this way was referred to in upland dialect as "to work as a *santri*" (*nyantri*). The term conveyed uplanders' perception of orthodox Islam as an outside and hierarchical faith, and their dislike of dependent labor. *Santri* laborers worked long hours for wages that local people regarded as exploitative—daily rates one-half those paid by European employers. Such debt-indentured labor had never before been seen in the uplands. It is important to note that the commercial expansion it supported was based in part, therefore, on unfree labor, which is to say, noncapitalist relations of production (cf. Hart 1986, 8).

Outside of the European estates and the immigrant merchants' farms, wage labor was less common, and at first it was subject to social restrictions. Village norms, for example, distinguished between cash crops and maize. The latter was referred to as "food" (*pangan; kangge ditedo*) rather than a market crop (*kanggo didol*, "to be sold"). Wage labor was proper only for cash crops. In principle, food crops, by contrast, had to be cultivated using household and *sayan* cooperative labor, and they were not supposed to be sold on the market. After 1900, however, demand for upland maize expanded significantly as a result of roadbuilding, food shortages in the lowlands, and government efforts to encourage the rural poor to consume food staples other than rice. Growing market demand led some midslope farmers to make a commodity of maize, selling a portion of the crop in lowland markets. This undermined the normative distinction between labor used to grow food and that for commercial crops. Following the lead of the merchant farmers, some midslope natives began to hire wage laborers for maize cultivation, again contrary to traditional norms. Others viewed the innovation as improper; to this day, in fact, some midslope smallholders insist that hired labor must not be used for the cultivation of maize.

In the upperslope region, the prohibition of coolie labor for maize cultivation remained in force for a longer time, surviving into the 1970s. It was not just a matter of the upperslope peasantry's greater traditionalism. At higher altitudes, maize could not be double-cropped, and upperslope production was insufficient to provide much of a surplus for market. The preferred market crop was vegetables, therefore, and there was no prohibition against using coolies for their cultivation. Even as the prohibition against wage labor in maize cultivation remained in effect, then, farmers in Tosari and Ngadiwono made extensive use of coolies for the cultivation of cash crops during the commercial expansion of the 1920s (de Vries 1931).

It was at this same time that laborers from midslope and lowland communities first migrated to upperslope commercial centers, seeking work in the vegetable fields. The expansion of wage labor, however, was short-lived. With the depression and ecological difficulties of the 1930s, wage labor again declined. It would reemerge in force only in the 1970s, eventually displacing cooperative labor as the preferred means of mobilizing extrahousehold labor.

The reshaping of labor relations under the influence of commercial change has been a recurrent theme in economic studies of Java (van der Kolff 1936; Koentjaraningrat 1961; Breman 1983; Husken 1979; Hart 1986). More generally, some Marxists and dependency theorists view the commercialization of labor as the key ingredient in agrarian capitalism (Wallerstein 1974; Frank 1969). As in Lenin's discussion of rural Russia (Lenin 1899), the expansion of wage labor is thought to go hand in hand with polarization of landholdings, intensification of exploitation, and, invariably, growing class conflict. Some analyses of rural Java have similarly postulated that wage labor is the driving force behind the recent expansion of commercial agriculture, and see it as a harbinger of growing class conflict (Gordon 1978).

Contrary to these views, however, there is considerable evidence to indicate that Java's new commercial agriculture is not uniformly dependent upon impersonal wage labor, and its impact on class relations has been varied. In wet-rice areas of north-central Java, for example, Gillian Hart (1986, 1989) has shown that recent changes have reinforced the importance of noncapitalist relations of dependency, such as those seen in *kedokan* sharecropping. Under these vertical labor arrangements, landholders extend economic privileges to a small number of workers in an effort to control the quality of labor and to exclude poor people who might otherwise feel entitled to work on large landholders' farms. Rather than simplifying class cleavages and polarizing rich and poor, then, in this instance commercial agriculture has served to reinforce vertical dependency and selective patronage.

Elsewhere in Java, poor villagers' access to harvest work—long a vital source of employment for many poor (Stoler 1977)—has been similarly restricted, through the replacement of "open" harvests with closed contract labor (*tebasan*). Under these arrangements, a trader (*penebas*) purchases the rice crop in the fields, and then brings in a work crew to carry out the harvest. Once again, a vertical bond cuts across horizontal ties of class. In such situations, it is, in effect, in the interest of contract workers to carefully guard the tie to their patron and exclude rival laborers. The agreement provides a well-paying job for the worker and lowers the landholder's labor costs. But it does so only inasmuch as it excludes the mass of villagers who might otherwise expect to join in the harvest (Collier et al. 1973).

Whether based on patronage ties or special task groups, the spread of such restrictive labor arrangements was one of the most dramatic developments in lowland agriculture during the 1970s (Hart 1986, 4; Husken 1989), demonstrating that commercial agriculture does not always depend on impersonal wage labor. It can also invigorate dependency relations and strengthen vertical alliances, while weakening lateral ones.

Labor in the Tengger highlands has also experienced great changes in the past few years. Here, too, however, the impact of the new agriculture has been mixed, in a way that prevents us from speaking of simple proletarianization or "capitalist penetration." Rather than a uniform expansion in impersonal wage labor, both wage labor and patron-clientage have increased. In the upperslope region, the new agriculture has pushed up the demand for labor and greatly expanded employment opportunities for poor and middle farmers. Much of this demand has been met through ordinary forms of wage labor. For the first time in the region's history, however, patron-clientage is also becoming common. Although in the midslope region demand for labor has not increased, the incidence of patron-clientage has. As in the upperslope region, the new agriculture appears to have promoted forms of dependency previously uncommon in the highlands.

Hart (1986) has demonstrated that in the rural lowlands this kind of patronage can have a disastrous impact on poor villagers. Those who are so unfortunate as not to have a patron lose access to vitally needed employment. As a result, they are pushed out of agriculture into even lower-paying jobs in food preparation or petty trade. Thus far in the Tengger highlands, however, the impact of patronage has been much less severe. In this region, after all, there was no tradition of "open" harvests prior to recent changes. The expansion of patronage has therefore not closed off opportunities previously available to the poor. Equally important, at least in upperslope agriculture, the expansion of patronage has occurred in conjunction with a growing general demand for labor that has provided employment opportunities for clients and ordinary workers alike.

In short, the spread of a more intensively commercial agriculture has as yet had only an ambiguous impact on upland labor relations. On one hand, it has dramatically increased the incidence of patronage. But it has at the same time increased general employment and brought genuine benefit to the poor. Just as important, finally, the commercialization of agriculture has occurred in a social context quite different from that of lowland Java (and, for that matter, much of lowland Southeast Asia). Though pressed by shrinking landholdings, a middle peasantry survives. Its presence mutes the contrast between rich and poor and leaves a distinctive mark on class relations.

PRODUCTION RELATIONS IN THE NEW AGRICULTURE

Until recently, to be a "mountain person" (*wong gunung*) was, for most people, to be a farmer on one's own land, only occasionally dependent upon the help of neighbors and kin. When asked about mountain identity, the vast majority of uplanders speak as if this were still the case today. Mountain Javanese are independent farmers, they insist, neither subservient to nor exploitative of other people. They "stand on their own two feet" and "speak directly to others."

At first sight, survey data appear to confirm villagers' reports that highland agriculture is still primarily dependent upon household labor. In both mountain regions, for example, more than 70 percent of main-crop cultivation is done by members of the farm household itself. Only one-fourth is done relying on wage labor. The remainder involves some form of cooperative labor, performed by near-kin or neighbors. When one looks more closely at the figures, however, it quickly becomes apparent that these mean figures obscure vast differences between classes. The poor rely almost entirely on their own labor. But wealthy farmers use coolies to do the largest portion of their work (table 5.7).[8]

8. The figures on agricultural labor were obtained by asking each of the 492 survey households to provide a description of the number of workers used and the number of days or hours worked during each phase of cultivation for the four largest crops harvested in the past six months. From this question aggregate figures were determined for the proportion of household, wage, and cooperative labor used by each farm. The resulting information was based, of course, on memory reports, but field surveys of actual work teams confirmed that the recall data were largely accurate. Since the survey focused on primary cultivars (defined in terms of area cultivated), they slightly exag-

TABLE 5.7   Types of Labor for Major Cultivars,
by Region and Size of Holding

	Landholding (ha)						
	.01– .19	.20– .49	.50– .99	1– 1.99	2– 3.50	>3.50	All House- holds
Midslope							
% Household labor	88.5	79.6	76.6	30.5	32.6	11.8	69.6
% Wage labor	6.9	11.6	17.1	59.1	63.3	79.5	23.3
% Cooperative labor	3.8	8.4	6.2	10.2	4.1	8.7	6.9
Upperslope							
% Household labor	98.4	89.4	85.8	71.3	58.0	33.5	74.7
% Wage labor	0	5.2	8.9	21.6	37.3	63.6	19.8
% Cooperative labor	.7	5.0	5.1	6.8	4.4	2.8	5.1

SOURCE. 1980 and 1985 surveys of 492 households.

This survey of labor utilization reveals other important facts. High-landers regularly refer to the importance of cooperation (*gotong royong*) and reciprocal labor in their lives. They cite its prevalence as a key point of contrast with lowland society. Whatever its moral value as a symbol of upland communalism, however, in practice its role in agriculture is minor. Most agricultural work is done by household labor. Where extra labor is recruited, it is now wage labor, not cooperative exchange. This is especially true among large landholders operating commercial farms. Among those owning more than 3.5 hectares, for example, two-thirds (the upperslope figure) to four-fifths (the midslope) of all main-crop labor is performed by hired coolies. For these farmers, the primary challenge of agricultural labor is managing hired workers.[9]

---

gerate the importance of cooperative and hired labor. Less likely to be included among the crops reported, garden crops are cultivated using household labor only.

9. Given the fact that a larger portion of the area cultivated in the upperslope region is devoted to new, capital-intensive commercial cultivars, one might be surprised to see that wage labor in aggregate is in fact more common in the midslope region than in the upperslope area. The difference is owing to the greater incidence of wage labor among farmers owning less than two hectares of land. In midslope communities, even the land-poor use significant amounts of wage labor; their upperslope counterparts use it more

Aggregate figures on "own household labor" show the other side of this story. Much as one would expect, the land-poor rely almost exclusively on their own labor for cultivation. As landholdings increase, however, the proportion of household labor diminishes dramatically, to a mere II.8 percent among large midslope farmers, or 33.5 percent among their upperslope counterparts. These low figures are in part attributable to farm size, and the consequent inability of largeholders to do the work of cultivation on their own. But the figures also reflect the fact that the largest landholders have begun to reduce their direct involvement in agricultural labor, not only limiting their role to supervision of workers, but shifting their attention to activities outside of agriculture entirely. A similar diversification out of agriculture has been reported in many other areas of Southeast Asia (Hart et al. 1989).

Large landholders are involved in an array of off-farm activities, many more directly related to political and social interests than to economic production itself. They predominate, for example, in organizations like the association of female heads-of-household (PKK), local chapters of Golkar (the ruling national party), farm extension programs, the village family-planning committee (run by women), the boy scouts, the village guard, committees for national holidays, religious study groups, and a host of smaller committees and organizations. Though agricultural cooperatives (KUDs) have not yet come to play as important a role here as they have in the lowlands (Hart 1986, 48; Mears and Moeljono 1981, 33), where they do operate they have become another patronage resource for the village elite.

Although some of these associations existed on paper prior to 1965, most have become prominent in village life only since the 1970s. Most were established at the direct urging of the national government, which views them as instruments of development and agencies for monitoring rural society. Village officials are automatically expected to devote much of their time to such activities. Their wives often pay the largest social price, spending endless hours receiving guests and preparing elaborate meals.[10] Even people who aspire to play just a small role in village govern-

---

sparingly. The anomaly is explained by the fact that reciprocal wage labor among the midslope land-poor is common, whereas it is rare among the upperslope poor. In a fashion similar to the old system of *gentenan* reciprocal cooperative labor, poor farmers here share wage-labor opportunities with neighbors of similar economic standing. A similar practice has been reported in some areas of the wet-rice lowlands (see Jay 1969, 253). The difference in wage-labor practices makes net wage-labor costs for the land-poor in the upperslope region greater. Hence they use wage labor a bit more sparingly than their midslope counterparts.

10. The "new cuisine" in the highlands is one small symptom of the restructuring of economic culture. In an area where even the wealthy had long consumed the same fare as their fellow villagers (although not necessarily in the same portions), the introduction of high-status urban cuisine was a serious break with mountain tradition. Most of

ment are obliged to devote a substantial amount of time to these organizations.

The expansion of these government-controlled bodies stands in stark contrast to the relatively unregulated growth of political parties in the pre-1965 period (see ch. 7). It also distinguishes contemporary villages from the "flaccid indeterminateness" and "monotonous poverty of social substance" that Clifford Geertz found characteristic of Javanese villages forty years ago (Geertz 1963, 103). Rather than suburban anonymity, the Javanese village today has something of the feel of a well-disciplined high school.

Affluent villagers also restrict their involvement in agriculture so as to engage in lucrative off-farm enterprises. Here again, most of these activities are of recent origin. Since the mid 1970s, in particular, there has been a small explosion of stores, coffee shops, hostels (in villages located on tourism routes), trucking, and trade. With the exception of petty trade and food-stall operation, most of these enterprises require significant amounts of capital, thus limiting them to the wealthy. Most are family-run and provide little or no employment for other villagers. In general, in fact, there is still much less nonagricultural employment here than in the rural lowlands. Indirectly, however, many of these new enterprises have brought benefits to less affluent people by increasing competition among traders, lowering transportation costs, making available a wide array of store goods, and increasing farm-gate prices.

Inevitably, at any rate, the diversification of employment among wealthy villagers has limited their ability to play any more than an indirect role in the daily work of cultivation. For an agriculture dependent upon careful labor, this raises serious management problems. For a people who traditionally saw farming as central to their identity, the change has also challenged popular self-perceptions.

Gillian Hart (1986, 175) has discussed this problem of labor management in a lowland Central Javanese context. There, too, social and economic affairs are luring the affluent away from agriculture. In her village, Hart notes, farmers guarantee themselves a faithful and disciplined work force by hiring laborers on a sharecropping basis rather than by paying a straight daily wage. Under such arrangements, they end up

---

the new dishes require expensive ingredients previously unavailable in the highlands, and their preparation—always done by women, assisted in some households by maids, another innovation of the 1970s—is far more time-consuming than the traditional fare of maize meal, cabbage, potatoes, and salted fish. Hart (1986, 203) also takes note of elite women's role in cooking, receiving guests, and otherwise cementing relations between the village elite and supravillage authorities. There, as here, such activities play a critical role in the maintenance of village status. The shift of a high-status woman out of directly productive activities, however, is often accompanied by a lowering of the woman's role relative to that of the husband (see Hull 1982).

paying more than they would with straight wages. In a context of wide-spread landlessness and the threat of unemployment, however, the benefits they extend to these privileged workers ensure greater loyalty and more careful work. In the long run, Hart observes, such privileged contracts lower landholders' supervisorial costs and allow them to engage more confidently in off-farm activities (cf., for Thailand, Ganjanapan 1989).

To the degree that large landholders in the Tengger highlands are shifting to off-farm activities, they are doing so, interestingly, without having to depend on sharecropping arrangements. As with Hart's Suko-dono elite, upland farmers are concerned about work quality. Sloppy hoeing, careless weeding, or clumsy harvest practices have an even more deleterious impact on delicate hillside fields, they point out, than on paddy fields. To guarantee the quality of labor, however, these farmers look, not to sharecropping tenancy, but to new forms of wage labor introduced in the highlands in the 1970s.

Wage Labor in the New Agriculture

For the landless and land-poor, agricultural wage labor has become a vital source of income. Almost one-quarter of all male heads of household report that they have worked as coolies (*kuli*) in the past year. Almost as many indicate that one of their children has done so. In the upperslope region, the figures for women are comparable, though they are lower in midslope communities. There poor women are reluctant to trek up into distant upperslope communities for jobs. Little agricultural work is available locally, and it is difficult to coordinate daily migration to upperslope villages with childcare or housework (both of which are done largely by women). Upperslope women, by contrast, can easily secure agricultural employment without having to leave the village.[11]

As one would expect, class has a powerful effect on familial involvement in agricultural wage labor. Large landowners never work as coolies. Many of the land-poor, by contrast, look to wage labor for the largest part of their incomes. Again, the pattern varies somewhat between the two mountain regions (table 5.8). In upperslope villages, a larger proportion of smallholders work as coolies. But they are less dependent on wage labor as their primary source of income than their midslope counterparts. The reason for the difference is simple: given the profitability of

11. There is also a cultural dimension to this variation in women's wage labor. In the midslope region, it is considered more shameful for a married woman to work as a coolie than it is for a man; this is not the case, by contrast, in the non-Muslim upperslope region. Poor villagers in the midslope region make genuine economic sacrifices to ensure that if someone in the household has to work as a coolie, it is not the female head of household. As long as the employment is still in the village, there is much less reluctance among upperslope villagers to let an adult woman work as a wage laborer.

TABLE 5.8   Percentage of Persons Engaging in Agricultural Wage Labor, Percentage Identifying It as Their Main Source of Income, by Region and Size of Holding

	Landholding (ha)							
	No Land	.01–.19	.20–.49	.50–.99	1–1.99	2–3.50	>3.50	All House-holds
Midslope								
Male heads of house-hold	66.7	30.8	41.2	19.4	0	0	0	25.9
Female heads of house-hold	0	10.7	3.9	5.6	0	0	0	4.7
Children	50.0	35.0	35.7	20.8	7.7	0	0	23.8
Where wage labor = primary income source	66.7	35.0	29.4	16.7	0	0	0	24.0
Upperslope								
Male heads of house-hold	0	100.0	63.3	31.6	10.8	3.4	0	23.5
Female heads of house-hold	40.0	71.4	53.4	22.4	1.2	1.7	0	20.1
Children	25.0	83.3	45.3	22.0	10.4	3.8	0	19.7
Where wage labor = primary income source	40.0	22.9	12.3	1.1	0	0	0	4.4

SOURCE. 1980 and 1985 surveys of 492 households.

vegetable farming, smallholders in the upperslope region can generate good income even from a small plot of land (see ch. 4). As a result, wage labor for them supplements income from their own farming. The midslope poor have no such profitable crops, and wages play a more important role in their total incomes (table 5.8).

In recent years, two new forms of wage labor have come to play an especially important role in upland agriculture. The first type of laborer, known as a "monthly coolie" (*kuli bulanan*), is a live-in worker who resides with the landowner and is given room and board in addition to a

TABLE 5.9   Households Employing Client-Laborers, by Region and
            Size of Holding (Percentage)

	No Land	.01–.19	.20–.49	.50–.99	1–1.99	2–3.50	>3.50	All House- holds
	Landholding (ha)							
Midslope	0	0	0	0	17.6	44.4	50.0	6.8
Upperslope	0	0	0	6.8	16.1	28.3	77.3	16.1

SOURCE. 1980 and 1985 surveys of 492 households.

monthly wage. The second, known as a "steady coolie" (*kuli langganan*), maintains an independent household, but has a special, regularized relationship to an employer. The hiring of live-in coolies—most of whom are from the midslope region—is particularly common in the upperslope region. There the demand for labor has increased so dramatically that large farmers have had to turn to outside workers to meet their needs. Full-time or steady coolies (*kuli tetep; kuli langganan*) are also found in upperslope villages, but are more common in the midslope region. There, the pool of land-poor families is sufficient to ensure that most employers do not have to bother with the added expense of providing room and board to attract workers.

Whatever the arrangement used, the number of local farmers employing one or both types of client labor is high. In the midslope region, 6.8 percent of all farms employ at least one such laborer, while in the upperslope region over 16 percent do. Among the largest landholders, the figure swells to 50–75 percent (table 5.9). Figures from the midslope region would be considerably higher, one should note, had it been possible to include absentee landholders in the survey.

The prevalence of such dependent labor today is remarkable in light of its rarity prior to the 1970s. Indeed, few developments contrast as dramatically as this one with traditional economic culture. Once identified with the obsequious hierarchy of the lowlands, dependent labor is today a driving force in the highlands' emerging economy (table 5.9).

Although this dependency is built around the wage-labor relationship, it is not mediated by cash alone. Indeed, the difference between labor management here and in Hart's (1986) *kedokan* and sharecropping examples—where labor relations are not based on direct wages at all—is smaller than might first appear to be the case. Full-time wage laborers are linked to their employers by loans, gifts, and other forms of patronage. In hiring full-time workers, an employer is expected to make a cash advance, usually equal to about four months' wages. Advance payments then continue throughout the life of the relationship. This involves some risk on the part of the patron, particularly where, as in the upperslope region, the laborer may be from outside the village. In most instances, however, laborers themselves initiate the relationship, approaching the landowner after they have won his confidence through several months' faithful work as a daily laborer (*kuli harian*). The relationship thus builds on more than the impersonal ties of the marketplace.

In interviews, employers regularly underscore the personalized nature of their tie to special coolies. They point out, for example, that client workers are often given full authority over fields and workers when the employer is away. In this respect, they resemble the "close laborers" (*buruh dekat*) in Central Java of whom Hart has spoken (1986, 119). They, too, are accorded special privileges for their role in supervising other workers. Unlike the Central Javanese workers, however, privileged laborers here are not recruited in early infancy from the ranks of the poor. Nor is the relationship maintained indefinitely; in fact, the bond rarely endures for more than five or six years. The worker in the Tengger highlands preserves greater autonomy in the long run and is not reduced to indefinite servitude.

In private conversation, full time-laborers underscore these same themes of trust and personalized attention, insisting that they work not just for their wages but because of special kindness the employer shows. In part, of course, these comments are intended to put a good face on a demeaning situation. But the social implications for the labor relationship are real. The employer-become-patron assumes responsibilities beyond those of the wages he pays. He provides a new set of clothes each year, gives bonuses when his worker has a ritual festival, and allows time off with pay if the worker has family problems. Most important, the patron provides a significant measure of social insurance by advancing interest-free loans during difficult times. In the long run, these loans may not be repaid even if the employee severs ties with the employer.

Admittedly, the work load of a client worker is heavy. Like a family member, he or she is expected to work longer hours than ordinarily required of field hands—seven to eight hours each day, as opposed to the normal five and a half to six. In the case of a live-in coolie, he (almost all are male) performs one or more hours of domestic duties as well, gathering firewood, fetching water, and helping with house repairs.

For their efforts, midslope monthly coolies earned Rp 10,000–12,000 per month (U.S. $9.00–11.00) in 1985. Those in upperslope villages earned Rp 15,000–17,000 ($13.64–15.45). This compares to daily wage rates (without food) averaging Rp 500–550 for men and women in the midslope region, and Rp 650–800 for men and Rp 650 for women in the upperslope villages. Food and cigarettes add an additional Rp 7,000 per month to the laborer's benefits. Annual gifts of uncooked rice and clothing, finally, provide a bonus equal to about Rp 9,000 in the midslope region and Rp 15,000 in the upperslope area. By the standards of Javanese agriculture, these are respectable incomes for field labor. Though providing only a modest livelihood, regular employment and lump-sum payments create a compulsory savings mechanism, allowing many coolies to save money. That is what most aspire to do. Invariably, their dream is to work their way out of the dependent relationship and eventually establish enterprises of their own.

Whatever its material benefits, the status implications of coolie labor are overwhelmingly negative. Of the two types of full-time wage laborers, the live-in coolie is the more socially marginal. Having given up any pretense of maintaining an independent household, he also gives up any claim to social standing in the village. Live-in coolies are most common in the upperslope vegetable regions, and almost all come from communities below this highland area. This makes their dependence on their employers all the greater, as they are isolated from other villagers and confine their recreation to the employer's household. The depth of dependence in this relationship encourages most live-in coolies to identify their interests—and their chances for eventually escaping this demeaning role—with their employer rather than with other workers. This, too, makes them well suited to serve as labor supervisors.

In the eyes of live-in coolies, what makes the role less degrading is the fact that, for most, the work is done only when one is young and unmarried or married without children. Live-in coolies regard their position as a temporary indignity, to be endured for a few years until one has saved enough cash to return to one's own community and start a small business. Many of the peddlers who offer their wares throughout the highlands are, in fact, ex-coolies of this sort. They first developed their capital and social contacts while working as field hands in the region. Indeed, the dream of operating some kind of independent enterprise is realized by most special laborers. Unlike their lowland counterparts, few remain in their dependent role indefinitely.[12]

In the case of "steady coolies" (*kuli langganan*), the status implications of the role are less severe. Unlike live-in workers, steady coolies maintain their own households. They work regularly, but not continuously, for their patrons and are paid on a daily rather than monthly basis. All nonetheless receive loans and annual gifts from their patrons. Intermit-

---

12. There are occasional success stories among such ex-coolies. Puspo's wealthiest cattle trader, for example, worked for several years as a live-in coolie in the upperslope region, and eventually shifted to cattle trading, an enterprise in which trust and good name are vital. Though he had inherited no land and began with only his own savings, he proved so skilled at his trade that he was eventually able to invest his earnings in land, becoming one of Puspo's largest landowners. Though statistical evidence is lacking, I rarely encountered such success stories in lowland Pasuruan and suspect they are rarer.

tent employment reduces patrons' maintenance costs, but also allows the laborer to engage in outside work, such as farming (most own some land) or wage labor for other people. By maintaining a measure of independence, steady coolies are able to avoid the humiliation of the live-in worker's role. Significantly, they are not expected to provide petty services outside of agriculture such as fetching water or collecting wood. They *are* likely to work for their patrons on special occasions like religious festivals. But the negative connotations of this work are limited, because neighbors and relatives also help the ritual sponsors.

In general, in fact, steady coolies enjoy higher status than other wage laborers. Most reside in the same villages as their employers, and their relationship is more enduring. While less subservient, therefore, steady coolies tend to have stronger and more personalized ties to their patrons. Unlike in the case of the live-in coolie, this relationship may be reinforced by ties of fictive kinship, as expressed, for example, in the ritual exchange of food during holidays or the mutual (if still imbalanced) exchange of gifts and labor during ritual festivals. At harvest, the steady coolie may be given a gift of part of the crop, just as if he were a close relative. For a large landholder, the trust this relationship engenders makes the steady coolie ideal for supervising laborers in the owner's absence.

From the perspective of social class, of course, this special arrangement, like that of the live-in coolie, reinforces the worker's identification with the employer rather than with the field hands he may supervise. Its moral quality cannot, however, be reduced to the instrumental interests of labor control. Many patrons extend favors to their dependents quite beyond what would be required to win their allegiance. I knew several who had provided interest-free loans to ex-dependents now working on their own.

Aside from these two types of coolie labor, no other forms of institutionalized dependency are common in today's Tengger highlands. There are none of the radically asymmetrical tenancy arrangements so familiar in the lowlands, such as *kedokan* sharecropping. The debt-pawning of land is also extremely rare (cf. Hart 1986; Husken 1979).

In analyzing trends in the Tengger highlands, therefore, it is important to put the spread of wage labor and the growth of clientage in broader perspective, especially if we are to assess their broader impact on solidarity and conflict. Although wealthy landowners employ dependent wage labor, the majority of villagers still work their own fields and look to them for the bulk of their incomes. In this region of Java, then, one cannot talk, as Robert Jay (1969, 265) does of lowland east-central Java, of communities neatly divided into two separate camps, the one consisting of independent wealthy farmers and the other of their dependents. Nor, as is the case in north-central Java (Hart 1986, iii), are the majority of

smallholders mired in relations of debt. Mountain Java shows a more independent face and illustrates the peculiar situation of Southeast Asia's
middle peasantry.

A Middle Peasantry

Villagers in both mountain regions will quietly acknowledge that
there are "haves" (*sing nduwe*) and "have-nots" (*sing ora nduwe*) in their
communities. However, they vigorously denied my suggestion that there
might be an unbridgeable gap between rich and poor. I do not believe
this was simply an idealization of village ways. It also reflects the continuing prominence of a group that has received little attention in peasant
studies: the middle peasantry. Situated between the more visible agrarian elite and the mass of the poor, whose plight rightly catches our eye,
this group receives scant comment in many accounts of agrarian change.
Influenced by Marx's vision of social polarization (see ch. 1), scholars often assume that middle peasants are doomed to historical oblivion.

Whether this prognosis is accurate for Southeast Asia's peasantry in
the long run remains to be seen. In the meantime, however, if we are to
develop a plural model of class and status, we are going to have to
broaden our investigation and attend to social reality as it is. Part of the
problem with the middle peasantry is, as here in the Tengger mountains,
that it eludes our stereotypes. It is characterized by neither the servile dependence of a dominated underclass nor the collective solidarity romantically attributed to proletarians. The preoccupations of these peasants
seem more modest. Haunted by the image of lowland poverty, they seek
to preserve and, if possible, extend what modest independence they can
without falling into the all-too-familiar destitution of the lowland poor.

This social orientation emphasizes neither selfless collectivism nor
self-possessed individualism. Its animating ethos is an almost-
paradoxical mix of self-reliance and communalist commitment. Ideally,
in this view, each household guarantees its own welfare. Dependence on
others is regarded as a temporary evil at best. Outside of the supports
provided by close kin, there are few really substantial institutions to provide "social insurance" or "subsistence guarantees" (Scott 1976) for the
poor. Though its redistributive mechanisms are few, this is still a moral
economy, though in a sense different from that implied in recent literature on moral economy. Its norms are most apparent not in the realm of
production but in consumption and exchange. The traditional village demanded life-style conformity, not selfless sharing or the leveling of class.
One could acquire what wealth one wanted in outside markets. But in
the village its use had to acknowledge neighbors and a mountain way of
life (see ch. 6).

There is a distinctive perception of social relations at work here. Individuals are conceived particularistically, as members of families with familiar, individual faces, rather than as anonymous representatives of categorical groupings. It is only when they move outside of the village, to interactions with merchants, Chinese, tourists, or unfamiliar lowlanders, that people think in broader categorical terms and invoke the exclusive moral notions such relations imply. Local relations, by contrast, always wear a particular face.

This unwillingness to visualize local ties in broad categorical terms stands in stark contrast to more severe forms of class or status consciousness. In the latter relationships, people from different groups have difficulty seeing each other as anything but representatives of impersonal, and often opposed, communities.

From a comparative perspective, of course, the fact that upland villagers do not see themselves in such sweeping terms is not surprising. Even where it has entered popular culture, class is an awkwardly abstract concept. Both Marx and Weber recognized that in the industrializing West the concept of class seized popular awareness only in the aftermath of the destruction of inward-looking local communities. Its rise to popular consciousness went hand in hand with the development of mass production, communications, and anonymous urban environments. In this setting, daily interaction was no longer regulated by personalized ties of kinship, parish, and locality. A more anonymous space was created, in which abstract collectivities like class and nation competed to define new forms of community (cf. Anderson 1983a; Bendix 1969; Giddens 1973, 84). The conditions were created for the peculiarly alienated/liberated consciousness of modern life.

Though social relations are changing, community in the Tengger highlands has yet to be so thoroughly depersonalized. For the time being, highlanders are reluctant to speak of their neighbors in anonymous and categorical terms. They were uneasy, for example, when I asked them to categorize people by wealth. In fact, they knew the relative affluence of different families quite well. But an exercise requiring them to put their knowledge on public record proved to be extremely disconcerting. "You just don't talk about your neighbors that way," I was told. (Villagers showed no such reluctance, of course, when discussing lowlanders, Chinese, or Western tourists.) In part, no doubt, this attitude is related to the old and highly idealized characterization of the village as a spiritual association of equal and autonomous households, bound by spiritual descent to its founders (Hefner 1985, 70). But there was a practical sociological influence at work here as well.

In the traditional Tengger highlands, there were no corporate organizations other than those of family and village. There were no castes, aristocrats, formally organized status groups, social clubs, guilds, religious societies, or other groupings that might challenge the primary integrity of the village. Recent immigrants were not distinguished from descendants of village founders, as is common in the lowlands (Jay 1969, 313). At work sites and in religious festivals, it was considered impolite to distinguish real kin from non-kin, who, in the context of the work event, were referred to as relatives (*dulor*). Even close personal friendships were viewed askance, since their exclusivity violated the qualities of randomness and mutuality valued in village interaction (Hefner 1985, 76–82). Kin ties, task groups, and ritual exchange relations were all primarily organized within the boundaries of one or two mountain communities. In short, until recently, villages in the Tengger highlands were remarkably vital entities. They displayed an overlap of economic, kinship, and ritual bonds far richer than is typical of the modern lowlands.

This is not to say that upland villages were closed communities. In the last century they assimilated an enormous immigrant population. What made these villages distinctive was not the physical exclusion of outsiders, then, but the fact that they had a critical mass of institutions to influence how immigrants behaved once they had arrived. Even as one looked outside the village for market income and exchange, one turned inward for work, amusement, marriage, and alliances. In the village, the objective cleavages of class were crosscut by personalized ties of kinship, neighborhood, and exchange with a political and moral weight of their own. In such a context, the impersonal language of the market, class, or nationalism failed to capture the moral particularity of village life.

This individualizing (but not individualistic) perception, and the value of nondependence to which it is related, are central features of middle peasant culture here in the Tengger highlands. Curiously, this same personalizing and independent view of social relations influences the aspirations of even the lowliest coolies. Most of them see their chances for self-improvement, not in collective solidarity with anonymous class cohorts, but in personalized alliance with individual patrons. In this instance, then, economic realities are conducive to vertical alliances, not lateral solidarity. The poor coolie struggles not against his dependency relationship, but within and for it—to assimilate the role to that of a dependent kinsman or neighbor, linked to the employer by more than the wage nexus. The relationship works if it is transformed from that of an anonymous category into a particularized tie.

Client coolies, then, work vertically and particularistically. They accept the reality of subordination in a way that at first sight seems to resemble the peasant clients Scott (1976) describes in traditional Southeast Asia. As Robert Jay (1969, 267) has said of clientage in Central Java, however, such personalized subordination tends to impede "the growth of selfconsciously exclusive classes." The dependency relationship here in the Tengger highlands displays another distinctive feature. The dependence is instrumental, and self-consciously so. It is accepted with an eye toward eventually winning back one's autonomy. Unlike Jay's clients, therefore, special coolies limit the role's duration, or, as with steady coolies, make the dependency more diffuse by using its rewards to engage in other economic activities. Even the poor are driven by the dream of dignity and independence.

The aspiration of these uplanders is different from that emphasized in much research on peasants. The literature on class resistance in Southeast Asia, for example, often implies that peasants feel primary solidarity with others in similar class circumstances, whether they are able to act on that sentiment or not. Popular aspirations here in mountain Java, of course, are powerfully informed by a vision of community. But its core is less anonymous and romantically collective than the resistance model would imply. One seeks to stand on one's own and not be ordered about. Only in doing so can one be fully acknowledged as a member of the community. The simple achievement of respectful standing in a community of brethren is a valued end in its own right.

CONCLUSION

Since the nineteenth century, landholding and labor relations in the Tengger highlands have been shaped by a broad array of institutions. Here, as throughout the modern world, the state played an especially important role in economic expansion (cf. Skocpol 1982, 174; Migdal 1982, 73; Chirot 1986). The colonial state—not an independent bourgeoisie—colonized the highlands and reshaped its economy. Enticing people to the region with the promise of agricultural land, the Dutch transformed the highlands into a vast government estate. Since landholders were subject to the labor taxes that supplied workers for colonial enterprise, it was in the government's interest to preserve a pattern of smallholder farming. State policies thus reinforced the region's smallholding traditions.

This state-directed economy eventually paved the way for the expansion into the highlands first of private European farmers and, shortly thereafter, of native "merchant-farmers" with economic and cultural ties to the Muslim lowlands. As commercial activity expanded, it gave rise in some communities to greater land concentration and new forms of wage labor. As in other parts of Java (Husken and White 1989), the trend toward a more commercialized agriculture was aborted, however, with the political, economic, and ecological crises of 1930–65. Commercial agriculture would fully recover only in the 1970s, bringing with it outside investors, wage labor, and new forms of social differentiation.

The new agriculture has not resulted in simple proletarianization or the uniform expansion of impersonal wage labor. Some land alienation has occurred, but absolute landlessness remains low. Wage labor has increased, indeed dramatically, and older forms of cooperative labor have declined. In the upperslope highlands, however, the demand for labor has pushed up wages and created new employment opportunities for the poor. A significant portion of the new wage labor, interestingly, involves personalized dependency. With their off-farm commitments, large landowners have come to depend on labor supervisors (*mandor*). They cultivate the loyalty of these workers by providing credit, gifts, and steady employment. But they do so without reducing their dependents to the status of permanently indebted clients. Even dependent workers spurn long-term ties and aspire to the status of independent farmers or petty traders. They share the basic values of the middle peasantry.

This desire for social autonomy has always been a key feature of upland life. Though animated by a strongly antihierarchical impulse, traditional upland communalism did not emphasize poverty sharing, patronage guarantees, or the noble collectivism of class resistance. Its animating impulse was the simple desire to stand on one's own. Its economic foundation was the ability of all villagers to own land. Labor relations similarly emphasized household self-reliance. Throughout all, the most generalized aspiration of social life was to avoid being "ordered about." The contrary reality of lowland society was all too familiar.

Pressed by shrinking landholdings, and drawn more firmly into national markets and politics, this smallholder peasantry is today changing. In objective terms, a more class-stratified village is emerging. But its cultural consequence is still muted by the presence of middle peasants and by the aspirations of the poor to join their ranks. Early on in my research, one poor peasant described this situation with unusual insight. "Mountain people," he said, "care less about rank [*pangkat*] and whether one becomes rich. What counts is to have something of your own, so you don't have to depend on others and be ordered around. You want to be able to speak directly and look others right in the face." This modest aspiration has been a powerful force in the making of this mountain peasantry.

SIX

Consumption Communities

The changes sweeping the Tengger highlands have had an impact beyond property, labor, and protection. Consumption is also changing, in a manner that reveals with unusual clarity the altered bases of identity and community. Recognition of this fact requires that we dispense with the view that the utility of goods is, as neoclassical economics would have it, technically given in the object, and thus objectively apparent to all. Utility is in the eye of the beholder, and it is perceived only in relation to a particular social system and "socially organized forms of satisfaction" (Leiss 1976, 9; cf. Bourdieu 1984, 224). Consumption, then, is not an obscure private act driven by shapeless desire. It is implicated in identity, and informed by the uses to which goods are put in a particular social world.

Human need, similarly, is not just the internalized expression of natural necessity. Whether with potlatch among the Kwakiutl, luxury goods in the West, or ritual festivals here in highland Java, "the realm of needing becomes immersed within the domain of communication"; in using goods, people "communicate to others their relationships to complex sets of otherwise abstract social attributes (such as status), thus identifying themselves within social structures" (Leiss, Kline, and Jhally 1986, 243). The circulation of goods outlines society's primary groupings and indicates the rights and privileges that characterize each. It gives visible form to the often intangible judgments involved "in the fluid processes of classifying persons and events" (Douglas and Isherwood 1979, 67; Sahlins 1976, 178). In a word, goods signify community and help to constitute the relationships of inclusion and exclusion, valuation and devaluation, that everywhere define its contours.

This much said, it is important to recognize that the semiotics of consumption works in varied ways. Sometimes its meanings are deliberately

Straw man argument

and self-consciously conveyed. In upland villages in the late 1970s, for example, it suddenly became de rigueur for any man of social standing to wear a wristwatch. Something else was at issue here than the need to tell time. Random inquiries revealed that few people, in fact, were really able to read the hour. Watches were set at all different times; indeed, it made no difference if the device worked at all. The purpose of watch-wearing was less grossly instrumental than it was socially expressive. One more sign that rustic mountain ways were in decline, it served to convey an image of urban sophistication and man-of-the-world importance.

In other instances, however, it may not be sufficient to ask what a consumer intends to convey through the use of a good. Its meaning may be expressed unwillingly or unintentionally, behind the back of its owner. Highlanders forced by poverty into simple shacks and tattered clothes, for example, communicate important information on the nature of economic privilege and the consequences of scarcity. Against their wishes, no doubt, they signal their position in the village order.

All this is to say that the anthropology of consumption is an extraordinarily complex endeavor. It must look at both the intended and unintended meanings of goods; both give consumption its larger significance. There is, in addition, a third dimension to the circulation of goods, beyond their intended or unintended meaning. As with all social action, consumption creates situations and consequences that "feed back to be the unacknowledged conditions of further acts" (Giddens 1984, 49). It has practical effects that escape actors' awareness but nonetheless systematically constrain their actions and well-being. Using expensive ingredients imported from outside the region, for example, the cooking now favored by affluent highlanders expresses a social orientation different from that of a poor farmer consuming the traditional fare of maize meal and onions. Its expressive import is thus readily apparent. The differential effects of that diet, however, are also felt in domains of which actors are less keenly aware, as in health and physical development, or fertility and infant mortality. In this instance, then, the unintended effects of consumption become the unacknowledged conditions for future welfare.

The food example illustrates a larger truth. Even as it explores their cultural meaning, the anthropology of goods cannot be confined to their semiotic import alone. However rich their meaning, goods are never *just* signs. Practical and semiotic, instrumental and expressive, they are both communicative and constitutive, announcing the social order and also differentially supplying the matériel its actors need.[1]

---

1. In more theoretical terms, the point here is that the study of goods must be concerned with both their meaning and their systemic social effects. This requires that one transcend the opposition between interpretive and "practico-functional" analysis. See Giddens 1984; Bourdieu 1977, 1–30; Eickelman 1979.

Both features of social process—the semiotic and the practical—are at the heart of changes reshaping household consumption here in the Tengger highlands. The nature of these changes is the focus of the present chapter. In this mountain region, consumption is deeply involved in the communication of received and changing identities. But it is also implicated in the material sustenance of human lives. For all these reasons, consumption provides another useful vantage point from which to assess the impact of economic change on upland class and community.

FAMILY, HOUSEHOLD, AND THE DOMESTIC CYCLE

The household in rural Java is the basic unit of ownership, production, and consumption. The nuclear family at its heart is also responsible for the transmission of the most important forms of productive wealth (see ch. 5). Here, as in most of Java, there are no bounded kin groups other than the family (Jay 1969, 189) and no corporate property other than that transmitted within its framework. Because the household and family play such a central role in the organization of economic life, an understanding of their rhythms is essential to an appreciation of the uses of goods and the genesis of wealth and poverty.

For most villagers marriage is the first and most important occasion for parental transmission of property. At wedding time, parents are expected to provide their children with the productive resources they need to begin a household of their own. "If you're an adult, you've got to have a house," affirms one oft-cited aphorism ("ne'e dewasa, kudu ngumah"). This ideal of household independence is at the heart of inheritance practices in this region of Java and is a powerful influence on parent-child relations. An independent household is the basis for one's recognition as a mature adult. Without it one remains a juvenile in the eyes of the community. Newlyweds are thus eager to extricate themselves as quickly as possible from dependence on their parents. Ideally, inheritance is organized in such a way as to speed them on this course.

In the case of rights to land, the actual procedures for inheritance inevitably depart from this ideal where parents lack the resources to get the young couple on their feet. Under the best of circumstances (and excluding some Muslims who give boys larger shares than girls), parents provide all children with equal shares in the household estate. On their wedding days (or even earlier, in the case of some wealthy families), children are given as much of what they are finally to inherit as possible. Ideally, parents reserve only a small portion of land for themselves, eventually transmitting it and the parental house to the child (often the youngest daughter, though there is no firm normative rule) who arranges to care for them in their old age. If, in the course of their marriage, the parents acquire additional land, it too is eventually divided among their heirs. By the time all their offspring have married, then, parents are expected to have transmitted the bulk of their land and wealth to their children. Popular norms are clear on this point: parents are expected to make great personal sacrifices for their children. Even if it entails real personal deprivation, parents should provide their children with as much wealth as they can as early after marriage as is possible. This is to ensure that married children have the resources to stand on their own and become mature villagers.

Today, of course, many families have insufficient resources to provide each child with a plot of land adequate to operate a farm, and actual inheritance procedures are more varied than this ideal would imply. In the case of land-poor families, parents may be obliged to share their land with newlyweds, ultimately transferring the plot to only one among their children in old age. Landless or near-landless parents may not be able to provide their children with even these capital resources. Their gift to them may consist of little more than shelter and help with daily meals until the young couple are able to support themselves.

Sometimes even parents with abundant landholdings defer transmitting rights to land for several years after the wedding, obliging the young couple to work as juvenile dependents. In most such instances, the parents compensate them for their work on the farm by giving them a set share of the harvest. Worse yet in the eyes of the villagers, they may require the couple to eat in the same kitchen and to request money for their daily needs, as if they were still young children. Although almost unknown in the upperslope region, deferred inheritance of this sort is less rare among midslope families. Even there, however, most villagers regard such parental behavior as evidence of hard-hearted miserliness. It maintains adult children in a state of dependency, sacrificing the children's self-respect for the personal well-being of the parents.

Whatever the inheritance procedure, most people expect the bride's parents to play a larger role in helping the young couple to get established. If possible, each set of parents should give the young couple a plot of land, or, failing that, some piece of property like a bull or a goat, or even just a hoe and an axe, but the parents of the bride provide the lion's share of nonland resources. They are also more likely to give the newlyweds shelter during the first months of marriage.

In former times, this pattern of uxorilocal residence was related to the custom of bride service. Although there is no formal normative sanction requiring it, most marriages are village endogamous—75 percent in the upperslope region, 64 percent in the midslope. Almost 90 percent of all marriages in both regions occur within a two- or three-village radius. Despite the fact that the bride and groom usually come from the same village complex, the groom, it used to be thought, should be the one to leave his parents and take up residence with his parents-in-law. In so doing, he was expected to work on their fields for several months or even a year. Bride service is now uncommon in midslope villages, however, although still performed in some upperslope marriages. Even where it continues to be practiced, the custom is today limited to occasional assistance by the groom during periods of peak labor demand, such as at planting and harvest (Hefner 1985, 149).

Though bride service is now uncommon, the uxorilocal bias in marital residence is still widely respected, as table 6.1 shows. Almost three-quarters of all newly married couples go to live with the bride's parents, and for a surprisingly long time: 2.3 years in the midslope region and 3.7 in upperslope communities.[2] Only a small percentage of newlyweds go to live with the parents of the groom.

Where, by contrast, the young couple move immediately to a home of their own, the bride's parents are still more likely to play a leading role. In about 60 percent of all cases, the bride's parents supply most of the funds for construction of the young couple's home; the groom's parents do so in only one out of every five marriages.

As table 6.1 indicates, the bias toward uxorilocal residence varies little by class. Poor and wealthy couples alike tend to live with the parents of the bride. The only notable deviation from this pattern occurs among large landholders in midslope villages, a group that, as we have seen, has been innovative in other domains as well. Among them a significant number of young people go to live with the groom's parents. The higher incidence of virilocal residence among the land-wealthy is reportedly a recent development, related to their growing conviction that it is more proper for the "woman to follow the man." Some midslope villagers insist that this residence rule is more consistent with Islam, but the majority simply identify it as "modern" (*moderen*). Whatever its social precedent, the practice again underscores the growing tendency of affluent villagers to identify with nontraditional customs and to distance themselves from village ways.

As long as a young couple reside and eat with the parents, in the community's eyes they remain children, not adults. In upperslope communities, where the ideal of social independence is still unqualifiedly resilient, the couple usually attempt to extricate themselves from this disesteemed

2. These average figures exclude those instances where a couple inherit a parent's home and land, and thus never move from the parental home. Though comparative data from across Java are lacking, it is interesting to note that Robert Jay's study in east-central Java saw a similar bias in residence patterns. Though villagers cite no normative precedent, Jay reports that 63 percent of all nuclear families live close to the relatives of the wife (Jay 1969, 40).

TABLE 6.1   Marital Residence, by Region and Size of Holding
(Percentage)

	No Land	.01–.19	.20–.49	.50–.99	1–1.99	2–3.50	>3.50	All House-holds
				Landholding (ha)				
Midslope								
Wife's parents	66.7	67.9	74.5	83.3	70.6	44.4	50.0	72.0
Husband's parents	0	10.7	17.6	5.6	17.6	33.3	33.3	14.7
Own house	33.0	21.4	7.8	11.1	11.8	11.1	16.7	12.7
Other	0	0	0	0	0	11.1	0	.7
Upperslope								
Wife's parents	75.0	100	76.1	71.2	72.9	74.6	81.8	73.9
Husband's parents	25.0	0	4.2	13.7	8.2	11.9	4.5	9.2
Own house	0	0	18.3	13.7	16.5	11.9	13.6	15.3
Other	0	0	1.4	1.2	2.4	1.7	0	1.5

Source. 1980 and 1985 surveys of 492 households.

position as quickly as possible. Even prior to moving to a house of their own, they take steps to signal their independence, often setting up a separate kitchen and food storage area (*pedharingan*) in the parents' house just a few weeks after their wedding. The separation of food stores sends a clear public message that henceforth the young couple will provide their own food. Some couples take even greater pains to underscore their new status. Not content merely to eat separately from the parents, they erect an impassable wooden partition in the middle of the parental kitchen, creating two separate hearthholds, each with its own entrance, oven, and stores. The parents and young couple are subsequently crammed into two closed-sized rooms.

From a purely economic perspective, of course, such an arrangement is inefficient and wasteful. Whereas joint households provide economies of scale—with parents and young people pooling resources to work the fields, buy food, collect firewood, wash clothing, and cook—after such a partition each couple must do everything on its own. This declaration of social independence thus has very real economic costs. But its consequences for personal prestige are equally real. From that point on, no one will fail to recognize that the newlyweds are economically self-reliant. Only at that point can they be invited to *slametan* festivals, *sayan* work parties, village council meetings, or any of the other events that mark one as mature. They have become adult villagers—a valued end in itself—and can expect the courtesies extended to all mature members of the community.

Family Types

The sense of autonomy evident in examples like this is one of the most basic and compelling concerns of village life. To be reduced to the status of a dependent lodger (*penumpang*; *wong mondok*) in another's home—a lowly but quite common position among the lowland poor (Jay 1969, 313; Breman 1983, 9)—is tolerated among highlanders only if absolutely necessary, and only among kin. Even then it should be for as brief a period as possible. Married lodgers among unrelated people are virtually unknown. Above all, even if one is obliged to live in someone else's house, one should do all one can to maintain a separate hearth. To be an adult is, quite simply, to have one's own hearth and not depend on others for domestic resources.

In the midslope region, young couples are less likely to go to such extremes as partitioning the kitchen to signal their independence. In part because of this region's lower standard of living, they pool their resources with their parents longer than is common in the upperslope region. In addition, among the Madurese minority in the midslope region (a minority not represented in significant numbers in the upperslope communities included in this study), one sees genuine extended families—parents with one or more of their married children and their spouses, themselves sometimes with children, all sharing a kitchen and domestic resources even after the first years of marriage. Of the 16 percent of "extended families" in the midslope region (see table 6.2), about half are of this type, while the remainder are temporary marital residences for newlyweds. By contrast, in upperslope villages, only about 1 percent of all families are long-term extended families, the remaining extended families (some 6 percent of all families) being temporary arrangements until the young couple gets on its feet.

In his study of the regency of Pasuruan in the 1920s, Egbert de Vries (1931, 1:50) also reported that extended families were rare among Javanese, while common among Madurese. Using such arrangements to share their resources, he noted, Madurese were able to establish a more flexible and varied family economy, with some people farming, others engaging in trade, and still others working as coolies or migrant laborers. In the nineteenth century, this arrangement played an important role in facilitating pioneer settlement by poor Madurese in remote jungle areas of the regency.

De Vries's insight still applies to the midslope Madurese population today. Virtually all long-term extended families in this region are among people of Madurese background. The pooling of domestic resources frees some family members to work in enterprises involving travel, economic risk, or intermittent returns, activities that a poor nuclear family would find difficult to sustain on its own. In the majority of cases, women

TABLE 6.2   Household Types, by Region

Household Type	Midslope (%)	Upperslope (%)
Simple nuclear family	52.7	54.4
Nuclear plus one or more parents	11.3	14.0
Nuclear plus unmarried sibling or cousin	6.7	4.4
Extended family (parents plus one or more married children)	16.0	7.6
Female-headed household (no husband)	7.3	11.2
Male-headed household (no wife)	.7	2.9
Other	5.3	5.5

SOURCE. 1980 and 1985 surveys of 492 households.

NOTE. Average no. of people per household: midslope, 5.1; upperslope, 4.2.

maintain the household and farm so as to free men to work elsewhere. Sometimes, however, one woman takes responsibility for domestic tasks so as to free another (usually an older woman whose children are grown) to engage in petty trade or the operation of a food stall (*warung*). Many of the women who sell food in upperslope communities, for example, are actually Madurese women from midslope households of this type. Legendary for their hard work and self-sacrificing thrift, they return to their families only once every week or two so as to reduce travel expenses and not forfeit income while the food stall is closed. The idea of such extended separation from one's husband and children strikes upland Javanese as utterly unthinkable. Some are just as poor as these Madurese women, and they are willing to endure great personal sacrifices for the welfare of their children. But they refuse to give up the security and comfort of a household of their own. They are similarly reluctant to form extended families. For them, an extended family comes about only under force of circumstances, as when a couple are too young or too old and infirm to maintain a nuclear-centered household of their own. To have a home of one's own, or failing that, an independent hearth, is for them too cherished an ideal. It is, after all, the minimum requirement for adult social status.

While an independent household is the preferred arrangement, this does not mean that everyone lives in nuclear families of husband, wife, and children alone. At any one time, only about 50 percent of all households are inhabited by simple nuclear families.[3] Nonetheless, the great

3. In her classic study of families in east-central Java, Hildred Geertz (1961, 32) found a similar emphasis on the nuclear family. About 75 percent of her rural sample (but only 58 percent of her town sample) were simple nuclear families. In his study of a

majority of households are, one way or another, built around a core nuclear family. The more varied range of household types shown in table 6.2 reflects the fact that, while the nuclear family remains the central unit in most households, its organization varies with the life-cycle of its members and the needs of close kin. Many households temporarily accommodate relatives unable to constitute a household of their own.

Even in the formation of non-nuclear households, the influence of the nuclear family ideal—and the broader concern with social autonomy that lies behind it—is powerfully apparent. Elderly parents, for example, often delay moving into the homes of their adult married children as long as is physically possible for fear of compromising their status or becoming a burden on their children. In some instances, even where they are no longer able to work in the fields and provide for their own meals, they continue to maintain a sleeping area apart from that of the married child with whom they are forced to eat. Such is the value placed on personal autonomy.[4] Similarly, an unmarried sibling or cousin will move in with a married kinsperson only when forced to do so, most commonly at the death of his or her parents. To have to do so *after* one has been married and established a home, however, is another matter entirely, since it implies that one is still a juvenile, unable to support oneself.

Male-headed households in which there is no wife are an only temporary exception to this nuclear-family emphasis. Inevitably, this type of household is a stopgap arrangement while the widowed or divorced man searches for another spouse. Only where the man is extremely old is he unlikely to remarry. It is widely understood that no man can live by himself without a wife or daughter to cook, clean, and take care of household finances. A widow or divorcée (*rondo*), by contrast, can always set up an independent household, and some—almost always poor—even live alone. A widower or divorced man, however, is considered incapable of

nearby community, Robert Jay (1969, 53) found a similar pattern: 60 percent of all families were simple nuclear ones (husband, wife, and children, if present); and more than three-quarters consisted of a simple nuclear family augmented by one or more parents of one spouse. Benjamin White's (1977) study of Kali Loro in rural Central Java found a somewhat more varied pattern. About 50 percent of all households were nuclear, 13 percent were one-generation households of various kinds, 19 percent involved three or more generations, and 18 percent were matrifocal. The comparative analysis of the Javanese family remains to be done.

4. In instances where they slept separately from where they ate, elders were grouped as living with their child for the purpose of table 6.2. The survey's criterion for membership in a household is where an individual cooks and eats, not where he or she sleeps. Other researchers in Java have used a similar criterion, one noting that cooking and eating together implies a "general though not necessarily total pooling of the day-to-day resources, work opportunities, and social obligations even though the individuals concerned may retain separate control of landholdings and other forms of wealth" (White 1977, 10).

doing even the most basic domestic tasks, since these are strongly associated with women's status. Indeed, one of the only legitimate excuses for
not inviting guests into one's home is the absence of one's wife. Guests
have to be received with drinks and sweets (and, if they stay longer,
cooked food), and everybody knows that men are utterly incompetent in
the kitchen. For all these reasons, a widowed or divorced man turns to a
daughter or (less ideally) a female sibling for temporary residence until
he can remarry. Although some very elderly men never remarry, most
widowers and divorcés do so in short order. Some people, especially
women, look askance at older men marrying young women, but the arrangement is not uncommon if the man is not poor. Besides young
women, of course, the available pool of widows far exceeds the number of
widowers; marriages between these two categories of people are not regarded unfavorably at all.

By contrast, widows and divorcées enjoy fewer options. If they are still
young, pretty, or affluent, they are likely to find husbands; there is no
stigma associated with a woman having been married before. But a
middle-aged widow or divorcée who is poor is likely to spend the rest of
her life alone or living with a sister or female cousin.

About 7–11 percent of households are female-headed. For an older
woman with children already grown, the lack of a husband may not be a
great inconvenience; indeed some older women rather pointedly commented to my wife that they were relieved to be without the tiresome
bother of a man. A widow can call upon grown-up children for help in
agricultural labor and still manage to maintain an independent household. As long as she is not obliged to move in with one of her children
(or, worse yet, a more distant kinswoman), this does not compromise her
adult status. Where death or divorce shatters a marriage and she is burdened with children and unable to remarry, however, a woman of limited
means may face more severe options. She will probably have no choice
but to move in with a sister or even her parents. Even doing this she may
be effectively relegated to the ranks of the village poor. In a divorce, husband and wife take back the property each brought to the marriage
(known as *asal barang*). Wealth obtained through mutual effort (*gono-gini*)
is divided evenly.[5]

Except where the children are adolescent or older, they follow the
mother in divorce, and she assumes primary responsibility for their care.

5. As is reported in other areas of Java (H. Geertz 1961, 51; Jay 1969, 64), two principles of division of joint property are recognized in Java. One provides equal shares for
husband and wife, while the other gives the husband twice as much as the wife. The latter principle is often identified with Islamic orthodoxy. Although Hildred Geertz reports that it is the more common principle in her area of east-central Java, here in
upland East Java, the Muslim type is the rarer.

If her husband dies without having children, his property returns to his parents or, in their absence, his siblings. Here, as in many areas of Java (Jay 1969, 173), property always remains in the parental line. Where there are children, however, the widow technically has usufruct rights to her husband's lands and other property, in a trust that remains effective until his children are old enough to make use of it themselves. As throughout Java (Jay 1969, 78), children retain their rights to inherit the property of both parents even after divorce, and even if the parent remarries and has additional children. Children from an earlier marriage do not have rights, however, in *gono-gini* property acquired through the joint effort of spouses in a later one.

Ideally, the mother should divide their father's property among the children even before they marry. In practice, however, particularly if the inheritance is small, the mother may postpone its transmission until a child marries. Given the importance of "own-household" labor in upland agriculture, particularly for the land-poor (see ch. 5), a woman in such a household will still be at a great disadvantage if she lacks the labor to maintain household and farm. Divorce or her husband's death relegates her to the margins of village society, threatened not only with lowered social status but with economic misery.

Given these facts, it is not surprising that here, as in north-central Java (Hart 1986, 112), female-headed households are overrepresented in the ranks of the village poor. Indeed, of all the family types listed in table 6.2, female-headed households are the only ones consistently consigned to the ranks of the poor. In the midslope region 89 percent of all female-headed households own less than half a hectare of land. The figure in the upperslope region is 72 percent. In terms of basic assets (calculated, roughly, as the estimated value of land, livestock, home, and household goods), female-headed households have just 40 percent of the assets of the average family. This radical deviation from the mean is seen with no other type of family. In an economy where productive resources are controlled by marriage partners, women out of marriage are at a real disadvantage.

Except in such instances of personal misfortune, household organization varies most generally according to the maturational rhythms of the nuclear family. In early marriage a couple reside with one set of their parents until they can establish a home of their own. In middle age one of their parents or a poor relative may come to reside in their home. In old age people are obliged to relinquish their cherished independence and become dependents of one of their adult children. This is the usual rhythm of the family, one that fluctuates with age and economic circumstances. Throughout, however, the pattern is continuously influenced by the concern to maintain an independent household, with the status autonomy it implies.

Divorce

Whatever its practical rewards and appeal as an ideal, a stable marriage is not always achieved, least of all in a first marriage. As in other parts of Java,[6] many young people divorce once, twice, or even several times before settling into a stable relationship. Traditionally, uplanders married young—at seventeen or eighteen years of age for boys and fourteen to sixteen for girls. For villagers it is an accepted and normal fact that adolescents are preoccupied with sex, and concern that a girl may become pregnant outside of wedlock is a motivation for early marriage.

Over the past generation, however, the average age at marriage has risen. Though sometimes quietly ignored, government regulations today require that young people be at least sixteen years of age at marriage. In addition, those from elite families have begun to continue their education beyond elementary school, postponing marriage even further (see below). Among the latter, it is no longer unusual for a man to defer marriage until his mid twenties, and a woman until age eighteen or nineteen. Upon completing their education, however, such privileged young people are still expected to turn immediately to the task of establishing a family.

The majority of divorces take place in the first year of marriage; few occur after three or four years. Differences of temperament and personality, as well as disagreements over family finances, are among the most common causes of discord. Given the pattern of uxorilocal residence, divorce generally involves the groom's sudden and often unannounced departure from his wife's parents' home. Usually it is only later formalized with village officials. Midslope Muslims are familiar with the formal Islamic regulations for divorce. These make it easier for men to initiate the procedure through the simple pronunciation of the *talak* oath, "I repudiate thee" (see Peletz 1988, 251). In practice, however, most midslope Muslims follow the same custom as upperslope Hindus, where divorce is initiated by the simple act of leaving one's partner.

Since there is only the most perfunctory exchange of gifts prior to marriage (Hefner 1985, 149) and property brought to the bond is taken back at its dissolution, the economic consequences of a youthful divorce need not be severe. Divorce is neither difficult nor strongly stigmatized—as long, that is, as there are no children from the union. In recent years, however, the government's Office of Religious Affairs has tightened its rules, demanding that village chiefs and religious officials accede less

6. Hildred Geertz (1961, 69) reports that almost half of all marriages end in divorce. In her study of an area of southwestern Central Java, however, Jennifer Alexander (1987, 20) comments that the rate in her more staunchly Islamic region is significantly lower. The growing influence of Islam in nearby Malaysia is also reported to have played a role in lowering divorce rates there (Peletz 1988, 251).

readily to requests for divorce. The fee for registering divorce has gone up, from (again using 1985 rupiah) Rp 1,500 to Rp 6,000 (U.S. $5.45). In addition, it is now not uncommon for officials to require a waiting period or a meeting of family elders before acceding to the request of the couple. These initiatives appear to be having some impact on popular attitudes, and, though I lack statistical evidence, villagers insist that the incidence of divorce has gone down.

Nonetheless, the overall divorce rate is still high. In the midslope region, 31.1 percent of all people have divorced at least once, and the figure in the upperslope region is 38.9 percent. By their early thirties, most people have settled into a stable relationship. The arrival of a child, in particular, serves to cement their tie. As a result of this late-life stabilization, the percentage of people of forty-two or older who have divorced climbs only slightly above the figure for the population as a whole, to 42.9 percent in the midslope region and 41.1 percent in the upperslope area. Divorces after this age are uncommon.

As in so many spheres of social life, however, there is a class dimension to divorce. As in nearby Malaysia (Peletz 1988, 255), the incidence of divorce is notably higher among the poor than it is among the wealthy. Among people of forty-two or older and owning less than one hectare of land, for example, 47.2 percent of those in the upperslope region and 43.2 percent in the midslope have been divorced at least once. Among more affluent villagers owning two or more hectares of land, by contrast, the figures are 34.3 and 28.6 percent respectively. While the difference is not astounding, it does reflect the fact that, as villagers themselves acknowledge, a sound economic footing is essential for the stability of a marriage. Money is at the heart of many arguments, and these are particularly common among the poor. Virtually all of the spousal disputes I overheard concerned money, inevitably related to the husband's profligate spending of vital family funds. Gambling in illegal betting rings—the most notorious of which are operated by Chinese merchants in market centers below the highlands—is often the cause of the most extreme cases of financial hardship.

Another social influence is at work in these statistics on divorce as well. Though, by comparison with lowland society, few marriages are arranged, and even those that are must receive the approval of the boy and girl (Hefner 1985, 148), children from high-status families do tend to marry more strategically than the poor. The latter choose their mates on their own, usually on the basis of strong personal attraction. For them, then, marriage is primarily an affair between individuals, and only secondarily a matter of interfamilial alliance. Wealthier young people, by contrast, are more attentive to the concerns of status, and often heed the counsel of their elders concerning marital prospects. In such instances marriage reinforces lines of alliance between village families, even though it does not involve the elaborate exchange of goods seen in marriages in other parts of Indonesia or Malaysia. The social effect is nonetheless similar: interfamily ties add another stabilizing ingredient to the marriage, reducing the incidence of divorce.

The influence of class and status on marriage is a subtle one, of course, but is wholly in line with villagers' attitudes toward romance and marriage. Although real personal love may develop, and, even in love's absence a sense of intimacy and respect is considered essential, villagers display a down-to-earth realism about the marital bond. The relationship is not regarded as a strongly contractual bond, least of all between families. Instead, it is viewed in largely instrumental terms, as a means to a valued social end. It sets an individual on the road to social independence and the adult status that only a household and family can bring.

Fertility, Infant Mortality, and Adoption

The impact of class on household welfare is perhaps no more revealingly apparent than in childbearing. Here, as in other domains of social life, the wealthy fare considerably better than their poor counterparts. Data on births and child mortality reveal this clearly: large landholders have significantly more children than their poor counterparts (table 6.3). The correlation is even more striking when one controls for age by looking at births and deaths in households where the woman is at least fifty, and thus effectively past her childbearing years (table 6.4). Although the exact correlation varies somewhat between the two mountain regions, the general trend is the same. Wealthy women have more surviving children than their poor counterparts.

Given the size of the sample (492 households) and the lack of more detailed demographic information, the data in tables 6.3 and 6.4 must be regarded as somewhat tentative. The correlation between wealth and family size to which they point has, however, been noted by demographic researchers in other parts of Java (Hull and Hull 1976). The relationship is particularly striking in the midslope region, where wealthy landowners have much larger families than the rest of the population, in part by virtue of lower infant mortality (they lose only one infant per woman on average, or less than half the figure for the midslope population as a whole). Here, in short, is dramatic evidence of the hidden injuries of class.

The picture is more complicated in the upperslope region. There the land-wealthy also tend to have larger families than their poor neighbors, but the total number of surviving children is smaller than in the midslope region. Despite the very large number of births (8.3 per woman among landowners controlling more than two hectares of land versus 6.6

[handwritten margin notes: "– No sample size / small size – no Stat. significance" (top left); "Trend in mortality / No trend in fertility" (top right)]

TABLE 6.3 Infant Survival and Mortality,
by Region and Size of Holding

	No Land	.01–.19	.20–.49	.50–.99	1–1.99	2–3.50	>3.50	All House-holds
Landholding (ha)								
Midslope								
No. of surviving children	3.1	3.2	3.1	3.4	3.0	5.4	4.8	3.4
No. of deceased children	1.4	1.3	1.1	1.3	1.4	.7	.5	1.3
[handwritten row]	4.5	4.5	4.2	4.7	4.4	6.1		
Mean age, female head of household	43.7	42.6	38.8	39.3	44.6	50.4	48.8	41.5
Total no. of household residents	4.3	4.5	5.0	5.3	5.2	7.0	5.2	5.1
Upperslope								
No. of surviving children	2.6	3.6	1.8	2.2	2.2	3.1	3.5	2.4
No. of deceased children	2.2	2.4	1.6	1.8	2.0	3.0	2.6	2.1
Mean age, female head of household	54.2	47.4	38.6	35.5	35.6	36.3	41.2	37.3
Total no. of household residents	1.4	3.9	3.3	4.0	4.2	5.2	5.5	4.2

[handwritten margin notes at right: "No clear directionality"]

SOURCE. 1980 and 1985 surveys of 492 households.

NOTE. "Surviving children" only includes children still living or living until teen years; miscarriages before term are not included among "born but deceased."

for the same group in the midslope region), these upperslope women still have fewer surviving children than their counterparts in the midslope region: 4.3 versus 5.6 per woman in the midslope region.

In general, in fact, this regional contrast applies across classes. Infant mortality is higher for almost all upperslope economic groups than it is for the corresponding midslope ones. While women over fifty had had similar numbers of children (6.5 midslope, 6.1 upperslope), significantly more survived in the midslope region: 4.4 per woman, as opposed to 3.3 in the upperslope area. In infant mortality, in other words, region appears to be as significant as wealth and class. "Region" of course refers to

TABLE 6.4　Infant Survival and Mortality, Where Female Head of Household ≥ 50 Years of Age, by Region and Size of Holding

	No Land	.01–.19	.20–.49	.50–.99	1–1.99	2–3.50	>3.50	All House- holds
				Landholding (ha)				
Midslope								
Surviving	1.0	3.9	4.5	4.8	3.1	6.2	5.0	4.4
Deceased	2.8	2.5	1.8	2.8	2.1	1.0	1.0	2.1
Total births	3.8	6.4	6.3	7.6	5.2	7.2	6.0	6.5
Upperslope								
Surviving	2.0	3.5	2.4	3.1	3.9	3.5	5.4	3.3
Deceased	3.7	4.0	2.0	2.1	2.9	3.0	5.6	2.8
Total births	5.7	7.5	4.4	5.2	6.8	6.5	11.0	6.1

SOURCE. 1980 and 1985 surveys of 492 households.

a complex of proximate variables, including the upperslope area's harsher climate, less varied (and protein-poor) maize-meal diet, lack of vehicle roads, and, until the late 1970s, almost total absence of medical facilities. Health officials who work in the upperslope region have long complained of the high incidence of infant mortality there, and these statistics appear to bear them out.

Nonetheless, in both regions large landholders fare better in matters of infant birth and death than do their land-poor counterparts. They have more births and more children who survive than the poor. The consequences of class are strikingly apparent.

A similar class influence is seen, interestingly, in adoption. Following a pattern seen in much of Micronesia, Polynesia, and insular Southeast Asia (Carroll 1970; Levy 1973, 479), adoption (*anak angkat; pupon*) is quite common in Java (H. Geertz 1961, 36). In the Tengger highlands, fully 12 percent of all households have adopted one or more children. Like so much else, however, adoption is subtly influenced by class. Not only do large landholders have more children, but they are also more likely to adopt children.

The practice and meaning of adoption among Javanese, however, are quite different from in the West. Adoption by relatives carries little social stigma; it is rarely a legally arranged relationship; and it is often not permanent. In the highlands almost all adoption is between close kin. The most common relationship is between elder and younger sisters; less commonly, it may be between parents and their married children (adoption of a grandchild). In the former instance, the adoption invariably occurs because one of the two sisters is childless. In the latter case, elderly parents, living alone, may seek the companionship of a grandchild now that all of their own children have left to establish homes of their own. In both instances the recipient family takes the initiative in requesting the adoption, often (especially in the case of a childless couple) approaching the pregnant relative sometime prior to the birth. As several mothers confided with some sadness, there is little a pregnant woman can do in such circumstances other than assent to the wishes of the relative. To risk sundering one's tie to a sister or a parent is simply too large a price to pay for keeping the child. Still, as Robert Levy (1973, 474–78) reports of Tahiti (where about 25 percent of all children are adopted), one sees evidence of resentment and pain on the part of parents obliged to give up a child.

Only in those few instances where a child's parents die is adoption arranged differently. Even in those cases, however, the most likely candidates to adopt the child are still the married siblings of the parents (especially sisters) or its grandparents. While adoption between unrelated people does occur in rural Java (Jay 1969, 72; H. Geertz 1961, 39), it is rare in this mountain area. Extrafamilial adoption is stigmatized, and strongly so. Villagers regard it as unfair to the child (which they do not think to be the case with adoption itself) inasmuch as non-kin cannot be counted on to treat the child as they would an adopted junior kinsperson.

Another difference between adoption in Java and in the West is that the practice does not involve the natural parents' renunciation of all rights or responsibilities toward the child. Although the child is encouraged to call its adopted parents "father" (*bapak*) and "mother" (*mak; mbok*), the natural parents are not forbidden to see the child. While the child is young, they do so only intermittently, and usually only in the context of visiting the adopting sibling or parent. As the child grows, however, it learns of its natural parents and may take to regularly visiting them, especially if there are other children with whom it can play. Though the child may receive an inheritance from its adopted parents, it has no formal right to one. By contrast, it fully retains its rights to inherit a share of the estate of its natural parents. Not surprisingly then, as the child grows older, these residual bonds may become stronger. In early adolescence, for example, it is not uncommon for an adopted child to drift back to the home of its natural parents to play with siblings or even take up residence. In such instances, the adopted parents are expected to defer to the wishes of the child and let it choose where to live.

This flexibility is related to the fact that adoption usually links close kin and is as much a relationship between adults as it is between adults

TABLE 6.5   Percentage of People Adopting Children, by Region
and Size of Holding

	Landholding (ha)						
	No Land	.01–.19	.20–.49	.50–.99	1–1.99	2–3.50	>3.50	All House-holds
Midslope	10.1	10.7	3.9	13.9	17.6	22.2	33.3	12.0
Upperslope	0	0	12.3	10.2	11.5	20.0	31.8	13.7

SOURCE. 1980 and 1985 surveys of 492 households.

and child. As Levy (1973, 482) notes of Tahiti, the attitudes seen in adoption also bear testimony to the cultural view that "biological parentage does not imply a fixed commitment." Though the quality of commitment for these Javanese is not defined biologically, it does not appear to be as variable as Levy reports among Tahitians. Javanese villagers, especially those of Javanist persuasion, stress that parents provide the child's bone (from the father) and blood (from the mother); they are of one substance and one descent (*turunan*). In the Javanist view of the world, biology is spiritual, not just material. The tie of blood and bone establishes a relationship that can never be severed, even in adoption. Adopted children, therefore, remember the souls of their natural parents just as other children do.

Another social fact qualifies the arrangement's flexibility here in upland Java. Whatever the social relations between biological and adopted parents, it is considered improper for a child to be adopted into a family poorer than that of its birth. Except where both natural parents die, adopted children move up the social and economic ladder—to elder kin and/or to people of equal or higher economic standing. Statistics on the incidence of adoption cannot show this directly. They do show, however, that the wealthy adopt children more frequently than their land-poor counterparts (see table 6.5).

What is one to make, finally, of the differential reproductive abilities of wealthier households? The obvious conclusion is that, in an agrarian economy where the household is both the means and a valued end of economic life, well-endowed couples are better able to do whatever is necessary to create a stable and prosperous household. Class leaves a visible imprint on this most important of achievements.

The task of raising children, of course, involves more than their physical survival or material inheritance. It also involves the transmission of cultural skills. In earlier years, when almost all highlanders engaged in agriculture, the bulk of this practical socialization was carried out in the family. Today, however, more and more of this training occurs outside the family, in schools and nonfarm enterprises.

While one might expect that the displacement of socialization out of the family would reduce the influence of wealth on social achievement, its influence has, if anything, increased. Education, after all, is expensive, and the control of productive wealth is often a precondition for long-term schooling. Though its history is complex, education is a key element in the new economic culture taking shape in this upland region. It reflects clearly the tension between an older, village-focused economy and a new economic culture oriented to the moral and material markers of larger Indonesia.

EDUCATION AND STRATIFICATION

The first schools in the mountain subdistricts were constructed in the villages of Tosari and Puspo in 1914, just after the completion of the road linking midslope Puspo to upperslope Tosari. (Unlike the nearby lowlands, the highlands had no *pesantren* Muslim religious schools prior to this time.) Like most rural schools during this period, these were three-year "people's schools" (*sekolah rakyat*), designed to provide basic instruction in reading (Javanese), writing, and arithmetic. Education was neither compulsory nor free, and most of the twenty or so students who enrolled in each school during its first year were the sons of village officials. In theory parents who hoped their children might receive education beyond the third grade could apply for admission to expensive Dutch-language schools in the urban lowlands. Few, however, tried to do so. During the entire colonial period, only three men from the mountain subdistricts left the region to study in these elite primary schools.

Despite their limited enrollment, schools introduced new social styles into upland villages. The teachers were lowland Javanese, and the language of instruction was not upland dialect, but a standard Javanese that few in the mountains had fully mastered. In the upperslope region, villagers spoke a nonstandard dialect of Javanese, characterized by pronouns, pronunciation, verb markers, and a lexicon different from the standard (Smith-Hefner 1983, 1989). In the midslope region, immigrant influence had been greater, and language there combined elements of both the upperslope Tengger dialect and standard "low" Javanese (*ngoko*). By comparison with lowland villages, however, use of the status-differentiating high Javanese known as *kromo*—employed in the standard to address those of higher status and unfamiliar people—was uncommon in both areas, except in speech with outsiders (Smith-Hefner 1989).

The teachers who came to work in the region were unfamiliar with the local dialect. In their eyes, moreover, their elevated role required that they be addressed in formal high Javanese. Their insistence on the use of *kromo* inside and outside the classroom introduced the children of the elite to the more status-sensitive standard. In conjunction with the growing influence of wealthy immigrants (who rose to prominence about this same time), the linguistic innovation soon spread to other members of the midslope elite. In several communities in the prewar period, for example, village chiefs launched campaigns to rid local speech of dialect features traditionally associated with mountain society (Hefner 1985, 244; Smith-Hefner 1989). The schools were a major influence in this process of linguistic resocialization.

Eventually, the Puspo and Tosari schools grew to include about sixty students each. A smaller school was opened in Ngadiwono in 1927, and still another in Mororejo in 1937. In a region where the total population was over 17,000 in 1927, however, only a small percentage of school-age children ever attended school.

Mass education grew significantly with Indonesian independence after 1949, when regency officials instructed villages to construct schools and made attendance mandatory for all children. During the first years of the republic, however, qualified personnel were in short supply. Upland schools were staffed by local men who had had only a few years' schooling and, after independence, a quick course in teaching methods. By the late 1950s, however, upgrading programs had replaced these teachers with others who had undergone at least two years of high school. As in colonial times, most of the new staff were from the lowlands, and they again served as agents for the introduction of lowland social styles.

Nonetheless, throughout most of this period, few students completed more than a few years of school. Schooling beyond the sixth grade was especially difficult, because there was no middle school in either of the mountain subdistricts. To continue their education, therefore, students had to attend classes in the lowlands. Most parents could not afford this expense. Among the few who could, moreover, there was reluctance to send loved-ones off to live in the lowlands. For upperslope Hindus in particular, sending one's children to the lowlands was tantamount to encouraging their conversion to Islam. In addition, there were virtually no jobs in upland villages that required high levels of education. Youths who wished to put their education to good use were thus obliged to leave their natal village permanently. This was not a course most parents wished to encourage. Besides, villagers said, the income from a good-sized farm was better than that of a lower-level government official—and a good deal more secure in times of rampant inflation. For a rural elite still solidly attuned to local ways, therefore, there was no advantage to encouraging higher levels of education.

All this changed in the 1970s, as members of the village elite came to orient themselves more and more to the values and life-styles of larger Indonesia. The attitudinal change also reflected improvements in the infrastructure of upland education. The government constructed two middle schools (SMP) in the mountain subdistricts in 1978-79, one in midslope Puspo and another in upperslope Wonokitri. Several new elementary schools were constructed as well, and the staffs of existing schools expanded. In addition to these government initiatives, an Indonesian evangelical missionary opened a small Christian junior high school in Tosari in 1967; in the 1970s this was expanded to become the highlands' first four-year high school. A handful of its students eventually went on to college. Their achievement reflected broader changes in popular attitudes, especially among the upland elite. Whereas none had wished to see their children leave the village a few years earlier, many prominent families now encouraged their children to continue their education and seek jobs outside the region. For the first time, having a relative in business or government in the lowlands became an important marker of prestige. One more barrier between highland society and the lowlands had fallen.

These are recent developments, and, even by Javanese standards, mean educational achievement among the population as a whole remains low. In the more conservative upperslope region, the average male and female heads-of-household have spent only 3.4 and 2.7 years in school respectively. Among children who have more recently completed their education, the figures are only slightly higher, at 4.9 years for boys and 4.2 for girls (see table 6.6). This is a noticeable improvement over the parental generation, but is still very low, especially in light of the fact that people who receive less than two years' education are effectively illiterate. Even possessing three or four years of education does not guarantee lasting literacy.

Comparable figures for parents in the midslope region were barely higher than those in upperslope villages, at 4.1 years for men and 2.7 for women. Among the younger generation here, however, the force of changing aspirations is powerfully apparent. The average boy now spends 6.4 years in school, and the average girl 6.1 (table 6.6). Not surprisingly, this achievement varies significantly by economic class. Averaging just four years' attendance, most poor children are unable to stay in school long enough to become enduringly literate. In wealthy families, by contrast, the average child spends two to three times this number of years in school. A significant number go on to high school and college. In education, in other words, the differential consequences of class are becoming increasingly apparent. All evidence indicates that this variation in educational achievement is likely to become greater (table 6.6).

TABLE 6.6 Years Spent in School, by Region, Gender, and Size of Holding

				Landholding (ha)				
	No Land	.01–.19	.20–.49	.50–.99	1–1.99	2–3.50	>3.50	All House-holds
Midslope								
Male head	1.7	4.0	3.9	3.8	4.9	5.0	7.2	4.1
Female head	.7	2.8	2.6	2.3	3.4	4.1	2.3	2.7
Male child	4.0	4.7	5.9	6.0	8.1	8.0	11.0	6.4
Female child	4.0	5.1	6.1	5.2	7.3	6.8	11.0	6.1
Upperslope								
Male head	.6	1.0	3.1	3.0	3.5	3.9	4.1	3.4
Female head	.8	3.0	1.6	2.5	3.1	3.6	3.6	2.7
Male child	4.0	3.6	4.1	4.6	5.3	5.1	5.9	4.9
Female child	1.7	3.4	3.1	3.8	5.1	4.8	5.3	4.2

SOURCE. 1980 and 1985 surveys of 492 households.

The data on education also illustrate that educational achievement varies little by gender. Indeed, I noticed no variation on this point even according to the religious preferences of the parents; good Muslims are just as interested in seeing their daughters go to school as their sons. For all practical purposes, boys and girls today spend the same amount of time in school, unlike the male-biased pattern seen in the parental generation.

In sum, the most notable difference in educational achievement is not between the sexes but between different class groupings. More and more children of the elite see school as an avenue for personal advancement, providing access to good-paying jobs outside the village. The change reflects not only a practical adjustment to employment opportunities, but broader shifts in upland concepts of identity and distinction.

EMPLOYMENT OUTSIDE THE VILLAGE

The overall trend in employment today is much as it is in education. Growing numbers of better-situated young people look to more lucrative and prestigious opportunities outside the village. As in so many other spheres, the trend is especially strong in the midslope region, but it is slowly growing in the more conservative upperslope region as well.

Labor migration out of upland villages, of course, is not new. Since the 1950s (and even the 1920s in a few instances) the midslope poor have engaged in seasonal migration to supplement their modest agricultural in-

TABLE 6.7   Percentage of People Who Have Worked Outside the
             Village, by Region and Size of Holding

	Landholding (ha)							
	No Land	.01–.19	.20–.49	.50–.99	1–1.99	2–3.50	>3.50	All House-holds
Midslope								
Male head	33.3	15.4	8.2	11.1	11.8	0	0	10.3
Female head	0	10.7	9.8	5.6	12.5	0	0	8.1
Any child	40.0	65.0	42.9	30.4	30.8	50.0	50.0	42.9
Upperslope								
Male head	0	0	18.4	11.8	6.0	1.7	0	8.2
Female head	0	0	5.5	1.2	0	0	0	1.5
Any child	25.0	16.7	18.6	2.0	13.0	2.3	15.8	9.5

SOURCE. 1980 and 1985 surveys of 492 households.

comes, trudging off to the highlands in search of agricultural employment. What is new today is that affluent children have joined the poor in this outward exodus. They seek a different kind of work than do the poor, of course, in enterprises like transportation, trade (especially high-capital, long-distance trade), store operation, government cooperatives, schools, and best of all, regency or subdistrict government. In the 1950s and 1960s almost no uplanders had jobs of this sort. Today growing numbers do, and their aspirations are reshaping upland society (see table 6.7).

As the figures in table 6.7 show, this outward economic movement is especially common among young people in the midslope highlands. The trend here, one should note, is generally consistent with reports from other parts of Java. The 1970s and 1980s have witnessed a diversification of employment, with rich and poor moving out of agriculture into non-farm enterprises (White and Wiradi 1989). Unlike the situation here in the Tengger highlands, however, in the wet-rice lowlands the poor have been forced out of agriculture into even less remunerative petty trade and wage labor. The affluent, meanwhile, have been enticed into endeavors even more lucrative than farming (White and Wiradi 1989, 296). In the Tengger highlands, by contrast, the poor continue to secure agricultural employment, largely as a result of expanding labor demand in vegetable-growing regions. It is only children of the affluent who are moving out of agriculture entirely in large numbers.

The pattern seen in the midslope area is no doubt more representative of upland regions in other parts of East Java than is the pattern seen in the Hindu region, where commercial agriculture has proved so lucrative that it retains the interest of the affluent and reduces the need of the poor to look outside the village for employment. The Hindu faith of the upperslope population also dampens interest in external migration. Many people who migrate out of the region end by giving up their religion, a fact that makes some people wary of sending their children off to the lowlands.

If the experience of the midslope population is any indication, however, the incidence of migration among the affluent young will increase even in this Hindu region. The recent opening of upland villages has brought about a kind of status inflation. Achievements and goods that previously had great luster look dimly parochial today. Elite villagers in particular feel these pressures to conform to the styles and investments of greater Java. They seek to signal their participation in a more national community. Their aspirations are a powerful force for the transformation of upland society.

CONSUMPTION COMMUNITIES

Few developments in the Tengger highlands have been more striking, or more symptomatic of the changing spirit of the age, than recent shifts in conspicuous consumption. Few are more revealing of the complex linkages between economic life and social identity. None, in particular, better reveals the truth that at the heart of economic life there is always a social community, characterized by its own structure of inclusion and exclusion, "a sense of shared identity, and commitment to values, a sense that 'We are members of one another'" (Etzioni 1988, 5).

Nineteenth-century visitors to the Tengger highlands regularly commented on the remarkable lack of differentiation among villagers in matters of food, dress, and housing (see Domis 1832, 331; van Lerwerden 1844). People of all social standings, they said, ate the same simple fare of maize meal, potatoes, cabbage, and salted fish. Administrators complained that even high-status villagers dressed themselves in the simplest of clothes and wore them until they were in tatters. One elderly gentleman who had worked as a forestry officer in the village of Wonokitri in the 1920s, with whom I spoke in 1985, recalled his first impression of upperslope fashions:

> People in those villages weren't yet modern [*moderen.*] Even if they had lots of land or some gold back in their homes they wore the same clothes as other people; you couldn't tell rich from poor. Everyone spoke in the same way to everyone else too, no matter what their position. Children talked to their parents and even to the village chief using ordinary *ngoko*. No one bent down and bowed before others. But it wasn't that people

were impolite. That's the difference with the lowlands [*ngare*]. It was more polite not to talk in high language, and better to dress simple so as not to draw attention to yourself. It wasn't like today. People didn't know that you're supposed to dress to show yourself off; they didn't know what it meant to be modern.

Dutchmen and Javanese alike were fascinated by this way of life, so contrary to the hierarchical etiquette of aristocratic Java. For some, the directness of speech and the simplicity of dress were indices of "childlike simplicity" (van Lerwerden 1844, 68) and high virtue. "Lucky residents of Tinger! How little do you know the privilege you enjoy" (Domis 1830, 330). For others, however, this unpretentious peasant culture was "tattered and unmannered" (Bodemeijer 1901, 314). One might be "sympathetic with their frankness and simplicity, and their lack of faults, but they are nonetheless in large measure dirty and undeveloped, and their religion is clearly beneath that of Muslim learning" (326–27). Highland culture must give way to that of the Muslim lowlands, one Dutch *controleur* concluded, because in all cultural development "the weaker must...dissolve into the stronger" (von Freijburg 1901, 334). Late-nineteenth-century Social Darwinism was creeping into European perceptions of a changing East Java.

These were, of course, stereotyped characterizations of upland society. Behind these simplistic observations, one caught occasional glimpses of the fading contours of a more differentiated social order, with hierarchies unrecognized because cast in unfamiliar molds. The earliest visitors to the area, for example, noted that the village chief (*petinggi*) wielded such extraordinary influence that "all submit to him" (Domis 1832, 329). Similarly, although "undistinguished in dress," the non-Islamic priests of the upperslope region were said to be wealthier than their neighbors. They were the ones most likely, for example, to have two wives (Kreemer 1885, 347). Both roles were intimately related to this region's religious tradition, and both were restricted to people who could claim a relationship of descent (*tis; titisan*) through maternal or paternal relatives back to some prior holder of the office (Hefner 1985, 82). Hence while villages were not divided into *gogol* landholding classes as in the wet-rice lowlands, status distinctions did exist, and they played an important role in village religion and government. The sacralized positions of chief and priest, in particular, were the shattered remnants of a broader system of status hierarchy dating back to pre-Islamic times (Hefner 1985, 270).

The migration of lowlanders into the highlands complicated these social arrangements. Most of the immigrants were Muslims. Though the variant of Islam they professed shared much with upperslope Tengger, by the beginning of the twentieth century there were pockets of Muslim orthodoxy where people refused to abide by mountain customs. Led by the immigrant merchant-farmers who rose to prominence in the early 1900s, these highlanders maintained economic and cultural ties with lowland society. Ultimately, as we have seen, they helped to introduce new forms of labor organization and more exclusive patterns of investment and consumption.

For most of the mountain population, however, consumption remained geared to a less conspicuously differentiated village tradition. Despite notable differences in income, its display in everyday costume or habit was considered improper. "You were ashamed to make others feel as if they had less than you," one elder uplander explained. "Even if you were a 'big man' [*wong gedhe*] and were really wealthy, you still looked like a farmer and a mountain person like everyone else."

Ritual Giving and Festivity

There was, however, one exception to this undifferentiating pattern: the *slametan* or ritual festival. In a region where, until Indonesian independence, there were strong pressures against marked differentiation in dress, food, furniture, and housing, the ritual festival was the one arena in which conspicuous consumption was not only tolerated but enjoined. The exception was in part related to the fact that festivals were identified with popular religion. In giving food and worship to guardian spirits, these events could be justified as bringing benefit to the village as a whole. By inviting all neighbors to these events, the festivals also expressed the much-valued themes of inexclusivity and cooperative harmony (*rukun*).

The appeal of these consumption events, however, was also related to the way in which they were embedded in village life.[7] Though simple rituals can occur for a number of reasons (Hefner 1985), *slametans* with full entertainment and feasting are held on only a limited number of occasions. In the midslope region, these include circumcisions, weddings, and rites to bless a newborn child (*among-among*). Smaller celebrations might also be held to bless the mother and child in her seventh month of pregnancy, in a rite known as the *mitoni*. In the upperslope region, the list of occasions also includes ceremonies to bless the souls of recently deceased family members, an especially lavish rite known as the *entas-entas* (Hefner 1985, 163–88). The midslope ceremony of similar intent (known as the *nyewu* or, more rarely, *entas-entas*) might include meal taking, but it is usually celebrated without drinking or entertainment.

---

7. Since my concern in the present book is with the economic dimensions of household festivals, I do not here discuss festivals sponsored by the village as a whole. I have described the organization and significance of these elsewhere (Hefner 1985).

As these examples show, festivities are most commonly held during moments of passage in the life-cycle of a family. In part, of course, the festivals' appeal lies in just this fact, that they so effectively communicate basic changes in the status of a married couple. The cycle begins with the blessing of an infant in the womb. It culminates in the wedding of one's own child and, eventually, the blessing of one's dead parents and grand-parents (Hefner 1985). In so doing, ritual consumption maps out the life-cycle, announcing and celebrating each change of life.

Whatever their general intent, however, the meaning of these festivals is anything but general and undifferentiated. The statuses they celebrate are conventional, but the prestige they convey is not. People of high social standing take great pains to ensure that their festivals are the largest and most lavish of all. Thus, while the rite for a newborn child proudly celebrates an event valued by all couples, the fact that it does so to differing degrees of elaboration means that it also makes a more particular, positional statement about its sponsors' standing in the village. Here, then, is an arena in which the mundane sameness of everyday life gives way to a blatant concern for prestige.

Historically, of course, the degree of festival elaboration has varied with general economic prosperity. During hard times, as between 1931 and 1950, and again in the early 1960s, festivities were scaled back and expenses reduced. During times of economic expansion, as during the 1920s, the mid 1950s, and the 1970s, the average cost of a festival increased. In the late 1970s, as farm income grew with the new agriculture, the real cost of the average festival skyrocketed to five or six times what it had been in the late 1960s. The largest festivals involved thousands of guests, and cost three to four thousand dollars each (Hefner 1985, 219; Hefner 1983b)—significantly more than the average family's annual income. Prestigious events were incomplete without the slaughter of several cattle, generators for light and taped music, and the gay presence of *tayuban* dancers (Hefner 1987c) and *ludruk* theater troupes (Peacock 1968) from the urban lowlands.

Although these events were sponsored by individual households, the manner of their financing vividly underscores the fact that here, as in all societies, private preference is shaped in the organization of social life. The capital for festivals was accumulated through a network of investment and exchange known as *sumbangan* ("contributions"), whose mediating role in social life was every bit as important for Tengger highlanders as the legendary *kula* among Melanesian Trobrianders (Malinowski 1922).

Sumbangan are donations of goods and cash given by neighbors and kin to the sponsors of a ritual festival. The sponsors may request these gifts directly, or the donor may provide them without prior solicitation. Once given, however, their value must be remembered precisely; often it is recorded in a book (Hefner 1985, 223). The reason this is so important is that at a later date each gift must be repaid with something of equivalent or greater value. Equally important, the repayment can be made only when the initial donor himself or herself sponsors a ritual festival. Once placed in the *sumbangan* exchange network, in other words, wealth remains locked in a cycle of exchange with no possible use other than sponsorship of more festivals. The exchange system, a sort of collective savings and loan association, thus squeezes investment and consumption into a distinctive social mold.

The system is made all the more compulsory by the fact that all adults with any claim to social standing are obliged to make contributions to their kindred, neighbors, and acquaintances. Once given, each gift engenders another, creating a cycle of exchange that ends only in old age or, more rarely, with the severing of a social tie. Most individuals begin to establish these gift relationships just prior to or after marriage, anticipating the eventual birth of their own children and the need for ritual capital of their own. Giving *sumbangan* without prior solicitation enhances one's reputation in the village for being generous and sociable. In addition, even though the capital provided in such exchange cannot be invested in nonritual events, the goodwill that results is of broader benefit, reinforcing strategic ties. Not to exchange gifts, by contrast, invites severe censure, and condemns a person to social marginality.

As table 6.8 shows, most villagers today still have a large network of exchange partners. The figures also reveal that the burden of establishing partnerships falls most heavily upon people of higher economic class. Because of the greater frequency of requests, and their own interest in establishing a broad network of *sumbangan* partners (both as an index of rank and a means to sponsor large festivals in the future), wealthier villagers have more partners than the poor. They also give larger contributions to these partners, investing enormous sums of money in this socially mandated exchange.

In the midslope region, the average ritual contribution is only one-third to one-fourth the value of those given on average in the upperslope region. Hence, although the figures in table 6.8 show that midslope people have more partners, they nonetheless have less money invested in the exchange network. In 1980, for example, wealthy upperslope farmers had on average about Rp 455,000 (roughly U.S. $728, in 1980 rupiah) invested in the network. Even though they had more partners, the midslope wealthy had an average of only Rp 165,000 outstanding in theirs. By the standards of rural Java, one should emphasize, even this latter figure is substantial.

The picture of consumption that emerges from these data is striking. No area of social life rivaled ritual festivity in the volume of capital it con-

TABLE 6.8 Number of Ritual Exchange Partners,
by Region and Size of Holding

	No Land	.01–.19	.20–.49	.50–.99	1–1.99	2–3.50	>3.50	All House-holds
		Landholding (ha)						
Midslope	16.4	24.9	26.4	30.5	34.6	42.4	66.3	30.0
Upperslope	10.3	11.7	12.0	17.1	19.3	36.2	40.5	21.3

SOURCE. 1980 and 1985 surveys of 492 households.

sumed. Through it, economic investment was linked to religion and social structure, serving to reproduce ritual institutions integral to an upland way of life. The example reminds us again that needs are shaped, not in the solipsistic introspection of an anonymous *homo economicus*, but in community, with patterns of power and hierarchy, and "socially organized forms of satisfaction" (Leiss 1976, 9).

Consumption Communities in Economic Change

In a changing social context, of course, this focus on local relations to the exclusion of other utilities may present a problem. Religious festivals create prestige and goodwill well enough. But in an open economy, where previous restrictions on consumption have been weakened, they may suddenly find themselves competing with other utilities for scarce capital. They run the risk of losing their allure if and when villagers become less concerned with—and less dependent on—the good regard of their neighbors. Whatever their benefits for one's local prestige, after all, festival contributions do not provide capital for general investment. Nor is their disposition left to the discretion of their owner. In addition, the prestige they create does not carry much weight in outside markets. In this sense, to call prestige a form of "symbolic capital" (Bourdieu 1977, 177) is misleading if, as the term suggests, it implies that the symbolic is directly translatable to the economic. As the literature on fiesta systems in Latin America shows so well (Cancian 1965; Smith 1977), this is often not the case. It cannot be if a local economy is to survive.

Old arrangements worked well, of course, as long as concern for one's village standing was a compelling interest and strong sanctions could be brought to bear on those who ignored local norms and misused their wealth. At a time when most villagers lived, worked, and married in just one or two upland villages, and when highlanders strongly distinguished themselves from lowlanders, the loss of esteem resulting from nonparticipation in the system was sufficient to keep most people in line.

Outsiders who migrated to the region with independent resources could, of course, better afford to ignore the ritual-status system, and sometimes they did. Historical evidence indicates, for example, that in some lower-lying mountain communities the system was well on its way to collapse as early as the 1870s (Hefner 1985, 1987a). In most of the midslope mountain region, however, the process began several decades later and was extremely uneven at that. The Muslim merchant-farmers who rose to prominence in the early 1900s were virulent opponents of this Javanist custom. Fortunately for mountain traditions, however, their influence waned with the economic collapse of the 1930s. In most of the highlands, then, the *sumbangan* tradition survived. Indeed, the above figures on number of exchange partners show that it is still an important feature of village life today.

In the past few years, however, a new and more serious challenge to the festival system has emerged. This one comes from the very heart of highland society. For the first time, affluent villagers are speaking of the need to cut back on ritual exchange or abolish it entirely. They cite its expense, complaining that it contributes little to national development (*pembangunan*). Quite correctly, they note that it diverts scarce resources from other economic projects. In the midslope region, Islamic critics speak belittlingly of the religious tradition of which it is part. Where such reformist appeals have taken hold (see ch. 7; Hefner 1987c), the economic and religious critiques converge, creating powerful pressures for the abolition of the ritual tradition as a whole.

There is, of course, a larger logic at work here, more complex than the simple rationalization of factors of production. Economy always assumes community. Today the way of life associated with the traditional economy of the highlands is on the wane.

Ritual festivals found their meaning in a small world of familiar others, where both status and welfare were directly dependent upon carefully nurtured social ties. Yet it is precisely this feature of village life that has suffered most in recent years. Those involved in extraregional commerce have come to realize that relations in the larger world are not lubricated by the ritualized largesse of *sumbangan* exchange. As the rural elite has shifted its attention outside the village, therefore, it has had to manage its resources in ways consonant with the political and economic demands of the surrounding society. This "rationalization" of production is not driven by the abstract logic of the market, but by aspirations to, and the political-economic machinery of, an outside world once kept at a distance. It is the boundaries of community that have changed, as villagers aspire, or are compelled, to be part of modern Indonesia.

Television and Economic Culture

The spread of television in the highlands provides another example of this challenge to received consumption norms. The first television sets made their way into the mountain region in the mid to late 1970s. At that time, the government required every village to have at least one set as a source of news on national events and culture. As commercial agriculture expanded in the highlands, however, privately owned color television sets, which retailed in stores for the equivalent of U.S. $300–500, quickly became one of the most desired of luxury goods. In the village of Ngadiwono in 1980, there were twenty-nine private television sets in the central hamlet, or about one for every fifteen households. In more typical mountain villages, there was one set for every seventy households.

The way in which television sets were assimilated into village life showed the tension between earlier and emerging consumption norms. In the mid 1970s, everywhere one traveled televisions sets were still treated as a quasi-public good, on the model of *slametan* festivals. Owners positioned sets on the verandas of their houses, facing the street, so that villagers who might wish to watch could do so. Situating the set neither inside nor outside the house, the owners were able to fulfill the expectation that, as with the amusements during ritual festivals, neighbors would be able to enjoy the entertainment too. Positioned between domestic space and the outside yard, the television sets were balanced precariously between old and new consumption norms.

As if by proclamation, a different pattern had developed by 1985. Sets were now located securely behind windows, which were sometimes adorned with items previously unknown in upland homes—curtains and tinted glass. Now only guests to a home were allowed the privilege of watching television. When asked about the change, owners invariably said that they were embarrassed by all the people standing around their front doors, neither inside nor outside, neither guests nor passers-by. In a society where great value is placed on the proper reception of guests, this was an understandable source of tension. Though the dilemma, then, was real, its manner of resolution was typical of new trends. A more private ethic was emerging, one less responsive to the demand that wealth acknowledge neighbors. It is the constraining influence of this local tie that has weakened.

Ultimately, it is with consumer goods as it was with education and employment. Villagers, especially the affluent, wish to be viewed as modern members of the national community. To affect its styles and compete in its markets, they must pull away from the commitments of the past and invest their wealth in more deliberately productive capital goods. In practical terms, what this means is that investments like *sumbangan* exchange will continue to decline, while ownership of trucks and new types of consumer goods is bound to increase.

The nature of this economic change is not captured by characterizations of earlier ways as irrational or traditional, whereas new ones are individual, rational, and calculated, as some models of "modernization" might suggest. As the *sumbangan* example reveals, "traditional" consumption was highly calculated and thoroughly rational. But its rationality was defined relative to a local world, with its own patterns of value and need. New forms of investment look outward, not because the broader market is inherently more rational, but because it serves an expanded community of which well-placed villagers, in particular, wish to be part.

From a comparative perspective, of course, none of this is surprising. James Scott (1985, 173) has also remarked that ritual festivals in Malaysia have declined as villagers look to the outside and channel their wealth into capital goods. Indeed, changes of this sort are familiar from all parts of the developing world. It is the well-known story of a bounded, tightly knit community being integrated into a larger and more stratified national one. Whether by force or choice, the contours of identity change. Relations of rank and prestige previously based on local notions of distinction are suddenly harnessed to national markets. These have "absorbed the functions of cultural traditions in providing guideposts for personal and social identity" (Leiss, Kline, and Jhally 1986, 3). Here in mountain Java those who can afford stereos, motorbikes, urban-style homes, and "lowland" dress express their citizenship in a new consumption community. Their efforts have a ripple effect, as others, feeling obliged to keep up with the Joneses, adopt what they can of new lifestyles. Economic culture shows the standardized influence of nation and class more clearly, while regionalist symbols recede.

In a world shaken by the violence of 1965–66, and then suddenly opened to new commercial influences, it is not surprising that consumption events that celebrate the virtues of village and ancestors have given way to the national symbols of *pembangunan dan kemajuan* ("development and progress"). Upland tradition was never unchanging. Indeed, it has changed so rapidly over the past century that one could in a certain sense call it an "invented tradition"—to borrow a phrase from Hobsbawm and Ranger (1983)—perpetually adjusted to the challenge of the moment. Though fast changing, however, economic tradition has had a practical and moral significance that was neither crudely instrumental nor illusory. Its norms helped to define a local world by erecting political and moral barriers between inside and outside and placing limits on what happened within. *Sumbangan* exchange was at the heart of this social economy. It did not systematically level differences of class or wealth. But it did have a repressive effect on capital accumulation. Wealth brought prestige only when spent on certain kinds of luxury goods. There was a political economy of status and meaning operative here (Eickelman 1979), in other words, one that looked to local ritual and social relations for its measures of distinction.

There are no such political or moral barriers with the ideas of "development and progress." Ubiquitous in the commentaries of village officials, these terms struck me as vague and meaningless during my first months in the field. I heard them through the filter of a Western, postmodernist irony that assumes that the very project of progress is flawed. But my hearing was naively ethnocentric. For villagers who have lived through economic misery and horrific political calamity, the appeal of these terms is real, however imprecise their meaning. They are instruments for revising cultural self-perception. Looking to the outside and the future, they deny the authority of village and tradition. The local world commands less attention, because, in practice and imagination, the better-off spend less of their lives there.

Quite unlike the situation in the industrialized West, however, the integration of this local economy into a national one is occurring in a context of widespread poverty. As in most of today's developing world, the technology of communications and the machinery of state have outstripped production. Politics and communications, not just production, drive this change. Poor villagers in the most remote communities have been made aware of new goods and needs. Unlike Western consumers, however, they observe these things with, as yet, little realistic chance that they will ever share in their pleasures. Hence, as the appeal of local community declines, the consequences of class become more apparent. The plate-glass windows and curtains of upland nouveaux riches are one response to this awkward fact.

Some poor people have responded to this dilemma by attempting to present themselves as the guardians of traditional ways. When they spoke with me of new styles of clothing, furniture, and cooking, they defended their dignity by insisting these goods were a betrayal of upland tradition. "I am just a farmer [*wong tani*], a mountain person [*wong gunung*]," I was told time and time again. Always it was with a directness that made clear the modest defiance those self-ascriptions implied. Even a few years ago these appeals to local allegiance and unhierarchical ways still carried great moral weight. Unfortunately for the poor, however, their arguments evoke no such consensus on community today. The barriers to the outside have been destroyed, and its goods and meanings have poured in. There is no going back to the upland village of old.

In another place or at another time, perhaps, this controversy might have given rise to a more overtly political contest. One of the ironies of contemporary Java, however, is that while there has been far-reaching social and economic change, public discussion of its form and meaning has been vigorously suppressed. The memories of the 1965–66 violence are still powerfully present. So, too, are the mechanisms of state it helped to usher in. They form the unspoken background to everything happening in Java today.

SEVEN

Politics and Social Identity

The 1965–66 Violence and Its Aftermath

Since Hindu-Buddhist times the Tengger highlands have been a subordinate territory within a state whose political and cultural heartland lay elsewhere. In the late eighteenth century the area, which had been peripheral to the rising Muslim principalities of the sixteenth and seventeenth centuries, was decisively integrated into what would eventually become the dominant political entity on the island, the Dutch colonial state. Though a regionalist tradition survived, highland identity never achieved the dimensions of ethnic separation characteristic of upland populations in much of Southeast Asia. Politically and culturally, the Tengger mountains were too much part of larger Java.

Indonesia's independence in 1949 seemed to promise to further integrate the highlands into the politics and culture of the surrounding lowlands. In fact, however, this did not occur. As national parties penetrated the countryside, the cleavage between the two regions, if anything, only hardened. The Muslim lowlands became the strongest center in all of Java for Nahdatul Ulama, the party of Muslim traditionalists. The Javanist highlands, by contrast, were dominated by the Indonesian Nationalist Party (PNI) and, to a lesser degree, the Indonesian Communist Party (PKI).

A similar process of polarization along sociocultural lines occurred in other areas of Java at this time (Mortimer 1982, 60; Liddle 1978, 190; Jay 1963). Religious symbols "came increasingly to be identified with ideas of the definition of the nature of the state and with the way social and material resources should be distributed" (Lyon 1970, 37). In rural Pasuruan the cleavage between Muslims and Javanists took an extreme form because it coincided with long-standing tensions between upland and lowland society. As we shall see, highlanders regarded the conflict that culminated in the bloodletting of 1965–66 as but the latest phase in a struggle pitting them against the stronger, more hierarchical Islamic lowlands.

The causes and consequences of that violence are the focus of this chapter. Though in some ways distinctive, the Pasuruan example provides insight into the dynamics of political conflict throughout rural Java before and after the bloodshed of 1965–66. More generally, it presents an unusually rich opportunity to reflect on the role of class and community in comparative political development. The example argues against the reduction of political violence to such polar alternatives as class struggle or cultural values. In their place, it demands a model that can recognize the cultural dimensions of class and the politics and economics of ethnicity, status, and religion. What is needed, in other words, is an interactionist model of politics and culture that acknowledges the multiple bases of allegiance and power. Such a recognition is at the heart of a non-economistic understanding of political-economic change.

The example also sheds light on the social forces that are realigning politics and identity in Java today. Driven by broad changes in the Indonesian state, recent developments have linked village to nation in a way unanticipated by observers of the old regime. As in much of the developing world, regional traditions are giving way to national culture. In so doing, they are creating the symbols and instruments for a standardized social hierarchy and the conditions for a broader struggle over the form and meaning of modern community.

POLITICAL COMMUNITY IN THE PRE-1965 PERIOD

The regency of Pasuruan has long been one of the most important centers of Islamic traditionalism in all of Java. Founded in East Java in 1926, Nahdatul Ulama, the party of traditionalist Muslim clerics, quickly came to dominate lowland political life. Its ascent was related to the area's earlier history of conflict and colonialism, which had swept aside Javanese traditions and laid the groundwork for the expansion of Islam.

Islam's rise in this region goes back to the eighteenth century. At that time—the dawn of the colonial era—the Pasuruan area was a "cauldron of warfare" (Elson 1984, 1). The most sustained violence pitted an alliance of eastern Javanese forces under the rebel Surapati against the combined armies of Mataram and the Dutch (see ch. 2; Kumar 1976). Even after their defeat in 1707, Surapati's followers continued to put up resistance for well over half a century, which suggests that the aristocracy had an only weak hold on the countryside. Eventually, however, the Dutch-supported rulers consolidated their control over the rich rice lands around Bangil and Pasuruan (Elson 1984, 12). No sooner was this done, however, than events again conspired to undermine their authority. With the indigenous population depleted by warfare, the colonial government encouraged a migratory influx of Madurese and Javanese. Fleeing the exactions of their own native aristocracy, animated by a commitment to Islam, and more proudly independent than their Javanese counterparts (de Vries 1931, 131; Elson 1984, 15), the Madurese who settled in the Pasuruan region were little inclined to defer to comprador Javanese aristocrats. The migration created a frontier society, with a more "freewheeling and open" social structure (Elson 1984, 16), and a less abiding respect for hierarchical ways.

In time, as population grew and the Dutch implemented their program for the forced cultivation of export crops, the lowland frontier closed. The earlier fluid social structure eventually gave way to a rigidly hierarchical colonial society, characterized by high rates of landlessness and a privileged rural elite (Elson 1984, 90–94; Alexander and Alexander 1979, 31). While strengthening state power, colonial programs did not enhance the independent authority of the gentry (*priyayi*). On the contrary, the gentry's role was thoroughly dependent on European might, and their actions were subordinate to European interests. As Sartono Kartodirjo (1972, 88) has observed of Java as a whole, the cooption of native *priyayi* only further estranged them from the mass of rural villagers, creating a vacuum of authority in popular society. In coastal areas around Pasuruan, some of the chief beneficiaries of this crisis were Muslim religious teachers (*kyai*). Untainted by association with the Dutch, they exercised influence across ethnic and territorial boundaries, becoming, in effect, the cultural brokers for a new rural order with ideals and commitments distinct from those of a discredited Javanese aristocracy.

Muslim influence was abetted by the expansion of religious schools (*pesantren*) in the lowlands during the last half of the nineteenth century. Mechanisms for the propagation of a more orthodox Islam, these schools were also central to lowland politics and social structure. Marital alliances linked wealthy families to *pesantren* teachers. Affluent villagers were expected to make gifts of money and land to religious teachers in support of school operations. With the pilgrimage to Mecca, sponsorship of Muslim activities became the preferred index of social standing, replacing the *slametan* festivals earlier prized in Javanese communities. In the process the mosque replaced the *dhanyang* spirit shrine as the ritual center of the village.

This ascent of the crescent over the banyan tree, to borrow a phrase from Nakamura (1983), represented more than the advance of an Islamic world view. It signaled the emergence of a new, less localized, social order based on interregional political ties, an alliance of religion and wealth, and a commitment to Islam that transcended Javanese and Madurese ethnicity.[1]

It is this historical background that explains why first Sarekat Islam (the Islamic Union; SI) and later Nahdatul Ulama (NU) grew so rapidly in the Pasuruan countryside at the beginning of this century. Sarekat Islam swept through Pasuruan in the mid teens, attracting a following among a peasantry hard pressed by declining circumstances (Benda 1983, 42; Elson 1984, 196). While it did not formulate an overarching political program, SI did serve briefly as a bureau for peasant grievances. Its vilification of the infidel government and *priyayi* officials (Benda 1983, 43) resonated strongly among Pasuruan's orthodox Muslims. Conversely, its promotion of "a purified and more devout practice of Islam" (Elson 1984, 199) ensured that its appeals were less sympathetically received in the Javanist highlands. Less hard pressed by economic decline, the latter region remained unmoved by SI's appeals.[2]

In the early 1920s Sarekat Islam's influence waned. Here, as in other parts of Java, this was in part the result of repression by *priyayi* officials, who deeply resented SI's charges that they were mere lackeys of the infidel government. The party was also racked by infighting, however, as orthodox Muslims vied with secularly oriented left-wing nationalists for control (Benda 1983, 44; Ricklefs 1981, 164–67). In Pasuruan, SI remained solidly in the hands of conservative Muslims. In nearby Malang, however, the left-leaning "red" faction won control of the organization (Elson 1984, 206). Long after SI's decline, in fact, Malang remained the one stronghold of left-wing and "secular" nationalist activity in this eastern region of Java. The contrast between a secular-nationalist Malang and an NU-dominated Pasuruan remained a characteristic of regional politics up through the 1960s.

Although the Great Depression had a strong effect on Pasuruan's export economy, the political climate in the regency remained relatively

---

1. Until well into this century, however, many Islamic communities continued to maintain shrines dedicated to the spirits of village founding ancestors. These often looked similar to Javanist *dhanyang,* with a large tree, an open grassy space, and a small shrine marker. Village origin myths stressed that the ancestors revered at these shrines were humans, however, rather than, as is often the case with Javanist shrines, guardian spirits of a nonhuman sort. In general, in addition, the primary indices of Javanism— prayer celebration by *dhukun* ritual specialists rather than a Muslim elder, food offerings for earth spirits, holy water, and drinking and dancing—were also less common.

2. Clifford Geertz's (1960, 128) comments on Javanist social organization (or the lack thereof) in the early 1950s apply equally well to that in Pasuruan at this time: the Javanist community had "nothing . . . which could even in the remotest sense be called a church or a religious organization. . . . [T]here is only a set of separate households geared into one another like so many windowless monads, their harmony preordained by their common adherence to a single tradition."

temperate. Beneath the calm surface, however, NU had quietly begun to expand its base. The combined repression of Dutch and *priyayi* officials had taken its toll on the leadership of other political parties, and there were few large demonstrations of anticolonial sentiment during this period (Elson 1984, 247). In the face of this repression, and in the aftermath of SI's decline, NU adopted a nonconfrontational strategy. Rather than directly challenging the government, it exploited its ties to rural religious teachers so as to promote its own style of religious politics. *Santri* students were sent into remote areas of the countryside, where they organized classes in Qur'anic study (*pengajian*), and laid the groundwork for new party chapters.

In characterizing NU's strategy in Java as a whole, Harry Benda has described it as a "consciously non-political course" (Benda 1983, 55). This may be true in the conventional sense of politics. But the initiative brilliantly reflected the organization's political priorities: not to foment immediate anticolonial resistance, but to disseminate orthodox Islam, winning the hearts and minds of a still weakly orthodox population. Unlike Indonesia's secular leaders, the *ulama*-teachers in the party leadership were untutored in Western ways and as yet unmoved by the vision of a nationalist Indonesia. They spoke not of nation and independence, but of moral regeneration in a countryside afflicted, in their eyes, by the twin evils of infidel colonialism and irreligious Javanism.

The quiet fruits of this strategy were already apparent in the late 1930s. Having begun with a base in towns and lowland villages, NU chapters spread to the lower fringes of the Tengger highlands, moving into communities where the contest between Islam and Javanism was as yet unfinished. Attacking *dhukun* ritual specialists, *dhanyang* spirit cults, and the ritual exchange system (Hefner 1987c), the party often shifted the balance of power to local Muslims. It was during this period, for example, that many villages at the lower periphery of the Tengger mountains discarded their Javanist ritual heritage. Through this mixture of proselytization and party building, NU expanded its rural base at a time when other political parties were in decline.

The Japanese occupation only served to strengthen NU's advantage. In Java as a whole the Japanese at first courted Muslim support more actively than they did that of nationalists or *priyayi*-aristocratics (Benda 1983, 201). As a result Muslims got a head start in establishing organizations that, after the war, would play a leading role in building Islamic political parties. Japanese support was crucial, for example, in the formation of Masyumi, a powerful federation of all-Indonesia Muslim organizations. Nahdatul Ulama executives were accorded a leading role in Masyumi's operation, and it eventually became a de facto part of the government through its involvement in the Japanese-created Bureau of

Religious Affairs. In 1944 these offices became operative in all residencies of Indonesia (Benda 1983, 161).

The final months of the Japanese occupation intensified the competition between Muslims and nationalists. A nationalist youth corps was established in mid 1944 and a rival Muslim one was founded a few months later (Benda 1983, 178). These became the core of Indonesia's first auxiliary military units. Rather than coordinating their activities, however, the two groups competed for control of the rural population. Organized in early 1945 as a military arm of Masyumi (Kahin 1952, 163), Hizbullah, the Muslim militia, launched a bold drive for mass membership in Pasuruan (and other parts of Java) during the first months of 1945, just prior to the Japanese surrender. Its success guaranteed Muslim dominance in lowland Pasuruan. The nationalists faltered in the face of this Muslim advance. The only large centers of population still outside NU's control were Javanist strongholds in the Tengger highlands. But these were so remote that the nationalists at first saw little advantage in attempting to organize a following there. For all intents and purposes, by the end of the Japanese occupation, Pasuruan was an NU stronghold.

The rivalry was complicated, however, by the struggle for national independence during 1945–49. By early 1946 Dutch patrols were moving unopposed through urban Pasuruan; by late in the year they made regular forays into the countryside. The military occupation forced republican resistance south, into the Tengger highlands and, beyond them, into rural areas along the southern coast in the regencies of Malang and Lumajang, where Dutch influence remained weak. The geography of resistance suddenly put Pasuruan's Muslim organizations at a disadvantage. The southern terrains were predominantly Javanist and had long resisted NU appeals. The situation thus presented the nationalists with a rich opportunity to expand their influence. Long castigated by lowland critics as primitive heathen, highlanders responded eagerly to nationalist appeals. Their role in the resistance laid the foundation for nationalist dominance in the region after the war. NU's advance had finally been checked.

Independence

Independence at first saw a relaxation of tensions in the regency, as villagers turned to the difficult task of rebuilding a shattered economy. Until 1953, in fact, Indonesian politics remained largely an elite affair, focused on parliamentary intrigues; little effort was made to draw the rural populace into the contest (Feith 1957, 10; Liddle 1978, 173). Party rivalries intensified, however, with the approach of the first general elections in September 1955. In the months prior to the elections, the major parties extended their recruitment drives into rural areas in an effort to drum up support, politicizing the countryside to a degree never before seen. In much of Java, the new mass organizations followed the lines of preexisting religious and cultural cleavages (*aliran*). Orthodox Muslims were drawn to Masyumi and Nahdatul Ulama, and Javanists rallied around the Indonesian Nationalist Party (PNI) or the Communist Party (PKI) (Jay 1963; Geertz 1965a, 148; Feith 1957). By comparison with other areas of Java, however, the political geography in Pasuruan was relatively simple, polarized between the NU-dominated lowlands and the nationalist uplands.

As Feith has observed (1957, 13), the 1955 electoral campaign was strongly colored by religious issues. Masyumi attacked the communists as atheists, while Nahdatul Ulama criticized Masyumi for its modernist reforms.[3] In Pasuruan certain factions within NU also attacked the PKI as an anti-Islamic organization, though some NU leaders were less concerned about the communists than they were about their reform Muslim rivals. The PKI and its peasant affiliate, the BTI (Barisan Tani Indonesia), also raised the banner of land reform at this time. For a variety of reasons, however, the issue did not catch on in Pasuruan. It was overshadowed by the question of whether Indonesia should become an Islamic state (*negara Islam*).

There were several reasons why religious issues were especially prominent in Pasuruan. Among Muslims and nationalists, first of all, there was a strong sense that a Muslim triumph was near. Nahdatul Ulama so dominated the local political scene that this party and its rivals had an exaggerated sense of its national influence. Campaign events also helped to push religious issues to the forefront. In several well-publicized incidents, Masyumi leaders and radical *kyai* from (the otherwise nonradical) NU demanded that upland ritual practices be outlawed. Allied with the nationalists in opposition to NU, village leaders in the midslope highlands responded warily to these attacks. They knew all too well that if Indonesia became an Islamic state, orthodox restrictions would fall especially heavily on them.

Hindu villagers in the upperslope highlands had reason to be concerned as well. Muslim party leaders in the lowlands flatly rejected the highlanders' claims that they were non-Muslim and thus should be spared restrictions imposed on Muslim believers. Citing the Hindus' practice of circumcision (regarded by most Indonesians as a Muslim rite) and their occasional participation in Muslim festivals (Hefner 1985), these lowland critics insisted that the highlanders were really Javanist

3. At the time of its founding under the Japanese, Masyumi grouped Muslim traditionalists and modernists in a single organization. Angry at the declining influence of traditionalists in the party, Nahdatul Ulama withdrew from it in 1952, leaving Masyumi to modernist Muslims (see Samson 1978, 199).

Muslims like those in the midslope region. They too, then, would be subject to the restrictions of an Islamic state.

As the election approached, tensions escalated, as did the tactics of some of the parties. Nationalist officials organized rallies in which they underscored the threat to Javanist religious traditions. Urban-based nationalist intellectuals created an umbrella organization for the defense of midslope traditions. In several of its leaflets, they denounced orthodox Islam as "un-Javanese" and called openly for a return to the non-Muslim "religion of Majapahit" (Hefner 1987c). The nationalist intellectuals also worked with midslope village chiefs to sponsor political rallies at several of the highlands' most famous *dhanyang* spirit shrines. Not surprisingly, NU leaders regarded these actions as a deliberate insult to Islam.

Just prior to the 1955 election, tensions reached a climax when a group of Muslim activists (loosely linked to radical factions in NU) invaded one of the most famous upland *dhanyang*, located amidst the ruins of a fourteenth-century Hindu water temple. The guardian spirit of this shrine was revered by midslope Muslims and upperslope Hindus alike, and pilgrims from the entire regency regularly flocked to its grounds. Under cover of night, the militants entered the shrine, smashed the faces of its old Hindu icons, and hauled off statues for disposal in a nearby river. Word of the attack spread terror through the highlands, but no counteraction was taken. Highlanders feared that it was but a small sample of what was to come.

In the end Muslim hopes for a national mandate were disappointed. The Islamic parties failed to win a clear majority of the national vote. The PNI and Masyumi emerged as the largest parties, capturing 22.3 and 20.9 percent of the vote respectively, while NU and the PKI won 18.4 and 16.4 percent (Feith 1957, 58). Nowhere in Java were Muslims more surprised than in Pasuruan, where the sheer dominance of NU had blinded Islamic party leaders to the national balance of power and caused them to expect a Muslim landslide.

Despite the disappointment at a national level, in Pasuruan itself the election results confirmed the unqualified dominance of Nahdatul Ulama. The party won an astounding 61.0 percent of the vote—the highest proportion in any of Java's regencies. Its main rival, the PNI, won only 22.1 percent, while the PKI and Masyumi obtained a mere 8.7 and 4.4 percent respectively (Alfian 1971). NU's share of the vote was almost as high in neighboring Probolinggo. The only region of Indonesia where NU's achievement was more stunning was in Madura, where its share of the vote was even larger than in Pasuruan. By comparison with other areas of East and Central Java, the Pasuruan results were also notable for the poor showing of both the PKI and Masyumi. The 1955 elections confirmed what was already apparent to many people: that the contest in Pasuruan was essentially a two-party affair, pitting the powerful, lowland-based Nahdatul Ulama against the much smaller, upland-based PNI.[4]

For Pasuruan's Javanist highlanders the election results meant that the most serious threat to their religious heritage was for the moment deferred. Subsequent political events reassured them even further. From 1957 on, the national influence of the most militantly reformist Muslim party, Masyumi, declined, with the dismantling of parliamentary democracy and the transition to "Guided Democracy" (Lev 1966; Ricklefs 1981, 243). During this same period, conversely, PKI influence grew. The 1957 elections for provincial councils resulted in substantial PKI gains in East and Central Java, largely to the detriment of the PNI (Lev 1966, 84).

Parallel to the PKI's rise, however, there was another development of equal importance. Alarmed by secessionist rebellions and the growing influence of the communists, the Indonesian military began to take a more direct role in national politics. Threatened by the military advance, but unsympathetic to the political leadership of the PNI, President Sukarno found himself looking more and more to the communists as a counterweight to the armed forces. Meanwhile, the national economy continued its precipitous decline. Not yet recovered from the war, rural commerce was disrupted in 1959 by an army order to expel all aliens (primarily Chinese) from rural areas (Ricklefs 1981, 255). Shortly thereafter, inflation began to increase, averaging 100 percent per annum from late 1961 to 1964 (Arndt 1971, 373; Ricklefs 1981, 259). As Mackie (1971) has noted, the impact of inflation was highly regressive, favoring those who controlled productive resources like agricultural land. This meant special hardship for Java's poor, who depended on patrons for access to land and on the market for rice.

Pressured in part by poor peasants hurt by the economic decline, but also hoping to seize the moment from its political rivals, including the military, the PKI responded to the national crisis by trying to expand its rural base. In late 1963 it announced a national campaign for implementation of the land-reform provisions of the 1960 Agrarian Law. In early 1964 PKI-organized peasants launched "unilateral actions" (*aksi sepihak*), seizing the land of large landowners and staging demonstrations in support of squatters and sharecroppers. The initiatives provoked strong reactions on the part of landlords and Muslim party supporters. Rural violence quickly escalated to new heights (Mortimer 1974, 309–28; Huizer 1974, 125).

4. In East Java as a whole, the overall percentages for the four major parties were: PNI, 22.8; PKI, 23.2; NU, 34.1; and Masyumi 11.2 percent. In Central Java, the proportions were: PNI, 33.5; PKI, 25.8; NU, 19.6; and Masyumi, 10.0 percent. See Feith 1957, 78. NU won first place in the vote in fourteen of East Java's twenty-nine regencies, and four of Central Java's thirty-two (Alfian 1971).

There is no question that class issues were central to much of this conflict. But their influence was qualified by the complex play of interests and organizations in the struggle. The PKI itself, for example, often protected landlords with party ties, while vigorously attacking landlords linked to its rivals (Utrecht 1969, 83). Muslim party leaders saw the campaign as a direct challenge to their authority, and thus characterized it as an assault on Islam rather than an economic struggle. Anti-Muslim outbursts in several well-publicized PKI actions (Walkin 1969, 828) lent credence to their charges.

The PKI was caught off guard by the strength of the countermobilization, and it was forced to rein in its followers. In late 1964 a compromise on implementation of land reform was achieved. For a while it looked as if some measure of calm might return to the countryside.

Tensions had risen to unprecedented levels, however, and the conflict left Muslim organizations both embittered and better-organized. In the months that followed, Muslim leaders felt further threatened by President Sukarno's continuing support for PKI initiatives. The die was thus cast for the events of 1965–66. In the aftermath of a failed left-wing officers' coup in Jakarta, the army and Muslim organizations moved against the PKI, rounding up and executing several hundred thousand of its supporters. These events laid the foundations for the New Order government.

PASURUAN: PRELUDE TO VIOLENCE

In 1964 East Java was the site of some of the most violent confrontations in all Java between Muslims and communists (Walkin 1969). Political conflict in Pasuruan's lowlands, however, was surprisingly restrained. There was some PKI activity around large sugar estates. There were also a few odd agricultural villages where the PKI was strong, especially in communities adjacent to the sugar estates where landless or land-poor laborers lived. Even at the height of the 1964 unilateral actions, however, the PKI in lowland Pasuruan found itself unable to mobilize support across broad segments of the rural populace. Its failure was owing to the fact that it faced the most powerful NU organization in all Java. Thus, despite their poverty and pervasive inequality, Pasuruan's lowlands saw fewer landlord-peasant confrontations than in neighboring Malang and Lumajang, where the influence of Muslim *kyai* was weaker and the PKI more powerful.

Faced with this impasse, the Pasuruan PKI focused its attention on the uplands, the one area of the regency where it looked as if it might be able to mobilize support. NU's influence was weak or nonexistent in most of the region, except in a few communities with Madurese residents. In addition, land-reform issues were beginning to attract more attention in the area. Squatters still occupied some 250 hectares of formerly European land, over which they had yet to be given legal rights. Though the PKI had not effectively exploited land-reform issues in the 1955 elections, they took on greater importance after 1957, when the government finally invalidated the land titles of Dutch landholders. Regency-level officials began to talk of returning the lands to the public domain, and rumors spread through the squatter community that they were about to be expelled from their holdings, breathing new life into the PKI's land-reform campaign. For the first time the PKI found itself able to rally poor uplanders to its cause.

Party efforts intensified after 1963 as the PKI began preparations for its national campaign. Its activities were concentrated in a handful of villages near midslope Puspo and Nongkojajar, and around Tosari in the upperslope region. The greatest portion of the squatter land (two-thirds of the total) was scattered around the Nongkojajar area, where Europeans had operated their largest estates. It was in this region too that the party attracted its largest following. The area of squatter land was smaller near Puspo and Tosari, comprising forty to fifty hectares around each village. In these communities, squatters made up only about 12–15 percent of the total farm population, and the PKI's following was more modest. By itself, this was clearly not enough to build a coalition capable of winning control of local government.

In the highlands the PKI faced a rival entirely different from the one it confronted in the lowlands. Local government was solidly controlled by PNI-supporters, not Nahdatul Ulama. PNI cadres were drawn from the ranks of the traditional Javanist elite, not a Muslim leadership. Wedded to village hierarchy in this way, the nationalists did not bother to build an independent party structure, but merely appropriated local reins of power. Their intravillage organization remained nominal.

Nahdatul Ulama had a smaller, but more vocal, following in several midslope communities, primarily recruited from the ranks of the Madurese minority. Inevitably, the NU minority controlled the village mosque, and this gave them a visibility beyond their numbers. They used the mosque as a base for criticizing PNI tolerance of spirit cults and such Javanist aesthetic traditions as *tayuban* dancing (Hefner 1987b). PNI leaders, meanwhile, championed the local cult of guardian spirits, using services at village spirit shrines (*dhanyang*) to symbolize their opposition to the religious policies of the NU minority. Religious officials still today acknowledge that the politicization of religion during this period resulted in a precipitous decline in Friday mosque attendance (Hefner 1987b).

Not surprisingly, given its small following, the highland PKI adopted tactics that were moderate by comparison with other areas of East Java.

There were no militant seizures of private land and no calls for a full-scale reform of village landholding. Instead, the communists limited their appeals to a demand for fair distribution of the European holdings.

The party's unwillingness to call for broader land reform was not just a matter of organizational timidity. Under recently passed national legislation, the limit for private holdings of rainfed land in this region was 8–10 hectares per household, which only a handful of households in the highlands exceeded. In the face of this fact, the PKI wisely confined its efforts to supporting squatters. As a result, however, the party had few grounds for appealing to people in villages where there was no squatter land. In such communities its following remained negligible.

Where it could exploit the squatter issue, and where it was able to develop a fledgling party structure, however, the PKI eventually extended its influence beyond the squatter community. For example, in several villages the party attracted an unusual following among rich farmers and traders, some of whom eventually went on to become cadre leaders. For these people the party was not primarily an organization of class struggle, but an alternative to a local PNI-elite regarded as conservative and backward.

Observers elsewhere in Java have also noted that the PKI sometimes attracted a more affluent, urban-oriented following on similar leadership grounds. In assessing the background of PKI leaders in Javanist villages around rural Pare (in the Kediri region), for example, Robert Jay (1969, 434) has commented that many of the leaders of the PKI, BTI (the peasants' union), and other communist affiliates came from the ranks of the "well-to-do." Analyzing the 1955 elections, Herbert Feith (1957, 35) notes that "unaccommodated youth" sometimes used party competition to legitimize their "conflict with the old hierarchy or hierarchies of the village."

Not coincidentally, the villages in which the PKI was most active in the Tengger mountains were, by upland standards, relatively cosmopolitan. The most important centers were located near upland market sites; by comparison with most of the highlands, these villages had an unusually large resident community of traders, craftsmen, and outsiders. They also had a larger number of young people who had completed elementary school and gone on to high school in the lowlands. These were communities, then, in which urban ideas had a greater hold than elsewhere in the highlands. They were the only villages in which a better-educated, well-traveled, and thus moderately detraditionalized "unaccommodated youth" had a noticeable presence. It was from the ranks of these relatively cosmopolitan villagers that the local PKI recruited its most prominent followers.

This fact was particularly clear in one small community near upperslope Tosari that I will call Sesari. There the PKI leaders were known as "merchant communists" (*bakul komunis*) because they included in their ranks some of the most successful vegetable traders in the whole highlands. These men came from families that had pioneered the vegetable trade in the 1920s. Despite their wealth, most of these traders were not members of the elite families that had traditionally dominated upperslope politics. Entrance to leadership positions was restricted to people who could trace descent back to earlier village chiefs or Hindu priests (Hefner 1985, 82). Having achieved their status through unconventional occupations, the merchant communists challenged the village establishment's monopoly of power and its traditionalist principles of exclusion. They also complained that the PNI elite was old-fashioned and inept. It did nothing, they said, to promote education, new forms of agriculture, or any of the other measures needed to yank the highlands into modernity.

The situation was more complicated in the midslope region. There, the most prominent "merchant-farmers" of the 1910s and 1920s had not been indigenous, but lowland immigrants. Most had also been devout Muslims. In the 1950s and 1960s the descendants of these men became leaders in the midslope region's small NU faction. In this area, too, however, there were youths from the ranks of affluent families of Javanist persuasion who resented the stranglehold of the conservative PNI on local government and looked to the Communist Party as an enlightened alternative. Because of this region's historic antagonism to orthodox Islam, it was inconceivable that they would turn to Muslim parties to express their antiestablishment sentiments. For them and other disaffected youth in the region, the PKI was the only alternative to the old-fashioned PNI.

Modern political parties, however, are complex national institutions. No matter how parochial they may appear when examined at a local level, their popular dynamics can never be reduced to village forces alone. This simple truth was dramatically apparent in the political struggles that swept Pasuruan in the 1960s. As party rivalries at the national level intensified, the strategies of the local-level PKI also changed. The focus of their attention shifted from what had been a largely intraelite rivalry to a contest involving a wider range of villagers. The issue around which the new lines of conflict were cast was the still unresolved matter of what to do with the old European lands.

The squatters had grown anxious about their situation, and with good reason. After officially invalidating European land titles in 1957, regency officials instructed subdistrict and village-level leaders to conduct a survey of the now-nationalized properties. They were to determine the precise area of the affected lands and the identity of their current occupants. The survey was carried out in a casual, haphazard fashion, however, and ultimately nothing came of it. The squatters continued to occupy their lands. In late 1963 and early 1964—apparently in response to the PKI's national campaign for land reform—regency officials issued similar directives, accompanied by instructions that each subdistrict and village form a committee to oversee disposition of the lands. Throughout Indonesia the constitution of such committees was a key element in the land-reform process (Utrecht 1969, 77). Not surprisingly, selection of their membership was often a hotly contested issue, since the committee was ultimately responsible for deciding who was to receive land, and how large an area.

In mountain Pasuruan the new directives caused great confusion. In announcing committee formation, PNI officials made no statement as to just what was to be done with the lands. In several instances, in addition, they packed the reform committees with their own followers in a brazen attempt to award themselves the lion's share of lands. By early 1964, therefore, alarm was spreading among the squatter population as rumors circulated that they were going to lose their lands. The situation was particularly tense in one midslope village, where half of the squatters were landless peasants from outside the region, mostly from villages at the lower fringe of the highlands. They had migrated to the area during the independence struggle hoping to obtain a plot of land from among the European holdings. The outsiders' presence had always been a source of tension, since many highlanders felt that the European lands were rightfully theirs. The local PNI leadership exploited this fact in an effort to divide the squatter population and seize lands for themselves.

In this one village, PNI leaders devised an ingenious plan to accomplish their goal. They announced that all outsiders on European land should surrender their holdings for redistribution to local villagers. The village chief then approached each of these families privately, offering them a small cash payment and house plot of one-tenth of a hectare if they complied with the decree. This offer, they were told, was purely the largesse of the village chief, and should it be refused, the regency government was under no obligation to provide further compensation. Meeting publicly with villagers, subdistrict officers (all PNI) backed up the village chief and hinted the outsiders might be arrested if they resisted. Eventually, about half of the outsiders relinquished their holdings. While some of this land was redistributed to local villagers, a large portion was quietly sold to lowland investors or given to regency officials for private use.

News of this treachery enraged the squatter population in neighboring communities and galvanized the PKI leadership. After several strategy sessions with their lowland superiors, the upland PKI called for mass protests against PNI corruption. Finally, it seemed, the party had found a cause to give it an appearance of strength in a regency where it was notoriously weak. The PKI announced it would support the cause of the upland squatters by bringing in several hundred lowland followers for demonstrations. By the standards of upland society, this was an unprecedented move. It violated the long-unspoken rule that, no matter how serious, local problems were best handled by local people. Even some people sympathetic to the PKI were alarmed by this flagrant violation of village tradition.

Ultimately there were three PKI rallies, and for each one, protestors were transported in from around the regency. The show of force was overwhelming: more demonstrators showed up than there were adult residents in any of the upland villages. The initiative succeeded brilliantly in its goal of intimidating PNI village chiefs. It is important to remember that at the village level the PNI really had no independent organization, having been grafted on to the existing social hierarchy in a relatively ad hoc fashion. Similarly, unlike their counterparts in many lowland communities, village chiefs could not call on a reserve of sharecropping dependents to come to their aid. Nor could village leaders stigmatize their opponents as anti-Muslim heathens, since the PKI and PNI shared the same Javanist views. Nor, finally, could the imperiled PNI chiefs expect support from landowners or party leaders in nearby NU communities. After years of abusive exchanges between the upland PNI and the lowland NU, the PNI chiefs were in no position to turn to Muslim neighbors for help. In this instance, therefore, religious antagonisms prevented the rural elite in the two regions from organizing along class lines. "Economic" interests alone were insufficient to bring the two together. The inability to organize along (lateral) class lines because of countervailing ties of religion and party has been widely noted in discussions of the PKI and the poor (Mortimer 1974, 327). It has been less widely appreciated that the same problem plagued rural elites, who were also split by religious and political commitments.

In the end the PKI won a notable, if local, victory. Although, in the midslope region, squatters who had already lost their land received no further compensation, the PNI land scam otherwise came to a halt.[5] Lo-

5. In the midslope community where the PNI land scam had been most massive, however, the PNI leader forced thirty recipients of land to return it to him after the violence of late 1965. His technique was similar to that used in 1964, but now it was all the more effective because of the fear squatters had of being accused of being communists. Approaching each family privately, he offered them a small house plot, explaining that if they did not give up the remainder of their landholding, he would denounce them as communists. On receiving land, he then sold it to outside investors or gave it to regency officials. Eventually the PNI leader was replaced by a Golkar village chief. This man had actually supported the squatters and was one of the most decent village officials I ever met. He was unable to reverse the land deals, however, since several of the people involved still had influential government ties. The corrupt village chief died a lonely man, openly despised by the villagers, who, once he was out of power, called him a thief to his face.

cal communists were given seats on the land committees, and the reform program proceeded smoothly. Many squatters had to resign themselves to receiving smaller landholdings than they had initially controlled. But no more people lost their land, and many poor people who had previously been excluded from the old European lands received a share.

Class and Power in the Pre-1965 Contest

Between the mid 1950s and 1965 the upland PKI moved from being the instrument of a progressive, if still affluent, counterelite to being a mass party mobilized around economic issues. With its affiliates, the PKI eventually counted several hundred supporters in the mountain region, with a core party cadre (concentrated in a handful of villages) of about one hundred people. Until the end, however, its leadership was primarily recruited from the ranks of traders and affluent peasants. Although it promoted issues of interest to the poor, in organizational terms it remained a complex alliance of people from varied class backgrounds.

Other evidence similarly confirms that class was not the only influence at work in the conflict, even where the issues in question were apparently economic. Some large landholders, for example, deeply resented the effort by PNI leaders to steal squatter land—so much so, in fact, that several threw their support to the PKI. Village officials, after all, were not acting in the interest of these wealthy villagers. The officials had no intention of sharing the land they seized with other large landowners; they were in cahoots with subdistrict- and regency-level bureaucrats. The primary basis of their power, then, was not class or property as such, but their privileged role in a different mechanism of power, the state. Its machinery provided village officials with access to the disputed European lands and with influence beyond that based on control of the means of production. "Certain forms of political power can be generated independently of class power," we are again reminded, "and can indeed annihilate the power of social classes" (Parkin 1979, 140). There was no better illustration of this important truth than the political behavior of these PNI elites.

The PKI's influence provides a similar lesson about the complex interplay of organization and allegiance in the political struggle. The decisive element in the party's competition with the PNI leadership was not its class base among the squatters, but its ability to appeal to an extraregional party organization in an area heretofore characterized by a marked lack of interest-group mobilization. This organizational advantage, then, was not reducible in any direct way to control of the means of production. It also depended on the greater initiative and skills of the communists relative to the less dynamic upland PNI.

In appreciating the dynamics of this political contest, then, we must avoid the romantic urge to discount the independent role of party organization and to overemphasize class. As Theda Skocpol (1982, 169) has noted, this error is commonplace in the literature on peasant political resistance. In class terms, after all, the local Communist Party was really an alliance of people from varied class backgrounds, even though poor people predominated in its lower ranks. In part because of this, the upland PKI never presented its effort as a pure class struggle. The central demands in its revived campaign were for an end to corruption and the removal of all functionaries implicated in misappropriation of lands. The party made no demands for the wholesale redistribution of property, or anything else that might have aggressively challenged local class structures.

This "nonclass" emphasis was owing in part, perhaps, to the preponderance of wealthy villagers among the PKI leadership. In part, too, however, it may have reflected the very correct sociological assessment that the real issue here was *not* just one of production and class, but also the abuse of office. In an area where villagers still retained strong regional allegiances, the village chiefs had violated public trust by turning their backs on their neighbors and throwing their cards in with district-level bureaucrats. They thereby made clear their primary allegiance. From this perspective, whether intentional or not, the PKI's emphasis on corruption, and its reluctance to portray the campaign as a class struggle, correctly underscored the fact that the rights and responsibilities at issue here were not merely those of property and class, but of state and society.

Though class influenced the political contest, therefore, it was not the sole basis for the conflict of interests, and it was not the sole source of power for its resolution. Village-level PNI leaders were nothing without their links to PNI officers in district and regency government. These were not lines of class per se, but relations specified by structures of state and party. In bringing popularly based extravillage institutions to bear on local rivalries, the Communist Party had also introduced a form of political organization that was not simply derivative of class. Unwittingly, however, its appeal to extravillage allies also anticipated the kind of power that would presently be fatally used against the party itself. All players in this local contest were soon to be reminded that their fate was all too much bound up with the affairs of larger Java.

THE VIOLENCE

The violence that swept across Java following the abortive left-wing officers' coup in Jakarta the night of September 30, 1965, caught the Pasuruan PKI by surprise. The coup and subsequent leftist army rebellions in Central Java were crushed in a few days (Mortimer 1974, 413–17; Crouch 1978, 97–157). Shortly thereafter, the armed forces began internal purges of leftist officers. Not long after this time, Muslim organizations in Central Java launched bloody attacks on PKI strongholds (Huizer 1974, 135). Muslim youth groups quickly followed suit in East Java. There ANSOR, the youth wing of Nahdatul Ulama, was reported to be at the forefront of the killings. But modernist Muslim organizations also supported the slaughter. The modernist social and educational organization Muhammadiyah, for example, issued a *fatwah* referring to the extermination of the PKI as a religious duty (Boland 1982, 145–46). Other noncommunist organizations also volunteered or were compelled to participate in the campaign (Anonymous 1986, 136).

In the Pasuruan lowlands, youth organizations associated with militant NU leaders initiated the attacks even before the army or local government was in a position to coordinate or restrain their actions. The first targets of the violence were labor organizers, fishermen, estate workers, and others directly associated with the lowland PKI. At this stage of more "spontaneous" or uncoordinated violence, the attacks were undisciplined and brutal, destroying whole families and involving widespread mutilation and torture. Heads, sexual organs, and limbs were displayed along the side of the main road outside of Pasuruan. Canals were choked with bodies. In the Pasuruan regency it was more than a month before the armed forces were able to move in to effectively focus the violence. Even then, it is said, gangs of lowland youths continued to operate independently of military guidance, so much so that army commanders in more than one instance intervened and detained religious leaders whom they accused of undisciplined killing. By the time the bloodshed was brought under military control, most of the lowland PKI cadre had been killed.

In the area of the regency where the party had had its most solid base, however—the highlands—there was no violence during this uncertain time. Not yet grasping the enormity of the bloodshed, most uplanders regarded the killings as a temporary, if terrifying, breakdown of law and order. National news was at first unclear, but villagers expected that calm would be restored in a few days. Indeed, during this first phase of the bloodshed, the upland PKI had the temerity to stage several demonstrations, demanding an end to the killings and punishment of their perpetrators. As the violence continued, however, party members realized that something far more serious than they had initially realized was occurring. Demonstrations stopped. Key PKI officials went into hiding. Several who were not native to the upland region took flight, hoping to find refuge in their natal homes. The party structure slowly dissolved as uplanders began to comprehend the scope and ferocity of the violence.

PNI leaders in the villages were anxious too. This was Pasuruan, after all, home of the strongest NU organization in all Java, and NU— longstanding rival of the smaller upland PNI—was at the forefront of the violence. Reports from the lowlands were sketchy for the first weeks. Rumors circulated that PNI Javanists were among those being rounded up for execution; others bluntly warned that after the PKI had been destroyed, the PNI was next. The rumors were fueled by the fact that ANSOR youth in the lowlands called their actions a *jihad,* or holy war. Its purpose, they proclaimed, was not just the destruction of the PKI, but the creation of a Muslim state. Rumors of anti-Javanist violence appeared confirmed when, early on in the bloodletting, several PNI members active in anti-Muslim religious organizations were captured and executed (Hefner 1987c).

Such anti-Javanist attacks struck terror into the upland population. In midslope villages, services at *dhanyang* spirit shrines were quietly suspended, and attendance at Friday mosque services swelled. In the upperslope Hindu communities, there was even greater confusion. People here could not make the least pretense of professing Islam. Some villagers argued that the only defense against the massacres was mass conversion to Islam. Others replied that this could never be done; if that were the only choice, then everyone should prepare to die. Most people, however, were simply immobilized with terror, awaiting the bloodshed they now knew was to come.

The violence did finally reach the mountain region. However, it had little of the spontaneity or anarchic indiscipline of the earlier lowland purges. It was carried out in a planned, coordinated fashion; with only a few exceptions, its victims were confined to communist ranks.

The timing and organization of the violence reflected its difference from the killing that had originally swept lowland Pasuruan. Its agents here were neither members of the local landed elite nor the local Muslims who had long done battle with PKI neighbors. In fact, they were not local people at all. The key players were a momentary alliance of regional and national organizations, dominated by NU and its affiliates, but armed and directed by representatives of the East Javanese military. With the exception of two small incidents near Nongkojajar, none of the violence against the PKI, astonishingly, was initiated by the local population.

This fact highlights the organizational dynamics of different phases of the anticommunist campaign throughout Java. While encouraged and in some instances even armed by agents of the state, lowland activists in the first stages of the killing acted with considerable independence of the government or military. The second phase of the violence, by contrast, resembled the later killings in other parts of Java. It was less spontaneous and more dependent upon the support of the military and civilian arms of the state. Its targets were Javanist strongholds where anticommunist groupings were unwilling or too weak to carry out the purge alone. Outsiders had to be brought in to get the roundup going, and threats of violence were used to secure cooperation from a population that was often unwilling. In the end, then, the violence in highland Pasuruan was not in any simple sense a product of local class or religious cleavages. It was thoroughly regulated by agents of the state and included in its ranks representatives of a variety of nongovernmental organizations, especially Nahdatul Ulama.

Days of Terror

It had been almost two months since the coup when Muslim groups from the lowlands, armed and accompanied by a smaller number of army supervisors, arrived in the region to begin carrying out the blood purge. Three weeks before their arrival, village officials had been ordered to place local-level PKI members in detention, shaving their heads to identify them. Village officials who refused to cooperate with this order were threatened with execution on grounds of hiding communists. In the face of such threats, there was little resistance to the directive. By the time the screening teams arrived, local communists were under house arrest, guarded by a terrified local militia.

There were no Javanists, Hindus, or, for that matter, village officials from the mountain region on the coordinating committee for the purge. It consisted instead of lowland youths from student action groups (see Boland 1982, 142; Crouch 1978, 165), NU, and its ANSOR youth affiliate, all under the technical supervision of army officers. Local officials and villagers were required, of course, to aid in the identification of PKI leaders. Nonetheless, village leaders were not regarded as willing allies in the purge. Indeed, there was some tension between NU leaders, who were hostile toward the local PNI, and the army coordinators, who were more interested in flushing out communists than condemning anti-Muslim Javanists. The NU representatives wanted nothing to do with the PNI leadership, and in several well-publicized instances they called for the execution of PNI leaders linked to Javanist organizations. Ironically, one such village chief had himself been the focus of a PKI demonstration; he had been one of the most notorious players in the PNI land scam. In the end, the man was spared, after army enquiries confirmed that he was not a communist at all, but merely a Javanist of considerable renown.

Here again, the decision in this case provides a dramatic example of the changing nature of the violence. During the more spontaneous killings several weeks earlier, an individual like this Javanist village chief would have been executed without a moment's thought. ANSOR youths *had* been able to execute several leaders of a prominent anti-Islamic organization known as "Javanese Buddha-Visnu Religion" (Hefner 1987c). Its headquarters was located in a Javanist village in an area otherwise dominated by NU, at the foot of the Tengger mountains. In this instance, AN-SOR youths had taken the initiative, without securing clearance for the action from the government or military. Now, however, as the violence was extended into areas where NU was too weak to act on its own, the support of the military was more important. The price for such support, however, was that stricter guidelines be used in targeting victims; a man's having been a vociferous promoter of Javanism no longer sufficed to condemn him.

Nahdatul Ulama's calls for holy war and the highly charged presence of its leaders in the purges still gave many uplanders the clear impression that what was really at issue in the conflict was religion. Clearly, from an organizational perspective, this was a misperception. Nonetheless, given the long history of regional antagonisms, the prominence of NU leaders in the roundup, and Muslim declarations that the violence was intended to usher in an Islamic state, it was easy for upland villagers to come to this conclusion.

Nowhere was this sense of primordial antagonism more clearly felt than in the Hindu upperslope region. In some nearby mountain communities, the screening teams required local militias to carry out the executions, but this option was ruled out in the Hindu region, apparently because the situation was considered too volatile. It was not that the PKI was stronger there. In fact it was smaller, and its cadres had always been rather timid in their actions. Its leadership, after all, was thoroughly dominated by the "merchant communists," many of whom came from some of the region's most distinguished families. Army leaders concluded, however, that the prominence of lowland Muslims in the purge of a non-Muslim region risked antagonizing the local population to the point of rebellion. Reportedly they also feared that the Hindus had dangerous magical powers that could be used against their enemies. Hence the military coordinators of the roundup decided to remove the local communists as quickly and quietly as possible and complete their task in a non-Javanist community below Puspo.

In some ways, the army leaders' assessment showed an astute perception of local tensions. Even more than the people of the midslope region, the upperslope Hindus had reacted to the violence with communitywide terror. During the first days of lowland killings, several PNI village officials had taken the unusual step of calling on their people to prepare to defend themselves from Muslim attack. Grossly misperceiving the organization of the violence, one PNI village chief (who had been active in the Republican guerrilla army) made a personal appeal to army officers in the lowlands to intervene and protect his threatened village. In another community a PNI village official who had long opposed the PKI nonetheless ordered that the small communist cadre in his village be protected from ANSOR violence. When screening teams entered his village a few weeks later, he paid for this directive with his life. These and other incidents help to explain why many uplanders saw the bloodshed as an act of Muslim violence against highland Javanists and Hindus. It was, many people said, *ngare* lowlander against Tengger highlander.

As the screening teams prepared to move into Hindu villages, whole communities were swept by incidents of spirit possession. Individuals were seized by ancestral and guardian spirits—the spirits invoked in every major ritual, and regarded as responsible for protecting the well-being of family and community (Hefner 1985, 70). The spirits spoke through the possessed, vainly urging reconciliation and an end to the violence. Such traditional religious instruments for dispute resolution may have been well suited for village feuding, but they were utterly ineffectual in the face of the machinery of state. Overwhelmed by a sense of impending doom, other villagers were found possessed along the sides of roads or outside their homes, shaking or crying catatonically. They remained possessed until friends, neighbors, and the village priest presented offerings to distraught ancestral spirits. No one could recall any such incident of mass possession before this period, and none has happened since.

The communists were finally moved to Sesari, where they were interrogated, and those deemed leaders were separated from the rest. When the day finally came for taking the prisoners away, a small crowd gathered quietly in the main square of the village where the PKI men were held. Guarded by anxious militia youths, two trucks (confiscated from one of the merchant communists) stood ready to carry away the forty suspects. As the men appeared, heads shaved, blindfolded, thumbs tied behind their backs, someone in the crowd let out a low moan, and then someone else another. Soon a handful of villagers began sobbing, shaking, and crying out furiously, their bodies stiff with the force of possessing spirits. Fearing violence, other villagers tried to restrain them and restore order. Alarmed by the outbreak, the screening-team leaders ordered local militia to push back the crowds. There was no resistance, only the gasping voices of ancestral spirits calling for peace and the release of loved ones. The trucks left without further incident.

For weeks afterward, a wave of collective possession swept neighboring communities as the souls of the ancestors cried out against the violence that had taken away relatives and loved ones. The prisoners who had been removed were never heard from again. Several days after their departure, the clothes of a few were quietly returned to relatives by a midslope villager who had witnessed the killings lower down the mountainside. The trucks had proceeded out of the highlands to an NU stronghold just below Puspo. There the men had been unloaded, and forced to dig a large pit. Then, one by one, they were beaten with bamboo clubs, their throats were slit, and they were pushed into the mass grave.

Many highlanders feared that this was just the beginning of a larger assault on their region. For weeks after the killings, rumors circulated that an ANSOR army was moving up the mountainside arresting and executing anyone who did not swear allegiance to Islam. The rumor, of course, was unfounded. No such ANSOR army materialized. For many people, nonetheless, the events of 1965–66 seemed to suggest a sad, but unavoidable, conclusion. It was the end, they said, the end of an upland way of life. A contest of generations had reached its conclusion. The people of the mountains had lost.

THE CHANGING BASES OF RURAL POLITY

Highlanders' assessment of their desperate situation ultimately proved inaccurate. Whatever its religious dimensions, the conflict was not in any organizational sense exclusively or even primarily about religion. The role of the state, or certain branches of it, was pivotal, as were an assortment of nongovernmental organizations.[6]

In the end too, the upperslope Hindus were not obliged to convert to Islam. They were required to establish formal ties with nationally recognized Hindu organizations, however, and to accept ritual and doctrinal reforms that reflected new state policies on religion (Hefner 1985, 247–65; cf. Lyon 1980). Similar changes occurred in the midslope highlands. Just two years after the bloodshed, Javanist Muslims in that region let up on

6. There is perhaps no more revealing document on the uncertain alliance of military leaders, party organizations, civil politicians, police, and religious groups involved in the anti-PKI purge than the anonymous eyewitness intelligence report on the violence in East Java written in November 1965; the picture that emerges from this confirms that in East Java the NU formed "the vanguard of the movement to crush the PKI and its mass organizations" (Anonymous 1986, 142). But it also indicates that there was hesitancy about the killings even within NU's ranks. This is a useful reminder of the fact that NU has often operated more as a loose alliance of religious leaders and their civil representatives than as a centralized party. Similarly, while the report shows that the military and the police took the initiative in coordinating attacks on the PKI, their efforts were at first handicapped by nationalist and leftist supporters in their own ranks. Elsewhere, the document shows, military and police units provided only follow-up support for bloodshed that was initiated by nongovernmental organizations. The document also confirms that during the first days of violence there was considerable regional variation in the scale and organization of anti-PKI activity. As in Pasuruan, this variegated organization took on a more coordinated, disciplined form only after the military settled scores in its own ranks.

mosque attendance as fears that they would be condemned as communists diminished. Later developments in this same area, however, undermined Javanism. Required by law to profess an officially recognized
religion (of which Javanist Islam was not one), many young people in the
mountains, especially those from affluent backgrounds, came to see little
point to traditional customs. Less attracted to the ways of the village, they
were drawn to the alluring images of modern Indonesia. An important
aspect of their new cultural citizenship was the profession of an official religion; for them that meant Islam. Ironically, the late 1970s saw a home-
grown movement for Islamic orthodoxy take shape right at the heart of
this Javanist stronghold (Hefner 1987c), another sign of the post-1965
diminution of antagonisms and realignment of social allegiances.

The emerging pattern of politics and community remains a complex
one, but already some trends are apparent. Developments since 1965–66
have systematically altered the economic organization of upland society
in a way that has battered down barriers to the outside. With roadbuilding and agricultural intensification have come new consumer goods, increased travel, and electronic media, all of which have provided
highlanders with increased exposure to outside ways. Education is also
on the rise, although in a fashion highly stratified by class. More young
people than ever are looking for employment opportunities outside the
region or to economic activities without precedent in the earlier, more
solidly agricultural, era. These developments have blurred the distinction
between uplander and lowlander and weakened the force of in-group allegiance (see ch. 6). They have also changed the form and bases of power
in rural society.

Lured by new goods, blessed by growing income, and backed by a
more powerful state, affluent villagers have responded enthusiastically to
these changes. Today they depend more for their standing on extravillage
institutions and less on the good regard of their neighbors. Not all members of the elite have turned away from the village; in the upperslope region, in particular, adherence to a minority religion presents a barrier to
wholesale appropriation of outside ways of life. Nonetheless, what James
Scott (1985, 177, 314) has noted of rural society in contemporary Malaysia
is broadly true here too: the affluent are less concerned to show off and
make a big name in the village because they spend more of their political
and economic lives elsewhere.

The National Framework for Rural Change

These local changes in community and power have been facilitated by
national developments. Early on in its rule, the New Order government
launched a variety of programs designed to restrict political activity and
weaken and redirect old allegiances. The first and most basic of these

measures was the destruction of the Indonesian Communist Party. Its elimination silenced a virulent, if often compromised, opponent of agrarian inequity. This ensured that future government initiatives would not be bothered by mass-based leftist foes.

But the government's political reforms extended further. First banning a number of the old parties, it then moved (shortly after the 1971 elections) to consolidate the remainder into two umbrella parties. One party (the "Party of Unity and Development") united all moderate Muslims under a label and platform stripped of any explicitly religious program (Samson 1978, 210). Muslims who had worked with the military to crush the PKI were disappointed to learn that they were as much subject to the new controls as everyone else. The other party amalgamated followers of the nationalist, Christian, and regional parties under a similarly domesticated platform. Candidates for leadership positions in these parties had to win government approval for nomination. The government exercised this right vigorously, intervening directly in party congresses and manipulating selection of party chiefs (Hering and Willis 1973, 6–9). Above both parties stood Golkar, the purportedly nonpolitical party of government functionaries. From the nation's capital to the most remote villages, officials were required to profess "monoloyalty" to this bureaucratic party. This policy effectively ended political pluralism within government (Ward 1974, 32–71; Emmerson 1978, 100–106).

In rural areas the guiding principle of these political reforms has been the doctrine of the "floating mass," according to which the rural population should not be distracted from the task of economic development by the intrusive activities of political parties except during those brief periods when electoral campaigning is allowed (Ward 1974, 189). Political parties are forbidden to establish branches below the regency level, restricting their operations to urban areas. In ex-PKI strongholds, village chiefs have been replaced with retired military commanders. Nationally, the doctrine of *dwifungsi* (dual function) legitimates such direct military involvement in political affairs by asserting the permanent responsibility of the armed forces in both national security and social development (Ward 1974, 28).

One consequence of these changes is clear. The political parties that penetrated the countryside in the 1950s, and that Western observers often regarded as the foundation of "a fundamental social reorganization" of rural life (Geertz 1965a, 127), have, for the moment, become massively irrelevant to agrarian political culture. In appreciating the significance of this, one must remember that it has occurred against a backdrop, not of rural quiescence, but of sweeping social change. The political organizations of old, in other words, have disappeared precisely when rural society has been most forcefully integrated into national structures. Village institutions provide little help in such radically detraditionalized circumstances. Neither can the political parties of pre-1965 days. Whereas the 1950s saw economic stagnation and a flowering of political organizations, the 1970s and 1980s have seen far-reaching social and economic change with few popularly based organizations to respond to its challenge.

As events in the Pasuruan highlands show, the one important exception to this general pattern is religion. It has now been a quarter century since the violence of 1965–66. All of the militantly anti-Islamic organizations that once operated in this mountain area, promoting the repudiation of Islam and a return to "the religion of Majapahit," have long since been outlawed. A generation has come of age that has little or no firsthand knowledge of the political antagonisms that pitted uplander against lowlander and Javanist against *santri* Muslim. It is a generation that, after 1966, was required to undergo compulsory education in one of the five religions recognized by the government: Islam, Catholicism, Protestantism, Hinduism, or Buddhism.

For Javanist highlanders these new strictures meant they no longer had the option of withdrawing their children from Islamic classes as formerly allowed (Boland 1982, 196; Noer 1978, 37). The related arrangement, once common in the uplands, of allowing Javanists to serve in schools as teachers of religion was also suppressed. The teachers who now provide religious instruction in midslope schools are graduates of Islamic teacher-training schools, institutions that have experienced significant expansion in the New Order period (Boland 1982, 197). The result has been that the quality and orthodoxy of Islamic instruction in midslope schools have increased significantly (Hefner 1987c).

Regarded under the old regime as a wing of Nahdatul Ulama, since its staff was recruited from that party's ranks, the Department of Religion has also come to play a more interventionist role in upland religion. Early on in the New Order, the department was "depoliticized." Its cabinet minister was recruited from the ranks of Golkar rather than Nahdatul Ulama, and, as with all government employees, its staff were required to swear their allegiance to the government party (Emmerson 1978, 96). Despite its "Golkarization" the department's budget has swelled, and its representatives have not let up on their promotion of adherence to recognized national religions. In East Java, especially, the department has earned a reputation for zeal in its promotion of *dakwah* (Islamic revitalization). Not surprisingly, the department has targeted Muslim areas of the Tengger highlands as one of several "weak zones" for which it allocates extra resources (Labrousse and Soemargono 1985, 222).

Ironically, the department's depoliticization may only have enhanced its effectiveness in promoting Islam in areas like the midslope highlands. A generation ago villagers openly defied the department's directives on religious education, since they viewed it as a tool of Nahdatul Ulama. Now when it urges villagers to attend mosque services or engage in Qur'anic study, as it has done here, it speaks with the authority of government. Its message is received by villagers who hear of the importance of religion in schools, the media, and village meetings. They hear this at a time, moreover, when the immensity of recent changes has convinced many people that the time has come to put village ways behind them and develop more modern social attitudes. The department's diatribes against *dhukun* ritual specialists and wasteful *slametan* festivals have struck a particularly responsive chord among middle and affluent farmers attracted to new forms of status and investment.

The time seems ripe for religious change, and it is occurring. After declining in the late 1960s, attendance at mosque services in midslope villages is again growing. "Javanist" villages now organize collection of the annual *zakat* (alms). Bright new prayer houses (*musholla*) can be seen in hamlets where years earlier no one performed daily prayers. Evening classes for Qur'anic study—rare in the midslope region prior to the 1970s—are training large numbers of mountain youths in ritual ways once contemptuously dismissed as *ngare*-lowlander.

Political and Religious Islam in Disjunction

These developments suggest that there may be a disjunction between the role of Islam in national politics and in popular religious culture. Nationally, the government's restrictions on party activity, and its requirement that Muslim parties renounce any plan of working for the establishment of an Islamic state, suggest that the organized influence of Muslim parties has declined. Similarly, it is well known that many high-ranking civilian and military leaders are avid enthusiasts of Javanist mysticism and deeply suspicious of Islam (Ward 1974, 123; Sundhaussen 1978, 77; Emmerson 1978, 96).

Although some observers view these facts as proof that Islam is everywhere in decline, other information suggests a more complicated picture. In some areas, after all, Golkar officials have worked closely with organizations promoting Islamic orthodoxy (Ecklund 1979, 260; Ward 1974, 82; Labrousse and Soemargono 1985). As Tamara (1985) has emphasized, the late 1970s and early 1980s have seen Islamic revival in large sectors of Indonesian society, and certain governmental bureaus have actively supported the effort (cf. Raillon 1985, 249).

Given the "bureaucratic pluralism" (Emmerson 1983) of the Indonesian state, of course, it would be a mistake to attribute a uniform practice to government officials. No state is a single agent, and, despite the best efforts of some despots, none is ever wholly monolithic. Here in Indonesia, it appears that some officials in the Department of Religion have promoted policies the long-term consequences of which might be objectionable to others in the government. For the moment, at any rate, this much is clear: Islam as an organized political entity may be in decline, but as a popular religious force it shows clear signs of good health.

All this is but one more sign that the "integrative revolution" (Geertz 1973b, 260) redefining the ties of village to nation has taken a somewhat different course from that widely expected thirty years ago. Although some political groups still promote alternative definitions of what the nation is to be, the range and intensity of debate have, for the moment, been decisively restricted. Today, the only popularly based nongovernmental organizations active in rural areas are religious ones. At the same time, rural society has been opened to a wide range of political and market forces, wreaking havoc with village traditions and creating tastes for more "national" life-styles. The changes in religious culture, then, are not happenstance events occurring independently of political and economic developments. Both have undermined the authority of the village at the same time that they demand, and provide the vehicles for, a new and more national identity.

It is not what one might have expected in the heyday of Indonesian parliamentary politics. In rural areas the promoters of the new economy and the new religion are drawn from the ranks of an elite that in an earlier era might have channeled its leadership energies into rival national parties. Now, if they play a formal role in government at all, chances are it is as members of the ruling party. If they are active in religious organizations, at least in the midslope region, it is in Islamic ones. In Muslim and Javanist areas alike, the members of this elite find themselves drawn to the same Honda motorcycles, television sets, and urban house styles. Strongly differentiated by class, this economic culture is less clearly marked by religion than was the case two generations ago. It bridges communities once separated by different status and ritual goods. In muting communalist differences, then, the new economy makes those of class all the more apparent. This, too, seems a distinctive feature of the emerging national culture.

The diminishing divisiveness of religion is reflected in other ways. In the midslope highlands former nationalist foes of the Muslim parties today speak loudly of the importance of Islam. Golkar-supported village chiefs promote an Islam purged of a Javanism that their counterparts two generations ago did their best to defend (Hefner 1987c). The Islam of which they speak, of course, is a ready-to-wear version that owes less to local ritual traditions or pious *santri* Muslims than it does to a generalized sense of national identity, and the importance of religion within it. It is also an Islam that at the moment wants little of political activism. Nonetheless, NU leaders in the nearby lowlands welcome these signs of Muslim piety on the part of their upland neighbors. They see it as proof that, whatever its setbacks in national politics, as a religious force, Islam continues to grow. For them, one must remember, Islam was never merely a means to a political end. It was a valued end in its own right.

In the upperslope highlands, these trends toward a more national religious culture have been less certain because of the local population's identification with Hinduism and continuing fear of Islam. Nonetheless, the response by leaders of this community has not been to close in on themselves, but to look outward to Hindu brethren in other parts of Indonesia (Hefner 1985, 247–65). The result is that even here a new, more "Indonesian" religiosity is slowly taking shape. It emphasizes belief in a supreme being, the need to replace "wasteful" ritual festivals with simple acts of devotion, and stricter bureaucratic controls over rural religion.

Some people refer to this new style of religiosity as *agama pembangunan,* "development religion." Like the changes in consumption shaking the modern highlands, this curious creation points to the "rationalization" of popular culture. As with those changes in consumption, however, the key to this process lies not in the abstract advance of an independent reason, but in changing state-society relations and, more particularly, the moral and political challenge of incorporation into the modern nation state.

CONCLUSION: POLITICS AND SOCIAL IDENTITY

During the 1950s and 1960s observers of the Indonesian scene spoke of the emergence of new forms of political integration, identified with the term *aliran* (from the Indonesian word for "current" or "stream"). Popularized in Indonesian studies by the anthropologist Clifford Geertz, the *aliran* concept emphasized that political organizations in independent Indonesia were built on preexisting allegiances of religion and community. Rather than grouping people by class, these cut vertically across social strata, distinguishing people along lines of Javanism, Islam, and, more generally, political ideology. It is important to emphasize that the *aliran* were not pure ideological entities for Geertz, as some of his critics have suggested. Each *aliran* segment had its own leaders, party structure, and associated social organizations, and it was their institutional interconnectedness, not ideology alone, that gave the *aliran* their social force (Geertz 1963, 15–17; 1965a, 127–29).

As Herbert Feith emphasizes (1982, 47), the concept of *aliran* was useful because it provided "the first really valuable tool for understanding the ways in which the ideas of national parties related to cultural patterns at the grassroots level in any part of the country." In the Javanese context in particular, the *aliran* idea seemed to make sense of the cleavage between, on one hand, Muslim parties, with their base in *santri*-dominated areas, and, on the other, the PNI and PKI, with their support in Javanist regions.

In Geertz's early work the *aliran* notion was also linked to a peculiar vision of nation-state development, strongly influenced by the seminal ideas of the sociologist Edward Shils (Shils 1957, 1960). Geertz saw the *aliran* as a "transformation of the santri, abangan, and prijaji traditions into modern universalistic ideologies." Recast in this more generalized format, the *aliran*, Geertz speculated, would eventually provide the symbolic framework for a "fundamental social reorganization" of rural allegiances (Geertz 1965a, 127). In short, the *aliran* were an integral part of an emerging national culture. It was to be built on a "civic sensibility" that superseded parochial ties of language, religion, and ethnicity, allowing for a broader, more consensual political dialogue (Geertz 1965a, 126).[7]

In recent years the *aliran* model has been widely criticized for its purported neglect of class (Anderson 1982, 79), confusion of ideological constructs with actual social structure (Kahn 1982, 92), and failure to recognize that patron-client exchanges often superseded ideological loyalties in determining *aliran* allegiances (Wertheim 1969, 10). Though the substance of some of these criticisms is debatable—Geertz most certainly did not think of the *aliran* as purely ideological or wholly independent of class, but argued that they were ideologically marked forms of social organization that incorporated and cut across class lines—these criticisms are right to demand that we reflect on the causes and consequences of the 1965–66 violence. In comparative and theoretical terms, the debate requires us to rethink the role of class and community in political conflict. A quarter century after the bloodshed, these issues must be at the heart of any effort to understand what Java was, and what it has become.

Class, Community, and the Sources of Social Power

The political history of Pasuruan provides insight into these complex issues. As we have seen, prior to 1965, political organization here did coincide in broad outline with long-standing cleavages of region and reli-

7. It is easy to discern the influence of Parsonian models of national development, with their emphasis on the importance of normative consensus as the basis for society, in Geertz's rather optimistic assessment of *aliran*. In fairness to Clifford Geertz, however, it is important to note that, unlike with Parsons, this emphasis was as much an expression of hope for Indonesia as it was a belief that such a consensus could ever be achieved; the vision was tempered by a realistic fear that things might go wrong. In one of his last works before 1965–66, for example, Geertz spoke sadly of the *aliran*'s "failure to make party politics work" (1965a, 150). Rather than domesticating political passions, the *aliran* seem only to have heightened them: "With each tremor at the national level local equilibrium was disturbed and all the hard-earned agreements, arrangements, and understandings were dislodged."

gion. NU dominated the Muslim lowlands, while the PNI and PKI vied for support in the Javanist uplands. To acknowledge that there was such a coincidence of religious and political affiliations, however, is not to imply that religion was their sole motive or organizational basis. Social groups often identify themselves in terms of shared cultural criteria such as religion, ethnicity, or ideology. But this does not mean that such criteria alone explain why actors come together as a solidary group. To emphasize that politics in pre-1965 Java was often played out along religious lines, then, is not to say that religion was the sole or even the primary cause of the conflict. As Michael Moerman (1967, 167) has argued for the study of ethnic groups, to understand the dynamism of status groups, one must look at them not only in terms of how they see themselves (though this too is a critical element), but also in terms of what they do, the interests they serve, and their relationship to other lines of social cleavage.

To rethink the history of the Javanese violence, then, we must clarify just what we mean when we say that the lines of political conflict sometimes coincided with religious community. "Religious solidarity" is almost always a misnomer or sociological synecdoche, inasmuch as what it involves is never just spiritual belief or ideology, but involvement in and identification with a whole community. As the history of highland Pasuruan shows, the compellingness of that identification is never just a spiritual or ideological fact. It emerges from participation in a social world, with its distinctive patterns of morality, class, and power. Religion in this broader sense, therefore, is always an index of more than itself. However rich its meanings, its authority is never just ideological. It depends, too, upon the social and political structures in which it is embedded and their ability to reproduce commitments to its ideals and life-ways.

This point is essential for an understanding of events in pre-1965 Pasuruan. From the 1950s on, religious issues—invariably in conjunction with party rivalries—exacerbated tensions between highlanders and lowlanders. These were not mere surrogates for an interclass struggle for control of the means of production. The social issues with which these disagreements were concerned—on the nature of religious community, the proper forms of worship, the rights of villages to regulate their own customs, the public display of female sexuality in dance and dress, and so on—were compellingly real in their own right.

To acknowledge the irreducibility of these cultural issues, however, is not to say that they were free of economic interest or consequence. Within each region the party structures that took shape "along religious lines" were often used to advance the economic interests of competing actors. Once in place, moreover, these political organizations achieved a measure of power and influence in their own right. Lowland landlords used Nahdatul Ulama's youth corps as a vehicle to defend their rights to land. Nationalist leaders in the uplands used their ties to district government to seize a portion of the disputed European lands for themselves. Though economic interests were at issue in both cases, the power wielded to advance them was not based on class organization alone, but on political structures of a more complex sort.

Similarly, even where class position might appear to have specified a common interest, political and religious allegiances often prevented members of the same class in different regions from working together. From the point of view of class, after all, it would have made better sense in 1964 for elites in both highland and lowland Pasuruan to put aside their religious differences and make common cause against their PKI rival. Clearly, this would have been to the particular advantage of the upland PNI leaders. Facing a vigorous communist challenge, they found themselves unable to rally around (lateral) class interests and call upon Muslim landowners for help.

The lesson is simple but important. Political solidarity is grounded in large part in the ability of communities and organizations to inspire commitments and penalize deviancy. As social anthropologists, in particular, have long been aware (Douglas 1970), the range of organizations capable of doing so is quite varied. We grossly oversimplify the origins of social power and the grounds for allegiance, then, when we automatically assume that their real basis is class or market position.

For the peasantry in the Tengger highlands, differences of religion and party affiliation were rightly viewed as reflecting far-reaching disagreements on what form social life should take and the nature of power and privilege. Religion and party, in other words, were indices of two very different ways of life, each with a slightly different culture, and each with its own mechanisms for inspiring and enforcing social allegiance. In a small way, one might say, it was here as it is in warfare between nation states: each side had its own class structure and internal political hierarchy, and the contest united people from different classes under a broader social banner.

To see this fact as evidence of a "false consciousness" on the part of the poor (or wealthy), or, even more misleadingly, as evidence of the absence of class influences, is to misconstrue class, substituting a unitary model for the more complex way in which class usually works. It would imply that the political influence of class is somehow more real when it operates independently of other social cleavages (which it never does) and results in conflict groups neatly polarized along lines of property ownership.

As has been widely noted, Marx believed that class would evolve along just such lines in the industrializing West, clearing the ground of religion, ethnicity, and other "archaic" status allegiances. With such traditionalist loyalties extinguished, politics would become a simple contest between two groups, the owners of the means of production and their propertyless laborers (Giddens 1973, 30; Parkin 1979, 5). Within the framework of such an idealized history, it was easy to believe that religion and ethnicity were spent forces, incapable of inspiring commitment or enforcing a political will. Similarly, to identify the forces that ultimately underlay social evolution, it seemed to make sense that one need only look to relations of production. Herein lay the hidden key to political and economic life alike.

Like the history of Europe since Marx's time, however, politics in Pasuruan shows that class is neither a unitary force nor the sole ground for social allegiance. This point is essential to the noneconomistic understanding of class. Class can work in conjunction with other social forces to create segmentary conflict groups, linking people of different classes but common race, religion, ethnicity, or whatever, against rival organizations also incorporating people of diverse class backgrounds. As Max Weber (1968, 926–39) emphasized, in other words, status groups identified in terms of religion, ethnicity, nation, or life-style can engender interests that bridge objective class groupings and have a moral and material integrity of their own. Although their identity appears grounded in noneconomic criteria, status groups of this sort invariably become important players in the contest for power and resources. We should not be fooled into thinking, therefore, that "economic" conflict is synonymous with class struggle. Competition for control of productive and cultural resources can be cast along more complex lines.

Our modern egalitarian values aside, then, there is nothing illusory about arrangements that link people of diverse class backgrounds in common cause. Nor, by extension, is it in any sense irrational or fetishistic for one to give one's life for one's nation, one's religious community, or some other social grouping irreducible to narrow economic advantage. Modern Java, and modern history generally, remind us all too often that men and women sacrifice themselves for more varied interests.

To say, then, that politics in pre-1965 Pasuruan was influenced by religion and regionalism, then, is not to imply that class in its circumstantial sense (see ch. 1) had little political influence. In fact, the contrary is the case. Class played a strong role in the political contest, but its impact was mediated through other social organizations in such a way that it sometimes worked to create segmentary alliances between classes, rather than neatly polarizing them in the way Marx envisioned in Europe.

In lowland Pasuruan, for example, the influence of land scarcity, rice shortages, and inflation worked to restrict the political options of the poor, forcing them into alliance with their NU patrons. Even working within an economistic framework, one can see that it was certainly in the best interests of a peasant in an NU-dominated lowland community to ignore communist appeals, even if they made moral sense and he or she was not a particularly pious Muslim. To join the PKI in such a village would have been tantamount to social suicide. Hence this actor's self-interest did not coincide with his interest as defined in a dichotomized class model, pitting owners of the means of production against laborers. A wider balance of forces than class has to be examined to determine actors' "economic" interests.

Clearly, in this instance, for example, the strength of rival parties would have to be factored into any assessment of the costs and benefits of different political options. So, too, would the influence of religious organizations and the state. Given this complex equation, the fact that an individual might choose to ignore PKI appeals is not necessarily evidence of false consciousness. It shows instead that more than relations of production must be considered when assessing an actor's social position and the structural interests it entails.[8]

It is important to note, finally, that both the *aliran* and productivist model of Javanese politics fail to grasp the importance of modern Indonesia's most critical political institution: the armed forces. Here is an organization grounded in neither cultural primordialism nor control of the means of production alone. Yet from 1957 on, it played a growing role in the nation's political and economic life. Since 1965 the armed forces have been the dominant force in the New Order polity. Their influence again underscores the important fact that all sorts of organizations can inspire and enforce allegiance, and that power does not flow from relations of production alone. The same point was made a half century ago by Weber (1968, 926; see also Giddens 1973, 43) in his analysis of the organizational distinctiveness of the state and the plural bases of social power. Modern political history only demonstrates the continuing relevance of this truth.

---

8. Wallerstein (1979, 172) makes a similar point, noting that status groups are not just based on shared identity, but often function to allow people to compete for resources. Having correctly recognized that status groups can play such practical roles, however, Wallerstein goes on to draw the mistaken conclusion that, in the end, status groups must be "blurred collective representations of class" (1979, 181). This sounds vaguely Marxist, since it keeps class in the foreground. But in fact it distorts Marx's own views on class, which always begin from relations of production. For Wallerstein, it would seem, any social group that competes for resources is a class. Besides confusing the concept of class, this argument fails to do justice to his own African examples. The point is that there are social organizations other than (lateral) class that can compete for scarce economic resources—political parties, ethnic groups, religious communities, and so on. Competition for resources can be based on a more varied array of groupings than class, and this fact requires us to attend to all solidary groups in a society, not just those specified by relations of production.

Here in modern Indonesia the state's intervention in 1965 marked the end of the *aliran* and the beginning of a new era in state-society relations. Its actions imposed new limits on the question of what Indonesia was to be. More than any other single institution, in fact, the New Order state created the foundation for the changes sweeping today's Java, transforming rural production, and challenging received ideas of community and authority.

EIGHT

Conclusion

Economy and Moral Community

In the final pages of his masterful *Javanese Villagers,* Robert Jay expressed the hope that his study would inspire comparative research in other areas of Java and the other nations of Southeast Asia. Some twenty years later, Jay's vision has yet to be realized even on the island of Java. We continue to make generalizations about Javanese culture and society based on what is, in fact, a narrow understanding of the island's regional variation. This much, however, is clear: highland communities must be accorded a greater role in any attempt to achieve a broader understanding of Javanese or Southeast Asian economy and society. Highland history is distinctive; its development sheds new light on the forces that have shaped Southeast Asia as a whole.

A SMALLHOLDER PEASANTRY

Though decisively influenced by events in the surrounding plains, society in the Tengger highlands differs from received images of the wet-rice lowlands. Here, as in upland areas of Central Java (Palte 1984, 11), the social order lacked the ranked class groupings found in lowland Java. Land tenure was based on individual fixed and heritable land rights, not communal ownership. The availability of land in the nineteenth century, and its low price during most of the twentieth, allowed residents to establish independent farms. In striking contrast to tenancy patterns in lowland Southeast Asia, the overwhelming majority of farms were owner-operated. The patron-clientage so widespread in wet-rice Southeast Asia was also virtually unknown here. The tone of upland interaction was set by an independent-minded middle peasantry. On an island where the consequences of destitution were all too apparent, the abiding concern of these highlanders was to maintain their autonomy so as to preserve their dignity.

Unlike Jay's lowland community in east-central Java (1969, 265), then, villages in the Tengger highlands were not "divided into two socially unequal parts" consisting of landowning patrons on one hand and their land-poor dependents on the other. A more appropriate image might resemble that painted by another author in a very different context: "A small holding, a peasant and his family, alongside them another small holding, another peasant and another family. . . . In this way the great mass of the French nation is formed by simple addition of homologous magnitudes, much as potatoes in a sack form a sack of potatoes" (Marx 1968, 172).

Contrary to Marx's impression of the French peasantry, however, this mountain population was not just a "vast mass, the members of which live in similar conditions but without entering into manifold relations with one another" (Marx 1968, 171). Traditional economy did not encourage extensive intraregional trade, a complex division of labor, or the development of class-based political organizations, features Marx cites to justify his disparaging remarks on the French peasantry. But highland society was not built around relations of production alone. In *sayan* festival labor, *slametan* celebrations, *sumbangan* ritual exchange, and everyday speech and etiquette, villagers created a richly textured social life. Though drawn into the politics and economy of larger Java, they maintained institutions and values of their own.

The Tengger region was never an undifferentiated society. Significant differences of class and status were apparent even in the tenth century, when this highland region was incorporated into a lowland-based state. In these precolonial times, priests and chiefs stood at the pinnacle of the local social structure. Both traced their roles back to status groupings based in part on descent (*tis*) (Hefner 1985, 270).

From the late eighteenth century on, landholding and labor relations were transformed by the European colonial state. Village leaders were rewarded for their cooperation with large grants of land, creating a new and more affluent elite. In this and other instances, political office was often a more important avenue to wealth and influence than the control of property alone. Indeed, in general, whether it was the conquest of the eastern salient by the Dutch (1706–80), the forced cultivation projects of the Cultuurstelsel (1830–70), liberalism and the emergence of private European farming (1870–1910), the closing of the forests (1910–20), or the destruction of the Communist Party (1965–66), state-level politics played a primary role in the making of this mountain peasantry.

Though reshaped by national policies, for much of its history upland society maintained a significant measure of social autonomy. Until barriers to the outside were pushed aside, for example, upland elites looked inward for guides to their values and investments. Villagers had long been involved in extraregional trade. But the uses to which they put their wealth showed the distinctive influence of local consumption norms, responsive to concerns more varied than the accumulation of wealth as an end in itself. Wealth had to acknowledge its neighbors if it was to reap a social reward. In this sense, the Tengger highlands resembled other "traditionalist" peasantries in Indian Mesoamerica, Africa, and southern Asia (Cancian 1965; Smith 1977; Wolf and Hansen 1972, 74; Douglas 1967; Barth 1967). Restrictions on the movement of people, goods, and ideas created strong barriers between the inside and outside world. The social borders allowed a community to survive with commitments and hierarchies of its own.

The autonomy of this upland society diminished as the modern era evolved. During the long middle ages from the fall of Majapahit to the coming of the Dutch, state control was especially weak, and the region preserved a religion and social hierarchy apart from those of Central Java. Had armies from the latter region not regularly invaded, and had Dutch colonialism not finally tipped the balance of power further, the native Javanese here and elsewhere in the eastern salient might have become an ethnic population separate from the Muslims of Central Java. In other areas of Southeast Asia, just such a process of cultural parochialization occurred. In particular, mountain terrains created barriers behind which ethnic minorities survived.

Conditions were not favorable to such an ethnogenesis here. The political economy of this mountain periphery was irreversibly transformed with the arrival of European colonialism. The Dutch brought with them a new kind of state. It systematically intervened in rural affairs, driven by a comprehensive vision of their usable wealth. Giving less leeway to native administrators, it replaced the central-point, "concentric-circle" pattern of the traditional Javanese polity (Anderson 1972, 22) with a more uniform bureaucratic web, "spun over the whole countryside, meshing it, more or less, into an administrative whole" (Elson 1978b, 42). Its primary purpose was to harness native energies to state enterprise.

Although in lowland Java it expanded and rigidified patterns of communal landholding, in the highlands colonialism reinforced extant patterns of smallholder production. The process was similar to that seen in coffee-growing areas of West Sumatra (Kahn 1980). There, too, the peasantry's incorporation into an international market did not polarize rural society into opposed classes of capitalist farmers and landless workers. Smallholding traditions survived, in part because they were consonant with European interests. Whatever its historical precedent, then, the Tengger region's smallholding tradition was not a product of timeless traditionalism. It survived in part because it worked so well with European colonialism.

One additional consequence of this incorporative revolution was the standardization of production, class, and communications across a once loosely integrated territorial expanse. This, too, served the extractive interests of European colonialism well. Unwittingly, however, it also created the conditions for new forms of native community. Here in eastern Java, the fragmented localism of the precolonial era gave way to more encompassing visions of ethnicity, Islam, and, eventually, nationalism. The vigor with which colonialism recast rural society paved the way for the system's eventual demise.

During the early years of Dutch rule, however, the people of the Tengger highlands were only marginally involved in colonial schemes, and they maintained their sense of being apart. As Java's population grew and the means were found to exploit the island's "waste lands," however, the highlands were brought into this same administrative grid. With coffee the most profitable export during the life of the Cultivation System (Van Niel 1972, 91), the demand for upland produce seemed limited only by the mountains' sparse population. Nineteenth-century population growth provided a ready solution to the labor shortage. Lowland immigrants flooded the highlands. In just a few years, they cut its jungles, killed off its game, and built government coffee estates. The transformation revealed for the first time the upland's environmental fragility. By the end of the nineteenth century, production fell as coffee was stricken with leaf blight. Large expanses of land showed telltale signs of erosion. Environmental problems forced the government to close the forests to further cultivation. The highland frontier disappeared, but not before providing alarming indications of its ecological limitations.

The subsequent evolution of agriculture was determined not by the interests of sustainable development but by the triple forces of government, population, and, fitfully, commercial enterprise. At the end of the nineteenth century, roadbuilding and land leases brought European farmers. Since they were few in number, their impact in the Tengger highlands was relatively modest. Shortly thereafter, however, native "merchant-farmers" arrived as well. They would have a more far-reaching impact. Though of Javanese or Madurese background, the merchant-farmers adopted the profit-oriented practices of Europeans and Chinese. Like the Europeans, they limited their role in agriculture to supervision, devoting themselves to off-farm activities like trade and transportation. Following the Europeans, too, they introduced more restrictive forms of wage labor. They also brought debt-indentured workers from the lowlands. The commercial expansion these Muslim immigrants pioneered was not built on capitalist wage labor alone, then, but on forms of indebted labor long familiar in Southeast Asia (Reid 1983).

As in other areas of Indonesia and Malaysia (Breman 1983, 35; van der Kolff 1936, 18; Geertz 1960, 131; Scott 1985, 18), *santri* or orthodox Muslims were disproportionately represented in the ranks of these managerial farmers. Although some of their agricultural innovations spread to the local population, particularly in the midslope region, other *santri* initiatives were resisted. Animated by different religious convictions, the Muslims built mosques, refused to join in ritual exchange, and campaigned against Javanist rites. The example is of comparative interest in Southeast Asian studies. Although at different times and in different places Islam has worked against sociopolitical hierarchy (Nakamura 1983), in this corner of Java it was in its vanguard (cf. Scott 1985, 14–22).

The commercial expansion, at any rate, was short-lived. The 1930s brought economic decline and the ruin of many Muslim traders. For the majority of mountain farmers, of course, commercialization had involved no more thorough reorganization of production than substituting cash crops for maize. In the face of the economic downturn, then, their reaction was simple. They cut back on cash crops and returned to subsistence cultivation of maize. In the upperslope region, the spread of a fungal blight in the 1930s gave added impetus to the commercial downturn.

The recession did not bring across-the-board disintensification, however; nor was it accepted with passive resignation. Pushed by shrinking landholdings, farmers responded with extraordinary initiative. They reduced fallow time, replaced the plow with the hoe, weeded more regularly, applied animal manures, intercropped, and opened even the steepest lands to cultivation. Erosion, leaching, and mudslides continued. Lacking the ecological durability of wet-rice *sawah*, *tegal* intensification increased short-term production, but also often violated long-term environmental interests. Though aware that, as they say, "the earth has lost its fragrance" (*ora wangi maneh*), farmers had little choice but to choose strategies that guaranteed a steady income, whatever their long-term impact. The challenge of sustainable development was all too clear.

The Great Depression was followed by the even greater devastation of the Japanese occupation and the Indonesian national revolution. The highlands suffered deforestation, road deterioration, and the depletion of livestock herds. They also saw the flight of Chinese capital, the destruction of the last coffee stands, the disruption of lowland markets, and the confiscation of the hard-won wealth of indigenous traders. Although there was a small commercial revival in the mid 1950s, it too was finally undercut by ecological decline and political disorder.

The three-decade recession did not eliminate class distinctions; indeed, in a few villages it may have accelerated their growth. Its cumulative effect, however, was to force most farmers into a low-risk subsistence agriculture, supplemented by cultivation of a few cash crops. The threat to popular welfare lay less in proletarianization than in pauperization, as landholdings and employment opportunities shrank.

In this upland region, then, history provides us with a partial answer to the Alexanders' (1982, 603) question as to how we are to explain the "non-reproduction of a landlord class" in Java—that is, why differences of wealth and power did not bring about greater inequality and more sustained commercial growth. In the Tengger highlands, nineteenth-century colonialism reinforced patterns of smallholder production. Though the 1920s saw growing economic stratification, the commercial intensification foundered on political, economic, and ecological obstacles. A middle peasantry survived, clinging desperately to its smallholdings. Local society awaited a more thorough integration into the national political economy.

In a few years, the changes of post-1965 Indonesia swept aside most of these obstacles. With the elimination of the Communist Party and the imposition of strict political controls, with roadbuilding and an expanded fleet of light-weight trucks, with ideological and administrative supports for commercial cultivation, and, finally, with green-revolution agrochemicals, a new social economy took shape. Reaching far deeper into native society than the commercial agriculture of old, the system transformed production. What ensued, then, was not merely a repetition of the trade expansion of the 1920s, but a genuine reshaping of technology, class, and consumption.

The consequences of this upland green revolution, it must be emphasized, were not uniform. Demand for labor changed little in the midslope region; in the long run, in fact, it may decline. In the upperslope region, however, labor demand expanded significantly, providing employment opportunities for the poor. In both regions, new forms of labor organization were not restricted to impersonal wage ties, but also involved the expansion of patronage. The latter, however, was of a less enduring and asymmetrical nature than commonly seen in wet-rice Southeast Asia (Hart 1989, 37).

In the midslope region the new agriculture attracted outside investment and inflated land prices. It made more firm the previously permeable barrier between rich and poor. In the upperslope region land prices also increased. But for the most part, the green revolution there actually strengthened the hold of small farmers on their land. In both mountain areas, finally, the majority of people remain at least marginally involved in farming their own land, cushioning their dependence on wage labor. For the moment, a middle peasantry survives, muting the gap between rich and poor, and restricting the development of a landless proletariat.

One point stands out from this economic history. It is that economic change here, and in Java as a whole, cannot be reduced to either of two familiar development stories: "capitalist penetration" or the unfettered expansion of free-market forces. A broader range of influences than either of these models acknowledge was central to upland Java's development. These included roadbuilding, improved communications, ecological degradation, population growth, religious change, and, very important, the ongoing adjustment of state-society relations. Indeed, if one had to single out one dominant influence in this whole process, it would be the activities of the state, not native capitalism or the autonomous dynamism of free enterprise.

Marxists and (Adam) Smithians alike overemphasize the independent role of the market and capitalism in modern economic change. Capitalism is not a self-sustaining entity; its precise operation is always mediated by social, legal, and political institutions. From its beginning, the expansion of European capitalism was critically shaped by the policies and intervention of the nation state (Giddens 1987, 159; Skocpol 1982, 176; Wolf 1982, 100). Somewhat paradoxically, the autonomy the market achieved in Western society would have been impossible without an array of extra-market legal and political supports, which have a complex history of their own. Similarly, in modern East Asia, most recent examples of capitalist industrialization have also depended on the supportive intervention of state agencies (Chirot 1986).

In Indonesia the market and private capital have rarely displayed even this degree of autonomy. In colonial times the state assumed primary responsibility for the channeling of investment and the mobilization of labor. Even today the state remains central in the formulation of development policies. It seems unlikely that any independent social grouping will emerge in the near future to challenge this monopoly of economic power.

A history that seeks to understand the dynamics of economic change, then, must attend to more than the logic of the marketplace or the interests of capital. It must, above all, understand the commitments and capabilities of different social actors, and the structures of authority and value that have made them what they are. Here, as in all societies, politics and culture are central to the process of economic development.

ECONOMIC DEVELOPMENT AND CULTURAL CHANGE

Since its beginnings in the nineteenth century, one of the central concerns of this interdisciplinary enterprise we call "social theory" has been to come to terms with the forces reshaping modern economy and society. Looking back at this intellectual heritage, it is surprising to note, as Anthony Giddens (1973, 10) has commented, how little progress has been made beyond the classical formulations of Marx, Weber, and Durkheim. As the "great transformation" moved from the First World to the Third, the field of analysis became vaster, and its moral urgency greater. Yet it is still more difficult for us to speak of the human consequences of modern economic development than it is of the formal characteristics of production and price formation.

Though neglected in mainstream economics, the concept of tastes or "preferences" provides a useful point of entry to this discussion (Bourdieu 1984; Hefner 1983b; McPherson 1983). It links what some analysts mistakenly see as opposed "spheres": economy and culture, the material and the meaningful. Anthropologists, of course, have long been interested in preferences, though in general they have not recognized the link to economists' ideas. Anthropology's approach to preference tends to be of a holistic or institutional sort, concerned with the meaning and value of cultural objects within a particular social context. Evans-Pritchard's (1940) comments on Nuer "interest in cattle," for example, explored not the aggregate consequence of individual preference for livestock, but the ecological, political, and symbolic conditions that made the interest culturally compelling (cf. Comaroff 1985, 68).

Neoclassical economics and its derivative political theories, by contrast, tend to take an individualistic perspective on the problem of preference. Rational choice from among preferred alternatives is, in effect, the primal act in neoclassical theory; economic man is above all a chooser (Popkin 1979, 31). The actual origins of those preferences, however, are of little importance to the overall neoclassical project. Their origins are viewed as inscrutably private and, in any case, relatively unimportant (Stigler and Becker 1977). They lie, it is assumed, outside the sphere of rational choice, somewhere in the "irrational" world studied by sociology and anthropology.

For a growing number of economic researchers (Felix 1979; McPherson 1983; Sen 1977; Etzioni 1988), however, the fact that preferences may originate in a process that is intersubjective rather than intrasubjective in no way relieves us of responsibility for their analysis. Rather than dismissing facts when they fit poorly in our models, we must confront them and expand our inquiry.

From historical examples like the one discussed in this book, it is clear that individual preferences are not conceived immaculate of society or culture. People receive social assistance in constructing their notions of the preferred and valuable, just as they do in formulating their attitudes of right and wrong (Shweder et al. 1987, 83). As here with highlanders' interest in ritual festivity, tastes are influenced by the structures of social life, with their peculiar organization of status, power, and investment (Sahlins 1976, 166–204; Leiss 1976; Hefner 1983b). Ultimately, too, they are related to the social "commitments" (Sen 1977) actors make to those around them, sustaining a moral sense of self in the process.

Although recalibrated in the practice of everyday life, these commitments inform each instance of individual calculation. They build on what social psychologists call "social referencing," or the anchoring of one's sense of self through identification and comparison with other groups and ideals (Sherif and Sherif 1969, 418; Feinman 1982, 445). "Self-interest," then, is not derived from rational deduction alone, least of all of the curiously solipsistic sort emphasized in neoclassical economics. It builds on a sense of self, with the social identification and comparison that sensibility implies.

To acknowledge that economic behavior is informed by social referencing means that our models of economic men and women must be more culturally and psychologically realistic. To begin, we must replace the abstract *homo economicus* with real people, situated in particular histories and cultures (cf. Keyes 1983b, 852). Then we must listen carefully to learn who they are and who they wish to be, and discover the implications of these commitments for economic choice. "The view of the person as a clear-headed maximizer over clearly defined preferences must give way to the image of a more complicated and less certain actor, attempting to sort out what is worth doing and what sort of person to be" (McPherson 1983, III). Consumption builds on this ongoing reference to self and community. Personal but not inscrutably private, preferences communicate a position in a social structure and an identification with a way of life.

Here, then, is a view that allows us to see economic processes as cultural and interactive from the start. It also provides a useful corrective to general models of social practice. We are encouraged to recognize the elements of deliberation and choice in behavior, long emphasized by economic theorists. From this perspective, actors are not social dummies motivated exclusively by the shared norms or "symbols and meanings" of their culture. To varying degrees in different social contexts, they also evaluate and reflect on alternate ends, at times questioning their culture's norms.

While introducing a deliberative dimension into our understanding of social action, the social-referential perspective enables us to avoid the narrowly individualistic viewpoint that informs most economic models (cf. Ortner 1983, 151). Actors are capable of reflective evaluation, but in doing so they do not simply consult some obscure calculus of desire. They also refer to their sense of self and their relationships to others around them.

This same insight provides a useful point of departure for comparing traditional economies with those that we see in the throes of modern development. The traditional-modern distinction, of course, is an ideal type. It refers not to actually existing social formations but to general tendencies, which we schematize so as to perceive more clearly the detail of different social orders. Above all, one must insist, the difference between traditionalism and modernity does not lie in the opposition between clearheaded "rationality" and a drearily unreflective "custom," as some models of modernization (including many Weberian ones) might suggest. The contrast lies in the way different social orders control preferences, inspiring actors to identify with some people while distinguishing themselves from others.. All social life, and all economic choice, builds on this economy of inclusion and exclusion.

Traditional social orders tend to be conservative in their management of tastes. It is not that actors are less rational, but that the social system that governs economic life depends upon a more tightly controlled circulation of goods, rights, and authority. It is the social structure, not individual rationality per se, that differs. Gender, status, and class are often distinguished by clearly demarcated life-styles. In such a context, aspirations are fitted to conventionalized social roles. Conformity to this "fixed need format" (Leiss, Kline, and Jhally 1986, 57) is seen as virtuous, while deviance invites the wrath of all those with a vested interest in received arrangements. In such circumstances, there can be no illusion that preferences are inscrutable private facts; their genesis is unequivocally related to the larger structures of everyday life.

As with ritual in the Tengger mountains, the association of certain consumption styles with a particular social group can be used as a badge of communal identity, creating a boundary marker between insiders and outsiders. This symbolization may impede the free flow of valuables from one society to another (cf. Douglas 1967; Barth 1967). In so doing, it creates a barrier behind which local economies and moralities can take hold. Invariably, however, these communal goods also have an internal distributional dimension. Rather than a free market of investment, the social order intervenes to regulate the circulation of valuables. People of high standing are expected to show their rank through the control and consumption of prestige goods. Through various social controls, other people are barred from their enjoyment.

Even in the most traditional of societies, of course, there is social mobility through the life-cycles of individuals and general social competition. In the traditional Tengger highlands, for example, there was social mobility in the *sumbangan* exchange system and the status order to which it was related. To overstate the point somewhat, however, the competition for prestige that these institutions served always ended by affirming received tastes. The perpetual reshaping of wants seen in modern capitalist societies would be out of place here, because the structure of society itself depended upon the stable correlation of preference and social position. In traditionalist economies from Tengger to the Trobriands, in other words, individual actors may rise and fall, but, if the larger system is to persist, their movement must validate the traditional correlation of status and goods. The social structure itself depends on this controlled circulation.

As the history of the Tengger highlands shows so well, commercial change need not undermine such traditionalist arrangements. A small-scale community may interact over extended periods with a capitalist economy without adopting all its features, least of all its perpetual adjustment of consumer tastes, or the class structure they imply.

Despite two centuries of involvement with the colonial economy, for example, the upperslope Hindus maintained a distinctive ritual and status scheme. Strict controls were placed on the movement of goods from the outside. Where wealth came into the village, it was carefully channeled into projects consonant with local forms of distinction. This did not mean that those who were wealthy always remained wealthy, and the poor, poor. In fact, there was considerable liberty in the pursuit of private fortune; individuals were free to become as rich as they could in trade. In this instance, social norms did not forbid the accumulation of wealth, but imposed strict limits on the uses to which, once acquired, it could be put. Moral barriers distinguished "lowland" from "upland" goods and barred certain types of consumption while enjoining others. Thus the competition for prestige seen in ritual festivals and *sayan* labor was to a significant degree open. But it always ended by reaffirming the compelling appeal of in-group ways. Private preference bore the visible traces of a people's way of life.

Where mobility beyond the in-group is weak, and internal controls are still strong, communities like those in the Trobriands, Indian Mesoamerica, or highland East Java can ensure a continuing identification with the group and the restricted investments it implies. As reference-group theorists noted a generation ago, however, where controls weaken and social mobility beyond the community increases, members of some social strata are likely "to contrast their own situation with that of others [outside], and shape their self-appraisals accordingly" (Merton 1968, 321). The political and moral boundary between in-group and out-group thus weakens. Some actors begin to look elsewhere than their community of residence for guides to what sort of person to be and what ends to pursue. The sense of self always implicit in economic choice suddenly becomes problematic. The search for new models of self-evaluation is on.

The causes of this weakening of boundaries may be varied—the product, for instance, of commercial growth, popular education, new communications, or a more intrusive state. But its impact on economic culture is everywhere the same. In the technical vocabulary of reference-group theory, social mobility and weakened in-group controls increase the probability that an actor's reference group need not coincide with his or her membership group (Merton 1968, 287). Values and preferences are suddenly opened to comparison with the outside, and local control over status and consumption is weakened. The village is drawn into the aspirations of the surrounding world.

Though cast in a technical vocabulary, the insight is an important one, and allows us to link economists' models of preference and anthropologists' notions of cultural value to the study of social and economic change. To explore the link, however, we must specify more clearly what we mean by culture, and its relation to preferences, agency, and human action.

Culture, Agency, and Economic Action

In interpretive social science we sometimes assume that individuals simply "internalize" the values of the group or community of which they are members. Culture in this view is something inherited from our predecessors, a more or less ready-made system of symbols and ideas, learned in rituals and other cultural performances, and used to understand and act in the world (cf. Geertz 1973a; Schneider 1976).

Though it points in the right direction, this is for most purposes a much too powerful model of culture. Not all the knowledge we learn in social life is transmitted in such a prepackaged and comprehensive format. A good portion of the knowledge we need to act in the world is, in fact, reconstructed by each of us as individuals. It depends, then, not on the passive internalization of prefigured symbols and meanings, but on an ongoing improvisation in the face of environmental demands and opportunities. The cognitive product of this effort can be similar for different individuals despite the fact that it is strongly dependent on individual construction. It is so, not because culture is an exhaustive guide to action and understanding, but because, endowed with similar minds and subjected to similar socialization, actors grappling with the same life-problems reach similar conclusions.

This is not to deny that a significant portion of our knowledge consists of shared formulas, categories, and perceptual dispositions, or that these influence our thought, perceptions, and actions. The point is simply that social life often contradicts received ways or poses new problems, pushing understanding beyond conventionalized forms (cf. Bloch 1989). The richness of thought is not exhausted, then, by the prefigured knowledge we acquire as members of a society. Rather than seeing culture as a relatively complete "template" for understanding and acting, we have to recognize that, from the perspective of social practice, it is cognitively deficient. In much of social life, it provides only a general, "qualitatively determined creative competence" (Sperber 1974, x–xi; cf. Bourdieu 1977, 2–17; Hefner 1985, 18–20).

By restraining our concept of culture in this way, and shifting some of the responsibility for meaning back to the agent, we can better address the challenge of economic behavior for social theory and historical change. As Weber best demonstrated, economic behavior involves preference, evaluation, and choice. Since we lack the ability to satisfy all our desires, we must in some circumstances evaluate our ends and the available means for their satisfaction. This is the simple essence of economic action. For general models of social action, it implies that there is a problem-solving and evaluative dimension to human behavior, as well as (and always in conjunction with) a "meaningful" one.

Interestingly enough, the economic dimension of Weber's social theory has received much less attention among his contemporary followers than has his emphasis on humans as culture-bearing beings. But the real achievement of Weber's work was his insistence that the two dimensions of human reality—the economic and the interpretive—are inextricably linked (Keyes 1983a). Though in the end he failed to come up with a definitive theory of their relationship, Weber's historical studies brilliantly demonstrate that economic action is everywhere influenced by the attitudes and dispositions acquired in the course of socialization. Rather than being an asocial rational calculus, economic choice builds on an identification with community and its ideas of value and reward. In short, social life presents problems that require choices in which we evaluate our preferences in light of who we are and what we wish to become. Identity and preference interpenetrate in the practice of everyday life. In so doing, they also confirm or reshape the commitments that define who we are.

The polarization in recent years between "softer" and "harder" versions of social science has blocked us from pursuing this insight. The consequences are familiar. Losing sight of the economic dimension of social action, interpretive social science "oversocializes" human beings, portraying them as animated by prefigured norms and meanings (Wrong 1961; Etzioni 1988, 7). Economic theory, meanwhile, undersocializes its actors. The rational capabilities of "economic man" show few signs of social or cultural influence.

In the end, there need be no such opposition between economic and cultural analysis. A more restrained notion of culture encourages us to recognize that, from the actor's perspective, culture is neither a finished system of symbols and meanings nor an exhaustive guide to action. It is the interpretive ground that makes possible further evaluation and improvisation. Its significance for social action is only fully realized in the efforts of individuals to define who they are and what they can do in light of the world's opportunities and constraints.

Economic Change as Cultural Reorientation

With such an agency-based view of culture, we can better appreciate the problems at the heart of economic life without alternately oversocializing or undersocializing our actors. Such an interactive, social-psychological view of culture also provides us with the tools with which to understand a problem at the heart of changes like those seen in the Tengger highlands.

Economic change involves a process of cultural reorientation, similar in some ways to alienation. The traditions of old are no longer compelling. New tastes push people toward new images of prestige and life-style. No one is quite sure where events are going. There is a sense of excitement and experimentation as new horizons appear. But the opening to the new also brings a repudiation of the old. Economic man and economic woman know more than their private desires; they are, in this instance, alienated from what they were.

The concept of alienation provides more than a metaphor for the analysis of economic change. It highlights a point of mediation between the changing macrostructures of political-economy and the altered commitments of community and personal identity. In a more technical vocabulary, alienation implies that people relate themselves to groups and ideals other than the one(s) in which they are immediately involved, sometimes using an "out-group" as the model for their aspirations and sense of self (Merton 1968, 287). Though cast in an unfamiliar idiom, this problem is at the heart of development in the modern world.

By itself, of course, the theoretical recognition of alienation is trivial, though it is distressing to note that theorists from George Herbert Mead to Margaret Mead have tended to neglect it, tacitly assuming that actors' frames of reference always originate in the social group to which they belong. What makes this truism more important, however, is the recognition that the conditions under which some people begin to look outside their membership group for values and guides to their sense of self are not random. In relatively small, stable societies, with a low incidence of mobility, reference groups and membership groups are likely to coincide (Sherif and Sherif 1956, 421; Merton 1968, 321). The integrity of the community creates a world in which political and moral constraints reinforce each other. The lack of alternatives to received life-ways, and the penalties for deviance, ensure their consonance.

Where, by contrast, outward mobility increases, national communications penetrate the local community, or, for whatever reason, the legitimacy of received ways is put in question, some individuals are likely to look outside their community for new ideas and aspirations. Once a local community is "opened" in this fashion—inevitably, it seems, with some of the elite custodians of the old order in the lead—the freer perception of juxtaposed worlds encourages some to aspire to life-ways with little local precedent. The boundaries of self and community shift; a new answer is found to the question of "what sort of person to be." This changed or changing sense of self and other transforms economic values and drives social change. We lose sight of this powerful truth when we substitute abstract models of "economic man" or "class interest" for a more sustained excursion into history and culture.

Here, then, is a clue to just how, despite centuries of interaction with the outside, the Tengger highlands maintained an economy and status system distinct from the lowlands'. The same insight explains just why this local system, and so many others in the developing world, are today in decline. In the Javanese case, changes in education, transportation, communications, and state policies reshaped rural life even before the transformation of production. Local elites played an especially important role in the changes. Drawn into the surrounding society, they were among the first to compare themselves with outsiders whose goods and investments had previously been stigmatized as "lowlander" (*ngare*). Catching wind of new ways, they shifted their investments into the currency of national markets and social structures. With the guardians of tradition defecting, the barriers excluding foreign goods collapsed.

The change obscured the clarity of in-group boundaries, and encouraged more and more people to embrace outside ways. The boundary between in-group and out-group, essential to any localized identity, thus weakened. So, too, did the structures of investment, exchange, and prestige that once defined an upland way of life. This was not just a moral or cultural event. At every moment it was informed by changing relations of power inside and beyond the village. From this perspective the long-trumpeted contest between political and moral accounts of economic change is a false one (Scott 1976; Popkin 1979). Each inexorably informs the other. Social change is nothing if not both.

Here, in a nutshell, is a cultural dilemma at the heart of development in much of the Third World. Even where production, property, and class are as yet untransformed, broader changes in consumption, communication, and government challenge local ways, expanding people's social references and unleashing a flood of new aspirations. The resulting crisis is as much moral and cultural as it is material and political. Changes in reference-group aspirations can, of course, work hand in hand with changes in production. In many instances, however, they precede them, stimulated by developments in media, schools, government, and life-style. To argue otherwise and insist on the priority of productive infrastructures is to lose sight of the power of government and communications. Both are key ingredients in this condition we call modernity. Notwithstanding economistic accounts to the contrary, neither is a mere epiphenomenon of industrial capitalism (Giddens 1987, 2; Skocpol 1985).

In the context of developing societies, social aspirations are volatile precisely because they can be stimulated far in advance of new forms of production. Penetrating more deeply into society, the state and communications transplant urban and elite values into even the most peripheral villages. Popular desires soon outstrip society's capacities to respond to their demand. It is for this reason, after all, that governments commit such vast resources to the management of cultural tastes. Through religion, language standardization, national rituals, and, above all, strict regulation of political life, states like the one here in Indonesia try to fit aspirations into acceptable molds. In other countries, responsibility for managing this reference-group revolution may be more broadly shared, and include businesses, religions, and other nongovernmental organizations. Whatever the precise pattern, the resources expended in this effort often rival those committed to technical aspects of economic development. From the perspective of national elites, of course, such expenditure makes good sense. Their privileges often depend on monopoly control of state resources or the tailoring of their citizenry's wants to the products of private enterprise. Hence they have a personal interest in this drive to domesticate popular desires.

As the Indonesian example suggests, however, questions of who to be, what to want, and what to share with one's fellows, are rarely answered in a free market of ideas. Amidst the turmoil of national development, rival groups arise proposing alternative solutions to the problems of a post-traditional world. The struggle for modernist identity is politicized. In Indonesia forty years ago, political parties were at the heart of this effort to redefine national aspirations. Today, with party activity frozen, and popular organizations repressed, state bureaus and businesses play a more pivotal role. The range of allowable ideas is also more limited. In such a context, it is not surprising that one sees a more privatized, "consumer" ethos than was typical in the old days. But what looks like the birth of an individualistic economy is itself the product of a long social history. Private preference always knows a social truth.

For the moment the Indonesian government appears to be in control of this reference-group revolution. In a certain sense, however, it has unleashed forces greater than it can understand. The government seeks to create a pacific "floating mass," unbothered by the political turmoil of the old regime. It urges villagers to respect village leaders and abide by the high-sounding, if rather remote, ideals of New Order policy. It speaks of the importance of *adat*-custom in social life and "traditional cooperation" (*gotong royong*) in economic affairs (Bowen 1986). Meanwhile, the economic and political changes it has promoted have only undermined the appeal of customary life-styles and rendered local traditions quaintly obsolete.

In so doing, the government has subjected previously separate regions to powerful currents of cultural standardization. Their impact is visible in the diffusion of luxury goods into regions where, two generations earlier, religious and ethnic goods marked clear communal boundaries. But the demise of local society has brought other changes as well. The penetration of orthodox Islam into Javanist areas of the countryside in particular shows that recent changes have sometimes played to Muslim advantage as well. An analogous process is unfolding in most of the developing world, where political incorporation has created new, more national, life-styles and broadened the debate on what society is to be.

From these examples, it is clear that national development engenders complex countercurrents. Local communities are drawn into a national grid. Status and class look to a larger market of values and investments. Even in remote villages, people become aware of their citizenship in a larger nation. With this awareness come new questions on identity and community. Through all this, then, development affects more than production and income. It unleashes a contest to redefine identity and community in a post-traditional world. This reference-group reorientation is a revolutionary force in its own right.

At this point in Indonesian history, and on the basis of this regional study, it is impossible to say what the consequences of this contest will be. This much, though, seems clear: here, as in most of the developing world, the certainty of appeals to local ways is destined to fade. Issues of community and identity, however, will not. Though political structures may limit their debate, the future will only underscore their urgency. Under these circumstances, the struggle to define community will remain at the heart of this process we call national development. It will be this way because it must be, for it is only through a sense of self and community that we define what is valuable, and what we must resist.

APPENDIX

A Note on History and Ethnographic Method

During one of my first visits to the Tengger mountains in the summer of 1977, I hitched a ride with a truck driver to the village of Ngadiwono, where he was picking up a shipment of cabbages. With great excitement, he explained to me that the people of that village—the most prosperous in the Tengger highlands, and eventually one of my field sites—were "just like Americans; they like to earn lots of money the capitalist way, then spend it real quick on things like televisions and motorbikes." By contrast, the people of a nearby community, he insisted, "like the social-ist way better; they do everything together and nobody gets rich, except the village officials."

Though the truck driver's assessment was far too simplistic, our con-versation that afternoon provided me with an introduction to the excite-ment and difficulties of historical ethnography. At the time, the Tengger highlands were still in the early stages of their economic transformation, and were barely a decade removed from the bloodshed of 1965–66. Al-though I did not realize it then, new changes were reviving old tensions in villages. Over the next years, as I became involved in village life, I be-came an unwitting player in a struggle to define what had happened in this region, and what it should become.

Collecting the oral histories that underlie important sections of this book, then, was not just a matter of tapping shared public truths. Some people were unwilling to enter the fray; for that matter, many felt awk-ward expressing their opinions on any topic. Though education and tra-vel are bringing great change, these mountain Javanese place much less emphasis on verbal skills than their lowland counterparts. There is here no real tradition of storytelling, and in conversations it is considered im-polite for any single individual to talk too forcefully. These qualifications aside, in my first months in the highlands it gradually became apparent that a good deal of behind-the-scene discussion was going on, and many villagers were partisans in a contest to define their history.

For some of the topics addressed in this book, such as agricultural techniques and labor organization, this controversy presented few problems. Other topics, such as the bloodshed of 1965–66, were more delicate, however, and required that I have an intimate relationship to the speaker. Even then, people disagreed on important details of history. To ensure both qualitative depth and comparative balance, then, I decided to use several different interview techniques in the course of my fieldwork, hoping that, in the end, they would provide me with some measure of ethnographic balance.

The most comprehensive historical accounts I gathered came from extended interviews with sixty village elders. Most of these were with men and women from the three main villages in which I lived, and four adjacent ones I regularly visited (see Preface). Interviews were conducted in several sittings over the course of many weeks, usually in the late afternoon and evening, but occasionally in the early morning, sipping sweet coffee or hot water. Focusing on a particular topic such as labor organization or village history, I used each interview to construct a general narrative with which to ask more informed questions of other villagers. Slowly, I made my way around a network of informants until, weeks later, I returned to talk to the first interviewees again, posing new questions in light of other people's accounts.

Having established a network of informants in my base villages, I then went into neighboring communities to raise similar questions and compare accounts from different villages and social groupings. In addition to the sixty core interviewees, then, I had extended interviews with another fifty or so individuals in the twenty villages that I visited for briefer, two-to-four-day stays (see Preface). Inevitably, the quality of these interviews was often poorer than my core interviews. In most instances, however, I was able to route my visit through a local villager whom I already knew, usually from prior visits or encounters while dancing at upland festivals. Though I got to know these people less well, their accounts proved to be an important source of comparative information for this study.

In addition to these in-depth interviews on history and culture, I also conducted 492 structured interviews on household economy (chs. 4–6). Though my sixty key informants were included in this interview, I knew most of the other interviewees less well. This was a highly structured interview, with over two hundred question items. Nonetheless, I took advantage of the occasion to ask open-ended questions as well. I conducted these interviews with my Javanese assistant, a middle-aged man from the lowlands. Before our interviews, we always divided our responsibilities.

One of us would record answers to our questionnaire on household economy, while the other would write down whatever unexpected information came up in the course of discussion. The household interviews thus provided both statistical and qualitative information. Equally important, they brought me in contact with individuals whom otherwise I might not have met.

In addition to these interviews, I met with a number of people from outside the highlands who were familiar with regency history and government. Among the most helpful were four Indonesian agricultural extension officers currently working in the highlands, and a fifth, now retired, who had worked under the Dutch. I also had the good fortune to interview three retired district officers who had first worked in the highlands during the 1950s, and another who had worked in the Forestry Department under the Dutch.

In all the interviews, my concerns were influenced by background materials that I had read prior to my research. Pasuruan has an unusually rich body of historical and archival commentary on both its uplands and lowlands. I drew heavily, for example, on Egbert de Vries's (1931) wonderfully comprehensive study of history and agriculture in the Pasuruan regency. His study is one of the finest of its type in all Java. It directed me to historical sources and presented a rich firsthand account of events during the first decades of this century. Robert Elson's (1978a, 1978b, 1984) masterful economic history of lowland Pasuruan also shaped my understanding of nineteenth-century political economy. Jan Palte's (1984) ecological history of upland Central Java, finally, cued me to many of the ecological problems of mountain agriculture. All this literature played a vital role in the formulation of my research program.

As my sense of history and culture sharpened, it seemed imperative to push beyond my core and household-economy interviewees and seek out individuals who had played central roles in different events. Three of the "merchant-farmers" who had migrated to the midslope region in the first two decades of this century were still living in the 1980s, and they provided me with detailed descriptions of their first years in the highlands. In the upperslope region there were eight elderly merchants who had been active over the same years. I was able to interview six. They provided me with accounts of the 1920s expansion, and the disastrous impact of the depression and great potato blight on trade.

Since this period left few written records but many bitter memories, my information on the Japanese and early independence periods came largely from local villagers, especially my sixty core interviewees. But I was able to draw on other voices as well. The native assistant-administrator to the Japanese-organized cooperatives (*kumiyai*) was still living in Tosari in the 1980s. After coming to understand that my purpose was not to criticize, he talked frankly about his work under the Japanese. Unlike most highlanders he still spoke admiringly of Japanese accomplishments. A lonely man, he was anxious to refute villagers' charges that he had been a party to their exploitation.

I was also able to interview eight men who had been active in the organization of militias just prior to the Japanese collapse; my interviewees included representatives from Muslim, nationalist, and leftist groupings. My best information on this troubled period, however, came from three individuals: one an upperslope farmer who had been active in the leftish Pesindo militia, the second a lowland gentleman who had played a central role in the Nationalist Party's upland initiatives, and the third a midslope villager with ties to Nahdatul Ulama.

The most difficult period on which to gather materials was that from 1959 to 1966, the period of party factionalism that ended with the destruction of the Communist Party. Sensitive to villagers' concerns that talking would only open old wounds, I decided at first not to ask questions about the violence. During 1977 and 1978–80, then, almost no one spoke to me in any detail about what had happened between 1959 and 1966. Though surprised by the great silence, I, too, preferred not to raise painful memories.

When I returned to Java in 1985, I sensed that my relationship with villagers had changed. People confided in me more regularly. In fact, they seemed to seek me out to discuss issues. Part of this no doubt was owing to the simple fact that I was older and thus, from a Javanese perspective, more deserving of respect. The change was also related to my returning to the highlands after an absence of several years. As many ethnographers can testify, returning to an earlier field site can have a profound effect on personal ties. It did in my case.

But there was a broader influence at work as well. Between the late 1970s and 1985, the changes that I had earlier seen in income, class, and social attitudes had taken hold throughout the highlands. By 1985 everybody was aware that the old ways were dying. The belief that, whatever their differences, villagers shared a common ancestry and collective tradition had been shattered. The crisis of tradition that I had noted in the 1970s had passed into popular awareness. Its force surprised even me.

I was especially struck by the change in attitude among members of the village elite. Though I developed close ties with many of them, in the 1970s most still adopted "official" lines in talking with me about sensitive matters like politics. By 1985 this had changed. To my astonishment, people on opposing sides of village disputes—like families with ties to the upperslope Communist Party, on one hand, and Nationalist Party leaders, on the other—sought me out to talk about what had happened. Over the years, of course, my assistant and I had developed a reputation as people interested in local history. Somehow our role now seemed clearer to villagers and we seemed more trustworthy. Many people approached us with their stories. Fearing that we might learn things that called their own positions into question, other people sought us out to legitimize their role in events. My assistant and I were, I feel, widely regarded as neutral observers. But it was clear that long-suppressed tensions were re-emerging, and that, in a minor way, we had become jurors in a trial of opinion. We had been drawn more firmly into village life, and our presence seems to have heightened the debate.

Tensions were particularly acute in some of the midslope communities in which I worked. One had been the site of a Nationalist Party land scam, in which European lands occupied by squatters were confiscated by a corrupt PNI village chief (see ch. 7). The openness with which poor villagers expressed their anger at the loss of their lands astounded me. It seemed to violate all of the standards of interactional harmony that I had learned in Java. I later realized that recent events had contributed to this spirit of openness. In this community the village chief who had ruled since 1946—and who had engineered the 1960s theft of squatter lands—had just been voted out of office and replaced by a younger Golkar leader. The new village head was not from an elite family and was popularly (and, I felt, correctly) regarded as uncorrupt.

What I was witnessing in this village, then, was the fall from power of the old elite. In many upland villages, of course, there was no such transfer of power with the arrival of Golkar; PNI leaders maintained their dominance by transferring into the government party. Subdistrict officials in this region, however, were sensitive to the old chief's unpopularity. They decided to let him go, allowing a younger man untainted by corruption to run against him. Villagers reacted to the change of regime with an explosion of goodwill. A key figure of the old village order had fallen, and people celebrated by speaking more freely of what had happened in the 1960s.

I was fortunate to have social ties to individuals on all sides of the 1965–66 violence. I was able to interview most of the leading PNI officers of the era (twelve men in all), who then put me in contact with three district-level PNI officials living in the lowlands. I unwittingly developed strong ties among ex-communists as well. The closest friendships I developed during all my months in the mountains were with the members of an extended family with whom I ate daily during 1979 and 1985. One evening, many months after accepting me into their family, they revealed to me that their father had been among those arrested and executed in late 1965. Through them, too, I met other people touched by personal tragedy. Now adult men, the elder sons in this family were the custodians of a veritable counterhistory of the village. Though politically leftish, they were now anticommunist, and felt that the PKI had used their father. Nonetheless, they demonstrated their independence from village leaders by converting to Christianity and talking enthusiastically about American-style democracy.

After several encounters at *slametan* festivals, I also became acquainted with two army officers (both from urban East Java) involved in district security operations since the early 1960s. I received my most detailed "government-side" accounts of the 1965 bloodletting, however, from an urban Muslim whom I first met during one of his vacation trips to the mountains. By an odd series of coincidences, this gentleman and I developed a friendship and met with some regularity. It was only after many months of interaction, in fact, that I learned that he had a bitter story to tell. As the leader of a Muslim student group, he had played a central role in the arrests and executions of communists in the highlands. Whatever his convictions, the memory of that period's human suffering haunted him. He seemed to use his conversations with me to relieve some of its burden. At first I was shocked to learn the grisly details of his involvement. But the honesty he showed in relating his story, and his moral pain, challenged me to understand his position.

My assistant, a devout Muslim, developed a close friendship with two key NU families in the midslope district, both of whom had been active in the 1950s and 1960s. Through him, I made their acquaintance and was treated with the utmost cordiality. They provided a frank assessment of their side of the conflict during 1965–66. I was also able to interview lower-level NU officials in two lowland villages just below the highlands. I was introduced to them by members of their family who worked as merchants in the highlands and had befriended my assistant and me.

There is no final guarantee to the comprehensiveness of historical ethnography. The best one can do is interview as many parties to an event as possible. Then one must check the plausibility of different accounts against each other, available written testimonies, and similar circumstances in other world areas. Ethnographic history, then, is not a matter of opening oneself to the straightforward inscription of others. Choice of informants, formulation of questions, and one's own identity in the community all powerfully constrain the dialogue.

I was interested in my research not only in local ethnohistory—the categories and narratives through which actors interpret temporal change—but also in determining what had happened and why, whether it figured in villagers' narratives or not. This concern for events was not motivated by commitment to an epistemologically naive conception of history or culture. Ultimately, it originated in what I can only describe as my sense of awe, and occasional sadness, in the face of what I was privileged to witness and hear. There was something larger and more compelling here than any single person's subjectivity, least of all my own. I felt it in the pain of my adopted family, who had lost their father in the 1965 killings, and in the moral doubt of my Muslim friend who had participated on the other side of those events. Moved by these conflicting perspectives, my hope was that the history I wrote would, somehow, speak to the truth of both their experiences.

BIBLIOGRAPHY

Adas, Michael. 1981. "From Avoidance to Confrontation: Peasant Protest in Precolonial and Colonial Southeast Asia." *Comparative Studies in Society and History* 23:217–47.

Alexander, Jennifer. 1987. *Trade, Traders, and Trading in Rural Java*. Singapore: Oxford University Press.

Alexander, Jennifer, and Paul Alexander. 1979. "Labour Demands and the 'Involution' of Javanese Agriculture." *Social Analysis* 3:22–44.

———. 1982. "Shared Poverty as Ideology: Agrarian Relationships in Colonial Java." *Man*, n.s., 17:597–619.

Alfian. 1971. "Hasil Pemilihan Umum 1955 Untuk Dewan Perwakilan Rakjat." Jakarta: Lembaga Ekonomi dan Kemasjarakatan Nasional.

Anderson, Benedict R. 1972. "The Idea of Power in Javanese Culture." In Claire Holt, ed., *Culture and Politics in Indonesia*, 1–69. Ithaca: Cornell University Press.

———. 1982. "Perspective and Method in American Research on Indonesia." In Anderson and Kahin 1982, 69–83.

———. 1983a. *Imagined Communities: Reflections on the Origin and Spread of Nationalism*. London: Verso.

———. 1983b. "Old State, New Society: Indonesia's New Order in Historical Perspective." *The Journal of Asian Studies* 42:477–96.

Anderson, Benedict, and Audrey Kahin, eds. 1982. *Interpreting Indonesian Politics: Thirteen Contributions to the Debate*. Ithaca: Cornell University, Southeast Asia Program, Modern Indonesia Project.

Anonymous. 1986. "Report from East Java." *Indonesia* 41: 134–39.

Arndt, H. 1971. "Banking in Hyperinflation and Stabilization." In B. Glassburner, ed., *The Economy of Indonesia: Selected Readings*, 359–95. Ithaca: Cornell University Press.

Bailey, Conner. 1983. *The Sociology of Production in Rural Malay Society*. Kuala Lumpur: Oxford University Press.

Barker, Randolph, and Robert W. Herdt, with Beth Rose. 1985. *The Rice Economy of Asia*. Washington, D.C.: Resources for the Future.

Barth, Fredrik. 1967. "Economic Spheres in Darfur." In Raymond Firth, ed., *Themes in Economic Anthropology*, 149–74. London: Tavistock.

Bellah, Robert N. 1957. *Tokugawa Religion: The Values of Pre-Industrial Japan*. Glencoe, Ill.: Free Press.

Benda, Harry J. 1983. *The Crescent and the Rising Sun: Indonesian Islam under the Japanese Occupation, 1942–1945*. Leiden: Foris.

Bendix, Reinhard. 1977. "Tradition and Modernity Reconsidered." In *Nation-Building and Citizenship: Studies of Our Changing Social Order*, 361–434. Berkeley and Los Angeles: University of California Press.

Bennet, Christopher, Darmawan, Sofjan Djalil, Ricardo Godoy, M. T. Muhammad, Nawir, and Wismoyo. 1987. "The Clove-Intensive Farming System in Maluku: A Cast Study of the Cultivation and Marketing of Cloves and Their Significance to the Local Economy." Jakarta: Ministry of Finance, Center for Policy and Implementation Studies.

Berger, Peter L., and Thomas Luckmann. 1966. *The Social Construction of Reality: A Treatise in the Sociology of Knowledge*. Garden City, N.Y.: Doubleday.

Biersack, Aletta. 1989. "Local Knowledge, Local History: Geertz and Beyond." In Lynn Hunt, ed., *The New Cultural History*, 72–96. Berkeley and Los Angeles: University of California Press.

Birowo, Achmad T., and Gary E. Hansen. 1981. "Agricultural and Rural Development: An Overview." In Gary E. Hansen, ed., *Agricultural and Rural Development in Indonesia*, 1–27. Boulder: Westview Press.

Bloch, Maurice. 1973. "The Long Term and the Short Term: The Economic and Political Significance of the Morality of Kinship." In Jack Goody, ed., *The Character of Kinship*, 75–87. Cambridge: Cambridge University Press.

———. 1989. "From Cognition to Ideology." In *Ritual, History, and Power: Selected Papers in Anthropology*, 106–36. London: Athlone Press.

Blum, Lawrence. 1987. "Particularity and Responsiveness." In Jerome Kagan and Sharon Lamb, eds., *The Emergence of Morality in Young Children*, 306–37. Chicago: University of Chicago Press.

Bodemeijer, C. E. 1901. "Rapport naar aanleiding van de Nota betreffende het Tenggergebied van den heer H. M. La Chapelle." *Tijdschrift voor Indische Taal-, Land-, en Volkenkunde uitgegeven door het (Koninklijk) Bataviaasch Genootschap van Kunsten en Wetenschappen* 43:311–30.

Boeke, J. H. 1953. *Economics and Economic Policy of Dual Societies, as Exemplified by Indonesia*. New York, N.Y.: Institute of Pacific Relations.

Boland, B. J. 1982. *The Struggle of Islam in Modern Indonesia*. The Hague: Martinus Nijhoff.

Booth, Anne. 1979. "The Agricultural Surveys, 1970–75." *Bulletin of Indonesian Economic Studies* 15:45–68.

———. 1985. "Accommodating a Growing Population in Javanese Agriculture." *Bulletin of Indonesian Economic Studies* 21:115–45.

Booth, Anne, and Peter McCawley, eds. 1981a. *The Indonesian Economy during the Soeharto Era*. Kuala Lumpur: Oxford University Press.

———. 1981b. "The Indonesian Economy since the Mid-Sixties." In Booth and McCawley 1981a, 1–22.

Booth, Anne, and R. M. Sundrum. 1976. "The 1973 Agricultural Census." *Bulletin of Indonesian Economic Studies* 12:90–105.

———. 1981. "Income Distribution." In Booth and McCawley 1981a, 181–217.

Bottomore, T. B. 1965. *Classes in Modern Society*. London: George Allen & Unwin.

Bourdieu, Pierre. 1977. *Outline of a Theory of Practice*. Translated by Richard Nice. Cambridge: Cambridge University Press.

———. 1984. *Distinction: A Social Critique of the Judgement of Taste*. Translated by Richard Nice. Cambridge, Mass.: Harvard University Press.

Bowen, John R. 1986. "On the Political Construction of Tradition: *Gotong Royong* in Indonesia." *The Journal of Asian Studies* 45:545–61.

Breman, Jan. 1982. "The Village on Java and the Early-Colonial State." *Journal of Peasant Studies* 9:189–240.

———. 1983. *Control of Land and Labour in Colonial Java: A Case Study of Agrarian Crisis and Reform in the Region of Cirebon During the First Decades of the 20th Century*. Dordrecht: Foris.

Brow, James, 1981. "Some Problems in the Analysis of Agrarian Classes in South Asia." *Journal of Peasant Studies* 9:26–39.

Cancian, Frank. 1965. *Economics and Prestige in a Maya Community: The Religious Cargo System in Zinacantan*. Stanford: Stanford University Press.

Carey, Peter B. R. 1979. "Aspects of Javanese History in the Nineteenth Century." In Harry Aveling, ed., *The Development of Indonesian Society: From the Coming of Islam to the Present Day*, 45–105. St. Lucia, Australia: University of Queensland Press.

Carroll, Vern, ed. 1970. *Adoption in Eastern Oceania*. Honolulu: University of Hawaii Press.

Chirot, Daniel. 1986. *Social Change in the Modern Era*. San Diego: Harcourt Brace Jovanovich.

Clifford, James. 1986. "Introduction: Partial Truths." In James Clifford and George E. Marcus, eds., *Writing Culture: The Poetics and Politics of Ethnography*, 1–26. Berkeley and Los Angeles: University of California Press.

Cohen, Jean L. 1982. *Class and Civil Society: The Limits of Marxian Critical Theory*. Amherst: University of Massachusetts Press.

Collier, William L. 1978. "Food Problems, Unemployment, and the Green Revolution in Rural Java." *Prisma* 9:38–52.

Collier, William L., Gunawan Wiradi, and Soentoro. 1973. "Recent Changes in Rice Harvesting Methods." *Bulletin of Indonesian Economic Studies* 9:36–45.

Comaroff, Jean. 1985. *Body of Power, Spirit of Resistance: The Culture and History of a South African People*. Chicago: University of Chicago Press.

Crouch, Harold. 1978. *The Army and Politics in Indonesia*. Ithaca: Cornell University Press.

Dahrendorf, Ralf. 1959. *Class and Class Conflict in Industrial Society*. Stanford: Stanford University Press.

Dixon, John A. 1984. "Consumption." In Walter P. Falcon, William O. Jones, and Scott R. Pearson, eds., *The Cassava Economy of Java*, 63–90. Stanford: Stanford University Press.

Domis, H. J. 1832. "Aanteekeningen over het Gebergte Tinger." *Verhandelingen van het Bataviaasch Genootschap van Kunsten en Wetenschappen* 13:325–56.

Donner, Wolf. 1987. *Land Use and Environment in Indonesia.* Honolulu: University of Hawaii Press.

Douglas, Mary. 1967. "Raffia Cloth Distribution in the Lele Economy." In George Dalton, ed., *Tribal and Peasant Economies,* 103–22. New York: Natural History Press.

——. 1970. *Natural Symbols: Explorations in Cosmology.* New York: Pantheon Books.

——. 1982. "Goods as a System of Communication." In Mary Douglas, *In the Active Voice,* 16–33. London: Routledge & Kegan Paul.

Douglas, Mary, and Baron Isherwood. 1979. *The World of Goods.* New York: Basic Books.

Ecklund, Judith L. 1979. "Tradition or Non-Tradition: *Adat,* Islam, and Local Control on Lombok." In Gloria Davis, ed., *What Is Modern Indonesian Culture? Papers Presented to the Conference on Indonesian Studies, July 29–August 1, 1976,* 249–67. Athens, Ohio: Center for International Studies.

Eickelman, Dale F. 1979. "The Political Economy of Meaning." *American Ethnologist* 6:386–93.

Eisenstadt, S. N. 1966. *Modernization: Protest and Change.* Englewood Cliffs, N.J.: Prentice-Hall.

Elson, R. E. 1978a. "The Cultivation System and 'Agricultural Involution.'" Research Paper No. 14. Melbourne: Monash University, Centre of Southeast Asian Studies.

——. 1978b. "The Impact of Government Sugar Cultivation in the Pasuruan Area, East Java, during the Cultivation System Period." *Review of Indonesian and Malayan Affairs* 12, no. 1:26–55.

——. 1984. *Javanese Peasants and the Colonial Sugar Industry: Impact and Change in an East Java Residency, 1830–1940.* Singapore: Oxford University Press.

Emmerson, Donald K. 1978. "The Bureaucracy in Political Context: Weakness in Strength." In Jackson and Pye 1978, 82–136.

——. 1983. "Understanding the New Order: Bureaucratic Pluralism in Indonesia." *Asian Survey* 23, no. 1:220–41.

Epstein, T. S. 1962. *Economic Development and Social Change in South India.* Manchester: Manchester University Press.

——. 1968. *Capitalism, Primitive and Modern: Some Aspects of Tolai Economic Growth.* Canberra: Australian National University Press.

Etzioni, Amitai. 1988. *The Moral Dimension: Toward a New Economics.* New York: Free Press.

Evans-Pritchard, E. E. 1940. *The Nuer: A Description of the Modes of Livelihood and Political Institutions of a Nilotic People.* Oxford: Clarendon Press.

Fasseur, C. 1975. *Kultuurstelsel en koloniale baten: De Nederlands exploitatie van Java, 1840–1860.* Leiden: Universitaire Pers.

Feeny, David. 1983. "The Moral or Rational Peasant? Competing Hypotheses of Collective Action." *The Journal of Asian Studies* 42:769–89.

Feinman, S. 1982. "Social Referencing in Infancy." *Merrill-Palmer Quarterly* 28:445–70.

Feith, Herbert. 1957. *The Indonesian Elections of 1955.* Interim Report Series, Modern Indonesia Project. Ithaca: Cornell University, Southeast Asia Program.

————. 1982. "The Study of Indonesian Politics: A Survey and an Apologia." In Anderson and Kahin 1982, 41–53.

Felix, David. 1979. "De Gustibus Disputandum Est: Changing Consumer Preferences in Economic Growth." *Explorations in Economic History* 16:260–96.

Frank, A. G. 1969. *Latin America: Underdevelopment or Revolution.* New York: Monthly Review Press.

Freeman, J. D. 1955. *Iban Agriculture.* London: HMSO.

Freijburg, G. G. L. von. 1901. "Rapport." *Tijdschrift voor Indische Taal-, Land-, en Volkenkunde uitgegeven door het (Koninklijk) Bataviaasch Genootschap van Kunsten en Wetenschappen* 43:331–48.

Furnivall, J. S. 1944. *Netherlands India: A Study of Plural Economy.* Cambridge: Cambridge University Press.

Ganjanapan, Anan. 1989. "Conflicts over the Deployment and Control of Labor in a Northern Thai Village." In Hart et al. 1989, 98–122.

Geertz, Clifford. 1959. "The Javanese Village." In G. W. Skinner, ed., *Local, Ethnic, and National Loyalties in Village Indonesia,* 34–41. Cultural Report Series No. 8. New Haven: Yale University, Southeast Asia Studies.

————. 1960. *The Religion of Java.* New York: Free Press.

————. 1963a. *Agricultural Involution: The Processes of Ecological Change in Indonesia.* Berkeley and Los Angeles: University of California Press.

————. 1963b. *Peddlers and Princes: Social Change and Economic Modernization in Two Indonesian Towns.* Chicago: University of Chicago Press.

————. 1965a. *The Social History of an Indonesian Town.* Cambridge, Mass.: MIT Press.

————. 1965b. "Modernization in a Muslim Society: The Indonesian Case." In Robert N. Bellah, ed., *Religion and Progress in Modern Asia,* 93–108. New York: Free Press.

————. 1968. *Islam Observed: Religious Development in Morocco and Indonesia.* Chicago: University of Chicago Press.

————. 1973a. *The Interpretation of Cultures.* New York: Basic Books.

————. 1973b. "Thick Description: Toward an Interpretive Theory of Culture." In Geertz 1973a, 3–30.

————. 1973c. "The Integrative Revolution: Primordial Sentiments and Civil Politics in the New States." In Geertz 1973a, 255–310.

————. 1983. *Local Knowledge: Further Essays in Interpretive Anthropology.* New York: Basic Books.

————. 1984. "Culture and Social Change: The Indonesian Case." *Man,* n.s., 19:511–32.

Geertz, Hildred. 1961. *The Javanese Family: A Study of Kinship and Socialization.* Glencoe: Free Press.

Giddens, Anthony. 1971. *Capitalism and Modern Social Theory: An Analysis of the Writings of Marx, Durkheim and Max Weber.* Cambridge: Cambridge University Press.

————. 1973. *The Class Structure of the Advanced Societies.* New York: Barnes & Noble.

————. 1979. *Central Problems in Social Theory: Action, Structure and Contradiction in Social Analysis.* Berkeley and Los Angeles: University of California Press.

————. 1982. *Profiles and Critiques in Social Theory.* Berkeley and Los Angeles: University of California Press.

————. 1984. *The Constitution of Society: Outline of the Theory of Structuration.* Berkeley and Los Angeles: University of California Press.

————. 1987. *The Nation-State and Violence: Volume Two of A Contemporary Critique of Historical Materialism.* Berkeley and Los Angeles: University of California Press.

Gilligan, Carol. 1982. *In a Different Voice: Psychological Theory and Women's Development.* Cambridge, Mass.: Harvard University Press.

Godoy, Ricardo, and Christopher Bennett. 1987a. "Diversification among Coffee Smallholders in the Highlands of South Sumatra, Indonesia." Working Paper. Cambridge, Mass.: Harvard Institute for International Development.

————. 1987b. "Coffee Quality among Smallholders in South Sumatra." Working Paper. Cambridge, Mass.: Harvard Institute for International Development.

Gonda, J. 1952. *Sanskrit in Indonesia.* Nagpur, India: International Academy of Indian Culture.

Gordon, A. 1978. "Some Problems of Analyzing Class Relations in Indonesia." *Journal of Contemporary Asia* 8:210–18.

Graaf, H. J. de, and Th. G. Th. Pigeaud. 1974. *De eerste Moslimse vorstendommen op Java.* The Hague: Martinus Nijhoff.

Hansen, Gary. 1973. *The Politics and Administration of Rural Development in Indonesia.* Berkeley: University of California, Center for South and Southeast Asian Studies.

Hart, Gillian. 1986. *Power, Labor, and Livelihood: Process of Change in Rural Java.* Berkeley and Los Angeles: University of California Press.

————. 1989. "Agrarian Change in the Context of State Patronage." In Hart et al. 1989, 31–49.

Hart, Gillian, Andrew Turton, and Benjamin White, eds. 1989. *Agrarian Transformations: Local Processes and the State in Southeast Asia.* Berkeley and Los Angeles: University of California Press.

Hatley, Ron. 1984. "Mapping Cultural Regions of Java." In Ron Hatley, ed., *Other Javas away from the Kraton,* 1–32. Clayton, Australia: Monash University, Centre of Southeast Asian Studies.

Hayami, Y., and A. Hafid. 1979. "Rice Harvesting and Welfare in Rural Java." *Bulletin of Indonesian Economic Studies* 15:94–112.

Hefner, Robert W. 1983a. "Ritual and Cultural Reproduction in Non-Islamic Java." *American Ethnologist* 10:665–83.

————. 1983b. "The Problem of Preference: Ritual and Economic Change in Highland Java." *Man,* n.s, 18:669–89.

————. 1985. *Hindu Javanese: Tengger Tradition and Islam.* Princeton: Princeton University Press.

————. 1987a. "The Political Economy of Islamic Conversion in Modern East Java." In William R. Roff, ed., *Islam and the Political Economy of Meaning: Comparative Studies in Muslim Discourse,* 53–78. London: Croom Helm.

————. 1987b. "The Politics of Popular Art: *Tayuban* Dance and Culture Change in East Java." *Indonesia* 43:75–94.

————. 1987c. "Islamizing Java? Religion and Politics in Rural East Java." *The Journal of Asian Studies* 46:533–54.

Hering, B. B., and G. A. Willis. 1973. *The Indonesian General Election of 1971.* Brussels: Centre d'Etude du Sud-Est Asiatique et de l'Extreme Orient.

Hobsbawm, Eric, and Terence Ranger. 1983. *The Invention of Tradition.* Cambridge: Cambridge University Press.

Hooykaas, C. 1964. "Weda and Sisya, Rsi and Bhujangga in Present-Day Bali." *Bijdragen tot de Taal-, Land-, en Volkenkunde* 120:231–44.

————. 1974. *Cosmogony and Creation in Balinese Tradition.* The Hague: Martinus Nijhoff.

Hoselitz, B. F. 1960. *Sociological Factors in Economic Development.* Chicago: Free Press.

Huizer, Gerrit. 1974. "Peasant Mobilisation and Land Reform in Indonesia." *Review of Indonesian and Malayan Affairs* 8, no. 1:81–138.

Hull, Terence H., and Valerie J. Hull. 1976. "Social and Economic Support for High Fertility in Indonesia." Working Paper Series No. 5. Yogyakarta: Gadjah Mada University, Population Institute.

Hull, Terence H., and Ida Bagus Mantra. 1981. "Indonesia's Changing Population." In Booth and McCawley 1981a, 262–88.

Hull, Valerie. 1982. "Women in Java's Rural Middle Class: Progress or Regress?" In Penny van Esterik, ed., *Women of Southeast Asia,* 100–123. De Kalb: Northern Illinois University, Center for Southeast Asian Studies.

Hunt, Lynn. 1989. "Introduction: History, Culture, and Text." In Lynn Hunt, ed., *The New Cultural History,* 1–22. Berkeley and Los Angeles: University of California Press.

Husken, F. 1979. "Landlords, Sharecroppers and Agricultural Labourers: Changing Labour Relations in Rural Java." *Journal of Contemporary Asia* 9:140–51.

————. 1989. "Cycles of Commercialization and Accumulation in a Central Javanese Village." In Hart et al. 1989, 303–31.

Husken, F., and Benjamin White. 1989. "Java: Social Differentiation, Food Production, and Agrarian Control." In Hart et al. 1989, 235–65.

Jackson, Karl D. 1978. "Bureaucratic Polity: A Theoretical Framework for the Analysis of Power and Communications in Indonesia." In Jackson and Pye 1978, 3–22.

Jackson, Karl D., and Lucian W. Pye, eds. 1978. *Political Power and Communications in Indonesia.* Berkeley and Los Angeles: University of California Press.

Jasper, J. E. 1926. *Tengger en de Tenggereezen.* Batavia: G. Kolff.

Jay, Robert R. 1963. *Religion and Politics in Rural Central Java.* Cultural Report Series No. 12. New Haven: Yale University, Program in Southeast Asian Studies.

————. 1969. *Javanese Villagers: Social Relations in Rural Modjokuto.* Cambridge, Mass.: MIT Press.

Kahin, George M. 1952. *Nationalism and Revolution in Indonesia.* Ithaca: Cornell University Press.

Kahn, Joel. 1980. *Minangkabau Social Formations: Indonesian Peasants and the World Economy.* Cambridge: Cambridge University Press.

————. 1982. "Ideology and Social Structure in Indonesia." In Anderson and Kahin 1982, 92–103.

Kano, Hiroyoshi. 1977. "Land Tenure System and the *Desa* Community in Nineteenth-Century Java." Special Paper No. 5. Tokyo: Institute of Developing Economies.

Kartodirdjo, Sartono. 1972. "Agrarian Radicalism in Java: Its Setting and Development." In Claire Holt, ed., *Culture and Politics in Indonesia*, 70–125. Ithaca: Cornell University Press.

Keeler, Ward. 1987. *Javanese Shadow Plays, Javanese Selves*. Princeton: Princeton University Press.

Keyes, Charles F. 1977. *The Golden Peninsula: Culture and Adaptation in Mainland Southeast Asia*. Philadelphia: Institute for the Study of Human Issues.

————. 1983a. "Introduction: Peasant Strategies in Asian Societies—Moral and Rational Economic Approaches." *The Journal of Asian Studies* 42:753–68.

————. 1983b. "Economic Action and Buddhist Morality in a Thai Village." *The Journal of Asian Studies* 42:851–68.

————. 1987. *Thailand: Buddhist Kingdom as Modern Nation State*. Boulder: Westview Press.

King, Dwight Y. 1982. *Interest Groups and Political Linkage in Indonesia, 1800–1965*. Special Report No. 20. De Kalb: Northern Illinois University, Center for Southeast Asian Studies.

King, Dwight Y., and Peter D. Weldon. 1977. "Income Distribution and Levels of Living in Java, 1963–1970." *Economic Development and Cultural Change* 25, no. 4:699–711.

Klaveren, J. J. van. 1953. *The Dutch Colonial System in the East Indies*. Rotterdam: Drukkerij Benedictus.

Knight, G. R. 1982. "Capitalism and Commodity Production in Java." In H. Alavi, P. L. Burns, G. R. Knight, P. B. Mayer, and Doug McEachern, eds., *Capitalism and Colonial Production*, 119–58. London: Croom Helm.

Koentjaraningrat, R. M. 1960. "The Javanese of South Central Java." In G. P. Murdock, ed., *Social Structure in Southeast Asia*, 88–115. Chicago: Quadrangle Books.

————. 1961. *Some Social-Anthropological Observations on Gotong Royong Practices in Two Villages of Central Java*. Modern Indonesia Project. Ithaca: Cornell University, Southeast Asia Program.

————. 1984. *Kebudayaan Jawa*. Jakarta: Balai Pustaka.

Kolff, G. van der. 1936. "The Historical Development of Labour Relationships in a Remote Corner of Java as They Apply to the Cultivation of Rice." Report C. Amsterdam: National Council for the Netherlands and the Netherlands Indies, Institute of Pacific Relations.

Kreemer, J. 1885. "Veertien dagen in Pasoeroeansch Tengger." *Tijdschrift voor Zendingswetenschap Mededeelingen van Wege* (Het Nederlandsche Zendeling Genootschap) 19:337–84.

Kumar, Ann. 1976. *Surapati: Man and Legend*. Leiden: E. J. Brill.

————. 1979. "Javanese Historiography in and of the 'Colonial Period': A Case Study." In A. Reid and D. Marr, eds., *Perceptions of the Past in Southeast Asia*, 187–206. Singapore: Heinemann.

Labrousse, Pierre, and Farida Soemargono. 1985. "De l'Islam comme morale du developpement: L'Action des bureaux de propagation de la foi (Lembaga Dakwah) vue de Surabaya." In M. Bonneff, H. Chambert-Loir, Denys Lombard, and Christian Pelras, eds., *L'Islam en Indonesia*, 219–28. Paris: Association Archipel.

La Chapelle, H. M. 1899. "Nota betreffende het Tengger-Gebied." *Tijdschrift voor Indische Taal-, Land-, en Volkenkunde* 41:32–54.

Leach, E. R. 1954. *Political Systems of Highland Burma: A Study of Kachin Social Structure.* Boston: Beacon Press.

Leiss, William. 1976. *The Limits to Satisfaction: An Essay on the Problem of Needs and Commodities.* Toronto: University of Toronto Press.

Leiss, William, Stephen Kline, and Sut Jhally. 1986. *Social Communication in Advertising: Persons, Products, and Images of Well-Being.* Toronto: Methuen.

Lenin, V. I. 1899. *The Development of Capitalism in Russia.* Moscow: Progress Publishers.

Lerwerden, J. D. van. 1844. "Aanteekeningen nopens de zeden en gebruiken der bevolking van het Tenggers Gebergte." *Verhandelingen van het Bataviaasch Genootschap van Kunsten en Wetenschappen* 20:60–93.

Lev, D. 1966. *The Transition to Guided Democracy: Indonesian Politics, 1957–59.* Modern Indonesia Project. Ithaca: Cornell University, Southeast Asia Program.

Levy, Robert I. 1973. *Tahitians: Mind and Experience in the Society Islands.* Chicago: University of Chicago Press.

Liddle, R. William. 1978. "Participation and the Political Parties." In Jackson and Pye 1978, 171–95.

Lipset, Seymour Martin, and Reinhard Bendix, eds. 1953. *Class, Status, and Power: A Reader in Social Stratification.* Glencoe: Free Press.

Long, Norman. 1977. *An Introduction to the Sociology of Rural Development.* Boulder: Westview Press.

Lyon, M. L. 1970. *Bases of Conflict in Rural Java.* Research Monograph No. 3. Berkeley: University of California, Center for South and Southeast Asian Studies.

———. 1980. "The Hindu Revival in Java: Politics and Religious Identity." In James J. Fox, ed., *Indonesia: The Making of a Culture*, 205–20. Canberra: Research School of Pacific Studies.

McCauley, David S. 1984. "Developing Java's Upland Agroecosystems— Opportunities and Constraints: A Summary Report of the Workshop on Agroecosystems Analysis for the Uplands of Eastern Java." Honolulu: East-West Center, Environment and Policy Institute.

Mackie, J. 1971. "The Indonesian Economy, 1950–1963." In Bruce Glassburner, ed., *The Economy of Indonesia: Selected Readings*, 16–69. Ithaca: Cornell University Press.

McPherson, Michael S. 1983. "Want Formation, Morality, and Some Interpretive Aspects of Economic Inquiry." In Norma Haan, Robert N. Bellah, Paul Rabinow, and William M. Sullivan, eds., *Social Science as Moral Inquiry*, 96–124. New York: Columbia University Press.

Mahoney, Timothy. 1981. "Local Political and Economic Structures." In Gary E. Hansen, ed., *Agricultural and Rural Development in Indonesia*, 180–95. Boulder: Westview Press.

Malinowski, B. 1922. *Argonauts of the Western Pacific*. New York: E. P. Dutton.
Mandel, Ernest. 1978. *Late Capitalism*. Translated by Joris de Bres. London: Verso.
Marcus, George, and Michael Fischer. 1986. *Anthropology as Cultural Critique: An Experimental Moment in the Human Sciences*. Chicago: University of Chicago Press.
Marx, Karl. 1968. *The Eighteenth Brumaire of Louis Bonaparte*. In Karl Marx and Frederick Engels, *Selected Works*, 95–180. Moscow: Progress Publishers.
———. 1973. *Grundrisse: Foundations of the Critique of Political Economy*. Translated by Martin Nicolaus. New York: Random House, Vintage Books.
Mears, Leon A., and Sidik Moeljono. 1981. "Food Policy." In Booth and McCawley 1981a, 23–61.
Meijer Ranneft, J. W. 1916. "Volksverplaatsing op Java." *Tijdschrift voor het Binnenlandsch Bestuur* 49, nos. 2 and 3.
Merton, Robert K. 1968. *Social Theory and Social Structure*. New York: Free Press.
Migdal, Joel S. 1982. "Capitalist Penetration in the Nineteenth Century: Creating Conditions for New Patterns of Social Control." In Robert P. Weller and Scott E. Guggenheim, eds., *Power and Protest in the Countryside: Studies of Rural Unrest in Asia, Europe, and Latin America*, 57–74. Durham: Duke University Press.
Mink, Stephen D., and Paul A. Dorosh. 1987. "An Overview of Corn Production." In Timmer 1987, 41–61.
Mink, Stephen D., Paul A. Dorosh, and Douglas H. Perry. 1987. "Corn Production Systems." In Timmer 1987, 62–87.
Moedjanto, G. 1986. *The Concept of Power in Javanese Culture*. Yogyakarta: Gadjah Mada University Press.
Moerman, Michael. 1967. "Being Lue: Uses and Abuses of Ethnic Identification." In June Helm, ed., *Essays on the Problem of the Tribe*, 153–69. Seattle: Proceedings of the American Ethnological Society.
Montgomery, Roger. 1981. "Employment Generation within the Agricultural Sector." In Gary E. Hansen, ed., *Agricultural and Rural Development in Indonesia*, 99–114. Boulder: Westview Press.
Montgomery, Roger, and Toto Sugito. 1980. "Changes in the Structure of Farms and Farming in Indonesia between Censuses, 1963–1973: The Issues of Inequality and Near-Landlessness." *Journal of Southeast Asian Studies* 2:348–65.
Mortimer, Rex. 1974. *Indonesian Communism under Sukarno: Ideology and Politics, 1959–1965*. Ithaca: Cornell University Press.
———. 1982. "Class, Social Cleavage, and Indonesian Communism." In Anderson and Kahin 1982, 54–68.
Nakamura, Mitsuo. 1983. *The Crescent Arises over the Banyan Tree: A Study of the Muhammadiyah Movement in a Central Javanese Town*. Yogyakarta: Gadjah Mada University Press.
Nisbet, Robert A. 1965. *Emile Durkheim*. Englewood Cliffs, N.J.: Prentice-Hall.
Noer, Deliar. 1978. *The Administration of Islam in Indonesia*. Monograph Series No. 58. Ithaca: Cornell University, Southeast Asia Program.
Noorduyn, J. 1978. "Majapahit in the Fifteenth Century." *Bijdragen Tot de Taal-, Land-, en Volkenkunde* 134:207–74.

Onghokham. 1975. "The Residency of Madiun: Priyayi and Peasant during the Nineteenth Century." Ph.D. thesis, Yale University.

Ortner, Sherry B. 1984. "Theory in Anthropology since the Sixties." *Comparative Studies in Society and History* 26, no. 1:126–66.

Palte, Jan G. L. 1984. *The Development of Java's Rural Uplands in Response to Population Growth: An Introductory Essay in Historical Perspective.* Yogyakarta: Gadjah Mada University, Faculty of Geography.

Parkin, Frank. 1978. "Social Stratification." In Tom Bottomore and Robert Nisbet, eds., *A History of Sociological Analysis,* 599–632. New York: Basic Books.

——. 1979. *Marxism and Class Theory: A Bourgeois Critique.* New York: Columbia University Press.

Peacock, James. 1968. *Rites of Modernization: Symbolic and Social Aspects of Indonesian Proletarian Drama.* Chicago: University of Chicago Press.

Peletz, Michael Gates. 1988. *A Share of the Harvest: Kinship, Property, and Social History among the Malays of Rembau.* Berkeley and Los Angeles: University of California Press.

Penny, David, and Masri Singarimbun. 1973. *Population and Poverty in Rural Java: Some Economic Arithmetic from Srihardjo.* International Development Monograph No. 41. Ithaca: Cornell University, Southeast Asia Program.

Pigeaud, Theodore G. Th. 1924. *De Tantu Panggelaran, Oud-Javaansch prozageschrift.* The Hague: Martinus Nijhoff.

——. 1932. "Aanteekeningen betreffende den Javaanschen Oosthoek." *Tijdschrift voor Indische Taal-, Land-, en Volkenkunde* 72:215–313.

——. 1962. *Java in the Fourteenth Century: A Study in Cultural History.* 5 vols. The Hague: Martinus Nijhoff.

——. 1967. *Literature of Java.* 3 vols. The Hague: Martinus Nijhoff.

Popkin, Samuel L. 1979. *The Rational Peasant: The Political Economy of Rural Society in Vietnam.* Berkeley and Los Angeles: University of California Press.

Rabinow, Paul, and William M. Sullivan. 1987. *Interpretive Social Science: A Second Look.* Berkeley and Los Angeles: University of California Press.

Raffles, Thomas Stamford, Sir. 1817. Reprint 1965. *The History of Java.* 2 vols. Kuala Lumpur: Oxford University Press.

Raillon, François. 1985. "Islam et Ordre Nouveau ou l'imbroglio de la foi et de la politique." In M. Bonneff, H. Chambert-Loir, Denys Lombard, and Christian Pelras, eds., *L'Islam en Indonesie,* 229–61. Paris: Association Archipel.

Reid, Anthony. 1974. *The Indonesian National Revolution, 1940–1950.* Hawthorn, Australia: Longman.

——, ed. 1983. *Slavery, Bondage, and Dependency in Southeast Asia.* St. Lucia, Australia: University of Queensland Press.

Republik Indonesia. 1983–84. *Nota Keuangan dan Rancangan Anggaran Pendapatan dan Belanja Negara.* Jakarta: Government of Indonesia, Department of Financial Affairs.

Ricklefs, M. C. 1974. *Jogjakarta under Sultan Mangkubumi, 1749–1792: A History of the Division of Java.* London: Oxford University Press.

——. 1981. *A History of Modern Indonesia.* Bloomington: Indiana University Press.

Ricoeur, Paul. 1979. "The Model of the Text: Meaningful Action Considered as a Text." In Paul Rabinow and William M. Sullivan, eds., *Interpretive Social Science: A Reader,* 73–101. Berkeley and Los Angeles: University of California Press.

Robson, S. O. 1981. "Java at the Crossroads." *Bijdragen tot de Taal-, Land-, en Volkenkunde* 137:259–92.

Roche, Frederick C. 1984. "Critical Lands in East Java: Development Problems and Potentials." *Economic Problems* 26:1–6.

————. 1985. "East Java's Upland Agriculture: Historical Development, Recent Changes, and Implications for Research." Working Paper. Malang, East Java: Brawijaya University, Agricultural Research Institute.

Rouffaer, G. P. 1921. "Tenggereezen." *Encyclopaedie van Nederlandsch-Indie,* 298–308. Leiden: E. J. Brill.

Ruthenberg, Hans. 1980. *Farming Systems in the Tropics.* 3d ed. Oxford: Clarendon Press.

Sahlins, Marshall. 1976. *Culture and Practical Reason.* Chicago: University of Chicago Press.

Sajogyo. 1977. "Garis Kemiskinan dan Kebutuhan Minimum Pangan." *Kompas* (Jakarta) 18, no. 11:77.

Sandel, Michael J. 1982. *Liberalism and the Limits of Justice.* Cambridge: Cambridge University Press.

Scherer, P. 1982. "Survey of Recent Developments." *Bulletin of Indonesian Economic Studies* 17:1–34.

Schneider, David M. 1976. "Notes toward a Theory of Culture." In Keith H. Basso and Henry A. Selby, eds., *Meaning in Anthropology,* 197–220. Albuquerque: University of New Mexico Press.

Scholte, Joh. 1921. *De Slametan Entas-Entas der Tenggereezen en de Memukur ceremonie op Bali.* Weltevreden: Albrecht.

Schrieke, B. 1957. *Indonesian Sociological Studies: Selected Writings.* Vol. 2. The Hague: W. van Hoeve.

Scitovsky, Tibor. 1976. *The Joyless Economy.* New York: Oxford University Press.

Scott, James C. 1976. *The Moral Economy of the Peasant.* New Haven: Yale University Press.

————. 1985. *Weapons of the Weak: Everyday Forms of Peasant Resistance.* New Haven: Yale University Press.

Sen, Amartya K. 1977. "Rational Fools: A Critique of the Behavioral Foundations of Economic Theory." *Philosophy and Public Affairs* 6:317–44.

Sherif, Muzafer, and Carolyn W. Sherif. 1956. "Reference Groups: Anchor Groups for the Person's Ego-Involvements." In *Social Psychology,* 417–37. New York: Harper & Row.

Shils, Edward. 1957. "Primordial, Personal, Sacred and Civil Ties." *British Journal of Sociology* 8:130–45.

————. 1960. "Political Development in the New States." *Comparative Studies in Society and History* 2:265–92, 370–411.

Shweder, Richard A., Manamohan Mahapatra, and Joan G. Miller. 1987. "Culture and Moral Development." In Jerome Kagan and Sharon Lamb, eds., *The Emergence of Morality in Young Children*, 1–83. Chicago: University of Chicago Press.

Skocpol, Theda. 1982. "What Makes Peasants Revolutionary?" In Robert P. Weller and Scott E. Guggenheim, eds., *Power and Protest in the Countryside*, 157–79. Durham: Duke University Press.

———. 1984. "Sociology's Historical Imagination." In Theda Skocpol, ed., *Vision and Method in Historical Sociology*, 1–21. Cambridge: Cambridge University Press.

———. 1985. "Bringing the State Back In: Strategies of Analysis in Current Research." In Peter B. Evans, D. Rueschemeyer, and Theda Skocpol, eds., *Bringing the State Back In*, 3–43. Cambridge: Cambridge University Press.

Smelser, Neil J. 1971 (1963). "Mechanisms of Change and Adjustment to Change." In George Dalton, ed., *Economic Development and Social Change: The Modernization of Village Communities*, 352–74. Garden City, N.Y.: Natural History Press.

Smith, Waldemar R. 1977. *The Fiesta System and Economic Change*. New York: Columbia University Press.

Smith-Hefner, Nancy J. 1983. "Language and Social Identity: Speaking Javanese in Tengger." Ph.D. thesis. University of Michigan.

———. 1989. "A Social History of Language Change in Mountain East Java." *The Journal of Asian Studies* 48: 258–71.

Speare, A. 1981. "Migration Trends." In Booth and McCawley 1981a, 284–314.

Sperber, Dan. 1975. *Rethinking Symbolism*. Translated by Alice L. Morton. Cambridge: Cambridge University Press.

Stigler, George J., and Gary S. Becker. 1977. "De Gustibus Non Est Disputandum." *American Economic Review* 67, no. 2:76–90.

Stoler, Ann. 1977. "Rice Harvesting in Kali Loro." *American Ethnologist* 4:678–98.

———. 1978. "Garden Use and Household Economy in Rural Java." *Bulletin of Indonesian Economic Studies* 14:85–101.

Strathern, Marilyn. 1987. "Introduction." In Marilyn Strathern, ed., *Dealing with Inequality: Analysing Gender Relations in Melanesia and Beyond*, 1–32. Cambridge: Cambridge University Press.

Sundhaussen, Ulf. 1978. "The Military: Structure, Procedures, and Effects on Indonesian Society." In Jackson and Pye 1978, 45–81.

Tamara, M. Nasir. 1985. "Islam as a Political Force in Indonesia: 1965–1985." Occasional Paper. Cambridge, Mass.: Harvard University, Center for International Affairs.

Thompson, E. P. 1978. "Eighteenth-Century English Society: Class Struggle without Class?" *Social History* 3, no. 2:133–65.

Timmer, C. Peter. 1973. "Choice of Technique in Rice Milling in Java." *Bulletin of Indonesian Economic Studies* 5:71–88.

———. 1981. "The Formation of Indonesian Rice Policy: A Historical Perspective." In Gary E. Hansen, ed., *Agricultural and Rural Development in Indonesia*, 33–43. Boulder: Westview Press.

———, ed. 1987. *The Corn Economy of Indonesia*. Ithaca: Cornell University Press.

Utrecht, E. 1969. "Land Reform in Indonesia." *Bulletin of Indonesian Economic Studies* 5:71–88.

Van Niel, Robert. 1972. "Measurement of Change under the Cultivation System in Java, 1837–1851." *Indonesia* 14:89–109.

———. 1981. "The Effect of Export Cultivations in Nineteenth-Century Java." *Modern Asian Studies* 15:25–58.

Vries, Egbert de. 1931. *Landbouw en welvaart in het regentschap Pasoeroean: Bijdrage tot de kennis van de sociale economie van Java.* 2 vols. Wageningen: H. Veenman & Zonen.

Walkin, Jacob. 1969. "The Moslem-Communist Confrontation in East Java, 1964–65." *Orbis* 13, no. 3: 822–47.

Wallerstein, Immanuel. 1974. *The Modern World System I: Capitalist Agriculture and the Origins of the European World-Economy in the Sixteenth Century.* New York: Academic Press.

———. 1979. *The Capitalist World-Economy: Essays by Immanuel Wallerstein.* Cambridge: Cambridge University Press.

Ward, Ken. 1974. *The 1971 Elections in Indonesia: An East Java Case Study.* Papers on Southeast Asia No. 2. Clayton, Australia: Monash University, Centre of Southeast Asian Studies.

Weber, Max. 1947. *The Theory of Social and Economic Organization.* Translated by A. M. Henderson and Talcott Parsons. Edited by Talcott Parsons. New York: Free Press.

———. 1968. *Economy and Society: An Outline of Interpretive Sociology.* Edited by Guenther Roth and Claus Wittich. Berkeley and Los Angeles: University of California Press.

Wertheim, W. F. 1969. "From Aliran towards Class Struggle in the Countryside of Java." *Pacific Viewpoint* 10, no. 2: 1–17.

White, Benjamin. 1976. "Population, Employment, and Involution in a Javanese Village." *Development and Change* 7:267–90.

———. 1977. "Rural Household Studies in Anthropological Perspective." Occasional Paper. Bogor, Java: Agricultural Development Council.

———. 1983. "Agricultural Involution and Its Critics: Twenty Years after Clifford Geertz." Working Paper Series No. 6. The Hague: Institute of Social Studies.

———. 1989. "Problems in the Empirical Analysis of Agrarian Differentiation." In Hart et al. 1989, 15–30.

White, Benjamin, and Gunawan Wiradi. 1989. "Agrarian and Nonagrarian Bases of Inequality in Nine Javanese Villages." In Hart et al. 1989, 266–302.

Wigboldus, Jouke S. 1979. "De oudste Indonesische maiscultuur." In F. van Anrooij, Dirk H. A. Kolff, J. T. M. van Laanen, Gerard J. Telkamp, eds., *Between People and Statistics: Essays on Modern Indonesian History,* 19–31. The Hague: Martinus Nijhoff.

Wolf, Eric R. 1982. *Europe and the People without History.* Berkeley and Los Angeles: University of California Press.

Wolf, Eric R., and Edward C. Hansen. 1972. *The Human Condition in Latin America.* New York: Oxford University Press.

Wrong, Dennis. 1961. "Oversocialized Concept of Man in Sociology." *American Sociological Review* 26, no. 2:183–93.

Yack, Bernard. 1988. "Liberalism and Its Communitarian Critics: Does Liberal Practice 'Live Down' to Liberal Theory?" In Charles H. Reynolds and Ralph V. Norman, eds., *Community in America: The Challenge of Habits of the Heart*, 147–69. Berkeley and Los Angeles: University of California Press.

INDEX

Acehnese War, 42

Adoption, 174–77. *See also* Childbearing

Agrarian law: of 1870, 50, 141; of 1960, 201

Agricultural involution: ecological qualities, 52; C. Geertz on, 15, 52; revisionist analyses of, 15n; and shared poverty, 114. *See also* Geertz, C.; *Sawah* (irrigated rice fields)

Agriculture. See *Sawah* (irrigated rice fields); *Tegal* (rainfed agricultural land)

Agrochemicals: for coffee and cloves, 94–95; credit for, 17; illegal distribution of, 83, 99; for maize and cassava, 84, 87n.3; production of, in colonial era, 63n; production of, today, 82–83, 84, 102n; use of, by class, 100–101, 103, 132–33; use in 1920s, 63; use in 1950s, 75; use today, 11, 13, 17, 99; for vegetables, 88–89. *See also* Green revolution

Alexander, J., 44n, 68n, 69n, 72, 129, 170n, 232–33

Alexander, P., 44n, 232–33

Alienation, concept of, 238, 241–42. *See also* Culture: theory

Aliran (political streams): literature on, 20n, 221–22, 226; role of, in 1965–66 violence, 20, 24, 221–22, 226–27; in rural Pasuruan, 193–94, 199. *See also* Class; Political parties; Status groups

Anderson, B., 20n, 28, 155, 222, 230

Ani-ani (harvest knife), 14, 61

ANSOR, 210, 212–13, 215. *See also* Nahdatul Ulama (NU)

Armed forces, 201, 210–11, 212, 226, 227. *See also* New Order

Asal barang (personal property), 168, *See also* Divorce; Marriage

Bailey, C., 14, 119

Bali, in relation to Tengger, 9, 22, 34–35, 37

Banditry, 38, 39, 74

Banking, 68

Banteng, 73

Barisan Tani Indonesia (peasants' union), 199

Bawon (harvest share), 115, 133n. *See also* Harvest

Becker, G. S., 235

Bellah, R. N., x

Bencar (deep-hoeing), 62, 62n.2, 108, 109

Benda, H. J. 196, 197, 198

Bendix, R., x, 19, 155

Bengkok (salary land), 119–20

Bennet, C., 91, 93, 94n, 97n

Berger, P. L., xi, xii

Biersack, A., xiii

Bima (god), 56

BIMAS agricultural program, 82–83, 84. *See also* Agrochemicals; New Order; Rice

Black market, 72, 83, 99

Blambangan, 36–38. *See also* Eastern salient

Blantik (cattle trader), 107

Bloch, M., 5n, 131, 135, 239

Blum, L., 5n

Booth, A., 13, 63, 85, 93, 130

Bottomore, T. B., 28n